ANXIETY VEILED

ANXIETY VEILED

Euripides and the Traffic in Women

Nancy Sorkin Rabinowitz

Cornell University Press

ITHACA AND LONDON

Copyright © 1993 by Cornell University

All rights reserved. Except for brief quotations in a review, this book, or parts thereof, must not be reproduced in any form without permission in writing from the publisher. For information, address Cornell University Press, Sage House, 512 East State Street, Ithaca, New York 14850.

First published 1993 by Cornell University Press.

International Standard Book Number 0-8014-2845-9 (cloth)
International Standard Book Number 0-8014-8091-4 (paper)
Library of Congress Catalog Card Number 93-17257

Printed in the United States of America

Librarians: Library of Congress cataloging information appears on the last page of the book.

♾ The paper in this book meets the minimum requirements of the American National Standard for Information Sciences—Permanence of Paper for Printed Library Materials, ANSI Z39.48-1984.

In loving memory of my sister Joan

Contents

Preface

"Where to stand? Who to be?" These questions, formulated by Hélène Cixous, have a special resonance for the feminist critic who is simultaneously a Hellenist. What is the place of feminist criticism in classics? What is the place of Greek tragedy in feminist criticism? Others have raised similar questions, but the problems are not easily solved. There are such radical differences between the two disciplines that they hardly speak the same language. In particular, while classics claims to be an empirical field of study, without a perspective, feminism is avowedly a perspective, a way of looking at the world. Whatever the variance between academic feminism and activist feminism, neither sounds remotely like the articles in classics journals. Nonetheless, I intend this book to be part of a conversation between feminist theory and the classics, a conversation I see as mutually beneficial.

Writing the book has been made difficult not only by this vexed relationship between feminism (or women's studies) and classics but also by what is happening within feminism. It seems that each phase of the contemporary women's movement has brought its own difficulties in "speaking as" a feminist; there was a time not so long ago when the rediscoveries of modern women authors made me feel both envious of those doing the discovering and apologetic about working on a canonized male author. Indeed, at a conference in the early 1980s, a distinguished feminist theorist asked my Chaucerian colleague and me if we didn't work on these authors because we wanted to sleep with the father. More recently, postmodern feminists and women of color have challenged the monolithic and universalizing claims of early feminists; although I am not nostalgic for the primordial *illo tempore*, these challenges have also made it more difficult to speak. Since it is very difficult to write from a multiplicity of perspectives, from a divided subjectivity, one must position oneself as some kind of subject—but what can we say if the words "woman," "man," "heterosexuality," and "sexuality" can no longer be used comfortably?

My own split identity, Hellenist and feminist, informs this book and will, I hope, make it of interest to my double audience. My training as a Hellenist (not my desire to sleep with Euripides) predisposes me to be committed to the continued study of Greek theater. Clearly, the dominant order has its reasons for attaching importance to ancient Greek literature: artistic excellence, transcendent human values, tradition. I hope to show that those interested in change, those away from the center, also have an interest in understanding these texts, precisely because of their position and the power they have exerted. Mythic texts such as the tragedies provide some of the underpinnings of contemporary ideology. By articulating the relationship between gender, power, and sexuality in tragedy, we can understand its ideological force; left unanalyzed, the dynamic at work in the plays may continue to seem to be universal and thus continue to reinscribe itself in the modern audience.

The discursive chasm between classics and feminism has certain very practical consequences, for each has its own ways of doing things. In order to make my work accessible to the non-classicist, I have translated all the Greek and have introduced Greek words only where necessary. While I prefer Hellenic spelling (for instance, *k* in Herakles; Hippolytos, not Hippolytus), where a Latinate version of a name is very widely known, I have retained the common spelling (for example, Clytemnestra). All line references to individual plays follow the Oxford edition of Euripides' texts. Except as otherwise noted, all translations are my own; readers seeking the complete texts of the plays in English can find convenient translations in David Grene and Richmond Lattimore's *Complete Greek Tragedies*, volumes 3 and 4 (Chicago: University of Chicago Press, 1959). The Loeb Classical Library (Cambridge: Harvard University Press) contains bilingual editions of the other ancient authors cited.

Another consequence of the doubleness is that I have many people to thank. I owe my interest in classics to my first Latin teacher, Irving Kizner, and my early Greek teachers, Stephen Daitz and Miriam Drabkin at the City College of New York; my interest in Euripides I owe to Anne Burnett, who taught me how to *understand* Greek literature. To a great extent, however, this book has been made possible by the women's movement and feminism, which have shaped my thinking about the classical material. Feminist work often grows out of a personal as well as a philosophical context, and this book is no exception, for the thinking and writing have been done in the good company of others, notably in the feminist reading groups of Hamilton College's Faculty for Women's Concerns. I thank the group as a model community for its support over the years.

Individual members, too, have been very important to my intellectual growth: Eve Kosofsky Sedgwick sparked much of my thinking about sex and gender, and many research groups provided prodding and encouragement. Director Carol Bellini-Sharp urged me to think about Greek tragedy as theater, and Patricia Francis Cholakian read every word (many more than once) and shared every thought. Without her, this book would never have been finished.

Feminism is a matter not only of research and politics but of teaching as well; I have been fortunate over the years in having wonderful students in feminist theory seminars whose challenging questions are reflected here.

Other colleagues—Evelyn Beck, Victor Bers, Mary-Kay Gamel, Barbara Gold, Shelly Haley, Janet E. Halley, Elaine Tuttle Hansen, Roberta Krueger, Tina Passman, Minnie Bruce Pratt, Amy Richlin, Carl Rubino, Charles Segal, Vicky Vernon, Froma Zeitlin, and Bella Zweig—have offered helpful advice. Ella Gant and Deborah Pokinski were visual consultants. The final stages were made almost pleasant by the speed with which Bernhard Kendler worked, the astute comments of Steve Nimis and Ann Michelini, and the excellent editorial work of Patricia Sterling.

One's spouse and parents often provide personal help, help not to be underestimated. In my case, Peter J. Rabinowitz has not only done the laundry and the child care but has also contributed more to the argument and prose than I usually acknowledge. And though it is obvious that a book cannot exist without a mother, in this case it is literally true, since Sophie Sorkin read and edited the entire manuscript. Finally I want to thank my children: Rachel, for telling me to go to my study and work now, and Michael, for sharing the computer with me.

Research support came partly from the National Endowment for the Humanities but most of all from a supportive administration at Hamilton College, which granted me two leaves and provided generous institutional assistance in many ways. It is impossible to do research at a small college without the help of others; I have been very fortunate in the cheerful assistance of an excellent library staff, in particular Joan Wolek and Cecilia Madigan in interlibrary loan. A small army of intrepid and invaluable student assistants have been initiated into the mysteries of *L'Année Philologique*; special thanks go to Goffredo Diana, Cecilia Madigan, Teresa Noelle Roberts, Melissa Tourtellotte, and Megan Wolf for organizational skills that far surpass my own.

I am grateful for permission to reprint those portions of the manuscript that have been previously published. An early version of the argument and its implications for *Alcestis* and *Hippolytos* was printed in *Theatre Studies* 34 (Winter 1989): 11–23. Part of Chapter 1 appeared as "The Strategy of Inconsistency in Euripides' *Iphigenia at Aulis*," *Classical Bulletin* 59 (1983); the original version of Chapter 5 as "Female Speech and Sexuality: Euripides' *Hippolytos* as Model," *Helios* 13 (1986); and Chapter 6 as "Renegotiating the Oedipus: Theseus and Hippolytos" in *Refiguring the Father: New Feminist Readings of Patriarchy*, edited by Beth Kowaleski-Wallace and Patricia Yaeger (Carbondale: Southern Illinois University Press, 1989).

NANCY SORKIN RABINOWITZ

Clinton, New York

ANXIETY VEILED

Introduction

It is all too easy for literary critics working on drama to ignore the fact of performance; thus I stress at the outset that Greek tragedy was made to be *performed* before live audiences in fifth-century B.C.E. Athens. It was not only a popular art form (unlike lyric, which was performed for the select few) but a public one, and intimately involved with the life of the polis. Specifically, to produce tragedies at the contest that made up the Great Dionysia was a *civic* duty. The festival was inaugurated by the presentation of tribute from the colonies to Athens; the city's own youth danced in army regalia.[1]

It seems probable that tragedy, as a public spectacle, was used like other cultural institutions to bolster the community, and given the predominant masculinity of Greek culture, that meant a community of male citizens.[2] In a brief overview of Greek theater, Sue-Ellen Case remarks: "As a result of the suppression of real women, the culture invented its own representation of the gender, and it was this fictional 'Woman' who appeared on stage, in the myths and in the plastic arts, representing the patriarchal values attached to the gender while suppressing the experiences, stories, feelings and fantasies of actual women. . . . 'Woman' was played by male actors in drag, while real women were banned from the stage. . . . Classical

---

1. For some implications, see Winkler, "Ephebes." For other treatments, see Longo, "Theater"; Goldhill, "Great Dionysia"; Gregory, *Euripides*, chap. 1.

2. Zeitlin, "Playing the Other," esp. pp. 66–67, refers to tragedy's role in constructing male subjectivity. Winkler, "Ephebes," speaks of the "notional or proper audience" as "one of men" (p. 39 n. 58). Karen Bassi's very interesting current project, "Gender and the Ideology of Greek Histrionics," involves demonstrating that tragedy was viewed as dangerous because it produced a "feminized" audience.

plays and theatrical conventions can now be regarded as allies in the project of suppressing real women and replacing them with masks of patriarchal production."[3] Even though relations between the sexes are central in tragic plots, the actors and writers were men; the theater, like the agora and the assembly, was a male space. The representation of conflicts between men and so-called women was, therefore, constructed from a masculine point of view.

If not much has been made of the fact that all the actors of tragedy were male, there has been an extensive debate about whether or not women were in the audience. The persistence of that debate itself is curious, since the evidence points strongly to the presence of women: references in Plato as well as some anecdotes in the commentaries indicate that women were in the audience, and although the testimony of Aristophanes may be somewhat contradictory, by and large it too seems to indicate women's presence. As we will see, women of the upper and middle classes did live a sequestered life, but they also had extensive ritual obligations that took them outside, and the festival of Dionysos might well have been such an event. The conflict, then, seems to result from the predisposition of the critics, not the evidence. As Arthur Haigh says, "In the treatment of this matter scholars appear to have been unduly biased by a preconceived opinion as to what was right and proper. Undoubtedly Athenian women were kept in a state of almost Oriental seclusion.... As a matter of fact the evidence upon the subject, if considered without prejudice, makes it practically certain that there were no restrictions of the kind suggested."[4] I accept, then, that women were in the audience; my aim will be to question the plays' effect on women in the audience, as well as their role in the consolidation of the male community.

Nonetheless, the debate over women's presence at tragic performance reminds us of how little we know about real women in antiquity; indeed, the sources are very sketchy. The archaeological remains are relatively uncommunicative; the fourth-century orators are unreliable, since they were trying to win lawsuits and so reported the details of women's lives only as they needed them; tragedy similarly represented the details of

3. Case, *Feminism and Theatre*, p. 7; see also her warning about the ways in which Greek texts have been canonized (p. 15).

4. Haigh, *Attic Theatre*, p. 324; see pp. 324–29, citing among other passages Plato *Gorgias* 502B–E, and *Laws* 817A–C, 658A–D. Pickard-Cambridge, *Dramatic Festivals*, pp. 264–65, discusses more problematic evidence. When Aristophanes describes an audience, his age groups apply only to men (*Peace* 50–53), yet other comic passages suggest women's presence (*Peace* 962–67; *Frogs* 1051), as does the somewhat dubious interpretation offered by the scholiast to Aristophanes' *Ekklesiazousai* 22, referring to a law providing different seating for free women and courtesans. On "orientalism," see note 24.

women's lives for its own purposes. Moreover, the evidence from the different sources is frequently inconsistent.[5]

Women in Fifth-Century Athens

Since this book does not claim to be a historical work, it is perhaps inappropriate to go into all the intricacies of the record we do have. Still, my argument about Euripides will be clearer in the context of a brief outline of the status of Athenian women in the fifth century (classicists can move directly to the discussion of theory). The Athens of tragedy was, as Pierre Vidal-Naquet put it, "a men's club."[6] Women were not citizens, were not listed in the census.[7] They were, however, recognized as natives of the city. The Periclean citizenship law of 451 B.C.E., which stated that both father and mother had to be from Athens for a child to be a citizen (Aristotle *Athenian Constitution* 26.4, *Politics* 33.5; Plutarch *Pericles* 37.3; Demosthenes 59, *Against Neaira* 16), suggests that although Athenian women had no political rights, they were essential for passing citizenship on to their sons.[8] The virtues of the two sexes as differentiated by the philosophers and reflected in custom suited them to the roles of warrior and wife respectively. At one Athenian festival, the Apatouria, for instance, boys—but not girls—born that year were registered in the phratry, or clan. Adolescents all cut their hair but did so in accord with roles specific to gender: the boys would then embark on military service; marriage feasts would be dedicated for the girls.[9]

5. For a historiographical overview of the debate about evidence and status, see Blok, "Sexual Asymmetry." Pomeroy, *Goddesses*, pp. 58–60, focuses on the difference between historical and literary evidence; Arthur, "Review Essay," p. 388, finds "the clue to the divergence of viewpoints...in ideological orientation." Foley, "Conception of Women," discusses the controversy about different sorts of evidence. A good recent summary of Greek attitudes toward women is Foley, "Women in Greece," with its bibliography.

6. Vidal-Naquet, *Black Hunter*, p. 206. Keuls, *Reign of the Phallus*, studies Athens as a phallocracy.

7. Harrison, *Law*, p. 65 n. 1; Gould, "Law," p. 46.

8. Harrison, *Law*, pp. 25–27; Lacey, *Family*, pp. 104–5. Sometimes *astē* (feminine of *astos*) is translated "citizen," but it means "one who has civil rights" as distinguished from "one who has political rights" (*politēs*); e.g., Demosthenes 57.54: "A boy is not a townsman if he is not born to a woman known to be of the city." The orator Isaios (8.43) uses the word for citizen; Aristotle and Demosthenes use the word for inhabitant of the city. For a subtle consideration of the law as the only reference to women as citizens, see Loraux, *Enfants*, pp. 127–29. Daladier, "Mères aveugles," in considering why women in tragedy do not recognize their sons, also argues that women were natives but not citizens (pp. 232–33). For a thorough consideration of the evidence, see Patterson, *"Hai Attikai"* and *Pericles' Citizenship Law*, on the masculinity of the phratry.

9. See Parke, *Festivals*, p. 89. On the Apatouria as a rite preparing each sex for its gendered

Questions about the status of Athenian women are in part also questions about marriage, since the respectable woman was a married woman. But here again, we find more ambiguity than clarity in the evidence. For instance, there was no one Greek word for marriage;[10] the result is considerable debate not only about what constituted a legitimate union but also about the legitimacy of offspring and the status of women. Though bride-price and exogamy characterized marriage in the heroic period, the classical period saw the transition to dowry and limited endogamy, as if the polis were anxious to conserve its resources within.[11] One essential part of Athenian marriage was a ceremony, known as *egguē*, in which the bride was promised to the groom; litigation about legitimacy (and inheritance) often refers to that contract as evidence that a lawful marriage did take place.[12] But the betrothal was followed by "the giving" (*ekdosis*), which could occur much later. Crucial to my argument is the fact that in both proceedings the match was contracted between the *kurios* (the man responsible for the woman; literally, the one in charge) and her husband-to-be. The bride was the object given; the *kurios* gave, and the groom took or received, as is clear in the ritual pronouncement "I give my daughter to you to plough for legitimate children."[13] As Jean-Pierre Vernant puts it, the function of marriage was not to bring pleasure but "to unite two family groups so that a man can have legitimate children who 'resemble their father' despite being the issue of their mother's womb."[14]

---

adult roles, see Zeitlin, "Cultic Models," p. 141; Schmitt, "Athéna Apatouria," pp. 1059–60; Vidal-Naquet, "Tradition d'hoplite athénien." For the role of initiation in socialization, see Vernant, "City-State Warfare," pp. 19–44, esp. 23.

10. Aristotle *Politics* 1.3.2.; Benveniste, *Vocabulaire*, pp. 239–42. Chantraine, "Noms du mari," p. 220, notes the instability of terms for husband and wife which results from the primacy of the parental role. On the equivalent ambiguity in modern Greek, see Herzfeld, "Semantic Slippage," p. 165.

11. A good recent summary is Patterson, "Marriage." On the change in marriage rules, see Vernant, "Marriage," p. 60, who believes it reflects a state of crisis; Gernet, *Anthropology*, p. 293; Harrison, *Law*, pp. 24–29; Wolff, "Marriage Law," p. 45. Bickerman, "Conception du mariage," pp. 24–28, discusses exchange and gift giving as a function in the polis. Aristocratic Athenian families according to Gernet also followed the old pattern. Bourdieu, *Outline*, pp. 52–57, notes that the modern-day poor marry those close by, whereas the wealthy make alliances at a distance.

12. Critics disagree about whether the *egguē* was sufficient as well as necessary (see Vernant, "Marriage," pp. 53–54). Bickerman, "Conception du mariage," p. 11, finds that it was not; Redfield, "Notes," p. 188, argues that it was. On the fluidity itself and attempts to fix it, see Vernant, "Marriage."

13. Clement Alexander *Stromateis* 2.23.1 = Menander *Peirikeiromené* 435–36 (ed. Koerte). The passivity of the wife is widely accepted: e.g., Harrison, *Law*, p. 21, calls the bride the "passive object of the contract"; *ekdosis* suggests that the bride was lent to the groom as new *kurios* (p. 30).

14. Vernant, "Introduction," p. vii.

Women thus moved from one *kurios* to another—father, husband, son—and never reached majority. Nor had they any independent economic status. Even though women who were not of the propertied classes did hold a number of jobs, they were apparently allowed to disburse monies only up to one *medimnos* (about enough to pay for three days' food) without the permission of a "guardian."[15] Nevertheless, since women seem to have given large gifts; the apparent contradiction leaves much room for speculation and interpretation. A. R. W. Harrison regards it as "largely a matter of definition whether we say that in Athens a woman's or a minor's capacity to own was restricted. Women, like minors, could not make legally valid agreements for the disposal of goods above the value of one *medimnos*, except through the agency of their *kurioi*. This limitation apart . . . a woman's or a minor's capacity to own either chattels or land was on all fours with that of a man who was of age, provided she or he was a properly qualified citizen."[16] Harrison, to my way of thinking, has a peculiar notion of "on all fours," since women did not have citizenship and needed the permission of an adult male to act.

Nor does the move from bride-price to dowry indicate financial independence. Although the dowry was to be used for the wife's maintenance and returned to her father in the event of divorce, her husband managed it for her; if he predeceased her, the money went with her back to her father or to the male children if they were of age. She had complete control only over the gifts, typically items of clothing or jewelry, given her at the time of the wedding.[17]

In *Against Neaira* (59.122) Demosthenes claims that men "have courtesans for pleasure, concubines to look after the day-to-day needs of the body, wives that we may breed legitimate children and have a trusty warden of what we have in the house." This famous passage underlines the fact that a respectable woman's importance lay in protecting the goods of the house in her lifetime and in producing legitimate offspring. We can see the importance of heirs in legislation regulating inheritance as well as in the situation of the so-called heiress (*epiklēros*). If a man died leaving a daughter but no sons, the daughter would be married ("with her portion," *epi-klēros*) to her nearest male relative, thereby keeping the wealth in the family. Clearly, she was not really an heiress but a connecting link between

15. See Schaps, *Economic Rights*.
16. Harrison, *Law*, p. 236.
17. They are called *anakalupteria* and are thus related to the removal of the veil, a gesture of disclosure (*anakaluptein*), and to the sexual consummation it symbolizes. On the relationship to veiling, see Sissa, *Greek Virginity*, pp. 93–94; Carson, "Putting," pp. 160–64. On female value and modern Greek dowry practice, see du Boulay, *Portrait*.

generations of men. Further, the rules governing the marriage of the *epiklēros* draw attention to the wife's tie to her family of birth: she bore responsibility to two lines, her husband's and her father's; if these obligations came into conflict—that is, if she were already married when her father died—the husband might lose her, and the "heiress" be divorced and remarried. Adoption laws reveal the same concern about the lineage. A man could adopt a son to be his heir; this son could also marry his adoptive sister, thus ensuring that the heirs would be blood relations of their (grand)father.[18]

We can link this concern with legitimacy to the seclusion of women: as W. K. C. Lacey puts it, "The importance of being able to prove legitimacy had two principal results; it made adultery a public as well as a private offence, and it made the Athenians excessively preoccupied with the chastity of their womenfolk, with the result that they were guarded in a manner nowadays thought to be intolerable."[19] There is ample evidence that women of property lived in the inner and darker regions of their houses; windows on the street were only in the men's quarters. Moreover, a well-bred wife was not supposed to eat with the men, and even male relatives would be ashamed to enter the women's quarters.[20]

Scholars continue to disagree, however, about the extent and significance of the "sequestration" of women. It was in any case class-specific and was as full of gaps as the Athenian calendar was full of religious holidays, since women had considerable importance in religious ritual.[21] Scholars' comments, nevertheless, have revealed the extent to which their beliefs and practices color their views of antiquity. A. W. Gomme, writing in 1925, said, "I consider it very doubtful if Greek theory and practice differed fundamentally from the average, say, prevailing in mediaeval and modern Europe"; H. D. F. Kitto echoed his sentiments, referring again to mo-

---

18. On adoption law, see Harrison, *Law*, p. 84. For a corollary among the Kabyle people, see Bourdieu, *Outline*, pp. 50–52.

19. Lacey, *Family*, p. 113; cf. p. 159: "It was of such overriding importance not to allow the least breath of suspicion to fall on young girls that they were not virgins, or on young wives that their child was not properly conceived in wedlock, that they were protected to what to our minds is a wholly unreasonable degree." Rousselle, "Observation féminine," p. 1092, notes that female sexual pleasure was exclusively related to reproduction.

20. See Walker, "Women and Housing." The orators Lysias and Isaios provide evidence of seclusion: Lysias 3.6, Isaios 313–14, Lysias 1.22.

21. For a vigorous and, I believe, wrongheaded approach, see Richter, "Position of Women." Dover, "Classical Greek Attitudes," p. 69, points out more moderately that "the thorough-going segregation of women of citizen status was possible only in households which owned enough slaves and could afford to confine [their] womenfolk to a leisure enlivened only by the exercise of domestic crafts such as weaving and spinning. This degree of segregation was simply not possible in poorer families."

dernity.[22] Donald Richter, writing in 1971, applauds Gomme for contesting the seclusion theory and adds: "The protective solicitude that did obtain was not extraordinary. It was occasioned by a quite normal measure of husbandly jealousy."[23]

To be sure, neither the existence of distinctive male and female roles nor the separation of women and men is necessarily equivalent to a negative valuation of women; separation need not entail contempt—or powerlessness, for it is possible that women exercised a form of power in the private realm.[24] And as contemporary anthropologists recognize, there is a problem in male ethnographers' reliance on male informants in getting at what is "actually" going on in a group.[25] In point of fact, however, in Athens the separation of the sexes did coincide with a widespread, if not universal, misogyny and a devaluation of the female realm. This was not only a sex-segregated society but also one in which the accepted virtues of woman and man were radically different in kind: his lay in courageously winning glory in battle, hers in bearing the pain of childbirth and loving her children.[26] According to Pericles, "Your greatest glory is not to be inferior to what god has made you, and the greatest glory of a woman is to be least talked about by men, whether they are praising you or criticizing you" (Thucydides 2.45.2). Sally Humphreys puts it this way: "The contrast between public and private life in classical Athens was sharp. Public life was egalitarian, competitive, impersonal. Its typical locus was the open

22. Gomme, "Position of Women," p. 25; cf. Kitto, *Greeks*, pp. 219–31, for the comparison of "Manchester" and Athens. See Versnel, "Wife and Helpmate," for a sophisticated consideration.

23. Richter, "Position of Women," p. 7.

24. Cohen, "Seclusion," considers differential roles and seclusion features that ancient Athens shares with modern Mediterranean cultures. Similar caveats are issued by Patterson, "*Hai Attikai*"; as she points out, absence of women from the political sphere does not mean their nonexistence. It does, however, signify a lack of a certain political power as Bourdieu, *Outline*, p. 41, argues strongly. Cf. also Zweig, " 'Primal Mind.' " On "orientalism," see Bernal, *Black Athena*, pp. 233–37. Because the phrase "almost oriental seclusion" is dotted throughout the literature, we must question the investment that not only male critics but Westerners have in a certain view of Greek culture.

25. A convenient summary is in Moore, *Feminism and Anthropology*, pp. 1–11. Just, "Conceptions," p. 154, notes: "For all of what we do know about Athenian women comes from the representations and ordinances of men. And that, in certain areas, it is so very little, becomes in this respect a salient fact." Winkler, *Constraints*, chaps. 1–2, raises the possibility that this extreme view is male boasting. Versnel, "Wife and Helpmate," puts the status debate into an anthropological perspective.

26. See Spelman, *Inessential Woman*, chaps. 1–2, on Plato and Aristotle; and Saïd, "Féminin," esp. pp. 93–96, for the difference of the male and female virtues in Aristotle. The work of duBois (*Centaurs*) and Lloyd (*Polarity, Science*, esp. p. 59; "Hot and Cold") shows that the tables of opposites included male and female, with assumptions about their relative value. For a modern example, see Bourdieu, *Outline*, esp. pp. 90–91. On sexual asymmetry in initiations, see note 9.

arena—market-place, law-court, theatre, gymnasium, battle-field. . . . The
oikos, by contrast, was in closed space, architecturally functional rather than
ornamental. Its relationships were hierarchic: husband-wife, parent-child,
owner-slave . . . women, children and slaves had no formal place in public
life."[27]

Yet even though middle-class women did inhabit a private sphere, divorced from the male arenas of marketplace and gymnasium, the private
and the public can never be totally demarcated even in the most rigidly
dichotomous of cultures.[28] In Athens as in our own time, the public and
the private were interwoven. Reproduction was clearly in the service of
the city. For example, selective enforcement of the legislation regulating
legitimacy helped the polis maintain the population it needed in order to
wage the Peloponnesian War. The Periclean citizenship law of 451 was
passed, according to Aristotle (*Athenian Constitution* 26.4), because there
were too many citizens. During the Peloponnesian War, however, enforcement seems to have been relaxed so that men in fact could have
legitimate citizen children from two mates (Diogenes Laertius 2.26). Legislation alluding to concubines "kept for the purpose of raising legitimate
offspring" (Demosthenes 23.53; Lysias 1.30–31) suggests the same possibility. Thus, when it was convenient, the concubine had an elevated
status; women's status was not stable but could be shifted to accommodate
the needs of the man or the city.

This brief example reveals the interdependence of city and family.[29]
Furthermore, Athenian polis organization depended on and was made up
of the individual households (*oikoi*). The interconnectedness of city and
family life draws attention to the problematic position of women as crucial
to and even identified with the house but irrelevant to the city's aggregate
of households. On the one hand, women were necessary: they produced
children, providing citizens and soldiers for the city as well as enabling
the family to reproduce itself.[30] On the other hand, they were a threat
because of their ambiguous relationship to the household: strongly identified with it, almost standing for it, yet imported from outside it and

27. Humphreys, *Family*, pp. 1–2.
28. On the problematic and powerful public/private dichotomy, see Rosaldo, "Woman"
and "Uses and Abuses"; Moore, *Feminism and Anthropology*, chap. 2; Comaroff, "Sui Genderis"; Sanday, *Female Power*. Cf. the work on contemporary Mediterranean society: e.g.,
Dubisch, *Gender and Power*; Bourdieu, *Algeria*, pp. 133–53.
29. On family and city, see Lacey, *Family*, pp. 73–79; Gardner, "Aristophanes"; Wolff,
"Marriage Law," esp. pp. 83–84; Patterson, *Pericles' Citizenship Law*, p. 10.
30. Vernant, "City-State Warfare," p. 50: the purpose in democracy was "to ensure,
through strict rules governing marriage, the permanence of the city itself through constant
reproduction."

maintaining their ties to another family.[31] Crucially, women's sexuality per se was necessary for legitimate procreation, but illicit sexual activity could dishonor the family name and pollute the lineage. Therefore, the ascription of sexual desire to women was problematic.

"Women" in Tragedy

Given the social, economic, and political condition of Athenian women, how are we to interpret the undisputed prominence of female characters in tragedy, and especially in Euripides, all but one of whose extant plays feature a prominent woman? Gomme takes the tragedies in general as evidence of the high status of Greek women and of the respect with which they were regarded. In contrast, Victor Ehrenberg rules out tragedy as evidence because of its highly conventional nature, but he does make an exception for the "realistic" works of Euripides.[32]

More recent theories of representation have, of course, made such old-fashioned criticism as Gomme's untenable. But can we say nothing about women on the basis of the representation of "woman" in the plays? Froma Zeitlin has argued that in fact "the feminine" dominates tragedy. She asks: "Can there be some intrinsic connections linking the phenomenon of Athenian tragedy, invented and developed in a historical context as a civic art form, and what the society culturally defines as feminine in its sex/gender system?"[33] Her answer to the question is "yes," and she identifies four areas where the feminine is significant: the representation of the body, the use of space, the plot itself, and the role playing so essential to tragedy.

I take another tack, assuming neither that the texts represent some specific external reality of female prominence nor that the feminine gives

31. Others have made similar points. See, e.g., Gould, "Law," pp. 55–57; Arthur, "Liberated Women," pp. 67–73. Mandel, "Sacrifice," p. 178, finds a similar insider-outsider status in modern Greek rural settings: "Here we see a paradox: the woman is expendable, yet her incorporation into the patrilineal group is essential to insure its continuity." On the identification of women and the house, see Vernant, "Hestia-Hermes," pp. 127–75. See du Boulay, *Portrait*, esp. pp. 102–36, on modern women in a traditional Greek village. Bourdieu, working in a setting where women constitute the possible site of a threat to male honor, makes similar observations in *Outline* and *Algeria*.

32. Gomme, "Position of Women"; Ehrenberg, *People*, pp. 200–206. But cf. note 5 above; Arthur, "Review Essay"; and Foley, "Conception of Women."

33. Zeitlin, "Playing the Other," pp. 64–65. For the trope of the feminine in modernity, see Jardine, *Gynesis*; on the feminine in Propertius, see Gold, "Ariadne." A well-worked-out statement of this concern about post-structuralist uses of the feminine is Spivak, "Displacement."

tragedy its shape; rather, I attend to the masculinity of Athens and stress tragedy's ideological function. As we have seen, Athenian women did not have independent economic and legal standing but were represented by their *kurioi*. Similarly, they did not produce the public images that appeared in tragedy or on vases.[34] Athenian women exemplify what Edwin Ardener calls a "muted" class, "muted simply because it does not form part of the dominant communicative system of the society—expressed as it must be through the dominant ideology, and that 'mode of production', if you wish, which is articulated with it."[35] In tragedy, then, the audience never hears women's point(s) of view, only what men think they would say.

But that is not negligible information. As Catherine Belsey says, "Fictional texts do not necessarily mirror the practices prevalent in a social body, but they are a rich repository of the meanings its members understand and contest. And in order to be intelligible at all, fiction necessarily ascribes certain meanings, however plural and contradictory, to subjectivity and to gender. It therefore constitutes a possible place from which to begin an analysis of what it means to be a person, a man or a woman, at a specific historical moment."[36] Given the masculinity of Athenian society and its anxiety about female sexuality, it makes sense to ask whether and how these representations of women served the male-dominated polis and the male imagination. Thus, Vernant observes the social functions of tragedy, and Zeitlin similarly holds that tragedy "can be viewed as a species of recurrent masculine initiations, for adults as well as for the young," and that drama "was designed as an education for its male citizens in the democratic city."[37]

Such an approach has the advantage of taking seriously the Greeks' belief in the didactic function of art and especially tragedy (see, for instance, Aristophanes *Frogs* 1009–10, 1054–55), a function that reveals its role in shaping Greek culture.[38] To rephrase the point in more current

34. Women were associated with weaving, most often a private form of representation, although robes were gifts to Athena at the Panathenaia and to Artemis Orthia. There was, nonetheless, a tradition of Greek women's poetry; see the work of Marilyn Skinner (e.g., "Sapphic Nossis" and "Woman and Language") and Jane Snyder, *Woman and the Lyre*. On double consciousness, see Winkler, *Constraints*, chap. 6.

35. Ardener, "The Problem Revisited," p. 22.

36. Belsey, *Subject of Tragedy*, p. 5.

37. Zeitlin, "Playing the Other," p. 66; she goes on to make the connection to the feminine. Cf. Vernant and Vidal-Naquet, "Tensions and Ambiguities": "Tragedy is not only an art form; it is also a social institution which the city, by establishing competitions in tragedies, set up alongside its political and legal institutions" (p. 9).

38. On the passage in *Frogs*, see Havelock, *Literate Revolution*, pp. 269–79. See also Gregory, *Euripides*, on his didacticism. Nussbaum's analysis of the relationship between

terminology, tragedy in its own time was viewed as "ideological." That is, it was not meant as a literal depiction of some physical or material reality (such as the lived experience of women's lives) but did have a determinable relationship to that reality. In Louis Althusser's often quoted definition, "What is represented in ideology is therefore not the system of the real relations which govern the existence of individuals, but the imaginary relation of those individuals to the real relations in which they live." Like other ideological structures, the plays "call forth" or "interpellate" individuals as subjects. As *interpeller* suggests in French, through its evocation of the police stopping a pedestrian, the subject who recognizes him- or herself in the "hey you" is subject to arrest. The subject is not "free" but rather subjected to ideology. Althusser says: *"The category of the subject is only constitutive of all ideology insofar as all ideology has the function (which defines it) of 'constituting' concrete individuals as subjects."*[39]

Michel Foucault's methodology, like Althusser's concept of ideology, reveals the simultaneous subjection of subjects; unlike Althusser, Foucault is interested not in ideology per se but in discourse and the body. Sexuality, "through becoming an object of analysis and concern, surveillance and control, engenders at the same time an intensification of each individual's desire, for, in, and over his body." Or, as he says later in another essay, "Rather than ask ourselves how the sovereign appears to us in his lofty isolation, we should try to discover how it is that subjects are gradually, progressively, really and materially constituted through a multiplicity of organisms, forces, energies, materials, desires, thoughts, etc. We should try to grasp subjection in its material instance as a constitution of subjects."[40] His method suggests that we ask how the "discursive practices" of Euripidean tragedy work to produce subjects.

There have been historically significant differences between men and women in their access to even an illusory subjectivity; Foucault and Althusser from *their* subject positions tend to overlook gender as a factor. Thus, Foucault notes in passing that the Greek code of sexual morality he analyzes did not apply to women; he concerns himself with how "Western man" has "been brought to recognize himself as a subject of desire."[41] A

Hellenistic philosophy and desire overlaps with mine; she argues that the philosophers held emotions to be "social artifacts, formations in the soul that result from the implantation of belief by society"; and that tragedy was one of the sources implanting those beliefs ("Therapeutic Arguments," p. 53).

39. Althusser, "Ideology," pp. 165, 174, 180, 171.
40. Foucault, *Power/Knowledge*, pp. 56–57, 97.
41. Foucault, *Use of Pleasure*, pp. 6, 22–23. For feminist critiques of Foucault, see Richlin,

feminist critic may use the Foucauldian method and subscribe to its liberatory agenda, but only by attending to the double subjectedness of female character and audience member. Thus, for instance, the discourse of tragedy gives male bodies to "female" subjects, leading perhaps to the continued subjection of women in the audience.

Althusser's concept of subjection is similarly in need of adaptation for deployment in the feminist arsenal. Criticizing Althusser's formulation, Teresa de Lauretis replaces the word "ideology" with "gender": "Gender has the function (which defines it) of constituting concrete individuals as men and women."[42] Her phrase "technology of gender" is a necessary corrective to Althusser.

To return to the significance of the foregrounded female characters, then, I shall assume that they were ideological constructions or, in Foucault's terms, discursive practices. Greek myth as formulated in tragedy was a "technology of gender"; that is, tragedy created gendered subjects in the audience, subjects who gained or assumed their subjectivity in a way consistent with their socially ascribed gender. Tragedy "hails" a subject in a certain way—but it was male subjectivity that was the goal. As a public art form, tragedy served the polis in part by describing, inscribing, and prescribing gender, transforming the biologically male and female into the socially masculine and feminine. The apparatuses of ideology present models of gendered behavior, particularly women's behavior, and give women reasons for complying with them. A key part of this ideological work is that the audience is constructed by the experience of participating in the drama; it is in the audience (modern as well as ancient) that some potential for opposition resides as well, for there is always the possibility that women will (or did) refuse to interpret them exclusively in this way. Texts can misfire.

While I would argue that all of tragedy shared this desired ideological function for the dominant order, it was not monolithic, it did not equally and at all times foreclose the possibilities of resistance; tragedy may even inscribe resistance.[43] Among the Attic tragedians we know, Euripides' plays have had the most vexed relationship to dominant beliefs and practices; his reputation has been most subject to change. Aristotle called his plots the most tragic of all (*Poetics* 13.8–10 [1453a30]), yet even Aristotle's praise is related to the blame Euripides must have received from

---

"Zeus"; Hartsock, "Foucault"; Bartky, "Foucault." Hekman, *Gender and Knowledge*, is more optimistic.

    42. De Lauretis, *Technologies of Gender*, p. 6.

    43. I thank Steve Nimis for suggesting that I strengthen this point.

others for his unhappy endings. That he won the fewest first prizes in tragic contests would seem evidence that he was unpopular with his contemporaries who judged the plays, but his work was the most reproduced in the fourth century. His fluctuating reputation may be related to his radicalism: along with the sophists and advanced thinkers of his day, he seems to have questioned the gods and opposed the Peloponnesian War.[44]

His intellectual and political radicalism was accompanied by aesthetic experimentation. So, for instance, he was parodied by Aristophanes for what might be termed realism, notably the bringing of "low" characters on stage; Aristotle too accused him of representing untragic characters (e.g. *Poetics* 15.8 [1454a29]; 25.31 [1461b22]). Moreover, his choruses were thought to be cacophonous and not to advance the plots of the plays (see Aristophanes *Frogs* 1301–59, for a parody; and *Poetics* 18.19 [1456a25–30]). Similarly, Aristotle and later critics drew attention to Euripides' use of the "machine" as a device to resolve the complexities of plot (*Poetics* 15.10 [1454b1]). In the nineteenth century these aesthetic "flaws" and philosophical tendencies brought him disfavor.[45] Modern critics, following their forebears' judgment, have been troubled by the plays' apparent lack of coherence; as a result, the quest for unity has dominated criticism of the individual plays, with defenders finding unity and opponents denying it. More recently, however, his unresolved endings and formal experimentation have made Euripides seem modern and a kindred spirit.[46]

Unlike Aristotle, Aristophanes based his criticism of these plays on their morality. And that brings me to my special interest in Euripides: he is the only one of the tragedians with a reputation on "the woman question," and yet that reputation is contradictory. Aristophanes' characters in *Thesmophoriazousai* blame Euripides' plays for making their husbands suspicious and thus causing them troubles at home (378–432; cf. 545–48); the character Aeschylus in *The Frogs* accuses the character Euripides of displaying only bad women (1044–46), of making women whores. This long scene is revealing, for Euripides asks how he has harmed the city (1049), and Aeschylus replies that he has persuaded the "noble wives of noble citizens" to take poison in shame (1050–51). His Phaedra was not un-

44. On Euripides and the Greek enlightenment, and the effect on rhetoric of changes in values, see Solmsen, *Intellectual Experiments*. Michelini, *Euripides*, and Vellacott, *Ironic Drama*, both speak to his role in the tradition.

45. Nietzsche, *Birth of Tragedy*, pp. 69–82, even accused him of bringing about the downfall of tragedy.

46. Michelini treats this tradition at length in *Euripides*, pp. 3–51. For an earlier summary, see Murray, *Euripides*, pp. 1–59.

realistic, but "such immorality [*ton poneron* 1053] ought to have been hidden away." In this century, on the other hand, critics have seen him taking the side of women and other oppressed groups.[47] Was Euripides a radical in depicting women's passion, and was he in that way a step before his time?[48] What, if any, is the relationship between his apparent opposition to war and his portrayal of women?

It would be a mistake, even a waste of time, to try to decide whether Euripides was a misogynist or a feminist. Instead of examining the overt images of women to see whether they are "good" or "bad," I look instead for the ways in which the plays structure audience reaction and thus impose a gender hierarchy consistent with and supportive of the sex/gender system of the time.[49] Euripides may indeed "invent woman" and "reverse traditional representations,"[50] but ultimately he recuperates the female figures for patriarchy. His plays perform this ideological work in subtle and complicated ways. To recognize this function is not to deny that he endows his female characters with great understanding and allows them to give voice to important ideas; nonetheless, their experience is shaped to the end of supporting male power. I argue that the plays establish two models of womanhood—sacrificial and vindictive—which speak to both women and men. On the one hand, they set forth codes of behavior giving women in the audience reason to participate in the culture; on the other hand, they reinforce men's need and right to continue to control women. Women in the ancient audience may have, like many later readers, resisted this structure proposed to them, by focusing on the power and the women's community behind the text.[51]

47. See, e.g., Masqueray, *Euripide*, p. 307; Murray, *Euripides*, p. 32; Pomeroy, *Goddesses*, pp. 103–12; Vellacott, *Ironic Drama*, pp. 6, 17–19. Simon, "Euripides' Defense," p. 42 n. 2, believes that he represents women "as human beings in a way completely contrary to conventional Athenian norms." Appleton, *Euripides*, devotes a whole chapter to his defense of women (see esp. p. 37); both he and Rose, *Handbook*, p. 178, mention the association of Euripides with emotion, and emotion with women. Cf. Le Maître, "De la prétendue misogynie." More recently, Assaël, "Misogynie," p. 92, has remarked on the sympathy that Euripides shows for his characters; she notes, nonetheless, that the reputation for misogyny is still current in a popular French handbook of mythology.

48. E.g., Masqueray, *Euripide*, pp. 296–325; Vellacott, *Ironic Drama*, pp. 16–20; Appleton, *Euripides*, pp. 37–38. Murray, *Euripides*, pp. 32–33, speaks of his making women less than ideal, giving them character.

49. See Webster, *Tragedies*, pp. 31–115, on Euripides' early plays, in which "a pattern seems to appear. Each year he produced one play about a bad woman, one play about an unhappy woman, and one play of a different kind" (p. 116); in the second group the pattern is not so clear.

50. Assaël, "Misogynie," p. 97.

51. See Zweig, " 'Primal Mind' "; Winkler, *Constraints*, p. 204, and chaps. 5–7 on women's culture as resistant. Both stress the role of ritual in providing a women's space.

The Exchange of Women

To explicate the relationship between Euripidean tragedy and the hierarchy of gender, I first use Claude Lévi-Strauss's model of the exchange of women. His extensive analysis of kinship is founded on several related and debated claims.[52] By exchanging women with men from another group, men form relationships beyond the family and thus establish culture. Lévi-Strauss argues that "the positive aspect of the [incest] prohibition is to initiate organization" (p. 43). In this system, women are commodities: "The exchange of brides is merely the conclusion to an uninterrupted process of reciprocal gifts, which effects the transition from hostility to alliance, from anxiety to confidence, and from fear to friendship" (pp. 67–68). The reciprocity underlying exchanges—for every woman that a man gives up, another is made available to him—is related to a fundamental aspect of gift giving in traditional cultures. "Exchange, as a total phenomenon, is from the first a total exchange, comprising food, manufactured objects, and that most precious category of goods, women" (pp. 60–61). Lévi-Strauss comes to this interesting conclusion: "Marriage is an eternal triangle, not just in vaudeville sketches, but at all times, and in all places, and by definition"; by this he means that "because women have an essential value in group life, the group necessarily intervenes in every marriage.... Considered in its purely formal aspect, the prohibition of incest is thus only the group's assertion that where relationships between the sexes are concerned, *a person cannot do just what he pleases*" (p. 43).

The Lévi-Straussian theory of kinship is highly relevant to antiquity, for not only was marriage explicitly negotiated between *kurios* and husband-to-be, with the wife constituting the object of the transaction, but also the exchange of gifts and hospitality were essential to Greek mores. Yet Lévi-Strauss's overt androcentrism, like that of Althusser and Foucault, makes it dangerous to swallow him whole. As Gayle Rubin and others have asked, even if marriage rests on the division of labor between the sexes, why do men choose and distribute women, and not vice versa? Who is the "person" who cannot do "just as he pleases"? Who is the "everybody"

52. This summary comes from Lévi-Strauss, *Elementary Structures* (page references are in the text). He draws heavily on the earlier work of Mauss, who observes that women (and children) are among the objects exchanged in obligatory gift giving (*Gift*, pp. 44–45). For critiques of Lévi-Strauss, see, e.g., Hartsock, *Money, Sex, and Power*, pp. 267–301; Rubin, "Traffic in Women"; Arripe, "Contribution," pp. 67–81; de Lauretis, *Alice*, esp. pp. 18–22; Irigaray, *This Sex*, p. 170; Cowie, "Woman as Sign," esp. p. 62, on what she calls "Lévi-Strauss' confusion" about the nature of this sign, for she argues that the "sign 'woman' in exogamy is not exchanged but produced in the exchange of actual women."

who gains "a claim to a number of women as large as possible" by renouncing "a limited or very restricted share in the women immediately available" (p. 42)? In fact, Lévi-Strauss's assertions about the universality of the incest taboo are shot through with his own masculine, Western biases; similarly, his assumptions about men's pursuit of women may result from his own placement within those structures.

This circulation of women is, according to Lévi-Strauss, comparable to the circulation of language. That is, sexuality is analogous to textuality: the one is organized in kinship, the other in language; both constitute culture. Women are thus in a paradoxical situation as both sign and generator of signs. Lévi-Strauss tries romantically to keep both notions in tandem, but his language reveals a problem:

> In this way, language and exogamy represent two solutions to one and the same fundamental situation. . . . The emergence of symbolic thought must have required that women, like words, should be things that were exchanged. In this new case, indeed, this was the only means of overcoming the contradiction by which the same woman was seen under two incompatible aspects: on the one hand, as the object of personal desire, thus exciting sexual and proprietorial instincts; and, on the other, as the subject of the desire of others, and seen as such, i.e., as the means of binding others through alliance with them. But woman could never become just a sign and nothing more; . . . in so far as she is defined as a sign she must be recognized as a generator of signs. . . . In contrast to words, which have wholly become signs, woman has remained at once a sign and a value. This explains why the relations between the sexes have preserved that affective richness, ardour and mystery which doubtless originally permeated the entire universe of human communications. (p. 496)

In practice, women's right to use language has been severely curtailed; in particular, their public speech has been prohibited. Thus, even though women as human members of a language-using group are part of the culture, their subordination has been marked by a differential access to speech. That is, women are not typically signatories to the social contract; they are exchanged as a sign that it has taken place. Similarly, in the tragedies, "women" speak only the words that the male playwright gives them and the male actor articulates.

The analogy between marriage and language, however problematic from a modern feminist perspective, is very revealing about antiquity. For, as I will show, Greek men's concerns about women's sexuality and their need to control female desire in order to obtain legitimate heirs had as their corollaries the seclusion of women and the attempt to control women's use of signs. This pattern is particularly clear in Euripidean plays that represent women as sexual actors who speak about their desire. Moreover, male anxiety about the authenticity of signs can also be displaced onto women.

But although Lévi-Strauss's theory does mesh well with Greek tragedy and does enable me to get at a source of male power as represented in the plays, its assumptions must be questioned. What is the precondition of the exchange of women? At bottom, it is that women be available to men. But how is that availability engineered? Psychoanalytic work on the process of becoming a woman has tended to assume the heterosexual imperative, positing that the normal female turns from her pre-Oedipal bond with her mother to make her father her new object of desire.[53] Writers such as Nancy Chodorow, Jan Raymond, and Adrienne Rich, however, stress the primacy of the mother-daughter bond;[54] its rupture then needs to be explained, as Rich points out, not taken for granted:

> If women are the earliest sources of emotional caring and physical nur-
> ture for both female and male children, it would seem logical, from a
> feminist perspective at least, to pose the following questions: whether
> the search for love and tenderness in both sexes does not originally lead
> toward women; *why in fact women would ever redirect that search*; why
> species-survival, the means of impregnation, and emotional/erotic rela-
> tionships should ever have become so rigidly identified with each other;
> and why such violent strictures should be necessary to enforce women's
> total emotional, erotic loyalty and subservience to men.[55]

Triangles, Congruent and Incongruent

Lévi-Strauss defines a triangle of man, woman, and group; he alludes also to the romantic triangle constituted by male rivals for a woman. But other triangles are involved as well, notably that comprising the man who gives, the man who receives, and the woman. This fact highlights a crucial consequence of the traffic in women. It places men in primary relation to other men but with the appearance of loyalty to a woman. Luce Irigaray and Eve Sedgwick have observed that the exchange of women creates a world in which relationships between men are formed and validated by women, who in some sense are then just a link—but, given normative

53. Freud, "Three Essays," esp. pp. 219–21, and "Femininity."
54. Chodorow, *Reproduction*; Raymond, *Passion*, esp. pp. 184–88 on mothers, and chap. 6; Rich, "Compulsory Heterosexuality," and *Of Woman Born*, chap. 5.
55. Rich, "Compulsory Heterosexuality," p. 145.

heterosexuality, a necessary one. Irigaray points out the duplicity of Western society's attitude toward male homosexuality: "Why is masculine homosexuality considered exceptional, then, when in fact the economy as a whole is based upon it? Why are homosexuals ostracized, when society postulates homosexuality? Unless it is because the *'incest' involved in homosexuality has to remain in the realm of pretence."* [56]

Rubin's important early essay, "The Traffic in Women," pinpoints the Oedipus complex as the structure subordinating the individual to the social process of exchange. She further asserts that compulsory heterosexuality is the reverse of the incest taboo. [57] To what extent can we use these terms derived from our own cultural milieu? Current work on sexuality in antiquity takes off from the work of Foucault and warns us against using our own categories to analyze premodern cultures. [58] In *A Rhetoric of Irony*, Wayne Booth establishes a class of stable irony and remarks that despite our current tendency to privilege contradiction, what is astounding is how often we do in fact understand one another. [59] I am taking a "stable constructionist" point of view here. To be sure, there are important differences between Athens and, say, New York, and these subtend the analysis in this book, but I think we can still use some of these words if we exercise reasonable caution. [60] I would argue that the Greeks did not live in a time "before sexuality," even if they did not exactly share *our* sexuality; that the Greeks did have a form of marriage that we would recognize as "heterosexual"; and that even if Greek men did not significantly classify their choice of sexual objects by gender, they married along gender lines.

For Greek men, the pressure to continue the family line and maintain the household did not prohibit same-sex desire. Rather it coexisted with a masculine code of behavior within which an older man's desire for a boy was normalized and praised. [61] Aristophanes furnishes ample evidence

56. Irigaray, *This Sex*, p. 192. I am very indebted to Sedgwick's formulation of male homosocial ties. In *Between Men*, p. 26, she criticizes Irigaray's "expensive" lack of historical specificity; for her analysis of the way several paradigms intersect, see her introduction and chap. 1.

57. Rubin, "Traffic in Women," pp. 192–200. Sedgwick, *Between Men*, pp. 3–4, modifies Rubin in important ways; on the difficulty of these terms, see her introduction, as well as the introduction to her *Epistemology*.

58. Halperin, Winkler, and Zeitlin, *Before Sexuality*; Halperin, *One Hundred Years*; Winkler, *Constraints*. For a critique, see Richlin, "Zeus"; she presented some preliminary findings on Roman homosexuality at the American Philological Association panel in 1991 in her paper "Not before Homosexuality: The Materiality of the *Cinaedus* and the Roman Law against Love between Men."

59. Booth, *Rhetoric of Irony*, esp. pp. 13, 133.

60. The warnings of Boswell, "Concepts," pp. 67–73, are salutary.

61. For the literature on same-sex desire, generally now construed as pederasty, see Dover, *Greek Homosexuality*; and Buffière, *Eros adolescent*, who says, *tout court*, "The Greeks con-

of prejudice against men desiring other men, but it seems to have been directed against individuals who transgressed the limits of that code, acted the sexual female, submitted to anal intercourse. Hence the "wide-ass" is the butt of many of his jokes (e.g., *Thesmophoriazousai* 200, *Knights* 639).[62] Since vase paintings commonly represent boy-man relationships, theorists such as K. J. Dover reconcile Aristophanes' blame with Plato's praise by presuming that only pederastic (cross-age) intercrural (not anal) sex was truly acceptable: "The reader who turns from Plato to comedy is struck not only by the consistent reduction of homosexual eros to the coarsest physical terms but also by its displacement from the centre to the periphery of Athenian sexual life; for comedy is fundamentally heterosexual."[63] The crime, then, says Winkler, was not to experience sexual longing for a male but to confuse "incompatible categories—those of male citizen and male prostitute. The *kinaidos* is a scare-image standing behind the more concrete charges of shaming one's integrity as a male citizen by hiring out one's body to another man's use. The three components of the accusation are promiscuity, payment, and passivity to another man's penetration."[64]

Any form of female desire could be perceived as a threat to the family and the Athenian polis—yet here we are faced again with the divergences between evidence from different locations and times. Although Spartan and Lesbian lyric poetry of the seventh and sixth centuries B.C.E. suggests that women were initiated sexually as well as ritually by women, there is no such evidence for fifth-century Athens. Sappho and Alcman sketch in a picture of girls in choruses who are erotically involved with one another; this subject of their desire is absent (if not actually taboo) in the discourse of Attic drama.[65] Female-female relationships are noticeably absent, given

---

demned homosexuality, which offended their taste and their aesthetic" (p. 7; cf. pp. 23, 617). Foucault, *Use of Pleasure*; Halperin, *One Hundred Years*, chaps. 1–3, 5; and Winkler, *Constraints*, chap. 2, all emphasize the Greek division of the sexual realm not by gender but along lines of domination and subordination; a citizen male could not engage in certain acts without loss of honor. Although Greek men may be said to have practiced pederasty, younger man pursued by older man, it nonetheless appears that first as youth (beloved) and then as mature man (lover), men could have been involved with other men for much of the period of sexual activity. If they behaved appropriately to their age and status, they received none of the opprobrium reserved for the sexual deviant, the *kinaidos* (on which figure, and the difficulties of translation, see Winkler, *Constraints*, chap. 2).

62. See Dover, *Greek Homosexuality*, esp. pp. 142–46.

63. Ibid., p. 148; cf. Halperin, *One Hundred Years*, pp. 29, 33, 35.

64. Winkler, *Constraints*, p. 46 (citing Halperin, *One Hundred Years*, pp. 94–98). He goes on to make the connection between the enforcement of the laws and the surveillance of politically important men, "the very restricted class of elite players in the high-stakes game of the city's policy management, where they were used as a weapon to knock opponents out of the game."

65. There is only one mention in Plato (*Symposium* 191e), where "Aristophanes" refers

that the public realm dominated by men was homosocial: it was founded on initiation into the military, which was associated with male "homosexual" acts; men also came into relation with other men through marriage. If female initiation was accomplished in female groups, it did not lead to public power, and it ended in marriage.[66] We see the very clear social consequences and dimension of "private" actions.

The kinship triangle constituted by the exchange of women works to prevent women from acting as sexual subjects. The staging of tragedy and the structure of representation in general can constitute another triangle: that between author, audience, and character in the production of gender. Of course, patriarchal power manifests and reproduces itself in representation as well as in the family. Catharine MacKinnon maintains that texts exert an epistemological power that makes the male point of view seem to be what *is*.[67] Laura Mulvey suggests that representation, as it has been practiced in the West, requires victimization; as she says, "Sadism demands a story."[68] Representation under male dominance—for example, in ancient Greece—places women in a position analogous to what Lévi-Strauss has analyzed as the exchange of women.

There is a further relationship between these two triangles. As we have seen, marriage by exchange placed men in relation to other men *and* in relation to women: that is, it gratified the homosocial desires *and* heterosexual demands of Greek culture. But such an institution was not easy to maintain. Might not a woman balk at the limits of heterosexuality and re-

---

to females who only love other females (*hetairistriai*). Dover, *Greek Homosexuality* (see pp. 172–73, 182, 181 n. 32), mentions that female same-sex desire does seem to deviate from the male pattern of dominance and subordination; see also Cantrarella, *Bisexuality*, esp. pp. viii, 4. Winkler, *Constraints*, pp. 162–65, notes that a general silence about female sexuality forms the context for the representation of and silence about lesbian sexuality in Sappho: "I simply begin my analysis with the fact that there was available a common understanding that proper women ought to be publicly submissive to male definitions, and that a very great pressure of propriety could at any time be invoked to shame a woman who acted on her own sexuality" (p. 163).

66. On the possibility of a female community behind tragedy, see Zweig, "'Primal Mind.'" There is direct evidence of male ritual homosexuality only among Spartans and Cretans (Plato *Symposium* 282B, *Laws* 1.636b–d, 8.836a–c; Strabo *Geography* 10.4.16, 20–21); on Sparta, see Cartledge, "Spartan Pederasty." There is debate about Athenian and Ionian parallels; Buffière, *Eros adolescent*, p. 76, finds early examples but on p. 197 denies military motivation, finding it intellectual and moral instead. Calame, *Choeurs*, pp. 421–38, 454, makes the connection between male and female patterns, noting that female relations with women are much less evident in myth (p. 432). On this absence, see Cartledge, "Spartan Pederasty," p. 30 n. 5; Sergent, *Homosexuality*. I am indebted to Ann Michelini's perceptive commentary on this point.

67. MacKinnon, "Feminism . . . Theory," p. 249.

68. Mulvey, "Visual Pleasure," in *Visual*, p. 22. For a development and refinement of this notion, see de Lauretis, *Alice*, esp. pp. 103–24.

fuse to identify with her husband's family? Might not a man refuse to set a limit to his relationships to men? In either case, from the hegemonic view, the continued life of the family would collapse. Thus, not only the exchange of women but men's and women's complicity in the system was necessary.

The role of tragedy as a public art form was in part to keep the system going. Even Euripides' radical plays do this cultural work, both revealing and disguising the system whereby men exchange women to institute culture, which then excludes them. The plays are informed by the pattern of the exchange of women, with the suppression of female subjectivity that that necessitates. They mimic the social structure, inscribing a heterosexuality that is seemingly absolute for women but consistent with, even predicated upon, homosocial behavior for men. Women are represented as torn from associations with other women which might be supportive; men are encouraged in their relationships to other men. Female identification with men supports male power by dividing women and making them seem to be the agents of their own suffering; men's same-sex relations similarly support male power.

On one level, the plots enact many analogues to the exchange of women. Just as the exchange of women places men in primary relation with other men (the father of the bride with the groom, not the bride with the groom), so, in Euripidean tragedy, different forms of the quest of male for male (friend, father, son) frequently underlie a plot that seems to foreground women. On another level, the performance of tragedy constitutes the triangle of author, audience, and character, in which even a strong female character mediates between the recipient and the sender of the message, both established as male.[69] The texts thus support the sexual hierarchy and the continued passivity of women, even while representing aggressive females.

This book does not pretend to be an exhaustive treatment of the plays of Euripides, for I have deliberately focused on those texts that depend on the exchange of women. To make clear the intricate ways in which these dramas yield additional meaning when studied from the standpoint of their ideological component, their work as technologies of gender, I have structured the text as follows. Part I analyzes the so-called sacrifice plays (*Iphigenia in Aulis*, *Hekabe*, and *Alcestis*, in particular), in which Euripides represents the female protagonists as choosing death and then glorifies them for their virtue. In this way, he dresses up the exchange value of women (acting as signs of male power or honor) as their own desire (acting as subjects in their own right). These figures strive for

---

69. On the object position of woman in representation, see Kappeler, *Pornography*, esp. chap. 5.

subjectivity when they volunteer to die, but they do not achieve it. I contend that in glorifying such moments of "freely chosen" victimization, Euripides bolsters the patriarchal system by disguising the objectification of women that is necessary for their exchange.

Part II addresses the way Euripides constructs the well-known strong women who resist the socially constructed norms imposed on them. Throughout these plays *Hekabe, Medea, Hippolytos*, there are female characters (Hekabe, Medea, and Phaedra for example) who disrupt, but in various ways their strength is eroded by the endings, which at the least attempt to deny them the audience's approval. The sacrificial heroines turn out to be models of what *to* do; the active ones turn out to be models of what *not* to do. If the figures who seem active only in their sacrifice present a model of what men would like women to be, these vindictive women, in causing the death of male youths, confirm Greek men's worst fears about women. Looking at the two paradigms together, we see that when mature male characters demand young women as sacrificial victims, the girls volunteer to die and are "glorified" for their nobility; when mature females murder male young, it is simply slaughter, for there is no ritual reason for or acceptance of such death.[70]

Part III, examining *Hippolytos* and *Ion*, shifts from the fantasized representation of women to the explicit consequences for the male characters. For the women, of course, are in fact a tool for the male author as they are for the culture; often, the underlying goal of the plays (and the culture) is the relationship between men. What Greek men, and not only Jason and Hippolytos, wanted was a way to reproduce without women. While in the other plays the exchange of women often reveals this structure to be at work (for instance, through bonds of friendship in *Alcestis* or of the military in *Iphigenia in Aulis*), in these plays the father-son dyad takes the place of the son's relationship to the mother.[71]

In Quest of a Third Position

The problems of positioning oneself as a feminist classicist are implicit in the very terms of my analysis. What does a feminist find in the past? Was it so awful as to be simply depressing? Should we take it as a cautionary tale, or should we look for something positive there? Euripides has con-

70. For a very different but related reading, consider Slater's *Glory of Hera*, itself the subject of controversy in classical studies.

71. See Poole, "Male Homosexuality in Euripides"; for the connection between father-son relationship and same-sex desire, see Grube, *Drama*, pp. 19, 21.

structed our belief in the characters' "freedom" *to some end*; what does he gain from that construction? What do we want to take from that construction? Simply to accept Euripides' glorification of the virgins seems to mean accepting the myth of female masochism; simply to deny their nobility seems relentlessly to call them victims and risks making them once again invisible. Similarly, simply to accept Euripides' vilification of the vengeful mature females implies an acceptance of the castrating mother; simply to reject the implicit evaluation seems tantamount to embracing a world where murder is acceptable. In celebrating their strength, am I tacitly accepting a morality that I actually find questionable?

As must be clear, feminist readers need at least a third position. I seek ways to see the strength behind the characters of Alcestis, Iphigenia, Polyxena and to recognize the strength of Medea, Phaedra, Hekabe without accepting the interpretation men have built into their constructions. We cannot practice wishful thinking, though, and should, I think, give up on reclaiming Euripides for feminism. We must first read the text with the ideology, as the author would have us do, in order to see and understand the forces that have made such representations compelling. Then we can read against that position in various ways; I have found myself increasingly emphasizing the female power that may well have inspired this male reaction.

In short, we have choices in how we position ourselves. In order to balance these two ways of reading, I need to rely on two further technical concepts: the "fetish" and the "uncanny." These terms have taken on a new constellation of meanings in poststructuralist and feminist literary theory. My claim is that in fact the sacrificial maidens are fetishized, while the murderous mothers are made terrifying by being made signs of the uncanny.[72] The former are rewarded with glory; the latter are punished with blame.

Marx takes the term "fetish" from nineteenth-century religious studies— where it indicates the assignment of will and power to an inanimate object—and uses it to denote a commodity taken out of its context of production and given value.[73] Psychoanalytic theory, on the other hand, relates the fetish to castration. According to Freud, the male child, viewing the mother's body and noting the anatomical difference between the sexes, fears for his penis, for he hypothesizes that his mother actually once had

---

72. Bal, *Death and Dissymmetry*, pp. 186–96, makes a similar correlation between sacrifice and the uncanny, or "unhomeliness," as she calls it.

73. Marx, "Fetishism of Commodities"; on Freud vs. Marx and the fetish, see also du Bois's introduction to *Sowing*. Outside the classics, see Williams, "Fetishism," pp. 24–30. Ellen, "Fetishism," pp. 213–32, brings religion, economics, and psychology together.

a penis herself but lost it. A little boy, according to Freud, may then develop the consoling narcissistic device of the fetish, which allows him simultaneously to understand that the woman before him does not have a penis and to endow her with one, thus reassuring himself about the security of his own. To quote Freud, "What happened, therefore, was that the boy refused to take cognizance of the fact of his having perceived that a woman does not possess a penis. No, that could not be true: for, if a woman had been castrated, then his own possession of a penis was in danger; and against that there rose in rebellion the portion of his narcissism which Nature has, as a precaution, attached to that particular organ."[74] In this schema, the commonly conceived fetish object, the shoe or foot, represents the missing phallus and makes it possible for the man to have heterosexual relations. In adoring the fetish, let us note, the fetishist is adoring not the woman but rather the aspect of her that he has chosen and that makes him comfortable, giving him the illusion of wholeness.[75]

It is my contention that the female sacrificial heroine functions as a fetishized object; the praise heaped on her is the corollary of the over-valuation of the fetish object, and as in the case of the adulation of such an object, it does not mean that women are positively valued. Quite the contrary. Male characters and men in the audience are in the position of the fetishist; their narcissism is also consoled, since the heroines sacrifice themselves for a masculine code of behavior. To the extent that male critics have participated in this glorification, they too have stood to gain from this structure of the fetish. And if a female member of the audience par-ticipates in the "glorification" of the sacrificial victim, she takes on a mas-culine subject position, allowing the disguised victimization to reassure her.

An alternative is to focus on the perceived strength that necessitates such measures of control. Freud links fetishism to the uncanny: "It is as though the last impression before the uncanny and traumatic one is re-tained as a fetish."[76] In several of the plays, fetishistic exaltation of the choices seemingly made by a passive woman is coupled with the punish-ment of other women who refuse to accept their own powerlessness and who will not be repressed or suppressed. This leads me to my second

74. Freud, "Fetishism," p. 153. He also refers to an "aversion, which is never absent in any fetishist, to the real female genitals" (p. 154).

75. On the double movement of adoration and denigration, see Schor, "Female Fetish-ism"; in tragedy the adoration is the glorification, which, since it is false, reinscribes castration. In a later essay ("Fetishism") Schor notes a connection between fetishism and irony in the nineteenth century. Euripides, too, was an ironist.

76. Freud, "Fetishism," p. 155.

term, the *unheimlich*. Although the usual translation of *unheimlich* as "un-canny" leaves out the root in "home," the term literally means "unhome-like." Yet as Freud points out, the *unheimlich* potential is already within *heim*. After surveying the semantic field, Freud gives this definition: "Thus *heimlich* is a word the meaning of which develops in the direction of ambivalence, until it finally coincides with its opposite, *unheimlich*."[77] In other words, too much privacy becomes secrecy. As we will see, it is significant that he gives as a Greek equivalent *xenos*, or guest-friend/stranger, the very word used to define Herakles in relation to Admetos in the *Alcestis*. "The familiar can become uncanny and frightening" in different ways, especially when "something repressed recurs" (p. 224). Further on he says, by way of summing up:

> We have now only a few more remarks to add, for animism, magic and sorcery, the omnipotence of thoughts, man's attitude to death, invol-untary repetition and the castration-complex comprise practically all the factors which turn something fearful into something uncanny.... It often happens that male patients declare that they feel there is something uncanny about the female genital organs. This *unheimlich* place, however, is the entrance to the former *heim* [home] of all human beings, to the place where each one of us lived once upon a time and in the beginning. ... In this case, too, then the *unheimlich* is what was once *heimisch*, home-like, familiar; the prefix "un" is the token of repression. (Pp. 243, 245)

Thus the uncanny is not something new but something "familiar and old-established in the mind that has been estranged only by the process of repression" (p. 241). As we will see in *Alcestis* and *Hekabe*, a ghost is a good example of the *unheimlich*.

These terms "fetish" and "uncanny" are closely related in feminist film theory, which can help us understand how they work to construct gender. Feminist film theory utilizes both the clinical and the everyday Marxist-derived sense of the word to theorize ways of looking, and this theory of spectatorship is useful for tragedy as well. Fetishism is typically viewed in both psychoanalytic and filmic terms as a masculine perversion, for the little girl would not feel the same threat of deprivation with respect to an organ she knows she never had, and the female viewer would not have the same distance from the female figure.[78] Instead of looking at images of women, I propose to look at the male fantasy and anxiety that require

---

77. Freud, "The Uncanny," p. 226 (subsequent page references are in the text).
78. On film and fetishism, see Mulvey, *Visual*; Doane, *Desire*, p. 32; Donaldson, "Miranda Complex." On the masculinity of the perversion, see Doane, *Desire*, pp. 15–16; Schor, "Female Fetishism"; Pajaczkowska, "Heterosexual Presumption," p. 83.

those images that are projected onto them. Mulvey alludes to a current realization that "the image of women that had circulated as a signifier of sexuality could be detached from reality, from referring to actual women, and become attached to a new referent, the male unconscious. The direction of the gaze shifted, satisfyingly, from woman as spectacle to the psyche that had need of such a spectacle."[79]

Mulvey and Suzanne Kappeler both suggest that there are only two positions for the female: she is either fetishized or punished.[80] In the sacrifice plays, a young and virtuous woman is idealized; she corresponds to the fetish. The virgins become objects of the male gaze; they reassure instead of threatening castration. Ultimately, they support male subjectivity. They are put to death, undergoing what would ordinarily be considered punishment without its seeming like punishment. In the plays with strong, older women the heroine is made to seem uncanny and guilty of some sort of excess. These figures are not consoling but dangerous; by making them seem excessive, Euripides encourages the audience to deny these uncanny older women their sympathy. For the time being, it is sufficient to note that in the plays featuring sacrificial heroines, the uncanny is present but separated from the virginal protagonist, displaced onto an older woman who is repressed by the play's struggle for closure.

Why should a feminist critic take on such critical theory and all the baggage that comes with it? In part because Freud is useful for understanding male fantasy, which I take tragedy to be.[81] Moreover, each of these particular features of the psychological landscape, the fetish and the *unheimlich*, involves a radical ambivalence: the fetish enables men both to accept and to deny castration; in the *unheimlich* the familiar is terrifying, and the terrifying is familiar. They are also devices that simultaneously acknowledge and control—acknowledge *in order* to control—female power. That is, the fetishized woman may console the observer, but only in the face of an anxiety at her strength, which is also represented; similarly, the uncanny woman is frightening in her strength, even if she is ultimately unsympathetic and punished.

This kind of shiftiness enables us to avoid the most obvious readings of these texts. The fetish and the uncanny are structures that acknowledge the possibility of a female power, even while they function as devices to co-opt that power, which men perceive as threatening. Through a fetishistic gaze, the male fetishist gains authority; beholding the desirable female

79. Mulvey, *Visual*, pp. xiii-xiv.
80. Mulvey, *Visual*, pp. 21–22; Kappeler, *Pornography*, pp. 51, 90.
81. DuBois, *Sowing*, Introduction, esp. p. 11, voices similar doubts and comes to a similar conclusion as to Freud's usefulness.

sacrificing for men, he gains assurance. By focusing on that fetishism, the female critic is enabled to take seriously (at least provisionally) the power controlled by this strategy. This fetishism, this castration, then, is not about the penis but about access to action and subjectivity.[82]

A Marxist as well as Freudian reading of the fetish is essential, for the fetishized woman is not only an object in a male sexual economy but also an exalted idol, a commodity, whose social construction is obscured. By refusing to forget that process, the modern reader is at least pointed again to the power (political this time) that necessitated the deception. This form of deconstruction is not nostalgic for the past, does not deny male control, but does recognize the female power behind it.[83] The multiplicity of possible interpretations indicates that Euripides and tragedy can be used in many different ways, depending on the intentions of the reader; we can emphasize what Euripides attempts to do as well as noting what he represents almost despite himself.

82. Schor, "Female Fetishism," argues that "the writer's fetishism becomes the critic's" (p. 301). See Kofman, *Enigma*, pp. 86–89, and "Ça cloche," pp. 132–45, on the generalized fetishism of Derrida. In the end, though, Schor has difficulty with the misogynist trappings of the word "fetishism," and I am uneasy even using the term "castration," although I am referring to a male fear that is allayed by a certain kind of use of woman.

83. See Rose, *Sons of the Gods*; and Jameson, *Marxism and Form*, pp. 118–20, for the related concept of the Marxist dialectical hermeneutic: "Art cannot manage that which it does not in some way reveal and evoke" (Rose, p. 36). We can choose to constitute ourselves as what Judith Fetterley calls "resisting readers."

PART I   *Fetishized Victims*

1 The Sacrificial Virgins: Iphigenia and Others

The extant plays of Euripides highlight *voluntary* sacrifice; furthermore, I would argue that they are the only Greek plays to dramatize that structure.[1] The death of Sophocles' Antigone, which seems like a model, is actually a punishment for the positive action she has committed, whereas for Euripides' characters death itself is the action taken. Although the Euripidean treatment brings out the metaphoric connection between marriage and death that is also prominent in *Antigone*, there is a crucial difference: Antigone prefers action to marriage; for Iphigenia and Polyxena the sacrifice is eroticized.[2]

I would hypothesize a connection between the importance of female characters and the importance of sacrifice in Euripides; women or effeminized men are the appropriate candidates for sacrifice.[3] Menoeceus in the

1. On sacrifice in Euripides, see Burnett, *Catastrophe*, pp. 22–27; Foley, *Ritual Irony*, esp. chaps. 1–2; Nancy, "Pharmakon sōtērias"; Pucci, "Euripides' *Hippolytos*," pp. 165–66; Roussel, "Thème du sacrifice"; Schmitt, *Freiwilliger Opfertod*; Vellacott, *Ironic Drama*, pp. 178–204. Michelini, *Euripides*, pp. 91–93, comments that such sacrificial virtue is not typically Greek and that the heroines' "outrageous virtue" structurally replaces vice.

2. Guépin, *Tragic Paradox*, pp. 102–3, observes the predominance of sacrifice in Euripides; he alludes to the parallel of Kore and Antigone as vegetation sacrifices, noting the other brides of Hades as well (p. 141). Rose, "Bride," makes the same connection to fertility ritual for Antigone. Burnett, *Catastrophe*, pp. 23–24, accepts Antigone as the model of the sacrificial heroine.

3. Cf. Vellacott, who thinks that the sacrifice of maidens points up or heightens the irony at work throughout the corpus, particularly indicating the hubris of the men performing the sacrifice (*Ironic Drama*, pp. 179–82). In Foley's view, there is a form of cultural work being performed, but ambivalently embraced: "These two plays [*Bacchae* and *Herakles*] create a fundamental social and poetic crisis and close with the emergence of a new order which makes survival possible, but at a cost so unbearable that their endings have been read as simply ironic or self-deluding" (*Ritual Irony*, p. 63).

Phoenician Women is the only male represented as willingly allowing himself
to be slain for a cause, while there are four women (in *Iphigenia in Aulis*,
Hekabe, the *Children of Herakles*, and the fragmentary *Erechtheus*). Since sacrifice too is a form of exchange (gifts are given to the gods, in order to put
mortals in advantageous relation to immortals), the sacrifice motif is especially relevant to my consideration of the exchange of women.[4] As proper
sacrifice is one way of constituting the community, so the literary representation of sacrifice does important cultural work: in the case of these plays, it
functions to reproduce a certain form of gender difference in the audience.

Why are maidens suitable victims? Walter Burkert believes that sacrifice
originated in the hunt; in discussing maiden sacrifice, he reasons thus:

> Hunting and war are sanctioned by social custom as tests of manhood,
> and they take precedence over courtship and marriage. Man declines to
> love in order to kill: this is most graphically demonstrated in the ritual
> slaughter of "the virgin," the potential source both of a happy union
> and of disruptive conflict within the group. In the maiden-sacrifice, all
> the tensions—the jealousy of the elderly, the strivings of the young—
> are released. An irreparable act transforms an erotic game into fighting
> fury.... In the period of preparation, maiden-sacrifice is the strongest
> expression of the attempt to renounce sexuality.[5]

Burkert accepts "man the hunter" and the related "development of a social
order leading to sharp sexual differentiation, which has even become a
part of our inherited biological constitution."[6] It seems, then, that the
sacrifice of girls is a corollary of their sex role. While Burkert's tendency
to universalize a modern bourgeois model of the home is problematic, his
correlation of sexual differentiation with hunting and therefore sacrifice
points out the role that the sacrificed virgin plays in a masculine culture.

Mieke Bal studies sacrifice in the Book of Judges from a different perspective but to similar effect. She argues that these virgins are appropriate
or necessary sacrifices because they are gifts to be given by the father.

4. On this primarily structuralist view of sacrifice, see Mauss and Hubert, *Sacrifice*; Detienne, *Gardens*, p. 4; Vernant, "Théorie," esp. p. 5; Segal, "Greek Tragedy" and "Mariage
et sacrifice," among others. Kirk, "Pitfalls," pp. 71–76, criticizes this broad generalization
and suggests that we distinguish carefully between modes of sacrifice. Guépin, *Tragic Paradox*,
sees both ritual murder (pp. 59–61) and gift (pp. 149–51) as formative.
5. Burkert, *Homo Necans*, p. 64. But cf. Hughes, *Human Sacrifice*, esp. pp. 76–79, on
the value of sacrifice as representing the ideal and related to initiation.
6. Burkert, *Homo Necans*, p. 17. Bremmer, "Scapegoat," p. 302, notes that the girls are
not the only victims and cites at least two examples where a prince or a king sacrifices himself;
he finds the king the "lonely marginal at the top" (p. 304). But the stake of the kings he
mentions is surely different from the girls'. As Schmitt-Pantel, "Histoire," p. 223, points
out, when men "die for the city," it is in the "highly valorised context of war."

Jephthah's vow (see Judges 11:30–40) is part of a "misunderstanding that encapsulates virginity in general and of which the daughter is a 'natural' victim rather than an accidental one." She argues that the status of the virgin "is first and foremost that of a potential object of gift, a subject of insecurity. How will the girl be given, and to whom? How will her next phase, yet unknown to her, end?"[7]

Bal points out that if a similar victim had "been given to a human victor, her fate would have been marriage."[8] She argues that in Hebrew "virginity" can have different meanings: for the father, it marks his daughter as an object to be given, for the maiden herself, it represents a time spent apart. The Greek word for maiden, *parthenos*, is also ambiguous. Significantly, maidenhood ended and the girl became a woman only when she was a wife, and only when she was lawfully given, not if she was raped or even pregnant but unmarried. There was, however, an exception: sacrifice could transform a virgin into a woman, as it does in the cases of Iphigenia and Polyxena. As Giulia Sissa has argued, the hymen is not the mark that modernity has made of it; defloration does not necessarily create a woman.[9]

Sacrifice and marriage may then serve the same function. Vernant, followed by many others, has argued that animal sacrifice and marriage are parallels: "At the same time that it is necessary, for survival, to eat the cooked flesh of the domestic beast sacrificed according to the rules, it is also necessary to nourish oneself with grain, with the cooked cereals of domestic plants cultivated by rule, and in order to survive oneself, to engender a son by union with a woman whom marriage has taken from savagery in order to domesticate by placing her in the conjugal hearth."[10] René Girard also believes that the goal of sacrifice is to salvage the group, to "reinforce the social fabric."[11] According to Girard, the sacrificial victim is a substitute, enabling the group to exercise violence without fear of vengeance; thus, for the sacrifice to be effective, the victim must be like

7. Bal, *Death and Dissymmetry*, p. 42.

8. Ibid., p. 49. The Hebrew tradition is not identical with the Greek, to be sure. For instance, the role of the Greek father is not always prominent, although it is in the case of Iphigenia, and there is almost always a strong female who threatens or enacts revenge (see Part II). Where Bal has to read in the avenging woman, she is clearly present in the Greek tradition.

9. Sissa, *Greek Virginity*, pp. 1–2, 76–78, 105–27; cf. her statement that *parthenia* "is a separate existence, which is ended by contact with the male sex" (p. 78). See also Calame, *Choeurs*, p. 65.

10. Vernant, "Théorie," p. 13. The first sacrifice and the first marriage are also connected to the duplicity of Pandora, the first woman. See Hoffman, "Pandora," p. 123. Cf. Vernant, "Myth of Prometheus," pp. 168–85; Mason, "Third Person/Second Sex."

11. Girard, *Violence*, p. 8.

the community but not identical to it. Marginal figures, then, children and slaves, are good candidates.[12] Married women do not make acceptable offerings because they could invoke the anger of two clans; by Girard's reasoning, virgins would meet the necessary conditions because—not yet married—they are marginal.

We can better understand the disproportionate number of virgins sacrificed by attending to the similarities between marriage and sacrifice as institutions.[13] Marriage centered on gifts and feast; sacrifice was itself an offering to the gods (a gift) as well as a feast for the community. Animal and bride were both garlanded. Marriage organized a natural phenomenon (reproduction) into socially acceptable behavior, orchestrating the relationships between male and female (as well as male and male, in the case of exogamous marriage by exchange), while sacrifice organized and sanctified a natural phenomenon (meat eating) and orchestrated the relationship between gods and humans and humans and beasts.

This functionalist approach, like the word "humans" above, leaves unexplored an underlying inequality between men and women in both institutions. Sacrifice and marriage were alike in constituting relationships through exchange; furthermore, both constituted hierarchical communities: men ate more than women at the sacrifice, and in marriage the woman sealed the contract but was not a party to it.[14] In the plays of sacrifice, the virgin is the sacrificial offering, as she is the ultimate gift in marriage. Just as the garlanded bride only appears to be the center of the marriage, so the garlanded sacrificial victim only appears to be the center of an action that requires but does not concern her. In sum, marriage is like sacrifice because in marriage woman is the offering through which culture is constituted.

Structuralists make another gender-blind proportion based on the metier to which each sex is dedicated: marriage is to women as war is to men. Initiation rituals produce men and women out of boys and girls, each prepared for his or her own role. But I would add that initiation for women leads to men, while initiation for men leads to men as well. The

12. Ibid., p. 12. See also Bremmer, "Scapegoat," p. 306, who points out that in sacrifice "a cheap or relatively superfluous animal . . . or a woman is sent away after being made more attractive than it originally was."

13. For a general discussion, see Vernant, "Introduction." I am deeply indebted not only to the work of Vernant but also to that of Helene Foley in *Ritual Irony*, chaps. 1–2. Segal, "Mariage et sacrifice," stresses the complementarity of the husband and wife; I would emphasize the asymmetry. As Schmitt-Pantel, "Histoire," pp. 226–27, observes, men as well as women marry.

14. Foley, *Ritual Irony*, pp. 32–36.

sacrifice of Iphigenia to Artemis may be a reflection of the death symbolized in initiation.[15]

A central and peculiar feature of Greek practice with respect to sacrifice was "willingness": the victim had to seem to walk up to the altar of its own volition, and various tricks were used to gain the appearance of consent. Jan Bremmer describes one: "Whenever the animal did not shake its head in agreement, wine or milk was poured over its head. When subsequently, the animal tried to shake this off its head, this was interpreted as a sign of its consent!"[16] The appearance of consent transformed what would have seemed a slaughter or murder into a sacrifice. If sacrifice was analogous to marriage, was the consent required any different? That is, was it required merely in order to transform rape into marriage?[17]

Tragedy has an important, albeit confused, relationship to sacrifice; they are alike in being offerings to a god.[18] As those involved in the meat sacrifice shared the feast and constituted a community, those at the tragedy were melded into a community by the experience. But in forming culture, as I argued above, both tragedy and sacrifice were most concerned with forming male subjectivity, in part through an articulation of gender and appropriate gender roles. Just as women were not equal members of the sacrificial community, so they were not equal members of the community formed by the performance of a play.[19] To the extent that tragedy formed a community, then, it was (in the case of the sacrificial drama) a community of men based on the representation of women's willing subordination; as a result, it allayed masculine anxieties about female strength.

The strength of the problematic *parthenos*, the woman not yet given in

15. See Vernant, "City-State Warfare," esp. pp. 23, 25; Dowden, *Death*, p. 36; Guépin, *Tragic Paradox*, esp. p. 138 on sacrifice and rite of passage. Vidal-Naquet, *Black Hunter*, objects sharply to assimilating the female to the male experience. See above, Introduction, note 9.

16. Bremmer, "Scapegoat," p. 308 nn. 49–50. On the voluntary nature of sacrifice, see Meuli, *Gesammelte Schriften*, pp. 993–96; Guépin, *Tragic Paradox*, pp. 100–101; Versnel, "Self-sacrifice," pp. 135–85; Henrichs, "Human Sacrifice," pp. 195–235. Vernant, "Théorie," p. 27, discusses the relation of murder and sacrifice, noting the omission of representations of the scene of death except in tragedy, which questions the human condition. For theories stressing violence as the root of sacrifice, see Burkert, *Homo Necans*; Girard, *Violence*.

17. For modern discussions of consent, see MacKinnon, "Feminism . . . Jurisprudence"; Pateman, "Women and Consent." On rape in antiquity, see Zeitlin, "Configurations." For further consideration, see Chapter 7, below.

18. On the sacrificial origins of Greek tragedy, see, e.g., Harrison, *Themis*; Burkert, "Greek Tragedy." Guépin, *Tragic Paradox*, defines tragedy as "a sacrificial ritual" (p. 16).

19. Though present, they were not there in the same numbers or the same capacity (they were not judges; they were perhaps seated differently) as men. See Introduction.

marriage, resided in the possibility that she might refuse marriage altogether and adopt the stance of the Amazon. Vernant puts the unmarried
girl (*korē*) at one end of a spectrum, the courtesan "entirely devoted to
love" at the other; they are mediated by the wife.[20] Either extreme can
then be dangerous to the institution of marriage. William Tyrrell argues
that the Amazon model emblematized the threat of what would happen
if the girl did not make the proper transformation.[21] Adrienne Rich, writing from a very different perspective, sees the virgin as "she-who-is-unto-
herself" and opposes that concept to the emphasis on the hymen (and a
logic of there/not there).[22] The self-sacrificing maidens of tragedy are
represented as reasserting a masculine warrior code, to which they then
sacrifice themselves. By so depicting this female power, the sacrifice plays
themselves work as sacrifices; as all tragedy is an offering to Dionysos,
these plays offer up their female figures to the audience.

   In the realms of Greek sacrifice, marriage, and tragedy, then, women
function as signs in a Lévi-Straussian sense; are they in any sense manipulators of signs and participants in the active making of culture? The
sacrifice motif would seem to lend itself readily to a paradigm of woman-
as-victim, man-as-victimizer; after all, what could be more objectified than
a human sacrifice? Yet Euripides presents his sacrificial heroines not as
helpless victims but as women who *willingly* give up life. This apparently
free choice is foregrounded in each case by the presence of an opponent
to the sacrifice. While the voluntary element conforms to Greek sacrificial
practice, the ritual requirement does not entirely explain Euripides'
practice.

   Is there in fact anything for women as such in this sacrificial model?
Women in the sex-segregated world of Athens, which stressed their silence
and nonparticipation, were denied access to heroism, among other cultural
values. Masculine virtues had to do with valor, *andreia*; female virtue had
to do with chastity. Male honor was rewarded with fame; female honor
was rewarded with the respectability of silence.[23] Silence *about* respectable

   20. Vernant, "Introduction," p. ix.
   21. Tyrrell, *Amazons*, pp. 64–67; cf. p. 73 on Hippolytos.
   22. Rich, *Of Woman Born*, pp. 107, 121, 249. Sissa's analysis of the Greek deemphasis
of the hymen (in *Greek Virginity*) challenges only one aspect of Rich's thinking. Loraux,
Tragic Ways, p. 33, points out the warrior quality of the chaste Artemis and Athena: "First
of all we should remember that, because she is ignorant of marriage and the works of
Aphrodite, the young girl is assumed by the collective imagination to have connections with
the world of war. Athena, virgin and warrior, comes to mind."
   23. Pericles' speech in Thucydides (2.45.2) is the classic formulation, for he basically says
that the only good reputation for a woman is no reputation at all; women should also be
silent. Sissa, *Greek Virginity*, p. 168, relates the two openings of mouth and vagina: "The
analogy between mouth and genitals, between sexuality and speech, could be deployed

women pursued them even to the grave, for women were not named on gravestones.[24] These maidens, however, could gain a kind of fame and glory ordinarily reserved to men. As Bremmer says about sacrifice itself, the victim looks "more attractive" than before; he points out that "in historical reality the community sacrificed the least valuable members of the polis, who were represented, however, as very valuable persons."[25] What is offered the virgins in tragedies of sacrifice is something seemingly quite different from the position they would have occupied in life. They escape from feminine silence without the implication of being loose in their morals, for the playwright gives them not only words but words calculated to win the very glorious reputation usually reserved for heroes.

The freedom that Euripides allows them, however, is as deceptive as the apparent presence of women on stage. Although the characters seem to be women who make choices and act, they are of course men dressed up in women's clothing.[26] Each female is thus absent while seemingly present. As a result, although (or because) Euripides makes his sacrificial victims seem like agents, he tells us nothing about what they want, only about what men require of them. In fact, we see the fetishization of woman; these figures are glorified objects which, by virtue of the very glory attributed to them, reassure men as to their own self-sufficiency. A grammar of the plays of sacrifice—who acts? who benefits from the action? who is acted upon?—will perhaps enable us to see through the constructed actions of these self-sacrificing heroines.

In fact, two sacrifices are enacted, one within the play, one enacted by the play's apparent granting of freedom and glory to these characters.[27] The apparently voluntary nature of these sacrifices obscures and mystifies what is at stake: the exchange of a young woman, and her objectification. In effect, by staging the spectacle of women willingly sacrificing themselves, Euripides reinscribes the sacrifice and thereby does considerable cultural work. First, he exculpates the men in the plays, for if women choose self-sacrifice, they have no one to blame but themselves. Second,

---

without limit." Sexual chastity as an ideal provided a model for the other opening: silence is golden.

24. Schaps, "Women Least Mentioned."

25. Bremmer, "Scapegoat," pp. 306–7; he continues: "In the mythical tales one could pass this stage and in the myths we always find beautiful or important persons, although even then these scapegoats remain marginal figures: young men and women, and a king." On the glory of the sacrificial heroines, see Loraux, *Tragic Ways*, esp. p. 47.

26. The men were represented too, but actual women were at another remove from reality; had the actors made no effort to change their voices, the disjunction would have been apparent.

27. On glory, see Loraux, *Tragic Ways*, esp. pp. 42–48.

in each play there is a sense that the men are morally bankrupt, but the sacrificial heroine gives new currency to outworn values by her investment in them. In effect, she shores up the status quo within the plays. Third, female spectators are given the illusion that they too can achieve subjectivity or even heroism if they identify with the sacrifice. (Herein lies the greatest potential for resistance, for it is possible that women or men—in the past and in the present—may choose to read against the text.) Finally, by praising the youthful female figures in these plays, Euripides also has a cultural effect on the men in the audience, who are reassured that this heretofore separate and independent "other" can be, even wants to be, used by and for men.

Iphigenia

In Euripides' *Iphigenia in Aulis*, *Hekabe*, and *Children of Herakles* the exchange of women is crucial, since in each play sacrifice replaces a wedding and, like marriage, builds a social structure through the use of a woman. Marriage is like death, as much as death is like marriage.[28] Because the plot of *Iphigenia in Aulis* devotes itself exclusively to the sacrifice, I start there.

Aeschylus's *Oresteia* provides a clear referent for the Euripidean *Iphigenia* and thus with a way of apprehending some of Euripides' aims as well. Aeschylus presented Agamemnon's sacrifice of Iphigenia as one cause of Clytemnestra's revenge against him; it is the first step in a forward-looking trilogy that includes Orestes' matricide and the establishment of a tribunal at Athens to try him. In the *Agamemnon*, we see Iphigenia only through the eyes of the Chorus as they look forward to Agamemnon's return. We see Iphigenia dragged to the altar, her cries stifled so that she cannot curse the expedition to Troy, for the sake of which she is to be offered up. In Richmond Lattimore's translation: "Her supplications and her cries of father were nothing, nor the child's lamentation to kings passioned for battle. The father prayed, called to his men to lift her with strength of hand, swept in her robes aloft and prone above the altar, as you might lift a goat for sacrifice, with guards against the lips' sweet edge, to check the curse cried on the house of Atreus, by force of bit and speech drowned in strength. Pouring then to the ground her saffron mantle she struck the sacrificers with the eyes' arrows of pity lovely as in a painted scene and striving to speak" (*Agamemnon* 227–43). The Aeschylean treatment renders Iphigenia pure victim, a lovely child who sang at her father's table,

28. For a similar view, see Segal, "Violence," p. 116; Keuls, *Reign of the Phallus*, chap. 5.

and emphasizes the irony of sacrificing the pure Iphigenia to regain Helen, the "promiscuous woman [*poluanoros gunē*]" (*Agamemnon* 62).[29]

In contrast, Euripides expands that moment into the whole plot of a self-contained tragedy, giving to the sacrifice and to Iphigenia a prominence they had not had in Aeschylus. More important, he introduces two innovations that seem at first contradictory: he has Agamemnon lure Iphigenia to Aulis with a promise that she is to be married to Achilles, a ploy that places in high relief Iphigenia's status as gift, object of exchange;[30] then, at a crucial moment he has Iphigenia, unlike her Aeschylean forebear, *choose* to die, which seems to undercut that objectification. I argue, however, that her choice is illusory and her glorification a form of fetishism. The marriage device points up the parallelism of sacrificial death and marriage for a woman; through either one a nubile girl in the liminal stage of virginity can become a woman. By making these changes, Euripides constructs ideal womanhood as heterosexual and self-sacrificing. It seems then that Aeschylus's description of Iphigenia's death romanticizes victimization, while Euripides' version eroticizes her willing sacrifice.

Iphigenia's choice of death has attracted much attention since Aristotle first pointed out its seeming inconsistency in the *Poetics* (15.9[1454a31]): "We have an instance of inconsistency in *Iphigenia at Aulis*, where Iphigenia the suppliant is utterly unlike the later Iphigenia." Indeed, her great speech of self-sacrifice does not fit easily into her characterization or into the play as a whole; it comes very late and very suddenly. Aristotle assumes a notion of character that is related to the humanist ideal of a unified individual; the fissures in her character, however, enable the modern-day critic to see that Iphigenia is actually, in Althusserian terms, being "called" as a subject. The father (or author) gives her a part to play that seems to make of her a subject, an actor. Looking at her choice in this way, we denaturalize it. The question to be asking, then, is not so much why Iphigenia volunteers, as why Euripides makes Iphigenia volunteer. What does he gain that is worth the appearance of inconsistency?

I suggest we take Aristotle's observation of the rupture between life-loving girl and martyr as a sign of the cultural and artistic construction

29. On the sacrifice motif in Aeschylus, see Zeitlin, "Motif"; Lebeck, *Oresteia*; and McDermott, *Euripides' Medea*, pp. 74–78. McDermott, however, finds the *Agamemnon* sacrifice not corrupt but rather normative in comparison with Medea's murder of her children (see below, Chapter 5). Despite (or because of?) her innocence, Iphigenia is made an object for the male gaze; thus, our attention is drawn to the "painted scene." On the eroticization of this scene, see Marsh, "(Other) Maiden's Tale."

30. For an extensive consideration of the marriage theme, see Foley's *Ritual Irony*, pp. 65–105, and her earlier essay on the play, "Marriage and Sacrifice"; Loraux, *Tragic Ways*, pp. 37–48 (on free choice, p. 43); Marsh, "(Other) Maiden's Tale."

under way. In the course of the play we witness the en-gendering of an
Iphigenia willing to be used in this way. Euripides gives Iphigenia (and
the audience) the illusion of her individuality, but the only action she can
perform as a subject is that of submission. As Bal points out, the biblical
virgins have a similarly constructed "choice": "The daughter cannot but
submit; within the limit assigned to her, however, she exploits the possibility left open to her."[31] As a nubile girl, Iphigenia is a commodity
made for exchange; in order to *be* exchanged, she must first be separated
from other women, for as Irigaray says, "*How can relationships among women
be accounted for in this system of exchange?*"[32] By willingly sacrificing herself,
Iphigenia seems to avoid her passive status as sacrificial object, and it is
precisely the allure of such an expression of her individuality that appeals
to her. Once she has complied, she is praised; in this way the playwright
gains the support of the women in the audience. In the course of the play,
Iphigenia is both subject and subjected; in fact, she is subjected by her
desire for subjectivity.

In order to highlight Iphigenia's choice, Euripides represents it as a
difficult decision, difficult for the audience and difficult for her. First, he
makes the audience suspicious of the cause in which she will die by spend-
ing the first third of the play undercutting the male hierarchy: the heroes,
their code, the war they are waging.[33] Euripides' Agamemnon begins by
rejecting intangibles that traditionally made life worth living for the Homeric warrior. He envies his slave and would prefer a life without danger
(*akindunon*, 17), even if it is without glory (*aklees*, 18); he envies those
with less honor (*en timais hesson*, 19). The ignobility of his position does
not go unmentioned; rather, Euripides underlines it by making his slave
reprove him: "I do not admire such statements from one of the best
[*aristeos*] men; Atreus did not beget you only for good [*agatha*] things,
Agamemnon" (28–30; cf. 20).

Euripides dramatizes the crisis of those in authority by displaying not
only an unheroic but also an indecisive Agamemnon.[34] He has sent for
his wife and child, falsely promising marriage to Achilles (98–105), but

31. Bal, *Death and Dissymmetry*, p. 68.
32. Irigaray, *This Sex*, p. 194. For female homosexuality in general, see pp. 170–97.
33. See, among others, Burnett, *Catastrophe*, pp. 24–25; Castellani, "Warlords and
Women"; Foley, *Ritual Irony*, esp. pp. 92–100; Siegel, "Self-Delusion" and "Agamemnon";
Walsh, "Public and Private"; Wasserman, "Agamemnon."
34. On the relationship between the indecisive prologue and the plot to rescue Iphigenia,
see also Foley, "Marriage and Sacrifice," p. 173; she connects the "unusual structure of the
prologue" and the "nature of the plot." Voluminous discussion of textual problems in the
prologue includes Bain, "Prologues"; Knox, "Euripides' *Iphigenia*"; Willink, "Prologue."
There is no uncertainty about Agamemnon's uncertainty, however.

as the play opens, he is inscribing a new tablet (*deltos*), this one telling his wife *not* to send Iphigenia to Aulis (107–10).[35] His torment is reflected in his actions; his servant wonders at what he is doing, as he throws out drafts of his letter (34–42; cf. *luonta kai sundounta*, 110). Later the folded *deltos* becomes a site for the acting out of conflicting claims, for Menelaus intercepts it, while Agamemnon claims that both tablet and servant stand for his honor as leader of his own house (314–16, 317, 322–23, 331). The internal struggle of Agamemnon is then repeated by the struggle between the brothers.

In their conflict the cause of the war is further undermined, for Agamemnon himself raises all the relevant objections to the war effort. He has already depicted it as a private vendetta, alluding to Menelaus's courtship of Helen and the oath of loyalty that her father, Tyndareus, demanded from the unsuccessful suitors (49–71, 78–80), and to the judgment of Paris whose choice of Aphrodite in a divine beauty contest won him the prize of Helen (71–77). Agamemnon further stresses the madness of his army, its folly in swearing such an oath. We have no corollary of the Aeschylean "will of Zeus" here; a failed marriage and a divine beauty contest have led to this conflict of armies, and therefore to the sacrifice of Iphigenia (587–89, 1308–9). Whereas Aeschylus does not even mention the beauty contest, Euripides brings it up repeatedly.[36]

Euripides, of course, might be praising this antiheroic Agamemnon, but the fight between the brothers challenges Agamemnon's account of his own behavior. According to him, he first refused to sacrifice his daughter but was persuaded by Menelaus (95–98); according to Menelaus, he immediately agreed, "willingly" (360). Moreover, Menelaus claims that the army was clamoring to go home (352–53), which upset Agamemnon, who wanted to go to Troy, even before Calchas spoke. How can we know if Agamemnon is self-deceived or a liar? How can we know if Menelaus is simply selfish? Euripides further undercuts the war by giving us Calchas's prophecy only in the dialogue of Agamemnon and Menelaus, and in any case, he demands the sacrifice only in order to "sail on," apparently not in order to go home (89–92, 358–59). What determines the sacrifice in the final analysis, is the brothers' fear of Odysseus's machinations, for he alone has heard the prophecy and he alone prevents any turning back (522–31).

35. On the rewriting and the word *metagraphein*, see Knox, "Second Thoughts," p. 244, who finds this unique word evidence of Euripides' innovation. On the whole, he is not bothered by the apparent inconsistency of Iphigenia and finds it part of an anti-heroic world that Euripides depicts.
36. On the theme in Euripides, see Stinton, "Euripides."

Thus there seems to be a cultural crisis at the heart of the play (private motive versus private motive, brother versus brother).[37] Agamemnon's activity of rewriting emblematizes the conflict. Nonetheless, the back-and-forth motion (the letter is written and rewritten, sent and retracted; the brothers switch positions) ends with the two brothers in harmony, agreeing that Iphigenia must die. It is clear that Menelaus values the ties of brotherhood above all others (471–84): "Having destroyed a brother, which was the last thing necessary, I would take Helen, exchanging evil for good" (487–88). Agamemnon echoes his sentiments: "Disturbances between brothers arise over eros or greed for establishments. I spit out such bitterness between kindred. But we have arrived at necessary events, the completion of the bloody murder of my daughter" (508–12). Their alliance is strengthened, and they unite against Clytemnestra, with Agamemnon saying, "Menelaus, as you go through the army, take care of one thing for me, that Clytemnestra not learn of these things" (538–40).

Once the brothers' strife has yielded to agreement, the conflict over the body of the letter (Menelaus had tried to grab it out of the old messenger's hand) shifts to a conflict over the body of the girl. As the letter's fate testifies to the power of Agamemnon over his own house, so does Iphigenia's death confirm his authority.[38] Folded like a vagina and receiving the incisions of the phallic stylus, the *deltos* itself stands for the body of Iphigenia, who will replace it as the contested site for the representation of male honor and power, and who will in her person receive the cut to the throat.[39] The first episode has two functions: on one level, it represents a culture in conflict with itself; on another, it leads the audience to question the war. While the first level resolves into male union against women, those other questions are left unresolved.

The undercutting of the motives for the Trojan War has led to a radical ambiguity of right and wrong; to settle it, Iphigenia must *volunteer* to die. Nothing less—not her murder or, as in Aeschylus, her forced silence—will do. Merely counting the play's uses of the words for murder and sacrifice reveals, however, that the interpretation of the event is not stable, and that from Agamemnon's point of view as well as Iphigenia's it *is* frequently a murder.[40] But in the end Euripides instructs us to construe

37. See Nancy, "Pharmakon sōtērias," pp. 23–24; and Foley, *Ritual Irony*, pp. 99–102, on a "Girardian 'sacrificial crisis'" in the play.
38. On this point Foley, *Ritual Irony* (esp. pp. 89–92), is considerably more optimistic than I am. It is not a good solution, but we are encouraged to read it as one.
39. On the word *deltos* as slang for vagina, see Aristophanes *Lysistrata* 151; Artemidorus *Oneirocritica* 2.45; Zeitlin, "Travesties," p. 326 (which refers to the body to be written on); duBois, "Horse/Men," pp. 41–42.
40. Sacrifice, forms of *thusein*: 91, 358, 531, 673, 883, 1185, 1262, 1272, 1398; kill,

it as a sacrifice by representing Iphigenia as nobly choosing to die: "It seems good to me to die; I wish to do this well and gloriously, putting away from me whatever is base.... Toward me all greatest Greece turns her eyes, for through me is the sailing of the fleet, through me the sack and overthrow of Troy, and in the future, no matter what the barbarians do, they will no longer be allowed to seize Greek women from blessed Hellas. The payment will be exacted for the destruction of Helen, seized by Paris. All these things, dying I will accomplish and my name will be famous and blessed for having freed Hellas. It is not right for me to love life too deeply; for you bore me for all Greece in common, not for yourself alone. ... It is fitting that Greeks rule barbarians, not barbarians Greeks. They are slaves, and we, Mother, are free" (1375–87, 1400–1401). Having first resisted death and called it murder, she *does* most magnificently come around.

It is easy to see that Iphigenia is, then, represented as choosing. But how are we to judge her act? After all, she gives her life for a cause that the text has rendered suspect. The process of undermining the heroes included undermining their motives for war; the conflict between Agamemnon and Menelaus puts each in the worst light possible. Thus it must be intentional irony when Agamemnon adopts Menelaus's position, which he had previously assailed, and even more so when Iphigenia echoes it later. When Agamemnon makes his speech to Iphigenia, is he a liar, and she a dupe? Does he believe his own words? Are we meant to? D. J. Conacher and Philip Vellacott represent alternative critical responses, Conacher accepting the nobility of both Agamemnon and Iphigenia at the end of the play, Vellacott finding the sacrifice another example of Euripidean irony. Helene Foley warns against reading "as strictly ironic a plot that is resolved through ritual," because of the "magnitude of the cynicism of such an interpretation."[41] Although I am not put off by cynicism, it seems that we can have it both ways: though Euripides does treat Agamemnon and Menelaus ironically, and therefore problematizes Iphigenia's motives for dying, the text nonetheless glorifies her.

We can see this glorification first in the reaction of the Chorus, which proclaims her noble (1402), then grants her fame (1504), and finally marches off calling on everyone to look at Iphigenia, the garlanded "sacker

---

forms of *ktanein*: 96, 463, 481, 490, 513, 880, 1015, 1131, 1166, 1178, 1193, 1207, 1232; death, *thanatos*: 1102; simple death, *katthanein*: 1375; Agamemnon as murderer, *phoneus*: 364; her death as murder, *phonos*: 512, 939, 947.

41. Conacher, *Euripidean Drama*, p. 262; Vellacott, *Ironic Drama*, pp. 176–77; Foley, *Ritual Irony*, pp. 92, 67 n.4. Older readings stress her nobility; current critics find it hard to see anything but irony.

of Troy and Phrygia" (1510–11). Achilles too lavishes praise on her: "O child of Agamemnon—if only I had won you as my bride, a god would have made me blessed. I envy Greece you, and you [your relationship to] Greece. You have spoken worthily of our country . . . And yet the more I see of your nature—for you are noble—the more desire for our marriage overcomes my spirit" (1404–7, 1410–11).

We may take Achilles in the beginning of the play as a self-important and unethical young man, but that does not give us license to discredit everything he says. His praise for Iphigenia is genuine, and she has an emotional impact on him, for where he had before cared only about his good name, he now cares about her. In fact creating an Achilles who measurably changes under her influence is one of the ways Euripides glorifies Iphigenia. The priggish, egotistic soldier gains heroic stature from her example.

The heroes do not match the heroism of the girl, but that does not necessarily mean that she is not held up as an example that they *should* emulate. Euripides gains the pathos he wants by juxtaposing the beautiful maiden with the jaded soldiers. Her very naiveté shames the cynical men; thus, it is not the value system itself that appears to be corrupt but merely their faulty embodiment of it. The text simultaneously demystifies their heroism and demands that we praise Iphigenia for her influence.

Iphigenia becomes willing to sacrifice herself by becoming a woman in the terms set out for her by the culture. Underlying the story of her sacrifice is a cult relationship between virgin goddess and mortal, and part of the dramatic irony of the play rests on Iphigenia's understandable confusion as to which sacrifice to Artemis is to be celebrated, that which precedes a marriage or that which precedes the war. As a goddess in charge of girls' initiation, Artemis was a suitable recipient of offerings at the time of marriage; the initiatory symbolism simultaneously links marriage and sacrifice, for what makes Iphigenia suitable for marriage also makes her suitable for sacrifice.[42]

Since the sacrifice is accomplished through the (false) promise of marriage, analysis of this text can be used to show the way in which women

42. See Lloyd-Jones, "Artemis and Iphigeneia," esp. p. 91. See also Dowden, *Death*, p. 62, for the relationship of puberty, marriage, and service to Artemis; Perlman, "Acting the She-Bear," p. 124; Jeanmaire, *Couroi et courètes*, pp. 258–63. On initiation of girls and marriage, see Van Gennep, *Rites of Passage*, esp. p. 116; on the parallel of war and marriage, Calame, *Choeurs*, p. 356. La Fontaine, *Initiation*, pp. 116–84, remarks that the commonest initiation for girls is marriage (p. 162). Iphigenia's initiation requires her separation from women, as is typical, while the male initiation prepares men for extensive politically significant homosocial ties. Cf. Vernant, "City-State Warfare," p. 23, on the difference between male and female initiation (also above, note 15).

and their sexuality are constructed to serve the ends of masculine culture. The representation of Iphigenia as dying voluntarily is an important part of the play's work as a technology of gender because it supports certain assumptions about what it means for a girl to become a woman. I return here to my claim that girls in becoming women give up an early tie to their mothers and other women in favor of a tie first to the father and then to other men. This play works out that structure, compressing two moments of the female development enforced by patriarchal culture. Iphigenia is inscribed as turning from her mother to her father, then from her father to her "lover"; as a result, she is willing to die for her father.

First we are shown Iphigenia shifting from the female world of her arrival, surrounded by her mother and girls of her age, to a male world of her father and soldiers. Not only does she enter in a chariot with her natal family, mother and brother, but even the heterosexuality of the marriage ploy emphasizes Iphigenia's relation to the family and women. For instance, the maidens of the Chorus receive her and her dowry; then her father sends her within to be with the maidens (678). Most particularly, she is shown in relation to her mother (*pareimi numphagōgos*, 610). Euripides makes this relationship a point of contention between Clytemnestra and Agamemnon, and Clytemnestra emphatically refuses to let Agamemnon take charge—insisting that her daughter's wedding is her ritual and cultural responsibility (728, 732, 734, 736, 740–41).

Euripides also gives Iphigenia a predisposition to desire the father. That she is her father's daughter is clear at her arrival and at her departure. Clytemnestra calls her "the most father-loving of all the children I bore to this one" (638–39). Her desire for her father is implicit in much that she says: she wants Agamemnon all to herself, wishes that he would stay home with his children (646, 656). When she pleads for her life, she calls on this reciprocal love, becoming more physical as she develops the theme: "I was the first to give my body to your knees and to give and receive your kisses" (*philas charitas* [literally, loving favors], 1221–22). As modern theory makes clearer, such a desire for reciprocity from the father is problematic for a young girl.[43]

When she chooses death, she completes this move toward her father and tries to protect him from Clytemnestra. She asks her mother not to be angry with Agamemnon and excuses him, saying that it is not easy for anyone to prevail over the impossible (*tad'adunath'*, 1368–70). Not only does she forgive him for his violence against her, but she sides with him against her mother, pleading with her not to hate him (1454) after the

43. On reciprocity, see Benjamin, *Bonds of Love*, pp. 111, 117.

killing has taken place.[44] As Agamemnon attempted to deny Clytemnestra
the right to lead the "bride" or to carry the torches, Iphigenia denies her
a part in the sacrificial ritual. Running from her mother, Iphigenia dedicates herself to her father, saying: "Who will lead me off, before I am
dragged off by the hair?" (1458). When Clytemnestra says "I will indeed
[be] with you," Iphigenia replies with a firm "Not you at all" (*mē su g'*,
1459). Iphigenia insists on her connection to Agamemnon: one of his
servants should lead her (*patros d'opadōn*, 1462), and she envisions a scene
with him at the altar (1471–72)—a scene she has desired from the
beginning.

When she first arrives in the camp, even though she adores her father,
the young "bride" is still passionately full of life and most emphatically
does not wish to die. As a result, we are not spared the sight of her
pleading for her life:

> O father—if I had the words of Orpheus, so that by singing I could
> persuade the stones to accompany me, or if my words could beguile
> those I wished, I'd make use of it now. Now, I will offer these tears,
> my only cleverness; may they suffice. I attach my body as a suppliant
> to your knees, the body she bore to you; lest you destroy me ahead of
> time, and lest you make me look on the world under earth, for it is
> sweet to look on the light. . . . To look on the light is the sweetest thing
> for human beings; the underworld is nothing; whoever wishes to die is
> mad. To live badly is better than to die well. (1211–19, 1250–1252)

This strong articulation of her will to live heightens the audience's consciousness of what is required to gain the acquiescence I have just sketched
in: that is, a combination of Agamemnon's reasoning and Achilles'
intervention.

The second moment of heterosexual development for women, the transition from father to another male, is crucial in the play; the "marriage"
of course provides the rationale for Iphigenia's presence at Aulis, but it
also ultimately convinces her to die. Like the women of the Chorus, who
begin by singing the praises of the Greek army, Iphigenia is smitten with
Achilles' bravery and wishes to be like him. Before he enters, she is still
mourning her prospective loss of life (1279–82), still wishes to hide from
men's eyes (1338–41). After his speech to Clytemnestra, she is transformed. She seems to feel for Achilles what Jessica Benjamin calls "ideal
love," in which, "as in other forms of masochism, acts of self-abnegation
are in fact meant to secure access to the glory and power of the other.

44. See Hirsch, *Mother/Daughter Plot*, pp. 37–38, for a consideration of maternal anger.

Often, when we look for the roots of this ideal love we find the idealized father and a replaying of the thwarted early relationship of identification and recognition."[45] It is, then, partly through Iphigenia's attraction to Achilles that she becomes ready to die. Her decision is cast in terms of a noble concern for reputation typical of a Homeric hero like Achilles: "It seems good to me to die [*dedoktai*]; I wish to do this very thing well and with good fame [*eukleōs*], putting out of the way everything that is ill-bred [*dusgenes*]" (1375–76).

Unlike Menelaus and Agamemnon, who between themselves at least recognize the army as a constraining threat, Iphigenia claims to die willingly. But how free is she? The appearance of choice obscures what is actually going on: she has no meaningful alternative. Having moved from mother to father and from father to lover, she is conditioned to make the choice she does. Moreover, she does not change her mind until she has seen and heard Achilles; yes, she falls in love with him, but she also learns of the force to be used against her: she will be dragged away by her golden hair (1366).

If her choice is an illusion, what then of the glory that Iphigenia desires and, as I have said earlier, seems to gain? The Iphigenia who was shrinking in front of Achilles (1340, 1341) and afraid to enter the public arena has taken on the desire for publicity now.[46] The notoriety she wants is forbidden to well-brought-up young Greek girls and granted only to men, as the play makes explicit. Separate male and female spheres are well defined in the text: Achilles is embarrassed to be seen with Clytemnestra; Iphigenia is expected to remain inside; the women are out of place in the army camp (568–72, 678–80, 740, 749, 830–32, 913–14, 1029–32, 1340). Although Iphigenia should not be seen (678–79)—indeed it was the fact that she was seen and gossiped about that made her death a necessity (427–32)—she now wants to be seen and remembered by all of Greece: "Look here, mother, how well I speak. Now all of great Greece looks to

45. Benjamin, *Bonds of Love* p. 117; as Phaedra imitates Hippolytos in her mad ravings (see Chapter 5), so Iphigenia imitates Achilles. In Benjamin's scheme, she wishes to be independent of her mother, and so throws her lot in with her father; the male child achieves independence from the powerful mother by identifying with the like parent, but the girl has to identify against her same-sex attachment (p. 111). On the relationship, see Smith, "Iphigeneia," p. 174; Castellani, "Warlords and Women," p. 4; and Chant, "Role Inversion," p. 85, who notes that Iphigenia is an Achilles among women.

46. On this point, without a gender analysis, see Walsh, "Public and Private," esp. pp. 294, 301–5: "Like the army, Iphigenia attains a harmony of personal and public motives . . . she resolves the dialectic of public and private with a new sort of feminine, acquiescent heroism modeled neither upon the old-fashioned, fearsome and uncompromising type Medea emulates nor the ungenerous pragmatism of Jason and Achilles." I give Achilles more credit for development.

me.... Dying, I will make possible all these things, and my reputation will be blessed for having freed Greece.... These things will make up a long-lasting memory, and my reputation will be my children and my marriage" (1377–78, 1383–84, 1379–99).

Euripides, however, grants her this stereotypically masculine and public fame without disturbing her femininity, by moving the private goals to a new register. First, she does not win fame as a hero would, through one-on-one combat with an equal. Rather, she achieves fame—that is, male success—by self-sacrifice, by submitting herself to her superior and opposite. Only in this way is female ambition acceptable. This path to the same goals is radically different from that of a male hero-warrior-knight like Achilles. Second, Euripides' Iphigenia does not defy the gender-specific code but reaffirms it, replacing children and marriage with fame (1399). The text's emphasis on her purported marriage to Achilles places Iphigenia between two marriages, one to Achilles, the other to Greece. Whereas she would have left her father to marry and have children, instead she leaves him for Greece, which now will be her marriage and children. We have seen her give her body to her father in supplication and have heard that she did so as a child; now she gives herself to all Greece (1397).

Finally, Euripides turns her into a fetish. Not only does Iphigenia gain only a female variant of glory, but, more interestingly, Euripides presents her craving for masculine reputation as a desire to be seen. Note, for instance, the repetition of words for "gaze" in the passage cited above: she tells her mother to *look* at what she is saying (*skepsai*, 1377) and that the whole Greek army *looks* at her (*apoblepei*, 1378); having been seen, she wants to be *spoken of* (*kleos* comes from *kluein*, 1383) and to be remembered (1398).[47] Her desire for the gaze redefines what might otherwise seem the Greeks' own murderous desire to look; she is exalted and praised as she is about to be victimized, denying their fault. Thus the fetish is operative in both senses. The glorification of Iphigenia takes her as a fetishized commodity, exalting her self-sacrifice by ignoring the attendant conditions of its production: that is, the exchange of women. She is also like an erotic fetish that comforts men in the face of sexual anxiety. As the fetish enables the fetishist simultaneously to accept and deny the girl's "castration," so the harm to Iphigenia (that is, the wound, psychoanalytically speaking) is denied not only by making her choose death but also by emphasizing

47. See Bal, *Death and Dissymmetry*, pp. 59, 62–63, on the significance of beholding the daughter of Jephtha. Sissa, *Greek Virginity*, pp. 97–99, argues that marriage (not intercourse) ends *partheneia* because it is public, to be seen (cf. Chapter 7, on secrecy and rape in the *Ion*).

the beauty of the throat that will receive the blow. The throat then becomes a focal point of audience attention:

> Look at [*idesthe*] her, the city-sacker of Troy and the Phrygians, as she
> walks, with a crown upon her head
> and dashed with the lustral waters,
> to the altar of the divine goddess,
> with streams of flowing blood,
> she is stained at the lovely [*euphuē*] neck of her body
> slain as a sacrifice. (1510–18)

In a final twist, though, the real glory is reserved for men. For while Euripides encourages the audience to think Iphigenia's death is her idea (by presenting her as making a choice) and therefore to admire her nobility, her death is merely a precondition for the glorification of the army and Agamemnon, who gain "the most renowned crown" (*kleinotaton stephanon*, 1529) and "imperishable reputation" (*kleos aeimnēston*, 1531). Theirs is the honor that she desired so.

As a woman in an exchange economy and a fetishized object, Iphigenia gains praise because she supports the masculine order—an order in crisis at the play's opening—by adopting the values of her father and the patriarchy. We need now to examine carefully Agamemnon's rhetoric. He persuades Iphigenia to die by presenting the war as a matter of freedom: "for we are less than this thing. It is necessary for Greece to be free, insofar as it is up to you and me, and not for barbarians to seize Greek women by force from the marriage bed" (1272–75). Iphigenia's "freely chosen" death is tied into the play's deployment of the theme of freedom, but at least the present-day audience must see that freedom is different for men and women.[48] She dies for the freedom of Greek men. The text suggests that Agamemnon and Menelaus are controlled by Agamemnon's letter or by the mob. But if these leaders cannot personally be free, they can still identify with a great and free nation. Thus, Menelaus displaces onto Greece the aristocrat's fear of being a laughingstock—or is it the cuckold's fear, given Menelaus's situation? He first alludes to the honor of Hellas, grieving

48. Women's lack of freedom is explicitly related to marriage. Not only did Iphigenia come to Aulis in order to be "married," but the marriage and theft of Helen are prominent motifs. Euripides explicitly raises the question of consent and violence. He asks if Thetis married Peleus willingly; he provides a new history for Clytemnestra in which she did not marry Agamemnon willingly but rather was a prize of war, her rape consummated with the killing of her child by the previous marriage. On Clytemnestra, see Marsh, "(Other) Maiden's Tale"; on familial violence, see Foley, *Ritual Irony*, pp. 73–75.

for his country, which "wished to do something noble but will let foreigners go laughing on account of you [Agamemnon] and this girl" (370–
72).[49] Agamemnon recapitulates and embellishes the theme when he urges
on Iphigenia the necessity for the war and her death. Here, male freedom
and female sexuality are explicitly intertwined. First Agamemnon says that
some Aphrodite has maddened the soldiers to fight in order to stop the
rape (*harpagas*) of Greek beds (1264–66). Then he asserts that they in-
dividually are less than the cause, that Iphigenia must be sacrificed whether
or not they wish it, because the freedom of Greece from barbarians—but
most particularly, freedom of the Greek marriage bed from attack (*sulasthai
biai*, 1275)—is at stake.

Agamemnon's public rationalization is an articulation of the ideological
basis of patriarchy, and of the very division into public and private: if
women are not safe within the home, the army must be mobilized. Two
assumptions underlie his statement: first, women must be controlled by
men, particularly with respect to sexuality and fertility; second, the male
sex as a whole is challenged if one woman can be taken from her husband.
This combination in turn leads to the further belief that men must "protect"
women; this protection (required by the need to control women) results
in the denigration of women and the aggrandizement of men. Not only
is nationalist rhetoric bound up with patriarchal assumptions, but both
are justified by the asserted culpability of Helen. In fact, however, men
are protecting other men, not women, as we see from the agreement that
the other suitors for Helen's hand would support Menelaus if she were
abducted. We must remember that rape is defined primarily as a crime
against the husband; *his* honor is at risk, *his* possessions.[50]

Ultimately, Iphigenia adopts the themes of her father and uncle, accepting Agamemnon's reasoning. As he shifts the ground from punishing
Paris to defending all Greeks, from retrieving Helen to protecting all
women, so Iphigenia makes the shift from love of father to love of fatherland (*Hellēsi*, 1386; *patridos*, 1388; *Hellados*, 1389; *Helladi*, 1397). In
her transfiguration, Iphigenia accepts the sanctity of Greek marriage beds
(*harpazein*, 1381) and the necessity for Greeks to rule foreigners; she
accepts the contrast between Greek freedom and foreign slavery (1400);
she agrees that the glory and freedom of Greece are dependent on the
chastity and safety of its women and hopes to achieve *her* glory (*eukleōs*,
1376; *kleos*, 1383) by securing *that* glory. The greater good for which she

49. For a working out of this concept in *Hekabe*, see Daitz, "Concepts."
50. Harrison, *Law*, pp. 19, 34, 36. The husband's honor is related to the sexual chastity
of his wife; he lives "without honor" if he remains with a wife who has been caught in
adultery (Demosthenes 59, *Against Neaira* 87 in particular).

dies, Panhellenism, is itself based on a limited form of exogamy: keep Greek women for Greek men. Thus Iphigenia dies for the freedom of all Greece, which means the maintenance of the hierarchical order: Greek over foreigner, man over woman. She dies "freely" to protect not her freedom but male freedom to possess women. The very emphasis on freedom, therefore, keeps women in a subordinate position. Agamemnon and Menelaus accuse each other of ignoble motives—sexual and political lust—but in public these attacks are forgotten, and in front of Iphigenia they give their desire acceptable, even noble, names. The first third of the play, however, has made us aware of the less flattering interpretation. Iphigenia must die not because of divine necessity but to keep women in the home, safe for their husbands.

In taking on the motives of the leaders, Iphigenia takes on a more explicit misogyny as well. For example, in frustration at his rhetorical defeat by Clytemnestra, Agamemnon says: "It is necessary for the wise man to keep his wife at home, good and useful, or not to keep one at all" (749–50). Moreover, the discussion immediately preceding Iphigenia's noble speech reinforces this message of female unimportance. The war is supposedly waged so that Greek women cannot be seized or raped, yet Iphigenia must be seized (*harpasas*, 1365; cf. 1266). Only Achilles is willing to defend her, and he has little hope of success (1358–66). Finally, Iphigenia's speech itself reveals the correlation between male values, denigration of women, and her action. Her solicitude is all for Achilles: "It is right that we praise our friend [*xenos*] for his quick spirit [or eagerness, *prothumia*], but it is necessary for you [Clytemnestra] to see to this, that he not be blamed by the army, since we would do nothing more for ourselves, and he would encounter bad fortune" (1371–73). She says that it would not be fitting for Achilles to do battle with all the Argives to prevent just one woman from dying (1392–93)—even though they will die to avenge Helen's abduction—and she strengthens the position further by saying that it is more important for one man than for thousands of women to continue to see the light (1394).

Iphigenia chooses "death with father" because her society predisposes her to condemn the women she has around her and consequently to condemn herself. Agamemnon scorns Menelaus for wanting Helen back even though he had a "bad marriage" (*kakon lechos*, 389), and when Iphigenia has not yet reconciled herself to death, she too blames Helen (1334–35). And as we have seen, the move away from her mother is accompanied by a similar judgment of women and their respective roles. Her attitude toward her mother is part of a more general denigration of the feminine.

Euripides creates a heroine who goes beyond the heroes in supporting the value system that condemns her to death. Agamemnon at one point preferred her to his honor (e.g., 16–19); she is made the Iliadic hero who prefers honor to life. As an outsider she might have seen the flaws in patriarchal hierarchy; instead she is made its spokesperson. As a fetish object, Iphigenia cannot be valued or value herself.

Once she is turned into this model woman, Iphigenia's role in the exchange threatens to exceed its boundaries, and at several moments the mythic plot is almost derailed; Iphigenia dedicates herself to fulfilling it.[51] As Menelaus and Agamemnon's struggle over the tablet resolves itself into a compact to work together to deceive Clytemnestra, so the putative relationship between Achilles and his prospective bride becomes a relationship of men when Achilles resigns himself to fighting Trojans and not Greeks. As is typical in exchange marriage, the desired connection is between men and is accomplished first by the false marriage plan. Here, the pseudolover is merely a stand-in for the father: Achilles' name is used to achieve Agamemnon's purposes. Is Iphigenia over the border of "givable"? is she already given? To what extent is the marriage already "real," since a "betrothal" (and remember that *egguē* might have been sufficient) has taken place? Can a duplicitous speech act accomplish marriage, which is only a speech act?[52]

Achilles actually mis-understands marriage to be between the two of them; his intention to give substance to Agamemnon's charade and his desire for Iphigenia (he wishes he were in fact married to her) almost avert the Trojan war. But Iphigenia refuses his protection, reinstating the patriarchal conventions of marriage in fifth-century Athens. She forces the antagonistic Achilles to support Agamemnon; she thus facilitates loyalty between men by not demanding or accepting loyalty to herself. Whether given in marriage or given in sacrifice, Iphigenia cements men's ties to other men. Even as an actual marriage would have facilitated the relationship between husband-to-be and father, so the honor paid her is in the interests of the male community; it is not hers at all.

The structure of the play, with its challenge to the heroic values in the first part and reassertion of them by Iphigenia at the end, suggests neither that Agamemnon has had a change of heart nor that Iphigenia's sacrifice is simply ironic. Rather, it suggests that Euripides' Agamemnon must give

51. Foley, *Ritual Irony*, p. 98, speaks of the "gradual movement back to the myth."

52. Foley, in "Marriage and Sacrifice" (pp. 161–63) and *Ritual Irony* (pp. 68–78), shows the elaborate references to the wedding; Roussel, "Rôle d'Achille" (e.g., p. 240), dwells on the extent to which the marriage is actually in process and the betrothal made. On marriage as a speech act, see Bal, *Death and Dissymmetry*, pp. 129–69.

his daughter something worth dying for. As noted earlier, Aeschylus's Agamemnon gags his daughter to ensure that she will not curse the house (*Agamemnon* 236–37); this Agamemnon goes even further and ensures auspicious speech rather than silence. Iphigenia is not simply a dupe; she is given reason to support the political organization that excludes her.

Iphigenia's choice supports the status quo on two levels. First, within the plot, it is to Agamemnon's and Menelaus's advantage, for if the girl is willing, then her death can serve to revitalize the values so badly eroded. Her sacrifice encourages the army and gives credence to the publicly held values that had been privately abandoned by Menelaus and Agamemnon. In fact, as we have seen, in this play the Trojan War comes close to not taking place, through Agamemnon's conscience or that of Achilles, but all is put back on track by Iphigenia's commitment of herself to those outworn ideals. We can best estimate the success of Agamemnon's strategy through the role of Achilles, who takes inspiration from Iphigenia and falls in love with her, envying Greece his bride.

Second, the text acts in a similar way on the audience. The steady improvement of Achilles in the course of the play, as well as his stature as a hero, must make his admiration of Iphigenia a model for the audience. Many critics feel about her the same way Achilles does, evidence that the "heroizing" reading is more than possible.[53] Through self-sacrifice, Iphigenia wins the apparent reward of fame; while keeping male power intact, her glorification gives women in the audience a plausible reason to go along with what is asked of them by their culture. Euripides presents an overt irony by contrasting happy "marriage" to the actual sacrifice, but the modern reader may find a deeper one in the similarity between the two. Both, in order to gain the requisite consent, appear to glorify the woman in question.

Interpreting that praise and apparent glorification as fetishism, we must first in Marxist fashion re-place Iphigenia within the structures of exchange that produce her willingness. Euripides represents her as a model of the young hero for Achilles, but an analysis of the interrelationship between sacrifice, marriage, and military motifs reveals the asymmetry between the female and the male hero. Iphigenia's death is too specifically feminized to stand simply for the loss of young life in war. If we further utilize a strategy of double reading, we can also see the possibility of a female heroism *not* in the pay of patriarchy and false patriotism. Taking the Freudian conception of the fetish but adopting a post-Freudian perspective, I would emphasize the power of the *parthenos* that the fetishistic

---

53. See, e.g., Bonnard, "Iphigénie à Aulis"; Bates, *Euripides*, p. 153; Rivier, *Essai*, p. 82.

strategies of marriage, sacrifice, and glorification seek to control. In this reading, the supposed threat of castration would come not from the male (mis)recognition of a woman's castration but from the recognition of the possibility of her *refusal* of castration. Euripides attempts to deny that possibility by representing Iphigenia not as an active soldier, not as an Amazon, but as a marriageable woman and thus an appropriate object of the fetishizing gaze. Reading with our own oscillation, we can reinscribe at least the outline of that figure.

Polyxena

Polyxena, in the *Hekabe*, has much in common with Iphigenia, but—in part because the action is more compressed than in *Iphigenia in Aulis*—the pattern of glorification for female self-sacrifice stands out more starkly. Iphigenia dies so that the Achaians can go to Troy; the ghost of Achilles demands the sacrifice of Polyxena to enable them to return. Both women are romantically associated with Achilles. Their difference in station (Polyxena, daughter of Priam, has been made a slave because of the defeat of Troy, whereas Iphigenia is a free woman and a princess) only underlines their similarity: each undergoes the same fate—that is, she is killed for men's benefit. Both are involved in quasi-pornographic scripts that work out the dynamic of active/passive, dominant/submissive, male/female by rendering them objects of the male gaze as well as of the knife (which also stands for the phallus and the law).[54] In the initial stages of the play, Polyxena is wrested from her mother by force and placed in the context of the Greek army; she too moves from the private female realm to the public masculine arena. And in *Hekabe*, sacrifice, like the marriage it replaces, is a founding moment of culture and functions through the exchange of women between men.

Most significantly, both Polyxena and Iphigenia are represented as *choos-*

54. On the similarity of the plays, see, e.g., Burnett, *Catastrophe*, pp. 24–25; Vellacott, *Ironic Drama*, pp. 178–79. On the possible invention of the connection between Achilles' ghost and the sacrifice of Polyxena, see King, "Politics of Imitation," pp. 48–49; Pearson, *Fragments of Sophocles*, 2:163; Conacher, "Euripides' *Hecuba*," pp. 3–5. Both King and Conacher review the ancient evidence, which is not conclusive; Conacher is dubious about the existence of a betrothal between Polyxena and Achilles, since all the evidence for it is late, but cf. Méridier, *Euripide*, 2:166. On the pornographic script, see Marsh, "(Other) Maiden's Tale." On dominance and submission, see, e.g., MacKinnon, "Feminism...Theory," esp. p. 245; her argument that vulnerability marks femininity as sexually attractive is also relevant to Polyxena's allure (see Gellie, "Hecuba and Tragedy," p. 32).

ing death, when it is clear that they will be forced to die in any case. This "willingness" appears to turn the woman from a sign into a manipulator of signs, but in fact it only makes her complicit in her exploitation. Like Iphigenia, Polyxena is represented as trying to act freely by choosing the inevitable; in her case it is even clearer that adulation is fetishization. In attempting to counter the violence that the army would do to her, she is despite herself cooperating with the ideology that mystifies the fact of her exchange. The necessity for myths of willing death suggests the complexity and complicity of the female position in this plot. Similarly, actual women are not simply victims: rather, through the representation of such heroines, they are given reason to participate in their own annihilation.

As a beautiful virgin, Polyxena has a particular kind of value for men. She is chosen as a gift to represent the army's respect for Achilles; she stands for his honor. Polydoros uses the word *geras*, meaning a gift of honor (41); Hekabe's dream repeats it (94), as does the Chorus in quoting Achilles (*ageraston*, 115). Although the ghost of Polydoros tells the audience that Achilles has demanded his "sister Polyxena as a sacrifice and prize" (40–41), we do not know why it is Polyxena who must be the victim.[55] Hekabe asks why they do not sacrifice cattle (*bouthutein*, 261)— or Helen, who would be suitable not only as the cause of Achilles' destruction (265–66), but also as the greatest beauty (269). Because Polyxena is a virgin, however, and thus untouched, as well as beautiful, she is the more acceptable sacrificial victim. Odysseus makes it clear that Hekabe herself will not suffice: "The phantasm of Achilles did not demand your death, old woman, but hers" (389–90). Hekabe is old and therefore no longer desirable, not worthy of exchange. Since Hekabe is due to die soon in any case, her sacrifice would not add to Achilles' honor. What he requires is the gift of Polyxena's beauty *and* of the long life she could have expected. The waste adds to his glory.

Polyxena's sacrifice for Achilles stands in place of her marriage. The connections of eros and this death are marked: Polyxena bemoans her status as unmarried girl (*anumphos anumenaios*, 416); she speaks of lying in Hades, or beside Hades (208–10, 418); and Hekabe mourns her as a "bride who was not a bride, maiden but no maiden" (612). Death is like marriage, and marriage is like death; although there is no father here to give Polyxena away, she is exchanged in death as she would have been in

---

55. Abrahamson, "Euripides' Tragedy of *Hecuba*," p. 122, nn. 8–9. Hogan, "Thucydides 3.52–68," p. 250, points out that since there is debate in the army, there can be no clear necessity for the death of Polyxena; King, "Politics of Imitation," p. 51, mentions that ambiguity but thinks it is of negligible importance.

marriage—otherwise why is she no maiden?[56] Iphigenia's journey to Hades
is enough like her voyage in marriage to allow Agamemnon to deceive
her (*Iphigenia in Aulis* 667, 669); death, the final crossing, is assimilated
to marriage as a change of estate. The likeness, however, sheds light on
both sides of the equation. It is legitimate for modern readers to ask what
Polyxena would have had to look forward to had she lived; the nature of
marriage in antiquity was such that it could be seen as death for the very
young bride.

For the girl Polyxena, then, the sacrifice replaces marriage. For the army,
it serves related cultural functions. Critics have tended to associate the
amorality of the play with the progressive degeneracy of Hekabe, but I
would suggest that the Greeks are in a state of crisis comparable to that
in the *Iphigenia in Aulis*.[57] In each, the undercutting of the heroes is set
off against the sacrifice and glorification of the virgin. Like its departure
from home, its return home puts the Greek army in a dangerous situation:
the soldiers will be at sea, at the mercy of the elements, and are thus
especially aware of the importance of luck. Moreover, the ships are once
again sitting idle (35–36); they are dependent on forwarding winds, which
Achilles has restrained (900, 1289–90). Hence, the Greeks attempt to
shore up the barriers between themselves and the unknown (both the dead
and the sea) by reinforcing custom, in this case the giving of gifts that
measure honor.[58] As in the Iliadic struggle over Chryseis and Briseis, the
gift is a woman, though one who is to be killed, not raped.[59] Imperishable
honor is, however, only another name for politics, as Odysseus makes
clear to Hekabe.[60] First, rewarding the best stimulates others to excellence
(307–16); second, the code of honor is part of the Hellenes' greatness

56. Sissa, *Greek Virginity*, p. 99, notes that Antigone and Polyxena are both promised
to the darkness; see also Loraux, *Tragic Ways*, pp. 37–42, esp. p. 39.
57. On the moral chaos of *Hekabe*, see e.g., Reckford, "Concepts of Demoralization,"
esp. pp. 126–27 on fortune (*tuchē*); Luschnig, "Euripides' *Hecabe*," p. 227. Abrahamson,
"Euripides' Tragedy of *Hecuba*," p. 129, calls it "a world of depravation and murder, of
betrayal and hypocrisy." For Thrace as a border zone, see Zeitlin, "Euripides' *Hekabe*." On
luck and virgin sacrifice, see Rose, "Bride."
58. On winds versus honor as motives, see Conacher, "Euripides' *Hecuba*," p. 2.
59. King, "Politics of Imitation," p. 53, finds the contrast between Briseis and Polyxena
central to Euripides' reevaluation of Achilles and "the Homeric system of using human prizes
as a measure of *timē* [honor]." As Christa Wolf's *Cassandra* (New York: Farrar, Straus,
Giroux, 1984) makes clear, it is hard for a modern feminist not to see these women as
analogues.
60. See Vellacott, *Ironic Drama*, p. 212, on the fall from heroic values. Adkins, "Basic
Greek Values," argues that the "competitive" values are still in force; Hogan, "Thucydides
3.52–68," replies convincingly; see also King, "Politics of Imitation." Matthaei, *Studies*,
pp. 128–40, finds a community *nomos* supporting the sacrifice; Kirkwood, "Hecuba and
Nomos," p. 64, thinks "it was not a capricious act of violence, but a deliberate measure
adopted for the good of the Greek army."

and distinguishes them from the outsiders (*barbaroi*, 328–31). In short, the woman is given to the hero as a sign of his honor; the gift functions explicitly to cement men together and reinforce the values of the society by setting them off from outsiders.[61]

Polyxena tries to avoid her status in the circulation of male honor and male meaning and to assert herself as a subject. She resists construction as victim, as is evident in many passages.[62] For example, Hekabe hopes that Polyxena will persuade Odysseus to pity her: "You see if you have greater powers than your mother; be earnest, use all voices, like the night-ingale, so that you will not be deprived of life. Fall at the knees of Odysseus most piteously and persuade him—use this argument, that even he has children—so that he will pity you" (336–41). But Polyxena refuses that form of action. In fact, she lords it over Odysseus, mocking his fear of the power that suppliancy would grant her: "Be brave; you have escaped my pleas to Zeus of the suppliants" (345).[63] She stands tall; she will not kneel to plead with him. That assumption of her full height is the corollary of her acceptance of death: she would rather be a corpse than a slave. She chooses to go along with necessity (346) because she thinks it good to die, desires death (347, 358) and sees no use in living (349). Her refusal to plead and her active embrace of fate are strategies of defiance.

Polyxena argues that she wishes to die as befits her station and before anything shameful happens to her (*prin aischrōn mē kat'axian tuchein*, 374); she thus puts herself in the Achillean position of the youthful male warrior for whom a short glorious life is more desirable than a long and uneventful one.[64] Like such a hero, she does not wish to be perceived as life-loving and low (*kakē* and *philopsuchos*, 348); whereas before her conversion she,

---

61. For a debate as to whether Euripides reaffirms or challenges those values, see Adkins, "Basic Greek Values," pp. 193–200; and Pearson, *Popular Ethics*, pp. 144–48. Adkins finds that the Greeks act within their own system of ethics; Conacher, "Euripides' *Hecuba*," p. 5, holds that Euripides "presents the sacrifice theme in such a way as to place the Greeks in the least favourable light." Pohlenz too, in *Griechische Tragödie*, pp. 287–92, finds that Euripides minimizes the horror of Polyxena's sacrifice and that it is in accord with a certain *nomos*. For the opposite position, see Abrahamson, "Euripides' Tragedy of *Hecuba*," pp. 123–24. Hogan, "Thucydides 3.52–68," notes that Odysseus weaves together traditional and contemporary values, "with a radically political base" (p. 246). Abrahamson, Hogan, King, Conacher, and Vellacott make the connection to the Peloponnesian War.

62. Conacher, "Euripides' *Hecuba*," p. 18 n. 27, sees her as an example of "existential heroism," comparing her to Antigone and Orestes. Cf. Ferguson, *Companion to Greek Tragedy*, p. 298, who also alludes to her "existential heroism" and compares her to "Alcestis, Macaria, and Iphigeneia . . . redemptive women, gentle, firm, attractive, courageous."

63. Daitz, "Concepts," pp. 219–21, compares Polyxena here to Hekabe in her scene with Agamemnon; cf. Michelini, *Euripides*, p. 134, who contrasts the two.

64. On the aristocratic code, see Rosivach, "First Stasimon," p. 359. The Chorus of slave women follows a path that the aristocratic "code cannot recognize" (p. 361). But rape is surely the fate of Polyxena if she lives.

like Iphigenia, spoke as if it were natural to love life, such attachment to life now seems to her ignoble. By dying at the peak of her powers, before she has had to live beneath her station, she hopes to become a heroine. At the same time, she reveals an aristocratic concern for appearances when she enjoins her mother from contesting what is about to happen, asking her to think how unseemly it would be for an old woman like herself to be dragged off by a young man (405–8).[65] For Polyxena, the question of *how* she dies becomes as important as *that* she dies.

The Chorus and Hekabe both approve of what they have heard from Polyxena: "Powerful and clear is the stamp that comes from nobility amongst mortals; the name of good birth increases even more amongst the worthy" (379–81). She is not only among the worthy but also among the beautiful and good (*kalōi*, 382) even though it hurts her (*lupē prosestin*, 383). The text seems to validate her version of her action, for the army and Talthybios are moved by her performance. We hear more about her freedom and nobility in Talthybios's report of her death. He says, for instance, that having been surrounded, accompanied, restrained, and consecrated, Polyxena speaks to say that she will die freely, as she has lived: "Willingly I die; let no one touch my skin; I furnish my neck with stout heart [*eukardiōs*]; release me, kill me as a free woman, let me die as a free woman; for as a queen I am ashamed to be called slave among the dead" (548–52). Talthybios believes that she has made her mother fortunate in her children, although unfortunate in other ways (581–82).

Talthybios is not alone in his reverence for Polyxena. He reports that after her speech the crowd roared, and Agamemnon bade the young men release her. Following her death, the soldiers give her gifts: "After she let out her breath in the deathly blow [*sphagēi*], no one of the Achaians stinted of their labor; some brought leaves in their hands to the dead girl; others bearing pine branches filled the pyre; whoever was not carrying something heard such insults from those who were: 'Do you stand there, vile one, not carrying any robe or adornment in your hands? Are you not giving anything to her, who is so outstanding in stoutheartedness [*eukardōi*] and nobility of spirit [*psuchēn t'aristēi*]?'" (571–80). She thus wins the reputation she had wanted for bravery and virtue.

Critics such as G. M. A. Grube agree: "Hecuba's sorrow was not unlike that she must have felt when her sons fell in battle. The nobility of Polyxena further raises the drama of her death to a higher plane of tragedy, and as Hecuba herself remarks, 'prevents excess of sorrow.'" Conacher also finds

65. Cf. Michelini, *Euripides*, pp. 174–76, on gesture.

her "converted from a passive victim to a heroic character in her own right," and he speaks of his "impression that Polyxena has taken charge of her own sacrifice.... Indeed, Polyxena's personal preeminence in this scene, with the Greek soldiers crowding about bringing reverent adornments for her body, calls to mind those mystic sacrifices in which, to the minds of the initiated, the roles of victim and divinity are centered in a single being." Vellacott too thinks the audience would have "witnessed a moving and solemn occasion whose cruelty was redeemed by Polyxena's heroism." Stephen Daitz finds that "the inner attitude of Polyxena... is crucial in transforming the revolting murder of a slave into a moving spectacle of human strength, dignity, and renunciation"; and Louise Matthaei sees the Polyxena episode as the play's only scene of "charm and pathos."[66]

There is reason to resist this glorification, however. Talthybios reports that she asserts her will at the point of death. But she is a lone young girl in the presence of the full army (*pas, plērēs*, 521, 522) at the sacrifice. The actors—Neoptolemus, son of Achilles, and her guards (525–27)— are male; she is the recipient of the action. What does it mean that in this context her audience, the army, gives her gifts? On the one hand it seems to signify respect: she has given herself up in honor of Achilles, and they in turn bring gifts to honor her. But their praise is itself a form of lust. The sexual component of that adulation is made apparent in Hekabe's fears that Polyxena's body will be defiled if the soldiers are near her: "Do you go and announce to the Argives that no one is to touch my child, but rather hold off the mob... lest some low-life do some outrage to the body" (604–8). Many critics believe that the death of the maiden has transfigured the mob;[67] Hekabe is more cynical. Hekabe's reading, although not stressed in text or criticism, interprets their gifts as a displacement of their desire. Polyxena, having refused to let anyone touch her, nonetheless suffers their touch via these gifts.

And what, we might ask, does she do with her freedom? According to Talthybios, "taking her robes from the top of her shoulder, she ripped them down her side to her middle and showed breasts and chest as beautiful as a statue; pressing her knee into the ground, she spoke the most piteous speech: 'Regard, young man, whether you wish to strike my chest; strike,

66. Grube, p. 221; Conacher, *Euripidean Drama*, p. 150; and "Euripides' *Hecuba*," p. 19; Vellacott, *Ironic Drama*, p. 192; Daitz, "Concepts," p. 220; Matthaei, *Studies*, p. 118 (cf. p. 126). Michelini, *Euripides*, pp. 158–70, treats the nobility of the girl but puts it into the context of sexuality and bad taste that she too observes in the play.

67. E.g., Luschnig, "Euripides' *Hecabe*," p. 231. For a view more like my own, see Michelini, *Euripides*, pp. 158–70.

if you wish, my throat; here is my neck ready for you' " (558–65).[68] Why
does Euripides have her bare her breast and strip to the navel? Why does
he have Talthybios say that she is as beautiful as a statue (*agalma*)? In so
doing, he has Polyxena turn herself into a spectacle for the internal audience, perhaps in recognition that her only power lies in her exchange
value, that is, in making herself desirable. Euripides gains the advantage
not only of conjuring up the image of Polyxena's nudity for the audience
but also of having her appear to be the agent of her own disrobing.[69] He
not only has her stress her role as object of the male gaze but underlines
it by having Talthybios use the image of the statue. This recipient of the
gaze, like Iphigenia, exposes herself simultaneously to the aggressive knife.

By dying willingly, then, Polyxena becomes not a subject, as she would
wish, but an object of sadistic, murderous desire; the adulation given her
is only a form of fetishism. As a freely acting sacrifice, she is, as was
Iphigenia, a glorified commodity removed from her specific context (in
this case, the slavery that results from war). The power imbalance is ignored
by seeming to give her a value. As an eroticized fetish, she is both mutilated
and adored. Her willingness to turn herself into her parts, breasts and
throat, enables the army both to accept and to deny what they take to be
women's castration. This model I think helps to explain a peculiar passage:
we are told that in dying Polyxena took care to hide "what should be
hidden from men's eyes" (570). Since she has already bared her bosom,
this imagined and covered body part must have been her genitals.[70]

In dying, then, she protects men from facing her difference—in psychoanalytic terms, her "lack"—and the possibility of their own castration.
But as I said earlier, this fetishism is not about anatomy but about cultural
constructions. On that level, she accepts heroic values and thus denies
sexual difference. Finally, her offering of herself saves the army from facing
the hideousness of what it has done. She wants to be a hero, and the
soldiers want to believe that she is one; they are complicit in denying the
disgraceful reality that her sacrifice is.

The range of possibilities open to Polyxena is very narrow, and in
praising her the text and critics cover up the system of exchange that
necessitated this act of "free will" (which is why I call it fetishism). There

68. There is a textual corruption here; *eutrepes* (made ready) and *euprepes* (most fitting)
have both been proposed.

69. Since the actor was male, the heterosexual erotic that I refer to could exist only in
the imagination; the homoerotic potential of the scene remains hidden under her robe, but
perhaps it is significant that this fetishistic desire for Polyxena is aroused only when "she"
seems to act like a male hero.

70. Again, this imaginary scenario is complicated by the masculinity of the actor.

is a paradox for Polyxena in that there is no nobility for the woman comparable to that available to the man on the battlefield; thus, she categorizes her
fate by comparing two sorts of marriage, the one (for which she was
brought up) to the son of a king, the other (her likely fate as a captive) to a
lowly slave (351–53, 365–66). The limits that the social order establishes
for her are clear: good marriage, poor marriage. In her death she is sold off
for Achilles' honor; in her life she would have been sold off for silver (360).
In her view, the choice is death with honor or life without honor, which is
no more than a sort of living death. In the actual description of her death,
this comes down to the difference between a cut through the breast or a cut
through the throat. Loraux has argued persuasively that the throat is the site
of a feminine death; since her throat is offered to Neoptolemus, and accepted ("he cut the windpipe with his sword," 567), she dies like a woman,
even though she tries to act the hero.[71]

In each of these plays, the woman is given as a gift to seal a contract,
to propitiate a spirit, so that a male endeavor can move to completion. In
acting "freely," both women subscribe to the ideology that values death
and war over life. Furthermore, they are objects in the service of male
subjectivity. Not only does the representation of her death undercut Polyxena's desires for subjectivity by making her an icon, an object of desire;
she is also repeatedly made the object of narration and, within that frame,
the object of view. Her sacrifice is reported first by the apparition of
Polydoros, then in Hekabe's dream, next by Odysseus, then by Talthybios.
In this way she is made a spectacle for the audience. She is exchanged not
once, but several times: given to Achilles, given to the army, given to the
audience as an object of desire.[72]

If, as Mary Ann Doane says, the spectator's desire is "delineated as either
voyeurism or fetishism, as precisely a pleasure in seeing what is prohibited
in relation to the female body,"[73] then the Greek army, the Greek audience,
and even we are teased by Polyxena's reported exposure and modesty. The
breast and neck (and mouth) are exposed, while the other, analogous
opening and canal are hidden. As her sacrifice replaces her marriage, so
for the audience the sacrificial death replaces her sex. Euripides inscribes
Polyxena's resistance, but in the end it comes to naught, for she is unable

71. Loraux, *Tragic Ways*, pp. 50–61.
72. The text is self-conscious about the number of times her story is told; Gellie, "Hecuba
and Tragedy," p. 32, points out that "Euripides expects high emotional dividends from the
reminders, and the same is true of the emphasis he places on Polyxena's youth and her
engaging vulnerability." Orban, "Hécube," p. 320, comments that Euripides pushes detail
almost to cruelty. Thus, the problematic voyeuristic sadism of tragedy—the audience taking
pleasure in someone else's pain—is heightened.
73. Doane, "Film and the Masquerade," p. 76.

to impose her subjectivity in any other way than through self-sacrifice. By understanding the text's fetishism, however, we can to some extent limit its potency.

Makaria and Menoeceus

Although they do not make up so much of the action of their respective plays, the sacrifice of Makaria in *Children of Herakles* follows almost exactly the model I have set out, and the lone sacrifice of a male—Menoeceus in *Phoenician Women*—further clarifies what is at stake in the sacrifice of women.

The *Children of Herakles* is a combination suppliant, sacrifice, and vengeance drama. The children of Herakles, with their aged leader Iolaus, have been pursued by their father's enemy Eurystheus, and have sought refuge in Athens; in order to gain the assistance of Demophon, the Athenian king, they must sacrifice a noble virgin. The first part of the play is then the story of a young girl who dies for her brothers.

Unlike Iphigenia and Polyxena, however, Makaria dies as a member of the category "female," for no one has asked specifically that she die; rather, Demophon announces that "One message stands out; they order me to sacrifice a maiden to Demeter's Kore, one who is of a well-born father" (407–9).[74] Demophon declines to kill one of his own children, thinking that to do so would start a civil war and make him look the fool, to boot. Enter Makaria. She is a modest young girl, aware of the potential impropriety of appearing in public. She is afraid of gaining a reputation for boldness (*thrasos*) simply by making this entrance (which is named an "exit from the inside," *exodois emais*, 474–75). In thus calling attention to her position on stage, she also draws attention to the artificiality of the stage and to the fact that in order for theater to involve female characters, "women" must behave anomalously and enter the public arena. She recognizes her position as a woman, which brings with it the obligation of silence and chastity (476); she recognizes her paradoxical situation—not the head of the family yet old enough to be responsible for her brothers and herself (479–83). Her desire to be effective is contradicted by her status as a female.

Makaria wishes to escape that contradiction by dying gloriously; once

74. As in the case of the sacrifice to Artemis, the relationship of virgin to virgin is underlined.

again, Euripides underlines that which gives the illusion of freedom.[75] Makaria, like Polyxena, tells the men not to be afraid (*mē nun treseis*, 500; cf. *tharsei*, *Hekabe* 346), "for I myself, before being ordered, stand here ready to die and for the sacrificial knife" (501–2). She is willing, not unwilling (531). She gives reasons reminiscent of those of other heroines. Like Iphigenia, who sees Achilles and the glory of Greece as more important than herself, she prefers the good of her family to her own private well-being. Like Sophocles' Electra in her conversation with her sister Chrysothemis, Makaria speaks of the difficulty of marriage for her if she does not act nobly (523–24). Like both Iphigenia and Polyxena, she sees this sacrifice as her way of achieving nobility consistent with her rank: "Is it not better to die than to accept such an unworthy fate?" (*toutōn tuchein anaxian*, 525–26). To let someone else die that she might live might be all right for other girls, but not one from such a distinguished family (*mē'pisēmos*, 526–27). Again, like both Iphigenia and Polyxena, Makaria wishes to be marked off from the crowd. She wants to be crowned and celebrated; she is not in love with life (*philopsuchous'*, 533; cf. Iphigenia, *Iphigenia in Aulis* 1385; Polyxena, *Hekabe* 348) but rather prefers the glorious death (534). And like the others, Makaria is praised for her decision: she has lived up to her ancestry (537, 540–41).

Euripides then gives her another moment of choice: the old man, Iolaus, horrified at the waste of such virtue, suggests a lottery among the sisters to see who will die for the family (*genous huper*, 545). But interchangeability of the members of the category does not please Makaria; she refuses to gamble with death by drawing lots: "I do not wish to die by chance" (547). In this play, where the culture merely insists that it be some noble girl, Makaria goes further and insists that it be she, for she feels that in that way she exercises her freedom: "For there is no graciousness [*charis*] in that [dying by lot]; you should not say it, old man. But, if you are willing to receive me and make use of me with good will [*prothumōs*], I willingly give my life for them, but not by necessity" (548–51).

Makaria clearly tries to evade the status of random female by claiming free choice. Her noble death marks her as a true inheritor of Herakles' courage; through this identification with masculine values, she appears to gain the sort of glory and reputation that a hero gains through valorous combat. First, her death is made to seem worthwhile because it leads to a victory (unlike Iphigenia's or Polyxena's); it also seems to lead to a good

75. Vellacott, *Ironic Drama*, p. 191, assumes that Makaria's death perfectly embodies the poet's irony, that we must know that something is wrong here. But irony is *almost* never that clear (see Booth, *Rhetoric of Irony*, for instances where it is clear).

reputation for women because she is so clearly more noble than the cow-
ardly Demophon and Iolaus.[76] She, like Iphigenia, is sacrificed to avoid a
cultural crisis: civil war between different factions in Athens (419). Second,
her death makes possible the continuation of her paternal lineage, something her life could not have accomplished, given the priority of male
offspring. By making Makaria a model of nobility, the text simultaneously
holds out the false promise that women can achieve success on the male
model and supports the value system that demands the death of maidens
so that men can wage appropriate wars. There is not much gain for Makaria, however, since her death is specifically on behalf of the men in the
family, and in the representation she is not accorded the praise lavished
on Iphigenia and Polyxena in their respective texts.

   There are, of course, cases that do not fit so neatly—Menoeceus, a male
victim—but even these help us to understand what is at issue in the
paradigm.[77] In *Phoenician Women*, when one of the members of the Theban
royal house must be sacrificed in order to win the war against the Argives
(931–41), Menoeceus, though a man, is suitable for the task, for like the
female victims he is unmarried and, unlike his more famous brother Hae-
mon, not promised to any bride (944–48). Thus, he still belongs only to
his country and can still be given away; in this way, he is like the girls.
Kreon, like Clytemnestra and Hekabe, is appalled at the idea and plans to
send him away (962–76). Menoeceus then volunteers. He wishes to avoid
cowardice (*deiliai*, 994) or treachery to his fatherland (996) and vows to
save his city (997).

   In this text the demand is not for a woman, named or nameless, but
for one of the descendants of Laius; thus a male is required, and as a result
the sacrifice plot works itself out differently in several ways. First, Menoeceus dies for his city, which is at war. By his death he can restore success
to the land; since he is in direct line for the throne, he is responsible for
the city. Thus, a close connection governs the choice of Menoeceus as
sacrificial victim, whereas the Trojan War has nothing to do with Iphigenia.
For the male, then, sacrifice stands not for marriage but for life as king;

76. Vellacott, *Ironic Drama*, pp. 188–91.
77. Antigone in Euripides' *Phoenician Women* provides a pointed contrast to Menoeceus;
through her we can see the difference between the two kinds of sacrifice, the one for the
family and the one for the public. While Menoeceus dies for the city, she lives for the family.
Of course, Sophocles' *Antigone* sheds light on Euripides' plays, but as I said earlier, his
Antigone cannot really be considered one of the sacrificial heroines, since she commits an
action for a cause that *then* entails her death; it is not her death alone that is demanded (but
cf. Loraux, *Tragic Ways*, pp. 31–32, 37, 47, who links her with the others through their
common "marriage to Hades" and glory).

it is a way of fulfilling his responsibilities to his people.[78] Menoeceus is like those for whom he kills himself; thus, while Iphigenia, Polyxena, and Makaria each dies for men—for a war of dubious value, for the honor of a dead hero, for her brothers, respectively—Menoeceus's death is for himself.

Consequently, and second, his motives are different. For instance, he does not think about his reputation or, as does Makaria, about who might marry him. His sacrifice most definitely does not constitute marriage for him. Third, although the women choose death, the threat of force hangs over them. But Kreon has already made a plan to rescue Menoeceus and is about to put it into action. Unlike Iphigenia and Polyxena especially, he has a real choice.

Finally, and most important for the representation, he kills himself, whereas the three women are killed. No matter how active Euripides makes them seem, in the end the women expose their bodies to the knife of some male official. In the narrative of Menoeceus's death, he is the actor, the one who delivers as well as receives the blow; as a soldier, he wields the sword himself (*sphaxas emauton*, 1010, 1090–92).[79] Even though the death is described as a ritual, no priest officiates. Thus, while the female protagonists are described as dying in a crowd of men, he is in isolation.[80] As a result, the voyeurism and fetishism of *Iphigenia in Aulis* and *Hekabe* are eliminated. There are only three lines devoted to his death, not even a complete sentence: "When the child of Kreon, standing on the highest tower, dying for this land, thrust his sword through his throat and became a savior for the land..." (1090–92).

When there is a civic consequence to a sacrifice, when it is a man sacrificing himself for his own people, there is no baring of beautiful breasts, no fulsome praise. That is because there is no need to seduce men into complying with that which is in their own interest, and not the same frisson of delight in seeing their vulnerability.

In the model of the sacrificial heroine, praised for her freedom and seen

78. Loraux, *Tragic Ways*, p. 42, remarks that marriage also marks growing up for a man, but not before he has already been in the military; thus, Vernant's equation about marriage and war in "City-State Warfare" is still informative. On this point, see Schmitt-Pantel, "Histoire," pp. 217–31, esp. 226–27. Bremmer, "Scapegoat," esp. pp. 302, 304, equates the marginality of the king in these legends with that of the virgins. I would disagree and, like Guépin, *Tragic Paradox*, pp. 207–8, see him rather as a sign for the city. (Guépin makes a further argument about the vegetation significance of the sacrifice.)

79. Like Deianeira in Sophocles' *Women of Trachis*, but unlike most female suicides in Greek plays, who tend to hang themselves. See Loraux, *Tragic Ways*.

80. Loraux, *Tragic Ways*, pp. 41–42.

as the analogue of the warrior hero, the contemporary feminist critic can find much food for thought. I have tried to avoid the two obvious paths—seeing the female figure as simply victimized or simply glorified—and to chart out a third course. Once we analyze the structure, we see that the culture needs women's compliance and gets it by holding out rewards for that compliance. One of those rewards is praise. Then, taking the praise itself as a form of fetishism, it seems to me that we can analyze the fetish in both Marxist and Freudian terms, both as a denial of the processes of production at work and as a psychological mechanism. Social and psychological needs come together. In the Freudian model we can see a possibility of female strength that the structure of the fetish seeks to control. If, to repeat Laura Mulvey's words, sadism demands a story, these texts demand female masochism to mask that sadism. We can resist the naturalization of such masochism first by revealing its construction ("this is what women desire"), then by redefining the apparent glorification as a form of fetishism designed to control the power of the woman not yet married.

There is a modern significance for my analysis of the ways in which tragedy constructs these characters constructing themselves as subjects, a construction that makes them seem to will their status as object of the male gaze. As feminist thinkers and writers, we too see ourselves as actors, as glorious heroines in the struggles we undertake. Which discourses are producing our resistance, and what power are they recuperating?

2 The Sacrificial Wife: Alcestis

Alcestis is central to my consideration of Euripides' work because it exposes in an especially clear fashion the ways in which sacrifice is used to help satisfy a male need for control, specifically by allaying male fears of both death and female sexuality. Death and sexuality are related not only in psychoanalytic but also in mythic or traditional cultural discourses, where the house can, in Pierre Bourdieu's words, "simultaneously and without contradiction be the place of death and of procreation."[1] Like the virgins, Alcestis is often taken to be "a hero and peer of the great culture-heroes," as William Arrowsmith says, or is glorified in some other way. Charles Segal argues that "her honor... is replaced, in Euripides' final act of substitution, by the honor that he gives her in the enacted commemoration of the play."[2] The model of female excellence is designed, however, to meet male needs.

Written as Athens was poised for the Peloponnesian War, with the long Samian siege in the background,[3] the play exhibits concerns that make it an analogue to Pericles' Funeral Oration celebrating the immortality of those who died defending the city at Samos. The fragmentary remains of that speech (Plutarch *Pericles* 8, 9) indicate that Pericles there articulated

1. Bourdieu, *Algeria*, p. 138; cf. Slater, *Glory of Hera*, p. 78.
2. Arrowsmith, *Alcestis*, p. 27; Segal, "Cold Delight," p. 221. In that essay and "Euripides' *Alcestis*," Segal focuses on the role of art, analyzing Admetos's statue to replace Alcestis in terms akin to my own; our interpretations are ultimately complementary, although quite different in intention. The treatment of much of the play's imagery in O'Higgins, "Above Rubies," is similar to mine, though not placed in the same context.
3. Ritoók, "Euripides: *Alcestis*," pp. 173–74, notes the historical connection; Arrowsmith, *Alcestis*, p. 24, also notes the parallel.

a model of male excellence, defined as death for the democracy.[4] The *Alcestis* played its role in supporting Athenian social goals by defining female excellence as dying on behalf of men and the family: that is, as a corollary to men's dying for the city.[5] The play is, then, political in that it participates in the process of recruiting women as wives and prescribes a model of female virtue useful to Athens on the brink of war. The text as a whole, with its inscription of both Alcestis's willing sacrifice and her return from the underworld, fulfills the triple male goals for exogamous marriage outlined in the Introduction: to extend the life of the lineage by providing heirs, to control female sexuality by placing it under the aegis of reproductive heterosexuality, and to establish acceptable ties between men.

The plot is simple. Apollo tells us in the prologue that in gratitude for the hospitality extended to him in the past, he granted Admetos the opportunity to prolong his life if he could find someone to take his place with Death; although Admetos's parents refused, his wife Alcestis agreed to do so. The play then opens with a confrontation between Apollo and Death in which Apollo tries and fails to rescue Alcestis from her pledge. After the servant has described her mistress's private farewells to house, children, and servants, Alcestis enters to take her leave of Admetos; on the point of death, she asks that he grant her one request and not remarry. He agrees and vows eternal mourning; he further plans to take a stone image of her into his bed. Despite his grief, Admetos welcomes as a house guest his friend Herakles without telling him who has died. When Herakles finds out, he retrieves Alcestis from Death and offers her as a gift to Admetos, but without revealing her identity. The play ends with a protracted scene between Herakles and Admetos in which the latter, attempting to be faithful to Alcestis's last wish, resists accepting this strange woman. Only when he finally receives her does he discover that she is his wife.

As is the case with many of the tragedies, there is more to the traditional story than Euripides makes use of. In fact, there are two story lines: that of Apollo and Admetos, and that of Admetos and Alcestis.[6] The first strand primarily elaborates concerns about death. Euripides gives this much back-

4. On the speech, see Loraux, *Invention of Athens*, pp. 40–42.

5. See the Introduction, pp. 4–9, on the relationship of public and private in Athens; see also Lacey, *Family*, pp. 21, 73; Vernant and the structuralists in general argue for the complementarity of the two spheres, marriage and war (e.g., "City-State Warfare," p. 25). Loraux, *Tragic Ways*, points out the differences between the deaths of men and women.

6. Lesky established the fairytale origins of the legend in his *Alkestis*. On the mythic background and the uneasy coherence of the two parts of the legend, see Séchan, "Dévouement"; and Conacher, *Euripidean Drama*, pp. 327–39. The ancient sources are Hesiod frag. 59–60 (West); Apollodorus *Bibliotheca* 3.10.3–4, 1.9.15; Plutarch *Amatores* 761e.

ground: Zeus killed Apollo's son Asklepios for bringing the dead back to life; Apollo retaliated by attacking the Cyclopes, who forged the thunderbolt that killed Asklepios; Zeus then made Apollo a servant to Admetos—the immediate backdrop to the play (1–9). The story of Apollo and Admetos is imbricated simultaneously in material that indicates the father's power. Zeus, the divine father, keeps the authority over life and death for himself; mythically, Apollo's servitude would stand for his death. Sex is not far from the surface, however: the thunderbolt as the emblem of the father's power is phallic, suggesting that the threat of death is also a threat to masculinity. The struggle between Zeus and Apollo, centering as it does on the thunderbolt, relates castration anxiety to a larger cluster of effects, including the desire for power, as well as a male's desire to arrogate to himself the power to give life.[7]

The second strand of the story raises the specter of terrifying female sexuality. While Apollo was in service to Admetos, he helped him yoke the lion and the boar to win the hand of Alcestis. But why was Admetos fated to die young? In Euripides we do not know, but other versions tell us that it was because he failed to sacrifice to the goddess Artemis; the presence of snakes in his marriage chamber either required or foretold his early death. The threat lurking in the wedding chamber in the form of snakes suggests the masculine perception of the female genitals as dangerous; since the inner space of the house (*thalamos*) is frequently identified with the female body, the snakes guard both spaces and keep off the male intruder. Euripides seemingly excludes this explanation, picking up the "narrative" only at the point where Apollo tricked the Fates into accepting a substitute for Admetos if he could find someone to die in his place (12–14).

As I hope to show, the omitted scene is nonetheless relevant to the anxiety Admetos experiences. This legend indicates a male sense of inadequacy coupled with anxiety about feminine sexuality, which is construed as threatening.[8] Admetos's inadequacy is reflected not only in the snakes but also in his marriage to Alcestis, which does indeed entail his death. In the end, Admetos's death is averted only because Alcestis is strong enough to replace *both* the omitted sacrifice and him.

Looking at other versions of the myth, we can see the great strength of Alcestis, who is after all the only mortal woman to make the journey to the underworld and return. According to Plato (*Symposium* 179b–d),

---

7. This is especially evident in the Apollo and Asklepios episode: when Apollo killed his unfaithful lover Coronis, he rescued his unborn son, Asklepios, and gave birth to him himself (Pindar *Pythian* 3).

8. Slater, *Glory of Hera*, p. 70, similarly sees fear of mature femininity in the snaky chamber.

Persephone respected Alcestis so much that she herself freed her. This version of the return to the upper world stresses Alcestis's relationships to other females and her status as a Persephone figure; thus, too, it strengthens the link between sexuality and death, since Persephone was raped by Hades and resides in his realm.[9] If we look to the East, we see a possible paradigm for Alcestis's variety of strength in the Sumero-Babylonian story of Inanna, who seeks her sister Ereshkigal in the Great Below and returns to her position in the Great Above only after remaining below for three days; her consort Dumuzi replaces her in the underworld.[10] Inanna (who incidentally celebrates her own sexual parts) then incorporates within herself both the upper and lower realms and is strong because of that inclusiveness. Alcestis is most akin to such a figure in those versions where she returns from the dead thanks to Persephone.

The mythic background to the events of the play, then, thematizes both death and female sexuality. The former is tied to a terrifying father-son rivalry and a symbolic form of castration anxiety, at least for the post-Freudian reader; the latter is tied to a sense of female potency that also threatens. The Inanna corollary points out that there could have been other views of Alcestis; while a hegemonic perspective has the ability to impose itself as the truth, a strategy of resistance could involve celebrating Alcestis's strength as Inanna's was celebrated.

Although no Greek play has escaped critical debates, the *Alcestis* seems to have aroused more than its share. To cite John Wilson's introduction to a collection of essays on the play, "Euripides' *Alcestis* has always been a critic's battlefield. Even the genre to which the play belongs is disputed—is it a tragedy, a satyr play, or the first example of a tragicomedy? Who is the main character, Alcestis or Admetos? And through whose eyes are we to see this wife and this husband? Is Alcestis as noble as she says she is? And is Admetos worthy of her devotion, or does he deserve all the blame that his father, Pheres, heaps upon him? And is the salvation of Alcestis a true mystery, a sardonic 'and so they lived happily ever after,' or simply the convenient end of an entertainment?"[11] The genre of the *Alcestis* (this

9. On the sacrificial pattern and connections to other goddesses, see Guépin, *Tragic Paradox*, pp. 120–42. The sacrificial maidens are modeled on Persephone's virginity. On these heroines as the sisters of Alcestis, see Roussel, "Thème du sacrifice"; Séchan, "Dévouement," pt. 2; Burnett, *Catastrophe*, pp. 23–27. On Admetos's similarity to Adamastos (one name of Hades), see Séchan, "Dévouement," pp. 493–98; and Foley, *Ritual Irony*, pp. 87–88. Conacher, *Euripidean Drama*, dismisses this connection.

10. Kramer and Wolkstein, *Inanna*.

11. Wilson, *Euripides' "Alcestis,"* p. 1. For a summary with bibliography, see Ritoók, "Euripides: *Alcestis*," p. 168. See also Bradley, "Admetus"; and Michelini, *Euripides*, pp. 324–29. As a result of these uncertainties, irony is a favorite approach: e.g., von Fritz, "Euripides *Alkestis*"; Smith, "Ironic Structure."

play was produced fourth in Euripides' competition entry for the year,
where one would have expected a satyr drama; as a result critics have
looked for and found comic elements in it) depends on gender. On the
surface, it is comic: death leads to life, and a funeral resolves into a wedding.
But is it a happy ending for Alcestis as well as for Admetos? Although
funeral and wedding may seem to be opposites, they come to much the
same thing for this woman.[12]

Recent criticism has focused on the play as a study of life and death,
specifically opposing those interpretations that dwell on it as a study of
marriage.[13] But it is precisely about the connections between death and
marriage (the institutionalized form of the sex/gender system, and responsible for the continued life of the family). Because she is a woman,
Alcestis is willing to die in Admetos's place: she sees her life as less important than his. And, because she is *willing* to die to save him, she not
only allows him to avoid death but also reaffirms male dominance. Finally,
the sacrifice is interrupted and death is avoided by a return to marriage.
When their re-union takes place, her subordination as a female in marriage
once again helps to reestablish the ordered limits of life and death, which
have been deranged by her premature death.

Even though Euripides does not utilize all the variants of the myth, the
same confluence of elements—father-son rivalry, male sense of inadequacy,
and female power—appear in the play. The text constructs female power
as liminal, therefore threatening, but it is controlled by gestures that claim
to celebrate it. I would argue, then, that Euripides puts the feminine into
play, only to cut off that play in favor of the consolidation of male subjectivity; the representation of Alcestis shifts between the uncanny and the
consoling fetish.[14] This chapter is organized around the oscillation between
threat and containment, a pattern that is inscribed three times: first when
Alcestis is offstage, next when she comes outside to say farewell, and finally
when she returns from the dead.

In stage one, Alcestis is depicted as a borderline figure, between life and
death, between the inside and the outside; through the sacrifice plot Eu-

---

12. Foley, *Ritual Irony*, p. 87, remarks on the presence of death in both marriage and
sacrifice—Alcestis's "promised sacrificial death for her husband recreates the primal experience
of the bride"—but believes that the marriage in the end is an improvement; I disagree with
the latter point.

13. See, e.g., Rosenmeyer, *Masks of Tragedy*; Gregory, "Euripides' *Alcestis*"; and Musurillo, "*Alcestis*," for the former view and Vellacott, "Woman and Man" for the latter.

14. The doubling that Freud associates with the *unheimlich* characterizes the myth and
the play *Alcestis*; see, e.g., Séchan, "Dévouement," who argues that "the story as it appears
from the classical period is made up of two separate elements" (p. 493). Castellani, "Notes,"
has argued that the entire text is double, with two prologues and structural repetitions. See
also note 6 above.

ripides assuages both Admetos's dread of death and a Greek male fear of
the potentially ex-centric and ex-cessive sexuality of the exogamous wife.
Most obviously, by volunteering to die in his place, Alcestis seems to allow
Admetos to avoid his fear of death. Cultural anxieties about the woman
outsider are simultaneously allayed because Alcestis is represented not only
as dying willingly but also as identifying totally with the house of Admetos.
In this stage, she is glorified as the best of women for having made that
choice; the text thus inscribes a fetishistic praise that promotes the ideal.

Nonetheless, Alcestis can still show a resurgence of power, as she does
in stage two when she asks Admetos not to replace her, not to remarry.
She is threatening in this scene, for she asserts herself as a speaking subject,
making demands counter to the commonsense perception of the family's
best interests. Admetos's inadequacy in the face of her power and his
conflict with his father make him an archetypal fetishist; his hyperbolic
speech of devotion does not actually elevate Alcestis but serves instead to
fetishize her, and thus bring her under his control.

Alcestis's return from the dead marks the third stage; coming back from
the "other side," she is clearly a liminal figure, now on two grounds. As
Maurice Blanchot says, "The image does not resemble a cadaver, but it
could be that the strangeness of a cadaver is also the strangeness of the
image. What we call the mortal remains evades the usual categories; something is there before us that is neither the living person himself nor any
sort of reality, neither the same as the one who was alive, nor another,
nor any other thing."[15] When Alcestis enters, she is on the margin and
an image; she seems to have become the fetish, the veiled object of Admetos's equally veiled desire, and is totally silenced.[16]

The residual power nonetheless immanent in such a figure is controlled
by making Alcestis the "subject" of a joke and turning her into an object
in an exchange of gifts between men. In this way, we will see, the play
deprives her of her potential strength and renders her a cipher—meaning
zero, and thus empty but nonetheless crucial as a place holder. Having
been glorified (or, as I claim, fetishized) for her self-abnegation in sacrifice,
she is turned into a simulacrum, the imitation of her own rival. This

15. Blanchot, "Two Versions," p. 81.
16. She functions like the Derridean *pharmakon*: "The boundary (between inside and
outside, living and nonliving) separates not only speech from writing but also memory as
an unveiling (re-)producing a presence from re-memoration as the mere repetition of a
monument; truth as distinct from its sign, being as distinct from types" (Derrida, *Dissemination*, pp. 108–9). Given the importance of Asklepios in the background, it is not surprising
to find reference to literal cures in the play; we can see that Alcestis attempts to save Admetos,
but instead she consigns him to a living death (see Gregory, "Euripides' *Alcestis*"). It is she
who is living and nonliving, inside and outside.

rhetorical and psychoanalytic structure is parallel to a ritual structure; in the next part of the chapter, then, I turn to the imitation of ritual that provides the overarching organization for the play.

Threat and Containment I: Fetishistic Praise

The play's opening gives a strong sense of Alcestis's liminality. As Apollo makes clear, her death is itself an aberration from the normal course of events: she is young and is dying before the old. In fact, Death wants her precisely because she is young and is "worth more" to him than someone who is due to die (52–55). While the unburied dead are typically taboo and contaminating, her marginality predates her actual death; since she has *promised* to die, she is both dead and not dead.[17] As a result, doubt marks the opening choral song; the Chorus does not know whether the queen is dead or living (80–83).

Alcestis is on the border in another sense as well, not only as a result of her extraordinary situation but as a result of her very ordinary status as a wife. It is important to the plot that she enjoys an ambiguous position: from the beginning, she is an outsider yet also at the center of the family. After her death, Admetos can convince Herakles to stay in his house even though he is in mourning, by playing on both ambiguities as well as on the fact that the same word means woman and wife. Herakles first asks if Alcestis has died; Admetos parries by saying she is both dead and yet living, because she is fated to die even if she is not yet dead (518–28). Then, since to be a woman is to be a wife, he can say that "his wife" died while seeming to say that "a woman" died. When Herakles asks if "the woman" was "an outsider or one of the family," Admetos answers an "outsider, but one necessary to the house" (531–33). Herakles stresses her outsider status again when he defends his rude and drunken behavior: he had believed it was only an outsider (*gunē thuraios*, 805; *othneiou*, 810) who had died.[18] Similarly, the praise for Alcestis underlines her position: her sacrifice is more noteworthy because she is not of the same blood as Admetos; father and mother are closer relations and should have been willing to die. "These were dear [*philoi*] in word, not deed. You, giving up what was your own and most dear [*antidousa . . . ta philtata*], saved me"

17. Buxton, "Voile et le silence," makes a similar point, concluding that her intermediary status explains her veil and silence at the play's end.
18. See ibid., p. 168, on the house as the house of death, and the "linguistic border" established by the Herakles scenes.

(339–41). He throws the fact up to his father: "You did not dare to die for your child, but let this woman, an outsider [*othneian*]" (644–46).

The *Alcestis* overtly thematizes the implicit goals behind the exchange of women, and Alcestis's position derives from the more general female condition discussed in the Introduction. The Athenian citizenship law of 451, which stipulated that only marriages between Athenians were legitimate, established an ideal of endogamy on the city level, but families were still exogamous within those limits. Although exogamous marriages do much for the culture (for one thing, they create ties between men of different families), any given marriage is nonetheless infected by the very disorder it exists to control. For instance, Hestia, the goddess of the hearth, is an emblem for the respectable wife because the wife, as the producer of children, is strongly identified with the hearth, itself a sign of the continued life of the household. But Hestia, the impossibly virginal daughter who never leaves the hearth, is also a problematic figure for the human wife who actually must leave her natal family and come to *stand for* the hearth of her husband's family.[19] Significantly, Hestia is also connected to the underworld and death, the very forces marriage would hold in check.[20] Moreover, the woman moves not only between life and death but also between inside and outside. Exogamous marriage brings an outsider woman into a new family. As a result, every family is made up of outsiders. This is strongly marked in Alcestis's case, for she was a prize that Admetos won in a contest; but the woman is a dangerous prize, as is demonstrated by the connection Nicole Loraux draws between the words for "marriage-bed" (*lechos*), "wife" (*alochos*), and "ambush" (*lochos*).[21]

How does the play (and culture) handle this threat? Stage one deploys several strategies. First, it makes Alcestis a sacrificial victim. Death says, "I go to her, so that I can begin the rite with this sword; for this one is sacred to the gods below the earth, whose hair has been sacrificed by this strong sword" (74–76; see also the reference to the priest, 25). Later on Herakles uses the language of sacrifice when he speculates that he will find Death or Hades drinking the victim's blood (*prosphagmatōn*, 845) at the tomb.[22]

---

19. Cf. the Introduction. I am indebted to the careful commentary of Ann Michelini for this observation.

20. For Hestia's role, see Vernant, "Hestia-Hermes," esp. p. 154. On the modern Greek parallel, see Bourdieu, *Algeria*, pp. 133–53.

21. Loraux, "Le lit, la guerre," p. 41.

22. Burnett, *Catastrophe*, treats the death as sacrifice (pp. 22–29). Gregory, "Euripides' *Alcestis*," discusses the slippage between the different descriptions (including suicide) of her death (pp. 263–65). While Alcestis is intended as an offering that will defer death, the fact of her death renders other sacrifice vain: "All has been done by the kings, the sacrifices

Like the plays of virgin self-sacrifice, this text also stresses the woman's volition: Alcestis is crucially defined almost as a suicide. Apollo first mentions her as having been willing to die when Admetos's mother and father were not (*ēthele*, 17), and the Servant says the same, expanding on the theme (153–55). The scene between Alcestis and Admetos further emphasizes the element of choice. Admetos overlooks his own responsibility; he acts as if Alcestis could at this point decide not to leave him. His peculiar confusion, when he presents himself as an abandoned victim, must not be taken simply as a device to reveal character, for it also has a rhetorical effect on the audience, suggesting that Alcestis has control. Her speech to him accomplishes the same rhetorical end: "I put you first [*presbeuousa*; cf. *protimōs'*, 155] and arranged it so that you would see the light in place of my life [*psuchēs*]; I die, on your behalf, when it was possible for me not to die, but to have some Thessalian man and to inhabit the blessed household of the tyrant" (282–86). By having her bring up the possibility that had she let Admetos die, she could have remarried, Euripides again makes it seem that she is an active agent.

The strength she reveals in her choice is nonetheless minimized by the motives given for the sacrifice: she dies out of devotion to the children and the house of Admetos.[23] She says that she would not want to bring the children up without a father: "I did not wish to live bereft of you with orphan children" (287–88). Alcestis does make a choice, one that allays male anxiety about the outsider woman: she is more devoted to the lineage than Admetos' own father is. Her actions demonstrate her devotion to the house of Admetos: she addresses herself to Hestia (162; cf. other references to the altar, *hestia*, 538, 545, 547, 589) and to the altars of Admetos's house (170); she takes leave not only of her children but also of each of the servants (189–95).[24] The servant makes a point of her taking her robe from "the well-maintained chests of cedar" (160–61); everything is in order here because Alcestis is a fitting keeper of the goods of the house, as her association with Hestia would also indicate. In the private scene, then, Alcestis is depicted as devoted selflessly to Admetos and his *oikos* and family, as well as to the marriage prospects of her children. The

---

dripping blood are full on the altars of all the gods; there is no cure for the evil" (132–35). Death cannot be avoided, and there are no more potions, only poisons.

23. Michelini, *Euripides*, pp. 326–27. Burnett, *Catastrophe*, pp. 34–36, emphasizes *philia* as opposed to erotic love; Sicking, "Alceste," asks whether she had any choice, because of what she owed to the family and children. But Dale, *Euripides: Alcestis*, p. xxvi, asserts that of course Alcestis loved Admetos: why else would she have agreed to die for him? The question, however, is about the nature of that love.

24. Burnett suggests that the veil at the end allows her to "return in the guise of Hestia herself" ("Virtues," p. 251). See also Vernant, "Hestia-Hermes," pp. 148–52.

sacrifice itself and the motivation for it define Alcestis as no longer a suspect outsider but rather a woman totally committed to the house of Admetos. Thus the problem of the outsider woman is eliminated by bringing her more securely within.

But this representation of Alcestis as *willingly* sacrificing herself obscures the culturally imposed limitations on women. While Euripides stresses her choice, I would at the same time underline the element of constraint, or those elements shaping her choice. Commitment to family does not counter devotion to Admetos; rather, the two coexist if we understand her relationship to her husband in terms appropriate to ancient Greece. Marriage was not about romantic love or desire but about the family; significantly, the inner reaches of the house are simultaneously the site of reproductive sexuality and the place, dedicated to Hestia, where its wealth is guarded. The Greek wife and daughter were generally identified with the hearth in the inner chambers, the *thalamos*. As Louis Gernet says, "The room where the ancient wealth of rulers was stored is called a *thalamos* (and it is worth noting that the word applies equally to the living quarters of the wife or daughter)."[25]

Therefore, although Alcestis is much more emotional when she retreats into those chambers, marriage, not some individualistic notion of love, is still the issue; Alcestis dies to fulfill her idea of marital obligation to her husband's family. She sheds tears when she approaches her marriage bed because she recognizes that it is her bed that has killed her: "O bed, where I let go of my virginal girlhood for that man for whom I now die, farewell; I do not hate you; you have destroyed me alone; I die because I recoiled from betraying you and my husband" (177–81). The bed stands for her marriage, which kills her in the play as much as it does in the myth, where the snakes in the chamber demand another sacrifice.

Euripides has Alcestis bring up the possibility of her remarriage to make the point that she did not have to die. But what would that marriage have yielded her? Another family to be responsible to? There would no doubt have been considerable pressure on a real woman in such a situation to remarry, but if Alcestis were to do so, what would become of her children with Admetos and what would become of the estate?[26] Recognizing her

25. Gernet, *Anthropology*, p. 101. See also Vernant, "Marriage" and "Hestia-Hermes," esp. pp. 148–49; Loraux, *Tragic Ways*, pp. 23–24 with notes.

26. For the dynastic argument, as to why Admetos should or would accept her offer, see Grube, *Drama*, p. 129; Roussel, "Thème du sacrifice," who says, "The chief of the line, whose existence is menaced, has the right and almost the duty to seek and accept the sacrifices addressed less to his person than to the collectivity" (p. 228); Séchan, "Dévouement," p. 343.

powerlessness as a woman surviving her husband, therefore without family and status, but nonetheless valuing her reputation, Alcestis plays her only card—her life. For dying is the only way she can guarantee the family honor: "And you my husband, boast to have had the best woman [as wife], and you, my children, to be born of such a mother" (323–25). Insofar as she did not owe her life to Admetos, and it would seem that she did not, it is indeed her will that is at issue, but it is the discourse of devotion to husband and children that makes possible this particular "assertion" (or consolidation) of self.[27]

Finally, we come to the last strategy of this section of the play, for not only does the text gloss over the constraints underlying Alcestis' self-sacrifice, but it simultaneously praises her for a "freely chosen" action that makes her an example to other women. There is no doubt that Alcestis is glorified in the text; she is "the best of women" because of her gesture of self-sacrifice. The Servant asks, "What could be more outstanding in a woman? How could one show that she honors her husband more than by being willing to die for him?" (153–55). The adoration of Alcestis is a clear part of the scholarly tradition on this play, as we can see in the reactions of critics as diverse as Loraux, who says that "Alcestis was devoted, loving, and virtuous, but she earned her 'glorious death' only through the male qualities of courage and endurance"; Herbert Musurillo, who finds no flaw in her; and A. M. Dale, who says that the "conspicuous glory is hers."[28]

In sum, Alcestis is inscribed first as shifting between categories and therefore, I would assert, as threatening. In this stage of the plot, however, even though her chamber and bed (*thalamon . . . kai lechos*, 175) are destroying her, she is represented as an ideal woman who identifies with the hearth and altars of Admetos's house. She then articulates the sensibility one would expect from a woman so identified with the interior and the private. She is made less threatening not only because she appears to choose to die but also because she chooses to die having identified totally with the family she has married into. In this way her borderline status is effaced, and the border is secured. More important still, she is praised and exalted for her dedication which is presented as if it were an action.

27. But cf. Nielsen, "Alcestis," on her distortion of aristocratic values. Myres points out in "Plot" that her view is anomalous; Admetos's is the norm. Michelini, *Euripides*, p. 92, argues further that the sacrifices of the virtuous characters are meant to challenge "social and aesthetic standards."
28. Loraux, *Tragic Ways*, pp. 28–29; Musurillo, "Alcestis," p. 284; Dale, *Euripides: Alcestis*, p. xxii. Weil, *Alceste*, p. 1, uses this play to defend Euripides against charges of misogyny.

Threat and Containment II: The Phallic Woman

When Alcestis appears on stage, there seems to be a radical shift, most obviously from tears to rational discourse. Much criticism of the play has centered on the supposed difference between the internal and external, private and public, representations of her. Is there a discrepancy between the two? Thomas Rosenmeyer seems to object to her serenity and finds her chilly, her speech to Admetos a way of giving him "a piece of her mind"; Charles Beye notes that she has no endearing words for her husband, only mistrust and coldness.[29] Is she in fact cold and "unattractive" when she is on stage, warm and loving in her own chamber?

Between the two major episodes is an important scene in which Alcestis is represented as almost completely "on the other side." The Alcestis who first appears on the stage has quite clearly shifted to the border regions between life and death. She sees the ship of the dead (252) and feels herself being led into the region of the dead (259–60). Furthermore, she announces that the children no longer have a mother (270–71). Euripides pulls her back from this extreme location with which she has just been so strongly identified, but it is nonetheless from that position that she makes her powerful speech to Admetos.

In her narrated address to her bed, Alcestis assumed that she would be replaced, that her bed would have a new occupant, no more chaste but perhaps more fortunate than herself (181–82). In fact, she has every reason to assume that Admetos will remarry. Her assumption indicates a truth about exchange marriage: only the function of wife, not the particular woman, counts. When she comes on stage, however, full of the power of having returned almost from the dead, she denies this common truth, resists being replaced. She negotiates with Admetos on the strength of what she is giving up for him; she feels that he owes her fidelity beyond the grave. When she comes to herself, then, she tries to assert some control over her fate.

Still this change does not reflect a change in motive. She remains committed to the good of the family, in particular her children; as her acceptance of death was based on her coming to terms with the limited options available to women, so does her demand of Admetos. Euripides depicts Alcestis as making the best of an imperfect situation at the same time that he inscribes the malice of the imaginary other woman. His Alcestis joins in the fabrication of the "wicked stepmother": "The boy has his father for

29. Rosenmeyer, *Masks of Tragedy*, pp. 224–26; Beye, "Alcestis and Her Critics," p. 123. See also Dale, *Euripides: Alcestis*, p. xxiv.

a tower of strength. But you, my child, how well will you pass your maidenhood? How will you fare with your father's new wife? She must not give you shameful reputation and ruin your chance of marriage in the height of your youth, because your mother will not be there to attend you at your marriage, nor to give you courage in childbirth, when there is nothing more cheering than your mother" (311–19). She is particularly worried about her daughter, both because she will not have her father in the same way that the boy has him and because little girls are more closely identified with and dependent on a mother. The father (a powerful "tower," or phallus) is available to the son and passes on to him; the daughter's part is to succeed through her ability to produce heirs.

Alcestis's request is excessive, though, and threatens to sabotage the very *oikos* she dies to protect.[30] As we will see in more detail later, the consequences of her death, the erosion of the well-being of the household, show up the problems that would spring from the permanent absence of a wife. Her assertive demand is then problematic in the terms set up by the play: if she dies for the good of the family, she should also want Admetos to remarry for the good of that family. Euripides represents Alcestis's power: she has returned from the brink of death and asserts herself. As a result, she is once again a liminal figure combining the insider and the outsider. When she claims that her act is an incalculable good, she claims a status for herself as a unique subject and asserts a self-sufficiency that may be perceived as threatening from the perspective of the dominant order. Sarah Kofman says: "Whether this self-sufficiency is real or only supposed to be real, it is what makes woman enigmatic, inaccessible, impenetrable."[31] Alcestis may be such an enigmatic figure.

The Freudian view of the *unheimlich* as the home that is not a home, the private place that is not safe, inheres in the Greek connection of wife (*alochos*), bed (*lechos*), and ambush (*lochos*). Since the female genitals are perilous for the male, the wife is a potential site of ambush. The portrayal of an inadequate and Oedipal Admetos is the corollary of this uncanny Alcestis. Admetos's masculinity is in doubt throughout the play: he is no traditional hero. He cannot even rescue his own heroine. He is indebted to Apollo for his bride in the first place, and to Herakles in the second.

---

30. Burnett, *Catastrophe*, pp. 37–38, 39. Gregory, "Euripides' *Alcestis*," points out the problem with the sacrifice as a whole.

31. Kofman, *Enigma of Woman*, p. 62; also p. 56 on narcissism, which she then relates to the *unheimlich*. The figure of the narcissistic woman that she highlights (p. 53) appears also in Derrida's *Spurs*, where he responds to Nietzsche's notion of the affirmative woman. On Hesiod from a Derridean point of view, see Mason, "Third Person/Second Sex," pp. 168–74. As I will argue, this feminine self-sufficiency—whether real or imagined—calls for masculine strategies of control.

In his reply to Alcestis' demand, he says he wishes he had Orpheus's power of song. But he does not have that hero's life-giving creative force, only his death-dealing gaze. Unlike Orestes in the *Oresteia*, who is suitably compared to Perseus, Admetos is a failed Perseus—or even the Medusa itself, since, in having the statue made, he would in effect turn Alcestis to stone.[32]

This anti-hero is significantly in violent conflict with his father and wishes him dead that he himself may live. He says, "You passed your youth in rule; as your son I am the appropriate successor to this house" (654–55). Admetos is like the protagonist of a Freudian "Family Romance,"[33] in which the child fantasizes that he has other parents than his own. "Can you ever have been the father of this body? Can she who says she bore me and is called my mother have given me birth? . . . I no longer count myself to be [*pephukenai*] your child" (636–38, 641). At this point he speculates that he may be the illegitimate child of a slave; later he claims Alcestis as a parent in their place, she "whom alone I count justly mother and father" (646–47).[34] In this romance, "Oedipus" gets to marry his "mother" and to live happily ever after.[35]

Having given Alcestis her moment of strength, Euripides proceeds to repress this female once more, thereby rendering the *unheimlich* simply homey. The response of his Admetos is to limit and control the *unheimlich* through a form of fetishism akin to the "glorification" I have just put forward.

When Alcestis makes her power play, it seems that she has won a victory, for Admetos meets her "demands" with hyperbole. He goes beyond her

32. It is one of those critical commonplaces to speak of the failures of Admetos (see, e.g., Blaiklock, *Male Characters*, pp. 1–20), although Burnett, "Virtues," makes a good defense of his character and thinks he is like Herakles and Apollo (*Catastrophe*, p. 43). On the feminization of Admetos, see Segal, "Euripides' *Alcestis*," p. 155; Foley, *Ritual Irony*, pp. 87–88; Loraux, *Tragic Ways*, pp. 28–29; Smith, "Ironic Structure," p. 133. See O'Higgins, "Above Rubies," for an analysis of the connection to the female Laodameia, taken up in a lost Euripidean play in which the woman lives and makes a statue that actually comes to life. We cannot say much more, given the fragmentary nature of the evidence (647–59 Nauck; Hyginus *Fabulae* 103–4). On Orpheus and references to art in general, see Segal, "Cold Delight," but he does not see Admetos as Medusa.

33. Freud, "Family Romances," pp. 237–41.

34. One might speculate that effeminacy is encoded in this speech as well, since it is typically women taken in battle who grieve in this way about their husbands (see Andromache, in Euripides' *Andromache*, and Tecmessa in Sophocles' *Ajax*). I am indebted to Ann Michelini for reminding me of these examples.

35. On the generally Oedipal structure of narrative in which the hero must recreate "*himself*" out of an abstract or purely symbolic other—the womb, the earth, the grave," see de Lauretis, *Alice*, p. 121 and chap. 5. The hero is established as male, one who crosses boundaries; the woman is the space at the boundary (p. 119).

simple request that he not marry, promising that his house will be in mourning for a year and that he himself will mourn throughout his whole life (328–68). He is extravagant in his despair: not only will he not marry, but he will have a statue of Alcestis as his bedmate and his dreams of her will be his only source of cheer. Like much else in the play, the statue is ambiguous, leading critics to opposite readings: is such a promise delicate (Burnett) or absurd (Bradley) or ludicrous (Beye)?[36] I would argue that Admetos's claims are already signs of betrayal. Having said that he will mourn forever, he simultaneously begins to look for consolation, for substitutes that will prevent him from suffering: "By the clever hand of an artisan the likeness of your form will be set up in the bed, on which I will fall, and enfolding it with my arms, calling your dear name, I will seem to have my woman/wife in my embrace, even though I do not. A cold pleasure [*psuchran . . . terpsin*], but all the same I will lighten the weight of my soul [*psuchēs*]" (348–54).

What is going on here? First, it is clear that Admetos uses art to console himself, not to keep his grief present. He will minimize his sense of loss by commissioning a statue that will replace the real woman and, by providing at least a cold comfort, prevent him from having to accept her absence. Moreover, as a representation, the statue will be under his control in a way that even as compliant a woman as the live Alcestis was not. In this way, the stone acts to restore Alcestis but especially to restore Admetos to himself.

It takes more than this, perhaps, to make the statue into a convincing fetish object, but we shall see that it conflates several uses of the term. First, Admetos seems to treat the statue as a traditional religious fetish, ascribing magical strength and human capacities to it. Second, it functions like the fetish in a Marxist sense: it is given a value apart from the conditions of its production. How could the statue comfort Admetos if he remained aware that it was a statue? In fact, he must forget, or pretend to forget, that it originated in his own desires in order for it to satisfy those desires.

And third, the question of desire brings me, of course, to Freudian theory, where the fetish works as a coping mechanism for men in the face of their "recognition" of the castration of the woman, which threatens their own castration.[37] Alcestis's death implies weakness (and by analogy, castration, impotence, or lack) and thus leads Admetos to fabricate the

36. Burnett, *Catastrophe*, p. 36 and n. 14; Bradley, "Admetus," p. 117; Beye, "Alcestis and Her Critics," p. 114. O'Higgins, "Above Rubies," considers the statue extensively. Segal, "Cold Delight," p. 224, takes the statue as emblematic, "standing as it does at the intersection of desire, death, art and absence."

37. Freud, "Fetishism," esp. pp. 154, 156.

fetish to reassure himself that *he* is still alive, still has the phallus. Another interpretation is possible, however. Freud hypothesizes that it is the sight of the mother's genitals that terrifies, but does the sight signify her castration or her power? Admetos seems to be faced not with a castrated woman but with the threatening phallic mother. When Alcestis asserts herself as a speaking subject, she takes the phallus and threatens Admetos with "castration" by denying him access to another woman. She has filled him with a sense of his own inadequacy, and her anxiety-producing speech then leads to his fantasy of the statue to protect him from that loss.

The statue is a fetish object that replaces the missing woman entirely; this strategy is familiar from contemporary film (and film theory) where, as Mulvey explains, one technique is the "complete disavowal of castration by the substitution of a fetish object or turning the represented figure itself into a fetish so that it becomes reassuring rather than dangerous."[38] Admetos's imagined reaction to the statue implies this usage.

Moreover, the statue defends Admetos against both sets of fears, sex and death. To begin with, it is sexually consoling; by commissioning the statue he symbolically regains control. Control is also represented in his hope that Alcestis will appear to him in his dreams (354–56), for the dream woman as a projection of his desires will presumably be responsive to them. First, Admetos plans to lighten his spirit and replace Alcestis's *psuchē* (soul, life) with a *psuchran terpsin* (cold pleasure), even as the more typical fetish object enables a form of heterosexual pleasure to operate despite male fear of the female genitals.[39] Getting into bed with the statue and calling Alcestis's name gives him a cold comfort; if that cold stiffens him, he will be a man with a man's power. Second, the statue as a chiseled object replaces the "phallus" Alcestis is presumed to have lost; insofar as it is phallic it replaces her in a reassuring fashion, totalized as a representation of the penis she did (not) have. Third, by representing her as phallic, Admetos reconstitutes her as like himself. His dream of going to bed with the statue thus fulfills his homo-erotic desires.[40]

On another level, the statue works to prevent Admetos once again from facing the thought of his own death; if Alcestis is replaced by her likeness in stone, then she has not simply disappeared but has been eternally fixed.

---

38. See Mulvey, *Visual*, p. 21.

39. Freud, "Fetishism," p. 154.

40. Freud would argue that the fetishist always feels aversion to the female genitals, and that the fetish prevents the homosexual object choice interdicted by the culture ("Fetishism" and "Medusa's Head"; see also Kofman, *Enigma of Women*, p. 84). It is possible that homosexual desire is also repressed; in Greek culture, such illicit desire would be for a man the same age, or for passivity, not all desire between men. Homoerotic attraction is displaced into the joking interaction between Herakles and Admetos.

In this way the statue is reminiscent of the grave markers of the day, which served somewhat inconsistent functions: like a song, they denied the death through memory, but they also affirmed the death by marking the place of burial and preventing use of the site for another grave.[41] Similarly, the statue both defers realization of death and turns the bed into the place of death, saving a place for "Alcestis."

Euripides' Admetos seems unaware of the distance between the live woman he has lost and the image he proposes to have made. In a situation characterized by exchange, there is perhaps not a great difference between wife and statue: if she is just a position, then the position can be filled by any "one." Although Admetos claims that no one else will be called his wife, he plans to call the statue by her name. As Dolores O'Higgins remarks, "Admetus' 'chill delight' may not differ much from the original."[42]

The use of a fetish object to control the woman who is fearsome because she appears to stand for both death and sexuality is consistent with a masculine desire for control over meaning in language. Thus it is fitting that Admetos completes his hyperbolic speech with the impossible wish that he could be the great artist Orpheus: "If the tongue and song of Orpheus were mine, [I would] establish your life in the light" (357–62). At the same time that he plans to employ an artist to fabricate an Alcestis for his bed, he wishes for an art that would both make him a life-giving hero and enable him to do for her what she has done for him. He would assume the creative role of savior, if not creative mother. Do Euripides and Admetos forget that Orpheus's gaze kills Eurydice?

Replacements proliferate. Alcestis was first a substitute for Admetos, taking his place with death and enabling him to live; then he made her a replacement for his parents; the statue has now replaced her. Thus it appears that the dynamic of threat and containment is ongoing; the continued need for fetish objects reflects an underlying anxiety. This alternation is similar to the structure of the Freudian conception of the fetish in two ways. First, the fetish enables the fetishist simultaneously to accept and to deny woman's castration. Second, fetishism oscillates between mutilation and adoration; to take Freud's example of the Chinese custom of footbinding, the feet are first mutilated, then turned into a fetish. One might say that the inscription of Alcestis's death corresponds to the "fact of castration" and mutilation, while her glorification by text and critics corresponds to the fetishistic denial of castration and adoration (see the In-

41. See Boardman and Kurtz, *Greek Burial Customs*, p. 218; O'Higgins, "Above Rubies," also treats this aspect of the play.
42. O'Higgins, "Above Rubies," p. 89; she also makes a connection to Pandora.

troduction). What, however, is the difference between these two moments? The adoration of Alcestis as the "best of women" itself inscribes her mutilation by rewarding her for passivity and the repression of all desire. The adoration is one element in persuading women to subscribe willingly to the mutilation.

If we take Admetos's speech as evidence simply of deep despair and the desire to keep Alcestis alive,[43] we may unwittingly facilitate the ideological work of the play, the project of encouraging women to accede to this system of sacrifice so as to gain the rewards of eternal life as a statue or in a song of praise. For controls cannot simply be externally imposed. Like the more modern woman on a pedestal, the figure of Alcestis accepts the code that trains her to make herself satisfying to male needs. The critics are not without reason when they see Alcestis as cold. In order to make her strong, Euripides gives her the appearance of impassivity. Has Alcestis undergone the operation that Luce Irigaray describes, becoming "fixed in the representation of 'femininity' prescribed for her? Is she a fetish whose corpselike beauty reflects a sexual indifference that has been won the hard way?"[44]

Threat and Containment III: The Return of the Repressed and Its Re-repression

In the conclusion to the play the balance between the characters shifts. Whereas before it was possible to analyze as threatening certain moves ascribed by Euripides to Alcestis, now she is so objectified as to make no move at all. Her silence highlights her status as a screen on which male desires are projected. As a result, the final scene is almost all "containment." In the protracted dialogue between Herakles and Admetos (see below) Herakles presses Admetos to accept the strange woman he has won in a contest. Despite his vows, Admetos is finally persuaded. Thus, in terms of the plot, Alcestis does nothing; she merely stands there, unrecognizable, and looks on.

Yet though the "happy ending" to the play depends on her return to

43. Grube, *Drama*, pp. 136–37, takes the love and sorrow as perfectly sincere and finds his language merely extravagant; Burnett, *Catastrophe*, mentions that he keeps his wife alive (pp. 36–37) "as far as possible." But Musurillo, *"Alcestis,"* p. 279, thinks we should not take it too seriously; and Rosenmeyer, *Masks of Tragedy*, pp. 228–29, sees the speech as an abnormal element.

44. Irigaray, *Speculum*, p. 127. Schor, "Female Fetishism," p. 368, refers to the impassivity of Lélia: "As cold and as chiseled as a classical marble statue, Lélia is an eminently phallic figure." Alcestis's *frigor* is similarly phallic and therefore threatening to her male audience.

life, which must be taken as reassuring, Alcestis's very being is nonetheless threatening. She is most obviously uncanny when she returns from the grave and makes her veiled and silent appearance, for here that which should be hidden comes to light. The battle between Asklepios/Apollo and Zeus has seemingly been reopened. Alcestis has transgressed the law of Zeus—established at the outset of the play—that Death will have his due; she has traversed the border between life and death.[45] This traversal is marked by her garb and her silence: like the cadaver, she is neither here nor there.

There are further grounds for taking her as uncanny. In the course of his interchange with Herakles, Admetos overtly experiences the *unheimlich*. He reaches out to touch the veiled figure and says: "Extending my hand, I feel as if I am cutting off the head of the Gorgon" (1118). In a staged version, he would presumably be averting his eyes from the dangerous woman, dangerous to his vows to Alcestis. Is it his own fear that makes him feel like Perseus ready to decapitate the petrifying Medusa? Is it that he, like Perseus, is a murderer, reenacting Alcestis's death by failing in his self-imposed obligations to mourn?

For Freud, the Gorgon is not only an anxiety-producing figure of the female genitals—prominent mouth and eyes surrounded by snakes for pubic hair—but also a sign of castration—the cutting off of the head standing for castration through displacement upward. Paradoxically, the many snakes and the freezing look offer reassurance, for the repetition replaces the threatened penis, and the freezing suggests erection. Karen Horney regards castration anxiety as an inadeqate explanation and hypothesizes instead a masculine "dread of woman" that is allayed by objectification, the creation of figures like the Medusa, and fetishism.[46] I find the interpretation suggested by combining both explanations more applicable to Admetos than either alone. Admetos's remark seems to be sexual because it links an image of extension—implying potency or at least erection—with killing the Gorgon, and because it is placed in a context of sexual innuendo. Admetos has been resisting Herakles' offer of this woman on the basis of her sexuality; we know from Herakles' suggestive nudges that Admetos is lustful, and he cannot imagine a safe place for this woman. Where can he put her? In the men's quarters, or in the chamber of his departed wife (1051–56)?[47]

45. See Gregory, "Euripides' *Alcestis*," on what this means for Admetos at the play's end and whether "back to normal" entails *his* death.
46. See Freud, "Medusa's Head," pp. 273–74, and "Infantile Genital Organization," p. 144 n. 3; Horney, "Dread of Woman"; cf. Slater, *Glory of Hera*, pp. 18–19, 318–20.
47. On lust, see Burnett, *Catastrophe*, p. 45. Beye, "Alcestis and Her Critics," p. 118,

In taking the Gorgon to stand for the female genitals and her effect of petrifaction as an instance of the shiver at the uncanny, we are of course face to face not only with Freud's emphasis on castration anxiety and the centrality of the Oedipal complex but also with a particular masculine perspective on Medusa.[48] The Gorgon's serpents, like the serpents in the marriage chamber, might suggest a powerful (so-called phallic) woman as well as the "castrated" mother, in the moment after the male "recognition" of her castration. As Philip Slater points out as well, not only do the many snakes belong to a female spirit, but in the end they find their way onto Athena's breastplate, where they defend her and act as apotropaic magic. Alcestis has been consigned to earth by her predestined death; as a result she might well seem gorgonish, that is, signifying power, *not* her own castration. Even when she does nothing, as is the case in this scene, there are signs of a residual female power.

The repetition that Freud points to as an important aspect of the *unheimlich* is prominent in the ending to this play and is a further sign of Admetos's anxiety. He says that he never wants to enter his house again, for it will inevitably remind him of returning there with his bride on their wedding night (911–25). But he is of course about to make that very return. Moreover, in so doing he returns (like Oedipus) to a double place: to the place where he was born and to the chamber where Alcestis gave birth to his children, a place consecrated to her and identified with her in the play, both because she addresses it at length and because she attributes her death to it.

Not only is his entrance doubled (and part of the structural doubling of this play), but through the device of the veiled Alcestis there actually seem to be two women involved: Herakles' proffered gift and Alcestis. Critics even speak of "Herakles' woman" as a girl, thus marking her distance from Alcestis, who is after all a matron.[49] How must Admetos feel, faced with this woman who reminds him of his wife: "You woman, whoever you are, know that you have the form and shape to the measure of Alcestis" (1061–63)? Looking on her, he seems to look on his wife (1066), and he begins to cry. The "two" women are unsettling in a way

---

notes Admetos's attention to the physical attributes of the "stranger"; Pandiri, *"Alcestis* 1052," p. 50, analyzes the word *strōphōmenon* as evidence of Admetos's "lascivious train of thought."

48. Cixous, in "Laugh of the Medusa," and other feminists see Medusa differently: e.g., Joplin, "Voice of the Shuttle"; de Lauretis, *Alice*, pp. 103–57. There is another side to Medusa, that of a woman raped by the god Poseidon and punished by the goddess Athena.

49. Beye, *Alcestis*, p. 7, calls her a "young maiden"; cf. Burnett, *Catastrophe*, p. 45: "The girl won at the games."

that the statue and the dream woman were not: they promised comfort; this physical replacement heightens his grief.

Nevertheless, Admetos represses the memory of Alcestis and accepts the woman that Herakles offers him. Crucially for my argument, even though he resists, he gives in before he knows that the woman is his wife. Alcestis's self-presentation in her earlier confrontation with Admetos was that of Irigaray's "fetish woman," but Euripides makes her still more fully that figure in the end, when she stands in for her own rival and, in her silence, poses like a statue to be unveiled. The displacement of the wife by the statue finds its sequel in Admetos's acceptance of a "new woman" from Herakles, while the exchange of women is disguised as a joke between men.[50] The movement between threat and containment is reiterated: her taboo, uncanny power, is brought under control and made reassuring to the male sensibility, its threat minimized through rhetoric and ritual.

The evidence that Alcestis is actually veiled is oblique and not textual. The summary at the beginning of the play says that "Herakles, having made Thanatos stand away, hid the woman in robes [*esthēti kaluptei tēn gunaika*]." Critics almost univocally refer to her as "silent and veiled," yet what she is wearing is just as likely the robe that she put on to die in (*esthēta*, 161). Of course, some kind of headgear is necessary to account for misrecognition or delayed recognition. More is at stake than the plot, however; the device works both for Admetos and for Euripides. First, the veil replaces Perseus's mirror, making it possible for Admetos/Perseus to face Alcestis/Medusa without being turned into stone; thus Euripides restores the gaze to him by veiling the monster, rather than by using the myth's obliquity and reflections.[51] Second, the veil has ritual functions in marriage: while hiding the face, it may well allude to the genitals, as its ceremonial lifting in the marriage ritual suggests. As Sissa says, "More precisely, the *anakalyptērion* represented in chaste, public form the scene that took place in secret at night."[52] She goes on to relate these veils to the veiling of the marriage bed, already identified with Alcestis in the early parts of the play.

In this ritualistic scene the woman is veiled and silent, making her like

50. Alcestis herself displaced, or was a substitute for, the mother who refused to give him life a second time. For a concise statement of the Freudian position on the wife as mother figure, see Freud, "Three Contributions," pp. 166–67; Irigaray, *Speculum*, p. 109. O'Higgins, "Above Rubies," discusses substitution.

51. Weil, *Alceste*, observes the similarity to the Gorgon's head (pp. 2–3) but finds the whole scene very amusing.

52. See Sissa, *Greek Virginity*, p. 96. Carson, "Putting," discusses the Greek wedding and seems to accept general veiling for women (160–64).

a statue about to be unveiled and, like the earlier statue, a fetish object. The double meaning of the fetish (different/same) can be seen here, too. Admetos gains power by being distinguished from the silent woman on the grounds of his masculinity and language. But the apparition also terrifies him by reminding him of Alcestis and his loss; he wishes he were dead and feels, as she did on the brink of death, that he is not really alive (1082, 1086). To the extent that he is mortal, not immortal, Admetos is not different from Alcestis but interchangeable with her.[53] The veil over Alcestis stands proleptically for the veil over death and human ignorance of it, or perhaps Euripides uses Alcestis to stand for the truth, also veiled.[54] The talisman works its magic, though, when Alcestis comes back from the dead; Admetos is once again protected from the recognition of the inevitability of death. He may have learned about divine generosity,[55] but he is prevented from achieving depth of learning by the return to him of the veiled Alcestis. The audience, never fooled about her identity, is also consoled (or should we say fooled?) by the possibility of evading death.

The play's objectification and fetishization of Alcestis is most at issue in the joke that forms the conclusion. Not only is she turned into the veiled imitation of herself, her own rival for her husband's affections, but she is made to serve in a masculine joke.[56] The plot merely requires that Herakles hand Alcestis over to Admetos, tell how he got her, and leave them to their bliss. Instead, he engages in a game similar to the one Admetos had earlier played with him. And in both instances, the audience has the experience of watching a prolonged interaction between men who use women as a source for their discourse. The identity of Alcestis is elided

53. Gregory, "Euripides' *Alcestis*," argues that Apollo's original gift was an avoidance of understanding the necessity of death and that the death of Admetos is implicit in the return of Alcestis. The ending does not, however, take the form of a recognition; Admetos returns to the ordinary mortal condition of ignorance as to the date of his death. Nielsen, "Alcestis," p. 95, refers to the Prometheus myth in this respect, and the play's removal of the veil of ignorance.

54. If Admetos could recognize and accept his own powerlessness, the way in which he is like Alcestis, he would free himself of the need to pretend to be "a man" and thus from the need to impose on others. On woman and truth, see Derrida's *Spurs*, in which he ruminates on Nietzsche's three kinds of women. For a critique of the poststructuralist use of the woman and the fetish as "figures of undecidability that suspend castration as an operation of truth," see Robinson, "Misappropriations," p. 49.

55. Burnett, "Virtues," p. 240: "Apollo has sent Heracles and he by a miracle brings to husband and wife a true *charis* (1101; cf. 1074), something far beyond the limits of mere justice."

56. Much of the criticism alludes to the joke or takes it for granted. See Beye, "Alcestis and Her Critics," p. 112; Grube, *Drama*, p. 144; Nielsen, "Alcestis," p. 99; Smith, "Ironic Structure," pp. 143–45, among others.

in each case: "Who is dead?" in the earlier scene becomes "Who is this woman?" in the later one.

Freud concentrates on the profit that comedy yields, and we would do well to concentrate on the excess of this scene and try to explain the gratuitous joke.[57] Whose interests are being served? How we understand the gain will depend, of course, on what we take to be the audience, and who we think is laughing or even smiling. Freud's analysis implicitly constitutes jokes as a male form. For instance, he finds one origin in smut: the joke replaces sexual activity with wordplay as a way of putting down a woman who has rejected the jokester's advance. He distinguishes a separate category of tendentious jokes, for which a silent third party is crucial. In this section, he tells many *schadchen* (matchmaker) jokes, which make a butt of the marriage broker; tellingly, he overlooks the bride, who is neither the speaker nor the recipient of the joke.[58] Freud distinguishes dirty jokes from tendentious jokes, but not all listeners will do so. In fact, depending on the context, the sexual innuendo may be intended as an attack on the (woman) audience; moreover, from a feminist perspective, it might appear that someone is indeed harmed (in particular, women) by the supposedly harmless joke.

How do these joke categories help us sort out the alleged humor of the scene before us? First, those who see Herakles making a joke at the expense of Admetos take the scene as an example of a "tendentious joke." This reading assumes that Herakles feels hostile to Admetos for having deceived him and that he therefore makes his own deception equal Admetos' trick on him.[59] He essentially makes a fool of Admetos, who does not know the identity of the masked woman. This tendentious joke requires the silent third party if it is to work. But we must ask if Alcestis, the audience on stage, actually finds it funny. What is her role in this scenario? Is she an audience or an additional butt?

Second, the humor may lie in the expression of repressed sexuality in, for example, Admetos's concentration on the desirability of the "stranger." In this reading, language replaces the sexual act as pleasurable; the two partners are the unknown woman and Admetos. The humor derives from

---

57. Freud, *Jokes*. See also Mauron, *Psychocritique du genre comique*.

58. As Mehlman remarks in "How to Read Freud on Jokes," p. 449, the triangle established is comparable to the exchange of women.

59. Smith, "Ironic Structure," pp. 131, 143, mentions the parallel in deception; Beye, "Alcestis and Her Critics," p. 117, talks about the "latent resentment of Heracles which seems evident at the close of the drama"; Galinsky, *Herakles*, p. 69, comments on the inversion of the two scenes.

the false identification of Alcestis as "other woman," thus forbidden but offered and accepted nonetheless. The exchange ultimately serves Admetos's pleasure by reassuring him that he can indeed have her, for she is not the wife's rival but the wife. But I would ask once again, what is Alcestis's role in this scenario? Does it serve her pleasure?

In either case, the joke puts Admetos and Herakles in prolonged contact; the woman is only an onlooker who cannot interfere. Theirs is the pleasure. As her role is enacted, Alcestis drops out to facilitate the interaction between the men. She is necessary, but she is neither the one who gives nor the one who receives.

What, then, is the work that the joke does? It turns Alcestis into a cipher, which she must be in order for Herakles' game to be effective. As I argued earlier, Alcestis should be at her most powerful when she returns from Hades; the ritual interpretation of her silence suggests the presence of a taboo. Taboos, however, generally exist as a hedge around danger,[60] and so I would ask, "What is the danger?" Alcestis is still dangerous because she is liminal, between life and death. The return of the woman full of a dangerous wildness, connected with death, is once again domesticated, this time by means of a joke. Moreover, the joke leads to a marriage, for Herakles' teasing of Admetos creates a triangle, one analogous to a typical matchmaking scene wherein parent (father) and matchmaker talk, but not the bride. The words Herakles uses, the emphasis on placing her in Admetos's hands (1113–15), are reminiscent of the betrothal, which takes place between the woman's *kurios* and her husband-to-be.[61] And the structure of the betrothal is always reminiscent of what Freud says about such jokes: the silent third party is crucial.

The analogy between the structure of the joke and the structure of betrothal, in that both render Alcestis an object to be given by one man to another, brings me to a cultural level of analysis. Hospitality was a major Greek social institution, and it is one that organizes this play: it builds up to the exchange of women and establishes the power relationships of the male protagonists. Euripides' use of Herakles emphasizes the element of exchange in the myth because it establishes a crucial male-male dynamic (Apollo-Admetos, Herakles-Admetos) at both ends of the story; Alcestis evolves into a sign manipulated by pairs of men. The

60. See Joplin, "Voice of the Shuttle," pp. 36–37, on this tendency, as well as Douglas's powerful *Purity and Danger*, chap. 9; cf. Freud, "Taboo of Virginity." On the play, see Buxton, "Voile et le silence."

61. On the marriage imagery, see Foley, *Ritual Irony*, p. 88; Arrowsmith, *Alcestis*, p. 117; and Buxton, "Voile et le silence," who relates marriage and death as moments of transition requiring the veil (p. 171).

Herakles-Alcestis-Admetos triangle established by the joke refers not only to marriage but also to an analogous structure of hospitality. As male bonds were preferred to mourning for the female dead in the first scene between Admetos and Herakles, so male obligations to men supersede fidelity itself in the end. In both moments where Admetos may be said to betray Alcestis (his "betrayal" is as hotly debated as almost everything else about this play), he does so in the interests of male friendship. Through the hospitality motif we see once more the way in which the play is a technology of gender, making women win their place by establishing ties between men.[62]

The theme of hospitality returns us as well to the Freudian *unheimlich*. Freud found the Greek analogue to *heim* in the word *xenos*: like *heim*, it contains within it its opposite, since it means both friend and stranger. The laws of hospitality are ways of converting the stranger, always a potential enemy, into a friend—ways, therefore, of taming the *unheimlich*. The laws of hospitality constitute a code making it possible to distinguish between friend and enemy. This code, like other rituals, protected men from an unfriendly world. In the *Odyssey*, for instance, *xenia* is a well-worked-out system organizing the relationships among aristocratic men obliged to undertake dangerous sea travel; *xenia* made sea travel safe by giving men of a certain class a home away from home. The changeable sea (epitomized in the shape-changing quality of such sea deities as Proteus and the Nereid Thetis) is a realm of the unknown, difficult to tame.[63] But in order to establish such secure ties, one had to exchange gifts: women would be the noblest of the gifts (see the Introduction) but not givers or recipients themselves.

Hospitality is the characteristic virtue of Admetos. It was to repay his graciousness as host that Apollo gained him the original reprieve from death, and the second saving is also based on hospitality. In the prologue Apollo predicts that Herakles will be entertained by Admetos and, presumably as a result, will save Alcestis (68). Not only is it Admetos's

62. On the hospitality theme, see Galinsky, *Herakles*, p. 68 ("exessive *xenia* is his most serious shortcoming"); Burnett, *Catastrophe*, pp. 38–40, 45, and "Virtues," pp. 242, 247, 249, 250; Conacher, *Euripidean Drama*, p. 338; Weil, *Alceste*, p. 4; Musurillo, "*Alcestis*," p. 280; Rosenmeyer, *Masks of Tragedy*, pp. 236–37; Golden, "Euripides' *Alcestis*," pp. 122–23; Jones, "Euripides' *Alcestis*," p. 55; Scodel, "*Admetou Logos*," pp. 51–62. Smith, "Ironic Structure," relates hospitality to Admetos's character as a gentleman: "His view of the host's office requires denying the status of guest to the woman who was more than life to him shortly before" (p. 135). But the woman is never a guest in the system of Greek hospitality, only a servant or a gift.

63. See Detienne and Vernant, *Cunning Intelligence*, pp. 107–74, 287–92, for the relationship between these deities, Metis, and the concepts of way and limit. On the relationship of *xenia* and Hestia, see Vernant, "Hestia-Hermes," p. 142.

characteristic virtue, but he adheres to an extreme standard, welcoming Herakles as a guest even though he is in mourning—and in opposition to the advice of the Chorus. When the Chorus asks him if he is not mad to be acting as host at such a time (552), Admetos replies that to turn his guest away would give him the reputation of being inhospitable (*axenō-teros, echthroxenous, xenou*, 556, 558, 559). Whatever lofty reasons he may have, he also has a very pragmatic one: whenever he goes to Argos, Herakles is *his* host (559–60). Is it an obligation or self-interest that motivates Admetos?

The text highlights the conflict between duties owed to wife and to guest; they do not comfortably coexist, for Herakles acts like the rowdy he is in legend, creating revelry in the house when Admetos has just promised Alcestis that he will have no singing. The servants, loyal to Alcestis, resent having to restrain their grief in order to treat the master's guest appropriately (761–64).

Yet Alcestis owes her life to the same obligation of hospitality, for Herakles goes to the underworld to retrieve her not for her sake but in recognition of Admetos's generosity (842, 854–57). The lie Herakles subsequently tells is very revealing: as if to underline the exchange aspect of the transaction, he claims to have won this woman in a contest; she is his trophy "thrown in with the livestock" (1032), and he presents her as such to Admetos. The latter accepts the woman from Herakles not out of overwhelming desire for her but out of desire not to anger Herakles (*sou promēthian echō*, 1054). If he accepts her, he affirms Herakles' quality as a guest: "Keep her and you will say that the son of Zeus is a noble guest" (1119–20).

Significantly, then, each of Admetos's failures to honor his oath to Alcestis is the other face of this much touted virtue of hospitality.[64] The relationship of hospitality does integrate Alcestis back into the family, but the active, desired relationship is not between man and wife but between the two men. To return briefly to the joke, one can speculate that Admetos humiliated Herakles when he deceived him into accepting his hospitality, and that Herakles gets back at him by insisting that he accept his gift of a woman (Alcestis in her veil).[65] In any case, one thing is clear: whichever

64. Burnett, "Virtues," pp. 251–53, finds the mixture part of the "drama of death and its reversal." Cf. Gregory, "Euripides' *Alcestis*," p. 265. As is typical of criticism on this play, different scholars cite the same passages as evidence for opposite conclusions.

65. See, e.g., Michelini, *Euripides*, p. 327; Beye, "Alcestis and Her Critics," p. 117. Gernet, *Anthropology*," p. 299, notes: "It is possible to 'give' away a woman (and she is a precious object) as a token of one's subjugation; but the giving of the gift could also be a sign of superiority and a means of exercising dominance."

man comes out on top, Alcestis is turned into a conduit between them, not a primary member but a term that binds them.

Ritual Superstructure

Up to this point my analysis has proceeded for the most part along psychoanalytic and rhetorical axes; however, as is evident from the similarity between the joke work and marriage, these discourses dovetail with the social and political.[66] Psychological structures synchronize with cultural structures such as hospitality. Thus the *Alcestis* also works through allusion to ritual and is organized around rituals of death and marriage. In another instance of doubling, the play falls into two parts, one ending with the formal funeral procession in which the shrouded woman is borne away, the other with the reenactment of her marriage ritual.

That description may sound as if these two rituals are complementary opposites, but they are not. Rather, they are similar when analyzed from Alcestis's point of view, for each is a transaction between men that requires her sacrifice. As the "joke" reveals, Alcestis's remarriage is tantamount to her death as any kind of speaking subject; thus while the ceremony resolves Admetos's anxiety about death and female sexuality, it completes the work of subordinating Alcestis. Though she was at least able to salvage honor and good reputation from her self-sacrifice, and was still able to enunciate demands of her own, the challenge presented by the conditions she sets is met in turn by having her remarry and resubmit herself to Admetos. He is the "Thessalian man" she marries.

As I argued earlier, Euripides establishes Alcestis's liminality; her questionable status also situates the play in a troublesome borderline area, because the Chorus's uncertainty as to whether she is dead or alive leads to discussion not only of her status but also of signs. In order to solve the enigma facing them, the members of the Chorus list the indicators of grief.[67] They emphasize custom and norms (*nomizetai*, 99; *nenomistai*, 111; cf. 609), but the anomalous Alcestis confuses the issue, since she is simultaneously dead and living.

The relationship between Admetos and his father, Pheres, also disintegrates because Alcestis dies instead of either of them. Admetos is unwilling to pay the debt to Death, and at the same time he believes he owes nothing to his father, since the father has acted badly toward him. In Greek

66. Cf. Rubin, "Traffic in Women," p. 198, on the Oedipus complex and the incest taboo, as well as my Introduction.

67. For a similar point, see Dale, *Euripides: Alcestis*, p. 59, on lines 86ff.

tradition the care given to one's parents was not only a sacred duty but a reassuring one, because that same code of behavior protected the sons in their own old age. When Admetos threatens to deny his father those rights/rites, he threatens that system.[68]

Finally, as a result of Admetos's hospitality to Herakles, the house is characterized by a mixture of songs that ought to be separate.[69] In first resisting Admetos's hospitality, Herakles says that such mixture is unseemly (*aischron*, 542), and Admetos promises that it will not take place (543). But as we can see from the servants' reaction to Herakles' carrying on, it does: "There were two kinds of music now to hear, for while this one [Herakles] sang, not at all thinking of the sufferings of Admetos, the household staff [*oiketai*] were mourning our mistress" (760–63).

The funeral, as a rite of passage designed to help mortals through dangerous transitions, should sort out and stabilize these ambiguities. In general the goal of such rituals is first to take individuals out of, then bring them back into the social group. During the marginal or liminal period, soul and survivors are polluted and experience some kind of overturn in role; the successful conclusion of the ritual reestablishes the pre-existing order. Part of the process is accomplished: Alcestis moves from being a person to being a corpse; thus, one form of ambiguity is resolved.[70]

At the midpoint of the play, however, it seems that disorder has won out; the sacrifice of Alcestis has only succeeded in making Admetos miserable. Burial is meant to resolve the instability implied by the presence of the cadaver, but this death initiates another set of ambiguities: the home is no home, the household is clearly in disarray (*ololen oikos*, 415), and the funeral ritual fails to reintegrate the survivors. Admetos cannot reenter the house[71] because it is so strongly identified with his wife and their wedding: "O, outside of my house, how shall I go in? how can I live with such a change in luck?" (912–14; cf. 941). If Admetos thinks that there is no profit in life (960–61), then ritual has failed to ward off the troublesome lack of distinction.[72]

68. But cf. Thury, who argues in "Euripides' *Alcestis*," esp. p. 200, that the passing on of the household control would have been typical, not atypical.

69. The songs of mourning and marriage in particular are contrasted (760, 765, 916, 922); for use of this pattern in the *Oresteia*, see Rabinowitz, "Paths of Song."

70. See Turner, *Ritual Process*; and the classic study by van Gennep, *Rites of Passage*, who observes that marriage and funeral have different emphases within an underlying similarity. See also Morris, *Burial*, p. 30, on the body's transition to corpse. On the doorway as a line of demarcation in both death and marriage, see Buxton, "Voile et le silence."

71. For another interpretation of this failure, see Burnett, *Catastrophe*, p. 38.

72. See Gregory, "Euripides' *Alcestis*," on death and lack of distinction, the sense that life has become death; she notes that Herakles is the restorer of distinction (p. 268).

Our sense of disorientation is resolved instead through the intervention of Herakles, who brings Admetos inside by staging another marriage. The funeral marks only the ritual stage of separation; marriage completes reintegration.[73] As I noted earlier, the betrothal stage of marriage (*eggue*) is imitated in the end, when Alcestis is literally handed over with the gesture of hand on wrist; her veils are a mark of marriage.[74] Funeral yields to wedding as Alcestis moves between two forms of garb, both ritually marked: from shroud to veil.

The opposition of funeral and marriage, death and new life, failure and success, is only apparent, however. Although Herakles' victory over death restores order, it does not undo the sacrifice of Alcestis but rather affirms the value of that sacrifice by seeming to reward her as well as Admetos. The three moments are analogous: initial marriage, sacrificial death, and symbolic remarriage. I would argue that Alcestis functioned as a prize and a sacrifice even in the earlier stages of the myth. She was initially the prize in a contest set up by her father Pelias. As the Golden Fleece is an object that confers rule on the possessor, so Alcestis is an object that seems to have a similar power: Jason yokes the beasts and wins the Fleece; with Apollo's aid, Admetos yokes the beasts and wins Alcestis. The Fleece grants rule; Alcestis grants life. Tracking down the mythical notion of value, Gernet makes a connection between elements important in this text, which may help to connect the sacrifice of Alcestis to her underworld voyage and return. "The object—as a rule the material for sacrifice—has religious value.... Just as other mythical objects, but especially prize objects, which by custom are symbols of wealth, have a necessary relationship with the other world postulated by religious thought, so one by one these objects descend into this 'other world' and rise from it."[75] The Fleece and the woman are alike in granting some good worth possessing; as a mythical object, Alcestis is worth sacrificing and makes the journey to the underworld.

At their first wedding, Admetos forgot to sacrifice to Artemis and thus was doomed to die, to become himself the omitted sacrifice. Alcestis then replaces him and is sacrificed to her marriage. What we have here is not death figured as marriage but marriage figured as death, for either bride or bridegroom. Though the Bride of Death image is circulating here, and

73. On death and marriage, see Foley, *Ritual Irony*, pp. 86–88; Redfield, "Notes"; Loraux, *Tragic Ways*, pp. 37–42, on the sacrificial deaths of maidens.

74. Critics' acceptance of "veil" instead of a more ambiguous term is interesting in and of itself; the effect is to remind us of marriage. See also Foley, *Ritual Irony*, p. 88; Arrowsmith, *Alcestis*, p. 117. Sissa, *Greek Virginity*, p. 95, (cf. pp. 122–23), alludes to her renewed chastity.

75. Gernet, *Anthropology*, p. 92. At least two of the tragedies presented with *Alcestis* (*Cretan Women* and *Alkmaeon*) seem to have been alike in being about women and a central object of value; see Webster, "Euripides' Trojan Trilogy."

though marriage may well have been seen as the death of the maiden and rebirth of the mature woman, in this case marriage is also the death of Alcestis as an individual and the birth of her as someone who lives and dies for another. She is entitled to act as a subject by virtue of willingly subjecting herself. In the play's conclusion, Alcestis's return to life is a return to marriage and must therefore recall the conditions of her first marriage.[76] What is in it for the woman? If we overlook the similarity of funeral and wedding, we risk seeing Alcestis as gaining something more than she does in coming back to life. If Admetos has learned that long life is not worth every cost, we might ask what Alcestis learns in the last scene of the play, and whether she would wish to return to life with that knowledge.

The play gives a strange answer to the question of what is in it for her, for while she is still "dead," Alcestis is promised two songs, one at the festival of the Carnea, the other at Athens (445–52). The Carnea, a festival of Apollo that marked the integration of young men into the life of soldiers, seems a strange choice.[77] It makes more sense if we stress the initiation aspect of the festival, given that Alcestis, a figure who comes back to life, holds out the promise of new life to others. The asymmetries of gender are nonetheless noteworthy: at the Carnea she will be remembered in a context that consummates men's ties to other men, just as she extends an initiatory hope to men. But her own initiation as a woman would have come about through marriage represented at the play's end. This juxtaposition of male initiation at Carnea and female initiation brings out the asymmetry of the male and female experiences. Moreover, if the play bearing her name is the song she is promised at Athens, it too establishes male ties to other men. To the extent that marriage forms a woman's rite of passage, Alcestis's initiation is made use of (in the joke and reconciliation) to connect Herakles and Admetos. Does the play's celebration of Alcestis fetishize her as Admetos does?

The homosocial ties of initiation are more explicitly homoerotic in late variants of the Apollo-Admetos story. The testing of Admetos by Alcestis's

76. It is plausible to take Alcestis as standing for womankind because she is presented as a model, "the best of women." Moreover, her situation inspires generalization about marriage: Pheres says that one should take only such an outsider to his hearth (627–28); Admetos wishes he had never married (880–81); and the Chorus recognizes that such a wife is rare but wishes for one like her (473–75).

77. Calame, *Choeurs*, p. 352. Conacher, *Euripidean Drama*, p. 331; and Séchan, "Dévouement," p. 352, view the allusion as evidence that the Alcestis part of the story has a connection to Apollo. Guépin, *Tragic Paradox*, p. 206, finds evidence for the connection of sacrifice and vegetation symbolism; he notes that the Carnea was a vintage festival. O'Higgins, "Above Rubies," sees the reference as part of the play's deployment of the fame theme.

father is a possible form of initiation, ending with his integration into the
adult world through his marriage to Alcestis. But that was an anomalous
trial, since he was already a king at the time, did not therefore have to
earn a throne, and had a god as his servant. Behind these atypical features
there are traces of a sexual relationship between god and king, in which
Apollo and Admetos exchange the reciprocal roles of lover and beloved
characteristic of some initiation cults. This male erotic is directly referred
to later when Callimachus (Hymn to Apollo 47–52) reports that Apollo
was burning with love for Admetos and served him out of desire, not as
punishment. Thus, perhaps Alcestis is to be honored at Carnea because it
was at the end of his period of homoerotic involvement with Admetos that
Apollo facilitated their marriage. That homoerotic phase is not over
for Admetos, however, but is sublimated into his homosocial ties with
Herakles. Pelias and Admetos, Apollo and Admetos, Herakles and Admetos: all are related through the exchange of Alcestis.[78]

Fetishistic Consequences

Is Euripides' own play the celebration Alcestis is promised at Athens?
If so, does the play's glorification fetishize Alcestis as Admetos does? The
answer has to be a qualified yes, to the extent that returning Alcestis to
life reinscribes the validity of self-sacrifice for women while seeming to
undercut it by making Admetos only questionably worthy of her. As a
proper woman she was dead even while alive, in part because she was
promised to Death but also because she squelched her desire for life and
even for her children, so that Admetos could be both father and mother
to them. In the end, Herakles says to Admetos, "Speak, since you have
gotten everything you desired" (*pan hosonper ētheles*, 1132). The hero seems
to get it all: long life and his wife, up to and including acting out rather
than escaping his Oedipus complex—marriage to his "mother," who is at
the same time a new woman. The satisfaction Euripides grants Admetos
must have been reassuring to males in the audience, for he is, as I said,
no hero but an ordinary man.[79]

Alcestis, however, has not gotten what she wanted; rather, her success

78. On initiation, see Sergent, *Homosexuality*, pp. 103–7. This is his interpretation of
the Carnea, corroborating that of Calame, *Choeurs*. On the feminity and transvestism of
Herakles, see Loraux, "Herakles."

79. On whether Admetos deserves his reward, see Segal, "Euripides' *Alcestis*," who observes some progress in him but notes that "Euripides has it both ways," for his hero is
rewarded a second time "for putting the demands of hospitality first" (p. 147).

is undermined, and male ties have been preferred to fidelity to her. On this level, *Alcestis* supports the status quo; fear of the uncanny woman, who is an outsider (*thuraios* and *othneios*), is settled by representing her as willing to die for her husband and by exalting her for that self-sacrifice—a model held up by later literature from Plato to Chaucer. In this fantasy of Alcestis's willing death, the psychoanalytic and historical discourses come together. For not only are Admetos's anxieties allayed, but the family is depicted as entirely self-contained as the endogamous Athens desired to be, according to the citizenship law of 451.[80]

The oscillation inherent in the conceptualization of the uncanny and the fetish implies that these structures are not absolutes: the repressed does indeed return, despite psychological and cultural devices bent on making sure that it will not. What, then, is the strength of the figure of Alcestis? It is not her inscribed willingness to sacrifice herself for Admetos but her negotiation of the boundaries and her claim that she has done Admetos an incalculable service through her sacrifice. The feminist reader can take comfort in her strength despite its definition from the male point of view as threatening and uncanny and needing to be settled through the fetish.

In a move to defer conclusion, I want to return to one of those unsettling doublings, that of Admetos and Alcestis, who are paired not only in marriage but facing death, since Alcestis has replaced him with Death, stood in for him. The interchangeability of Alcestis and Admetos indicates that the woman is *unheimlich* partly because she represents the objectification of masculine fears of death. The fact that there is a chain of replacements—Alcestis, the statue, the veiled mystery woman—reveals the instability of the "happy ending." Each surrogate is inadequate because the reality of death can only be put off, not eliminated. Alcestis takes Admetos's place, but he then briefly occupies her position and begins to have her realization that in some instances death is preferable to life. Euripides prevents Admetos from fully sharing her experience, though; he does not see what Alcestis sees when she comes close to death (252; cf. 259), and her relationship to death is clearly different from his in that she faces death and the truth bravely. Although Admetos may be deceived that there is truth behind the veil, the veiled woman is obviously aware of the lie.[81]

This deconstructive/psychoanalytic reading is both attractive and none-

---

80. Cf. Vernant, "Hestia-Hermes," p. 134.

81. See above nn. 16, 31, 54 on Derridean readings, also the interpretation of her early self-sufficiency.

theless problematic for me, for like similar discussions of the "feminine" it risks eliding real women and their very real pain, accepting textual power in lieu of political power. The character Alcestis is silenced, after all. What then is the appropriate position of identification for contemporary women in the current audience? Should we act as transsexuals and identify with Admetos, who survives?[82] Or do we accept the bribe held out by the praise for Alcestis? The only new position to speak from—one that would neither accept Euripides' glorification nor doubly victimize the figure of Alcestis— seems to be straddling the fence. Specifically, I want to stress that Alcestis does attest to a female power, but one that men may perceive as threatening and therefore seek to control. Textual praise of a woman who actively seeks her own passivity is one way to achieve feminine complicity with patriarchy. The modern-day reader must recognize the strategies of control for what they are in order to capitalize on the resistance that is inscribed in the myth; by attending to the interplay of forces, we may be able to avoid simply reinscribing a new form of the fetish ourselves.

82. Doane, "Film and the Masquerade," points out that Freud eliminates the female spectator when he theorizes "femininity"; as she says, in the cinema the woman is similarly the enigma. Doane hopes to escape "oscillation between a feminine position and a masculine position, invoking the metaphor of the transvestite" (p. 80) and a strategy of masquerade in which one would "overdo" the gestures of femininity (pp. 81, 87). Euripides' Alcestis, like the other characters, is a man in woman's clothing and an exaggerated example of femininity, but I am not sure how that helps me as a member of the audience.

PART II *Vengeful Destroyers*

3   The Terrifying
    Mater Dolorosa: Hekabe

I want to shift now to the second paradigm identified in the Introduction, the one centering on the violent figures who are paired with fetishized sacrificial heroines and who are made to seem excessively vindictive: Clytemnestra, Alkmene, and Hekabe. Although, from a defensive masculine point of view, as we have seen, even a virgin may be threatening and (in Mulvey's words) require "voyeuristic or fetishistic mechanisms to circumvent this threat,"[1] the older woman is conceived of as presenting another kind of threat and is consequently dealt with differently. She is not fetishized, because she is no longer desirable and cannot be exchanged; instead, she is represented as destructive, excessive, uncanny. While the plays considered in Part I grant virgins the appearance of subjectivity—by representing them as adopting the masculine value system and willingly subjecting themselves to the male gaze—they represent the older woman's assumption of subjectivity as violent. This form of tragedy is, in Julia Kristeva's terms, "a piece of music whose so-called oriental civility is suddenly interrupted by acts of violence, murders, bloodbaths: isn't that what 'women's discourse' would be?"[2]

In the *Iphigenia in Aulis*, Euripides' Iphigenia is shown turning from the older woman, Clytemnestra, to embrace her father and his value system, newly defined as Panhellenic as well as phallocentric. The sweet daughter takes her father's side; from that position she helps to effect a temporary repression of the maternal. Euripides changes Aeschylus's Clytemnestra,

1. Mulvey, *Visual*, p. 25.
2. Kristeva, "Stabat Mater," p. 114.

making her "bourgeois," everyday, a doting mother.[3] The innocent girl is
then set off against this maternal figure, taking a masculine heroic stand
against the more physically grounded (life-affirming) position taken by
the mature female.[4] Iphigenia fears that her mother's emotionalism will
impede her own heroism and begs her not to cry, not to mourn her
daughter in any way or to build a tomb for her (1433–44). In this speech,
Iphigenia's nobility denies Clytemnestra both the pleasure (and pain) of
physical closeness to her while she is still alive and a site at which to express
her grief. More important, these prohibited signs of emotion and mourning are connected rhetorically to the hatred that Iphigenia would prohibit
as well (1454–57). Thus Clytemnestra's anger is another one of those
messy, contaminating female emotions that Iphigenia avoids when she
identifies herself with her father.[5]

While the heroes fail and seem inadequate to the task before them, these
women are, in opposite ways, made models of power. Iphigenia's sacrifice revives male nobility; Clytemnestra's anger replaces it with visceral
strength.[6] The very attachment to the body that Iphigenia would repress
forms the source of the power that Clytemnestra will ultimately call on.
It is clear when we watch a modern production of the play that the sheer
guts are all hers.[7] Despite Euripides' "realistic" and everyday representation
of Clytemnestra, the audience knows that a monumental hostility smolders
barely beneath the surface. In fact, at the same time that Euripides represents Iphigenia as attempting to forestall Clytemnestra's revenge, he also
suggests another cause for that revenge by alluding to a former husband
and child killed by Agamemnon (1148–52). Moreover, the story of her
murder of Agamemnon was so well-known that Euripides could not create
a Clytemnestra who was not vengeful. As a result, when Iphigenia begs
her mother not to be angry with her father, and when Clytemnestra boasts
of her chastity as a wife, the audience conjures up the unchaste and angry
Clytemnestra who so dominates the tradition. We must assume that Eu-

3. Norwood, *Greek Tragedy*, p. 287, calls her a "thorough *bourgeoise*"; Grube, *Drama*,
p. 428, calls her "commanding and efficient."
4. Similarly, women of lower class, like the Nurse in *Hippolytos*, value life over honor.
The association with the flesh is perceived as limiting freedom to exercise excellence.
5. On these connotations of femininity, with passages from antiquity, see Carson, "Putting," pp. 135–70; cf. Spelman, *Inessential Woman*, chaps. 1–2 (on Plato and Aristotle).
6. Cf. Michelini, *Euripides*, p. 134; and Kovacs, *Heroic Muse*, who sees a comparable
heroism in Hekabe (esp. pp. 111, 116). Certainly Hekabe's vigor corresponds to that of
Clytemnestra, as opposed to the behavior of the Greek leaders.
7. In a performance at a conference at Santa Cruz (spring 1991), even someone as young
as the undergraduate playing Clytemnestra partook of that power, present in a magnified
form in Irene Papas's performance in the Cacoyannis film and in Don Taylor's BBC
production.

ripides knew his audience would see his Clytemnestra with these treatments as backdrop and that he aimed for the instability he achieves. Such strong mythic material resists repression.[8] Whereas in the *Alcestis* female power looms in the background but is tamed, in the *Iphigenia in Aulis* female power threatens and is contained but not eliminated. The play attempts to forestall Clytemnestra's future violence and define it as negative, but the sympathetic reader can find much that is "positive": that is, oppositional to the power of the dominant class and its ideology.

The "terrible" mother resurfaces in the *Children of Herakles*, in which the maiden is again sacrificed; here the old woman actually does the threatened harm. Significantly, the text emphasizes the proper role of women: the girls are inside with Alkmene (41–44); Makaria apologizes for coming out and speaking (474–77); and Alkmene recognizes that she behaves inappropriately (978–80). Euripides seems to have made two critical changes in the overall story. First, he is the only one to tell the story of the devotion of Makaria.[9] Second, in other versions of Eurystheus's vendetta against the children of Herakles, Eurystheus is killed on the battlefield; Euripides in contrast has the messenger bring him back alive for Alkmene's pleasure (*terpsai thelontes sēn phren'*, "wishing to give pleasure to your heart," 939). Alkmene demands his death (1045–52), even though the Athenians oppose her: if he must die, he should have fallen in battle, not been taken prisoner and then killed. Euripides goes still further by making Eurystheus more moderate than his own emissaries; as a result, his death feels like more pointless violence.[10] Given all this, it would seem that Euripides intended the audience to juxtapose these two sorts of females: nubile and mature, compliant and aggressive, praiseworthy and blameworthy.

Chiastic Plot and the Strategy of Displacement

The *Hekabe* provides the most developed example of this doubling of female roles. In discussing the similarities between Polyxena and Iphigenia

8. Obviously, not all mythic variants are equally as memorable, but given their prominence, the reiterated negative views of Clytemnestra would have been indelibly inscribed in the imagination of the Athenian audience of the *Iphigenia in Aulis*.

9. For a similar linking of *Herakleidai* and *Hekabe*, see Falkner, "Wrath of Alcmene."

10. Gladstone's introduction to his translation of the play (*Heracleidae*, pp. 111–12) makes the point neatly: "This abruptly changes the whole direction of the play and reverses our sympathies. From the beginning, we have been made to take the side of the innocent Heracleidae and their gallant protectors against the wicked king.... But when at last Eurystheus appears, he is nothing like his herald...it is Alcmene who turns horrible in her insistence on revenge.

(Chapter 1), I focused on the pornographic gesture with which Polyxena tries to take charge of her death (if not of her life), and the fetishizing response of the Greek army. There is more to the play than Polyxena, however; Hekabe too tries to achieve subjectivity and to escape from masculine domination, and she too is to some extent re-placed in the system she opposes.

As queen of the Trojans, Hekabe had both status and authority; as a result of the war, she has neither. She is an old woman who used to have everything but now merely has nothing to lose. She has lived beyond her usefulness to men and comes into a new power as a result, a power that is rapidly made terrifying. Initially, the audience is inclined to respond sympathetically to her because of her nobility and her loss of city, husband, and children. The play stages her final bereavement, the death of her two remaining children. We learn from the prologue speech of Polydoros, the last of her sons, that he has been killed and thrown into the sea by his father's "guest friend" Polymestor. He tells the audience that today Hekabe will discover his body and be forced to witness the sacrifice of her daughter Polyxena. Polydoros asks that Hekabe bury him.

Although Hekabe cannot save Polyxena, she once more resists her fate when she discovers what has happened to Polydoros. In a gesture of excess, she goes beyond giving him the burial he requests and wreaks vengeance on Polymestor, blinding him and killing his children. In the final scene, Polymestor significantly enough predicts that she will be transformed into a hound with fiery glance (*kuōn genēsēi purs' echousa dergmata*, 1265), that her grave will become a sign to sailors (*sēma, nautilois tekmar*, 1273), and that Agamemnon will be killed by Clytemnestra (1281).

From this summary it should be obvious that the *Hekabe* is the imitation not of one action but of two, a sacrifice and a revenge. The problem that has most consistently bothered critics about *Hekabe* is its apparent lack of unity or coherence; although some have found sources of unity (or alternatively attacked the whole quest for it), I suggest that we take the ostensible lack of unity as a sign of Euripides' intentions. This is particularly advisable because Euripides seems to have invented this version of Polydoros's death[11] and emphasizes his innovation by conflating that death at the hands of Polymestor with the sacrifice of Polyxena.[12]

---

11. See Conacher, *Euripidean Drama*, pp. 146–52, for the background.

12. For an excellent bibliography, see Michelini, *Euripides*; she finds unity in Hekabe, who links the two stories (p. 132). Kovacs, *Heroic Muse*, pp. 79–80, agrees and links the "shape of the play" to "the figure of the heroine. She appears to change from passive sufferer in the first half of the play to furious avenger in the second." Other sources of unity are structure (Conacher, *Euripidean Drama*), action (Conacher, "Euripides' *Hecuba*"), and theme

Euripides' version introduces a male figure into what would otherwise have been a woman's story, and with that move come certain elements of gender ideology.[13] After all, a sacrifice and a revenge could be almost seamlessly knit together if it were the sacrifice that was being avenged.[14] But the model of the mortal mother avenging the daughter is often interrupted. Aeschylus undercuts Clytemnestra's devotion to Iphigenia by giving her several motives for killing Agamemnon, and in Euripides' *Iphigenia in Aulis* the vengeance is in the future. Euripides attenuates the close female bond in a different way here; unlike Clytemnestra, Hekabe does not avenge the death of her daughter. She fights to save Polyxena, who would have been everything to her had she lived (281; cf. 669), and she mourns her, but she waxes philosophical in response.[15] It is the loss of the son whose life had been saved out of all the city, who would have been the "only anchor of the house" (*monos oikōn agkura*, 80), that makes her wish to take revenge.

Even if there are two plots, might we not still look at the juxtaposition of the deaths of two children as simply doubling Hekabe's pain? From this perspective, we would expect to see the woman of part one of the play break and turn into the vengeful monster of part two. But that is made difficult as well, for instead of building in a traditional linear fashion, the play seems to sheer off in a new direction in the middle. In fact, part one, the sacrifice, which could be a self-contained tragedy, replete with attempted persuasion, climax, and messenger speech, shifts into part two in a quite peculiar way. A body is brought on stage which Hekabe, understandably enough, assumes is Polyxena's. Instead, it is Polydoros's, washed up on shore as his ghost predicted.

In effect, Euripides has chosen a chiastic structure for the play: Polydoros/Polyxena—Polyxena/Polydoros. The ghost speaks first of himself, then of his sister; Hekabe too dreams vaguely of him, and then of Achilles' demand for the girl.[16] Mentioned second, Polyxena's story is enacted first.

(Daitz, "Concepts of Freedom and Slavery," and Kirkwood, "Hecuba and Nomos"). For the problem of disunity, see among others Pohlenz, *Griechische Tragödie*, pp. 287–97; Delebecque, *Euripide*, esp. pp. 148, 159; and Norwood, *Essays*, pp. 35, 47, and *Greek Tragedy*, pp. 215–19. Conacher, "Euripides' *Hecuba*," pp. 6–7, reviews the evidence for Euripides' invention.

13. Devereux, *Dreams*, p. 269, notes glibly that the Greeks were not really interested in young girls; though Euripides was, even he recognized that they existed only as supporting characters in a male plot.

14. Conacher, "Euripides' *Hecuba*," p. 26, asserts that "Hecuba avenges one child by betraying the other."

15. See Michelini, *Euripides*, pp. 165–70.

16. Devereux, *Dreams*, points out that in the dream's condensation both children and both enemies are present (p. 282); Greek ideas of dreaming would suggest that the ghost

Significantly, this particular chiastic plot works by making Polyxena give way to Polydoros; one crucial effect, as revealed in this moment, is the displacement of the female by the male. The slippage between these two bodies, made to occupy the same theatrical space, stresses similarity and difference. While Polydoros and Polyxena are both offspring and could be taken together in that way, they are also boy and girl; their fates are determined in part by their gender, and the plot is determined in part by their gender as well. As I said above, the fate of one leads to mourning, the other to vengeance.[17]

The strategy of displacement is symptomatic, for there is another displacement at work in this play, this time *onto* the female. After all, what drives the tragedy? The names of the children refer to the circulation of gifts and honor which is the glue holding the culture together. Polyxena's name suggests guest friendship, but she will be made a gift to Achilles; Polydoros depended on guest friendship, but his name stresses gifts, and gifts of gold went with him to the house of the *xenos*.[18] The deaths of the children—one killed in obedience to the warrior code, one killed in defiance of the code of hospitality—indicate that something is wrong in these systems themselves. While the chiastic double plot displaces female with male, the dangerous mother is subjected to analogous treatment; the spatial (scenic) displacement of the female by the male correlates to a psychic displacement; anxieties that might well be aroused by and on behalf of masculine civilization are displaced onto the female.

This displacement deflects audience attention from systemic failings to Hekabe's violence. Hekabe initially gains our sympathy when, caught in a totally masculine world, she uses the weapons it deems acceptable; when she goes beyond suppliancy to action, however, she loses the audience's approval because she is made to seem excessive. Let me stress here that this is the effect the play has had on a number of critics over the years. Typically, critics blame Hekabe and see her as being metamorphosed twice, once spiritually and once physically; she becomes a vengeance fiend and then a dog.[19]

that we see is her dream (pp. 271, 273); cf. his chap. 4 on the dream of the Erinyes, where Clytemnestra is also *eidōlon* and dream.

17. On difference of treatment, see, e.g., Kovacs, *Heroic Muse*, p. 99; Meridor, "Hecuba's Revenge," 34–35; Conacher, "Euripides' *Hecuba*," pp. 10–11; Pohlenz, *Griechische Tragödie*, pp. 287–88.

18. On the names, see also Zeitlin, "Euripides' *Hekabe*," p. 53.

19. Abrahamson, "Euripides' Tragedy of *Hecuba*," 121; Matthaei, *Studies*, pp. 118, 155, attributes the transformation to her frenzy; Luschnig, "Euripides' *Hecabe*," pp. 228, 232, calls her a "fiend" instead of a sufferer and sees her dehumanization as the meaning of the legend about her transformation into a bitch. Meridor, "Hecuba's Revenge" (p. 28 n. 3),

In the end Polymestor prophesies a position for her that will allay masculine fears aroused by the sight of this fearless old woman, who will stop at nothing because she has nothing to lose. Having tried, like her daughter, to avoid her status as object by speaking and then acting, Hekabe loses her ability to speak. Not only is she inscribed as changing from human to animal, but more important, she turns from a speaker to a feature in the landscape, as we can see from the prophecy that her grave will be a sign to sailors. Thus the story that Euripides' Polymestor recounts restores order to the masculine realm; the text as a whole accomplishes this work by projecting the difficulties of that world onto this woman and then by objectifying her.

Sympathetic Victim

Hekabe at first enjoys moral superiority as the victim of a hostile male environment.[20] That her world is defined as masculine we can see as early as the speech of Polydoros. Although he identifies himself through both mother and father—"I am Polydoros, son of Kissian Hekabe and father Priam" (3–4)—when he speaks of what has happened (as opposed to who he is), we enter the realm of the masculine, receiving a sketch of hospitality (*xenia*) and the code establishing it. Polydoros refers immediately to Polymestor's status as guest friend (*xenou*, 7), brings it up again (*patrōiōi xenōi*, 19), and finally names it even as the concept is betrayed (*xenos patrōios*, 26). This system of friendship need not be masculine, but it was so in Greek culture, where (as in the *Alcestis*) women were important as the most valuable gifts exchanged, making the ties of *xenia* into those of family (*philia*). According to Bourdieu, such an exchange performs important political functions: "To reduce to the function of communication, ... the exchange of gifts, words, or women, is to ignore the structural

cites the common response, that the vengeance is "an odious act of fury performed by a devilish creature, a view which seems to be confirmed by the prophecy about Hecuba's impending death in the shape of a bitch mentioned near the end of the play." See Wilamowitz-Moellendorf, *Griechische Tragödien*, 3:267 ("Teuflische Bosheit," devilish wickedness), Murray, *Euripides*, p. 89 ("kind of devil"); Lesky, *Greek Literature*, pp. 373–74 ("avenging demon"); Webster, *Tragedies*, p. 124 ("mad fury"). Hogan, "Thucydides 3.52–68," p. 256, notes the shift of sympathy. Kovacs, *Heroic Muse*, pp. 99, 108–9, resists this tradition; Zeitlin, "Euripides' *Hekabe*," notes its existence and tries to escape it (pp. 62–63). The fact that all these people have read the play in a certain way cannot simply be dismissed.

20. Zeitlin, "Euripides' *Hekabe*," sees this superiority too but focuses instead on the play's tension "between the stability of a singular self and the network of reciprocal relations... whose dynamics of operation it is the theater's vocation each time to explore in a given dramatic setting and with a given cast of characters" (p. 57).

ambivalence which predisposes them to fulfil a political function of domination in and through performance of the communication function."[21]
In this play, all three—gifts, words, women—are exchanged in order to
ensure the continuation of male power.

The masculine atmosphere is rooted in military mores: Polydoros was
"saved" because he was not old enough to bear arms in the Trojan War,
and his sharpest mourning is for his brother Hektor, who died in battle.
Weapons are mentioned repeatedly (5, 9, 14, 15, 18) in this brief statement. As the youngest male, Polydoros (like Hektor's son Astyanax) has
a life only as long as the city remains; his existence cannot be separated
from that public realm. In each scheme, hospitality or friendship and the
military, honor is central—honor disregarded by Polymestor, and honor
demanded by Achilles.

Hekabe's first opponent is Odysseus, a clear spokesperson for one set
of public values. His motives for complying with Achilles' request are
avowedly political: cities fail if they do not honor their best men more
than their worst; the Greeks must honor the grave of Achilles, who was
the best man (*kallist'anēr*) and worthy of honor (*axios timēs*), if they expect
other soldiers to follow his example (304–10). Odysseus is pragmatic:
one has to give soldiers a reason to die; praise, gifts, and honor are what
he has to offer. In addition to maintaining a hierarchy among the soldiers,
the sacrifice of Polyxena is also necessary because it distinguishes Greek
from barbarian (326–31).[22] The masculine code outlined here values the
dead more than the living, the soldier more than the citizen, the Greek
more than the foreigner, the male more than the female, the free more
than the slave. This table of opposites is Odysseus's model of the world.

Can these values be maintained? The political aftermath of the Trojan
War underlines both the norms and their problematic nature, for those
without power are particularly dependent on culturally established morality for protection. Hekabe has already experienced an Aristotelian *per-
ipeteia*, moving from good to ill fortune (*hōs prasseis kakōs hosonper eu pot'*,
56–57). Because of this radical shift, the Trojans, having lost city and
power, are without strength (798); these homeless wanderers, says David
Kovacs, are the "survivors of a vanished world of wealth, dynastic power,
and traditional morality, a world where family ties and personal allegiance

21. Bourdieu, *Outline*, p. 14. Scodel's stimulating "Old Women" notes Hekabe's role as
a negotiator in the exchange economy of the play, who succeeds by exploiting sex.
22. Segal, "Violence," p. 109: "[the play] explores the otherness of the female by combining it (as in the *Medea*) with the otherness of the barbarian." That code echoes too in
the speeches of Agamemnon and Iphigenia in *Iphigenia in Aulis*.

were important and where the gods stood surety for the sanctity of the basic human emotions of pity, gratitude, and honor."[23] But the fate of the living Trojans is also linked to sex: Hekabe's slavery results from her womanhood; if she were a man, she would be dead.

Polydoros was recognizably at risk at home, typically construed as a safe place; therefore he was sent away from Troy to the home of Polymestor, his father's guest friend. But he turned out not to be safe there either, for Polymestor undercut the code of guest friendship, which depends on the lawful exchange of gifts, gifts taken as signifiers of status and position. A literalist, or a greedy man, he prefers the money that accompanies Polydoros to what it supposedly stands for. The proper host should covet not the wealth but the honor; however, lust for possessions intervenes in the case of Polymestor, who therefore acts in an uncivilized manner. The normative world that Hekabe depends on in this initial stage is, thus, frail because of the questionable morality of men.

There is also a problem of definition. The masculine world that Hekabe faces depends on ties of hospitality (*xenia*) to exist, but as I argued in Chapter 2, the word *xenos* contains within it the very threat it attempts to eliminate. That is, the *xenos* is both a stranger and a friend, for the ties of *xenia* convert strangers into friends. Moreover, *xenia* and *philia* (friendship or love) are contested concepts in this play, as we see not only in Polymestor's breach of custom in killing his guest but in Hekabe's appeal to Odysseus on the basis of *philia*: she calls him one of those demagogues who put pleasing the masses before their friends (254–57), meaning herself. Although her family has been at war with the Greeks, she claims this relationship on the basis of the good she did him when she saved his life. Later, Polymestor claims a similar status with respect to the Greeks. Odysseus ignores Hekabe's claim, and Agamemnon ignores Polymestor's. The code depends on clarity, but in fact there is confusion of crucial terms: who is inside and who is outside, who is friend and who is foe, who is Greek and who is barbarian?[24] These questions are related to the much discussed debate about the respective influence of nurture and nature (*nomos* and *phusis*), which plays an important role in the text: humans are not

---

23. Kovacs, *Heroic Muse*, p. 84; he ignores gender, but cf. Matthaei, *Studies*, for whom Hekabe is a slave, helpless against power, and a "wronged woman...the same all the world over" (p. 130). Meridor, "Polymestor's Crime," p. 81, observes that Hekabe is without polity and thus without protection. On Hekabe and persuasion as the weapon of the weak, see Buxton, *Persuasion*, pp. 170–86.

24. Adkins, "Basic Greek Values," discusses the concept of justice founded on doing good to friends and harm to enemies.

"naturally" good or hospitable, but are constructed by custom (*nomos*) or power relations.[25]

As a non-Greek, a woman, and a slave, what is Hekabe's recourse in this situation? At first, she does not step outside the system but rather tries to use its logic to her ends. In her attempt at persuasion when she confronts Odysseus, for instance, we get a further sense of the value system at work. She uses the discourse of the masculine order, its language and techniques; she calls on law or custom (*nomos, logos*, 291, 294) and hospitality and sees herself as upholding those codes of behavior. Hekabe tries to establish her claim on Odysseus's loyalty because she once saved his life (239–53), but she does not dispute the purpose of sacrifice itself; rather, she suggests using an animal (260–61) or even another human— why not Helen, who has really harmed the Greeks and who is the most beautiful woman of all (265–68)? Hekabe, in short, accepts the values of the warrior code, while accusing Odysseus of failing to uphold them and acting instead as a demagogue.

The double plot displays Hekabe facing the male order not once but twice, on behalf of both Polyxena and Polydoros. In a parallel to her failed attempt to persuade Odysseus, she tries to persuade Agamemnon. She first calls on him to be the avenger of abused friendship, referring to Polymestor as "this man, this most unholy friend"; she stresses her previous hospitality to Polymestor and repeats the word *xenia* (790, 793–94). She next appeals to law or custom: by *nomos* we live and establish the boundaries between the unjust and the just (800–801). By having her speak in this way, Euripides makes Agamemnon and the audience sympathetic to her.

Hekabe is represented, then, as starting from a position within the boundaries of acceptable behavior, as behaving according to what is deemed civilized. Soon, however, Euripides depicts her as going too far in word and deed.[26] The doubling and displacement I noted earlier also dominate the play's development of character and help shape the audience response, for Euripides conveys the slipperiness of Hekabe through her movement between the doubles.

To take a concrete example, not just one but two ghostly emissaries come from the dead. Each ghost demands something, but the differences are as striking as the similarities: Achilles requires a victim; Polydoros merely wants the burial that is his due. Given this difference, it is significant

25. On *nomos* see Michelini, *Euripides*, pp. 139–42, with the observation that Hekabe's rhetoric also betrays her; Matthaei, *Studies*, p. 128; Kirkwood, "Hecuba and Nomos."

26. Michelini, *Euripides*, pp. 170–81, notes the reciprocity of revenge; I obviously disagree, but do agree that the play is about the shameful or *aischron*.

that Hekabe later gives her son sacrificial victims. This action is a crucial part of Euripides' creation of Hekabe's character and her development from victim to victimizer, for in this way he increases her resemblance to Achilles—the Achilles of the *Iliad*, who vindictively mistreats Hector's body.[27]

Hekabe not only replicates Achilles, whom she ostensibly opposes, but takes on the features she condemns in other Greek leaders. Odysseus is the entirely public man, good at what he does but heartless; he is a skilled speaker (*poikilophrōn kopis hēdulogos dēmocharistēs*, 131–32) who persuaded the army to make the sacrifice. Hekabe opposes Odysseus, but she is successful with Agamemnon only by imitating Odysseus the rhetorician.[28]

The chiastic plot with its doublings makes Polyxena both a foil for Polydoros in the category of child, and a foil for her mother in the category of woman. The pointed comparison of the mother and daughter underlines their similarity *and* difference, for though they are both women, they are of course at very different stages of life. Hekabe stands for the old; she is a crone, gray-haired (*graūn*), and walks with a cane or with assistance (59–67). In contrast, Polyxena is a virgin, young, only about to begin her adult life. The difference between the two is emblematized in the body, and more specifically in the breast, the sign of their physical likeness but difference. Mentions of Hekabe's breast signify mothering and nurture (142, 424); mentions of Polyxena's breast mark her as the object of the male gaze (560).[29]

The pairing of the women also underlies the anticipated reversal of their roles. For instance, they have come to the turn in the road where the younger will be the support of the elder; as Hekabe returns to infantile incapacity, her child will be "nurse" and "staff" to her (281). In a similar reversal, Hekabe says that she will cling to Polyxena like ivy to the tree, though we would ordinarily expect the mother to be the tree (398). And in an interesting turn, she urges Polyxena to have the tongue of the nightingale in order to move Odysseus to pity (337), but in myth the nightingale replaced the mother, Procne, who killed her male child.[30] Here not only are mother and daughter confused, but they are also related to the question of voice.

27. King, "Politics of Imitation."

28. On her similarity to Odysseus, see also Zeitlin, "Euripides' *Hekabe*," pp. 70–72.

29. See Zeitlin, "Euripides' *Hekabe*," pp. 74–78; Daladier, "Mères aveugles," esp. p. 236, on the breast as signifier of maternity and on the necessary rupture of the bond with the children.

30. On the contrast between the two and its relevance to heroism and the exposure of Polyxena's body, see Michelini, *Euripides*, pp. 158–69, esp. p. 169.

The two women are not interchangeable, however. Hekabe is aware that she cannot play Polyxena's role; when she tries to die in her daughter's place and thus save her (385–87), Odysseus makes it clear that an old woman will not suffice: "Not you, old woman, did the phantasm of Achilles bid the Achaians kill, but this one here" (389–90). For Polyxena is young, beautiful, and consequently desirable; Hekabe is not.[31] They stand in different relationships to the world of men and its exchange of women.

Knowing that she has no value in a system where women get what value they have either through marrying and reproducing (which she has already done) or by being objects of desire, Hekabe has recourse to another strategy. She tries to intervene in the masculine order by taking her own revenge; in order to evade her object status, she becomes a supreme rhetorician.[32] Making this move differentiates her morally from her daughter. Polyxena thinks death better than slavery; Hekabe, ignobly perhaps, is willing to be a slave if she can have vengeance. We seem to have two molds into which these females fit: while the young one is glorified as a sacrificial martyr (see Chapter 1), the old woman literally becomes a bitch. Yet ironically, in the play's economy their very different strategies have a similar effect: both become objects while trying to become subjects, but each in ways appropriate to her status. Critics explicitly note that the mother does not learn from her child, or live up to her example.[33] Thus, Polyxena's attempt at glory, because of its fetishistic status, makes up a large part of the critical attack on her mother, even though Hekabe was barred from using the daughter's devices. Through these pairings, then, Euripides shifts Hekabe from sympathetic character—one whose name is synonymous with suffering—to fiend: a bitch with glaring eyes.

The Uncanny Avenger

What is the threat, what is so frightening about Hekabe, who has so little to lose?[34] The first part of the play casts Hekabe in what we might

31. Similarly, Death wants Alcestis, not some old person who is ready to die anyway.

32. Luschnig, "Euripides' *Hecabe*," sees her as escaping victim status: "Hecabe's final reaction parallels their consistent actions: it is selfish, impious, inhumane; but through it she shows that she is capable of assuming power over her enemy, that the role of victim is not the only role she can play" (p. 233).

33. See, e.g., Daitz, "Concepts," p. 222; Conacher, "Euripides' *Hecuba*," pp. 10–14; Vellacott, *Ironic Drama*, pp. 210–12 on the debasement of Hekabe. See Luschnig, "Euripides' *Hecabe*," p. 229; Matthaei, *Studies*, p. 155, on the contrast between Polyxena and Hekabe.

34. Kovacs, *Heroic Muse*, p. 109, sees her not as threatening but as reassuring: "He,

call the Demeter role, the grieving mother, with Polyxena playing Persephone, who is taken from her mother by the sexual demands of an underworld figure. Demeter responds by punishing humanity with fruitlessness; she takes on the role of an old crone in her wandering and tries to make Demophon immortal.[35] Similarly, Hekabe is an old crone who punishes Polymestor in order to avenge her male child. While the goddess's destruction is devastating, it is at least part of the divine prerogative; moreover, it is ultimately countered by Zeus's power. When a mortal woman displays the fearlessness of the goddess, however, it is uncanny.

Demeter's fearsome rage is that of a sexualized mother; the sexuality of Demeter's cult is apparent from the related figures of Iambe, who in the Hymn to Demeter makes the goddess laugh with her mocking (and probably obscene) remarks (Apollodorus *Bibliotheca* 1.5.3.; Homeric Hymn to Demeter), and Baubo, who makes her laugh by showing her genitals.[36] Hekabe, turned into a baying hound, is like Baubo, whose name derives from the word *bauzein*, meaning a dog's bark.[37] Thus, though old and beyond the age of nursing, Hekabe is nevertheless a figure of female sexuality; perhaps we should see her fearlessness in the face of Polymestor's prophecy as a version of Hélène Cixous's call to "show them our sexts."[38] The laugh of Baubo, like Cixous's image of the laughing Medusa, makes a mockery of male fears of female genitals; Maurice Olender remarks that "the fixed stare and the absolute frontality of this public face express a self-sufficiency that excites laughter or fear in the viewer."[39] The goddess or a self-sufficient woman gets the joke, while the man turns tail and runs.

If the mother at the play's beginning reminds us of Demeter—the Mother who mourns, is responsible for grain, and is also sexual—the vengeance plot must conjure up other monstrous figures.[40] Behind the ref-

---

citizen of an order [that] cannot contain natures such as hers, will rejoice, at some level of his being, in the fact that she exists. He will contemplate with satisfaction her animal shape and her hero's tomb, both symbols of an elemental reality that brooks no denial." But the metaphor brings her under control, makes her useful to "him," whereas she had no desire to be so.

35. On this similarity, see also Poole, *Unity*.

36. Baubo figures in Orphic fragments, from Clement of Alexandria *Protreptikos* 2.20.2–21.2. For a current view, see Olender, "Aspects," with bibliography; on laughter and female ritual, see Winkler, *Constraints*, chap. 7.

37. See Zeitlin, "Cultic Models," pp. 144–45, on Baubo and barking.

38. Cixous, "Laugh of the Medusa," p. 289.

39. Olender, "Aspects," p. 105; on the element of terror, see pp. 103–4. As he points out, Bellerophon was turned back by the Lycian women's exposure, and the Persian women used it to motivate the army (Plutarch, *Virtues of Women* 9, 5). See Winkler, *Constraints*, chap. 7, for the connection of laughter, women's rituals, and the female subjective world, aside from the male view.

40. Euripides' Phaedra and Medea can be assimilated to this model, but in the background

erence to Hekabe's future existence as a hound may well be an identification of Hekabe with Hekate, which would underline the fact that the text inscribes a version of the crone. As Olender says, speaking still of Baubo, "Ugliness, obscenity, and the old woman are well suited to one another. Thus, among the upsetting demons familiar to those among the ancients who followed the paths of Hekate and her nocturnal Baubo, alongside Mormo, Gello, and Empousa, we also find Lamia."[41] In pre-Olympian religion, the triple goddess (Hebe, Hera, Hekate) was emblematic of a natural cycle of life and death, but that sense of periodicity has broken down by the fifth century. Death, separated from life, becomes more fearful, and the crone seems threatening because in her the nurturing aspect of woman has been cut away, leaving only mortality. Female power comes to seem violent, and what is feared most is a vengeful, castrating violence against the sons.[42]

There is a psychological analogue to this religious development, for fear of death, fear of female genitals, and fear of castration are linked in the Freudian concept of the *unheimlich* (uncanny). And the *Hekabe* begins and ends in the realm of the uncanny, specifically the otherworldly. Moreover, the play is permeated by those figures that Freud associated with the *unheimlich*: doubling, ghosts, death, castration anxiety (see the Introduction). An analysis of the uncanny elements of the play also enables us to measure the metamorphosis of the character Hekabe. In the beginning, she is associated with the human realm as it faces the *unheimlich*, but by the end she is instead viewed as a manifestation of the uncanny itself.

The physical setting of the play is, as Froma Zeitlin has said, "a mediate or transitional space between the world of the living and the world of the dead . . . a transitional place between the world of the past and the world of the future. . . . This Thrace is depicted then as a species of border zone, betwixt and between, a frontier territory in which barbarians dwell."[43]

In this limbo, the first voice, that of Polydoros, comes from the realm

---

is again Aeschylus' Clytemnestra, who also lost a daughter in order to gain propitious winds for the Greek army. The similarities are extensive, and the stories are explicitly linked when Polymestor (seemingly gratuitously) predicts Clytemnestra's murder of Agamemnon. See Meridor, "Euripides' *Hec.* 1035–38," on the connections between the blinding of Polymestor and the death of Agamemnon. Among textual echoes, not the least is the use of the Lemnian women, whom Hekabe takes as an example of women's strength, whereas Aeschylus has the Chorus of *The Libation Bearers* compare Clytemnestra to the Lemnian women and to Skylla, a hound, and Orestes takes Perseus fighting the Gorgon as his model (*Libation Bearers* 832–35, 1048). The Erinyes are uncanny figures, old like Hekabe, sexualized from their association with Clytemnestra.

41. Olender, "Aspects," p. 102.
42. On Hekate and Hekabe, see Jeanmaire, *Dionysos*, p. 271; Zeitlin, "Euripides' *Hekabe*," pp. 63, 90 n. 40. On the crone, see Walker, *Crone*, esp. pp. 19–29.
43. Zeitlin, "Euripides' *Hekabe*," pp. 53–54.

of the dead and speaks with supernatural authority about what will happen as well as what has happened. The ghost is a double, an image (*eidōlon*); thus the prologue situates the action in the realm of the *unheimlich*. Although the ghost tells the audience who he is, leaving no confusion on that score, his very appearance nonetheless confounds the living and dead by bringing a message from the other side.[44] "I come having left the receptacle (*keuthmōna*) of corpses and the shadowy gates, where Hades lives apart from the other gods" (1–2). These words emphasize the ghost's movement (*hēkō, lipōn*), as well as the conception of death as dark and apart from life. The proper place for the dead is in the underworld; burial is designed to keep them there and to restore the boundaries between life and death. Since Polydoros has no grave (*taphou tlēmōn tuchō*, 47), his spirit is at large; he arranges for his body to be found so that burial can take place (47–50). And even though the midsection of his speech is presented as naturalistically as possible and performs a conventional theatrical function, simply having the ghost of Polydoros as prologue speaker is unsettling.

Moreover, even though much of his speech is not particularly weird or eerie, he has an uncanny effect on his mother. As he leaves the stage, he announces that she is afraid of her vision of him (*phantasma deimainous' emon*, 54). The ghost is clearly identified with the dream he seems to have sent her; she shivers with fright at the phantasm (*deimasi, phasmasin*, 70; *phrissei, tarbei*, 86).[45] This shivering suggests that at the play's opening, Hekabe is confronted by the forces of darkness and death, summed up by Freud as the *unheimlich*. Her twofold dream is also ambiguous in meaning. In part one a fawn is pitilessly snatched from her knees by a wolf; in part two a phantom of Achilles appears on his tomb, demanding one (*tina*) of the Trojans as a prize (90–95).[46] As the use of the indefinite article suggests, the dream is less clear than the prologue: Polydoros has already announced to the audience that Achilles has demanded his sister.[47] The vagueness of the threat in the dream serves to increase Hekabe's anxiety.

44. Devereux, *Dreams*, p. 271, associates dream and uncanny: "In Greek drama the dream narrative is functionally akin to a Messenger's speech. It is, in a sense, 'News from Nowhere'— and the reporting of uncanny (dreamlike) occurrences by Messengers is even more characteristic of Euripides than of his two great peers." Cf. Vernant, "Representation of the Invisible," on the mediation of the opposition by the stone blocks called colossoi.

45. Jouanna, "Réalité," argues that the phantasm the audience sees is simultaneously Hekabe's dream vision and relates the dream/ghost to the Greek concept of the double, for the ghost iterates the appearance of the live person (p. 49). Cf. Vernant, "Representation of the Invisible," pp. 307–8. Moreover, according to Freud, seeing one's double causes the sensation of the uncanny.

46. See note 16 above, and Devereux, *Dreams*, p. 282.

47. Interestingly enough, Polydoros in speaking to the audience says "Achilles," but the phantasm of Polydoros sends the phantasm of Achilles to Hekabe (94).

Hekabe calls on Lady Earth (*potnia Chthōn*, 70), Blackwinged Mother of Dreams, to help her understand the dream that foretells Polyxena's death. Her prayers invoke earth in its capacity as underworld and, at the same time, make the commonplace Greek connection between sleep and death. The chthonic earth, recipient of the dead, is the source of dreams; dream phantasms are like ghosts or souls, and sleepers are like the dead. But her cry has further significance, for it conjures up an earlier, pre-Olympian era when the oracles (for instance, Delphi) were tenanted by women. With the dream, we are clearly in the realm of the uncanny but, even more, in the realm of a primordial female strength.

While she calls on that goddess, Hekabe is still differentiated from her dream and its spectral resonance. It is her dream, but in Greek thinking about dreams it is revealing about the world, for it comes to her from outside. She is neither part of it nor in control of it. Since its ambiguity terrifies her, she calls for an interpreter to tell her what the dream means. In calling for an interpretation, Hekabe uses the same word that Agamemnon later uses when he judges between her and Polymestor (*krinōsin*, 89; *krinein*, 1240). She wants someone to draw the line that will enable her to be certain, that will help her to distinguish between different meanings. But as the language indicates, that effort also entails a moral dimension. Confronted with undifferentiated dream material, Hekabe needs one of her children (Helenos and Cassandra are named—again, one son and one daughter) to help her find her way through the maze. The audience shares this experience of the uncanny, for it too is faced with the shifting positions taken in the course of the play and desires an interpretation that will make sense of what it has seen.[48]

In the earlier portion of the play, then, Hekabe is distinguished from the chaos around her because she is represented as contemplative, and in her response to Polyxena's voluntary death she reflects on the relative significance of nature and nurture in producing virtue. She does not take a simple position; she notes that with luck even bad soil can yield a good crop and that good soil produces poorly in bad circumstances. At the same time, however, she comes to the conclusion that there is an unchanging human identity, that the good remains good and does not corrupt its nature (*phusis*) under pressure of circumstances (*sumphoras*, 597–98). While Hekabe alludes to nature (*phusis*), she also believes in custom or law (*nomos*) and, as I mentioned above, bases her appeal to Agamemnon both on humanity's need of law and on his "virtue."[49]

48. On the audience's similar feeling of ambiguity in reading or viewing the *Hippolytos*, see Goff, *Noose*.

49. As Michelini points out (*Euripides*, p. 141), "If Polyxene's death appears to prove the truth of the unlikely proposition that aristocratic *physis* will persist through all the dyes

As more recent theorizing about sex and gender has shown, culture and nature are exceedingly difficult to separate: biological sex (or *phusis*) becomes gender (or *nomos*). Are the female characters in tragedy, such as Polyxena and Hekabe, constrained by their sex or their gender? To say that Polydoros and Polyxena are distinguished by their gender, not by sex, means that they are constructed in accord with cultural ideals of masculinity and femininity. The complexity of Hekabe's position in the *nomos-phusis* debate is related to her age and her sex. As a mother, she is well aware that both birth and rearing were instrumental in creating Polyxena's nobility. In the end, she seems to come down on the side of nurture: good upbringing teaches virtue; whoever has learned well, having learned the measure of the good, knows also what is shameful (601–2).[50]

Hekabe calmly considers the role of custom, but her own transformation reveals that custom is also mutable. According to Hekabe, the human is maintained by the recognition and establishment of limits (*kanoni*, 602). For all the legitimacy of her request—after all she only asks Agamemnon to support law or custom (*nomos*) and justice (*zōmen adika kai dikai' hōrismenoi*, 801)—her vengeance is coded as excessive and made to seem so to the audience.[51] After her discovery of the death of Polydoros, Euripides represents her as going beyond the limits of what was lawful for a woman— beyond what Greek men wanted to believe was in woman's nature to what they feared was in woman's nature.

The change can be measured in the paired scenes, for in the second scene of supplication Euripides identifies Hekabe not with theoretical discussion but with persuasion, and emphasizes the amorality and sexuality of such persuasion; these qualities then give moral coloring to the enacted scene with Agamemnon as well as the offstage vengeance action. When she confronts Agamemnon to beg him for assistance, she becomes a figure for rhetoric or persuasion itself, asking why mortals should learn any skill but persuasion, since Persuasion rules all, and everything comes to naught

---

of experience, Hekabe's life will turn out to prove the opposite, that human beings do learn and change."

50. Romilly, *Modernité*, makes the point that Euripides here has Hekabe participate in current debates (pp. 140–45); cf. Michelini, *Euripides*, e.g., p. 142, on the rhetorical cast to the play.

51. On excess vengeance, and comparison to Medea and Alkmene, see Falkner, "Wrath of Alcmene," p. 124; Collard, "Formal Debates," pp. 65–66. Pohlenz, *Griechische Tragödie*, compares her to Medea, as do Lesky, *Greek Literature*, pp. 373–74, and Gellie, "Hecuba and Tragedy," p. 40. Matthaei, *Studies*, pp. 152–54, sees it as "talionic justice" but feels that Polymestor nonetheless gains status as the outraged victim and thus replaces Hekabe as the one to be pitied. Meridor, "Hecuba's Revenge," points out that Euripides portrays Hekabe as consistent with Athenian law (pp. 30–31), but her vengeance is personal and thus does exceed it. Michelini, *Euripides*, reminds us that the Greeks had a different standard for revenge; she concedes that Hekabe nonetheless ceases to be sympathetic (p. 171).

without it (814–20). What is questionable in her position here would be familiar to the Greek audience; rhetoric of this sort presents not good arguments but deceptive ones. *Peithō* connotes the persuasion associated with rational discourse as well as that associated with sexuality; in both cases it has positive and negative poles; all are implicated in Hekabe's persuasion.[52]

Her somewhat baroque wish to be all voice—in arms, hands, hair, and feet—by some skill of Daidalus further suggests excess (838).[53] But what of the connection to Daidalus's automatic creations? These, like Hephaistos's automata, are all appearance and must remind us of Pandora, another of Hephaistos's creations.[54] Pandora, of course, brings with her the field not only of woman's ascribed duplicity but also of her beauty and sexuality. In Pandora and Persuasion, who as a goddess was also handmaiden to Aphrodite, desire and language come together; this fearsome combination is operative in Euripides' representation of Hekabe's access to power and revenge.

In the same passage Hekabe begins to spell out the erotic element of persuasion, particularly of her persuasion of Agamemnon. She brings up Agamemnon's pleasure with Cassandra as one reason he owes her a favor. Critics are sharp with Hekabe here. They find this allusion disgusting and even a form of pimping.[55] Her argument is part of the text's problematization of desire: it is early given as Agamemnon's hypothetical motive for objecting to the sacrifice of Polyxena; having been won over by his relationship to Cassandra (120–22, 127–28, 825–27, 855), he takes the Trojan side. But to act on the basis of desire for a woman is not seen as a good (compare the case of Menelaus).[56] Agamemnon fears now that people will say he is helping Hekabe because of Cassandra. At issue here

---

52. See Michelini, *Euripides*, pp. 142–57; Buxton, *Persuasion*, on Hekabe, pp. 170–86. Romilly, *Modernité*, summarizes Euripides' complicated relations to the sophists and discourse (pp. 155–63). On poetic language more generally, see Pucci, *Hesiod*; Walsh, *Enchantment*. On the seductive *logos*, see Pucci, "Euripides' *Hippolytus*," p. 167.

53. See Michelini, *Euripides*, pp. 152–53, on this line and its part in the bathos of the speech.

54. I am indebted to O'Higgins, "Above Rubies," for this connection between Hephaistos's statues, Pandora, and women. For interesting treatments of Pandora, correlating women, sexuality, art/language, see among others Bassi, "Helen," p. 12; Loraux, "Race des femmes"; Foley, "Conception of Women," pp. 145–46; Zeitlin, "Travesties," p. 207; Pucci, *Hesiod*, pp. 82–126; Vernant, "Myth of Prometheus," pp. 168–85. On Pandora, earth, and the jar, see duBois, *Sowing*, pp. 47–59; Hoffmann, "Pandora."

55. E.g., Michelini, *Euripides*, pp. 151–54; Conacher, "Euripides' *Hecuba*," pp. 22–23; Luschnig, "Euripides' *Hecabe*," p. 232; Kirkwood, "Hecuba and Nomos," p. 66.

56. On Bedouin male shame at needing a woman, see Abu-Lughod, *Veiled Sentiments*, p. 93; in the culture she studies, the man who needs women is a donkey or a fool: "The bestial insult is applied to the man who seems not in control of his sexual appetites."

is the way a woman can sometimes gain power over a man, even when men seem to have all the power. In ancient Athens this strategy redounded to the credit of neither: it made him seem less manly, and the woman immoral. In this scene, then, Hekabe is playing a man's game, imitating Odysseus as orator and using her only card, her daughter's desirability, to her son's advantage. But that rhetorical power in the hands of a woman is a sign of male inadequacy.

Once she has persuaded Agamemnon to allow her to summon Polymestor, she is made ever more unsettling, more threatening to men. First, Euripides encourages the audience to see her form of justice as double repayment. Polymestor killed her child; in retaliation, she not only kills *both* his children but also blinds him. In Polymestor's defense, it must be noted that he did not destroy Polyxena and the rest of Hekabe's children; the Greeks did that. Nor did he make Hekabe a powerless slave; the Greeks did that. By killing both his children and blinding him, she does to him what all the Greeks did to her; Euripides has her make him the scapegoat for all her wrongs. As the Greeks established order by projecting chaos onto a monster, who could then be killed, Hekabe has loaded all her rage on the one victim, for he is the only one she can act on.[57] The sight of any slave striking back might produce anxiety, but if she were not so excessive, her justice would be unassailable.

Second, the way she proceeds would make Hekabe particularly difficult for a Greek man to accept. She counters traditional expectations about gender and age: as Agamemnon says, how can a woman who can barely walk attack a grown man (876–78, 883–85)? More threatening still, she gets her power from the community of slave women of which she is now a part. The sexual component of the danger that women represent is clear in the analogies she cites: the Danaids, marriage resisters who (all but one) killed their grooms on the wedding night (886); the Lemnian women, who killed all the men on Lemnos for their infidelity (887). These mass murders set the stage for Polymestor's later misogyny, when he says that these women's deeds corroborate all other statements about women (1177–82).

Hekabe is rendered even more frightening by her use of socially prescribed feminine behavior as a deceptive mask, beginning with her show of shame at meeting Polymestor face to face in public (968, 975). She plays on his assumptions about female weakness, assuring him that he

---

57. For the view that the revenge is reciprocal, see Michelini, *Euripides*, p. 170; Gellie, "Hecuba and Tragedy," p. 37. For an excellent treatment of the doubleness of the revenge, see Zeitlin, "Euripides' *Hekabe*."

does not need his guard, for there are only women within (1016). Once they have him, the women work swiftly, relying upon clichés about women to disarm him and remove his children from him. They exaggerate their femininity to trap him: by admiring the shuttle work of *his* women, they lift his robe and strip him of his weapons; and by trading on their supposed motherliness, they hand the children from one to the other until they are beyond his reach (1152–56, 1157–59).

Given this thorough web of deceptive persuasion, Hekabe surely accuses herself when she accuses Polymestor of using rhetoric to his advantage: she must stand for the successful orator in the audience's experience. In this way, the feminine comes to occupy the position of specious speech. Hekabe is like Clytemnestra, who builds up walls of lying speech (Aeschylus *Agamemnon* 1374–76); Medea, who says what she has to; Phaedra, who writes a lie to gain revenge. In all these cases, women's discourse is false and allows the "weaker" parties to take advantage of their presumed (and enforced) feebleness.

At this point, Hekabe has become part of the uncanny which terrifies: she is made into a castrating female. Women's space, like women's genitals, which Polyxena so tenderly hid from men's eyes, ought not to be seen. It is the home that is no home, a dangerous region, as others have learned.[58] When he enters these inner regions, Polymestor, like Oedipus and Tiresias, is blinded. Made to hear the murder of his children but unable to protect them, Polymestor is rendered impotent in two ways: first by the blinding, a form of castration, and second by the loss of his heirs and the end of the lineage. His fate would surely send a shiver down the spine of any man in the audience.[59] Euripides' orchestration of these figures renders visible the fears underlying the castration anxiety that Freud thought was itself basic.[60]

But also like Oedipus and Tiresias, Polymestor gains a second sight and becomes a prophet.[61] While Hekabe laughs at him, he is given the power to see her. Moreover, the text, like the riddle of the Sphinx ("What walks on four legs in the morning, two legs at noon, three legs at night?"), gets at the question of what is human. Who is less human, Polymestor or

58. On the dangerous regions of the house, see Zeitlin, "Playing the Other," p. 73; on the tent here, see her "Euripides' *Hekabe*."

59. On castration, see Segal, "Violence," p. 122, with n. 41.

60. Flax, *Thinking Fragments*, p. 80, enumerates, as underlying the Freudian construct, "fears of annihilation, loss of love, our aggression and rage at the mother for her autonomy and power over us, and our desire to take that power for ourselves."

61. Gellie, "Hecuba and Tragedy," points out that he "is allowed to exercise a dramatic control over the play's ending" (p. 38), acting first as his own messenger, then as a *deus ex machina*.

Hekabe? The man who has killed and disdained the laws of hospitality is like an animal (1172–73) because of Hekabe's violence to him, but she will actually be turned into an animal. Hekabe has emerged in the play as an enigmatic, deceitful, and murderous speaker; the monstrous Sphinxlike threat that she poses to man is emblematized as her transformation into a hound with blazing eyes. She is not only the other defined as monster but also the old person who walks on three legs in the riddle. To the extent that the play and Oedipus identify the human as male, they are in trouble with the Sphinx.[62]

As the play began with a spirit from the dead, it ends in the realm of the supernatural with the prophecies of Polymestor.[63] The non-real dominates the chiastic structure of this play: when the ties of hospitality and the other rules that govern human existence are broken, mortals are thrown back into chaos. To allay anxiety about flaws in the system itself, however, the text displaces these onto the female (and identifies them with her sexuality). Hekabe is rendered part of the *deinos*, the unknown and terrifying regions that had frightened her in the beginning (*gunaikes ōlesan me, gunaikes aichmalōtides; deina deina peponthamen*, 1094–95). From the male point of view, women put men into relationship with death by involving them in reproduction. The language links the innermost regions of the house (cf. *Alcestis* 872, *keuthos*) and the underworld, women and death. The hiding place of the underworld (*keuthmōn*, 1) has unleashed Polydoros; the women's quarters hide a crowd of Trojan women (*kekeuthas'*, 880). In fact, Achilles' demand for honor and Polymestor's greed, both generated by the problematic system of male loyalty to other men, cause the difficulties, but by the end of the play Hekabe seems to be the problem.

In this play, then, Euripides exposes male fears of the repressed and oppressed woman by making Hekabe enact the anxiety-producing threat. A woman's maternal anger, aroused in part on behalf of her own daughter, is activated against a man's sons. In the time frame of the play she gets what she wants, and her revenge is sweet. In the future, however, she will be put in her place: having been a speaker and an actor, she will be silenced and immobilized as a dog (itself a signifier of female sexuality) and a sign

62. See Muriel Rukeyser's "Myth" (in *Collected Poems*, p. 48) for a modern feminist reworking of Oedipus.
63. Luschnig, "Euripides' *Hecabe*," remarks that "the drama takes place between two exotragic legendary events, the apparition of Achilles' ghost and the metamorphosis of Hecabe into a dog" (p. 227 n. 2); Luschnig also points out the atmosphere provided by the first ghostly appearance. Orban, "*Hécube*," p. 316, says that "the action inscribes itself between two phenomena which surpass understanding: . . . the apparition of the phantom of Achilles . . . [and] the metamorphosis of Hecuba into a dog."

to sailors. Thus, although she has resisted being a signifier to be manipulated by men, she, like Polyxena, fails and is incorporated into the male meaning machine. And the critical tradition has joined in the blame of Hekabe as a way of finding a single meaning for the text.

I have tried to give here a reconstruction of an authorial reading—that is, an analysis of the text's "intentions"—because it is on that level that it does its ideological work. It is possible, however, to resist that reading. One could, for example, refuse to accept the definition of Hekabe's revenge as double and instead revel in her success. That might seem to return us to a world where vicious revenge is acceptable, but those of us who cannot read this play without pitying Polymestor and his children can still accept Hekabe's victory if we remain conscious of the cultural desires that have worked themselves out by scapegoating her. We can use the figure of Hekabe (after all, a man in drag) to call the constitution of gender into question. By understanding the problems with patriarchal ideology and its representations, we can at the least resist their effect on us and at the best imagine the world otherwise.

4   Vindictive Wife, Murderous Mother: Medea

The *Medea* presents a structure strikingly similar to that of the *Hekabe* and, as we will see, the *Hippolytos*: a female victim initially sympathetic to the audience forfeits that sympathy by indulging in a vengeance made to seem excessive. And yet the *Medea* is also very different from the other plays treated thus far. First there is no sacrificial virgin, willing victim of the patriarchs, to set against the vengeful older woman. Instead, Medea kills Jason's bride-to-be, taking a virginal victim of her own. Second, this vengeful woman does not seem to pay any price for exacting vengeance: she neither commits suicide, like Phaedra in the *Hippolytos*, nor does she experience the more ambiguous fate of Hekabe. Far from being silenced, she speaks her final lines from a chariot provided her by the Sun himself. Third, although Phaedra is subordinated to her position as a woman in an exchange economy (see Chapter 5), and Hekabe has lived that life out fully, gaining new power from her very worthlessness (see Chapter 3), Medea seems to escape from such female entanglement altogether. Surely, Medea triumphs: as I have argued elsewhere, she is not the fetishized victim of a pornographic gaze but provides her own pleasure by scripting the death of her rival.[1]

Though some readers may take pleasure in Medea's revenge, I would argue that this text does not strive for that reaction but rather works toward reinforcing the traffic in women. As Marianne Hirsch notes, Medea continues to be problematic even in our own time: "Those who are heirs to Greek mythology are haunted by the specter of Medea, the woman

---

1. Rabinowitz, "Tragedy."

who turns her anger at her husband into violence against her children."[2] This is true because we are the heirs of a mythology handed down not by the Medeas of the past but by the Jasons.

As a mythic figure Medea is a force to conjure with, and critics approaching such figures often ignore the author responsible for the familiar version of the story. We must, however, be mindful of what the text does with the myth. In particular, it seems that Euripides invented the murder of the children. Moreover, he has constructed his character in such a way that the audience will be encouraged to perceive female sexuality and language as embodying a threat to male offspring. Euripides maps this play on a grid formed by axes of divine/mortal, masculine/feminine, and Greek/barbarian.[3] He represents an ambiguous Medea, both goddess and woman, foreigner and native; she is liminal and trans-gressive, crossing over the boundaries, with the result that the threat she poses seems a general contamination.[4] As Page duBois says, "Euripides offers, in the *Medea*, a continuous linear discourse about all the problems of difference, animal/human, Greek/barbarian, male/female. The single character Medea is marked in all ways as the other. . . . Medea is not a whole other culture, but the other within the city. . . . In Euripides' play one of the partners of the marriage is herself an enemy, one who unlike Clytemnestra cannot be eliminated."[5] I will show, however, that Medea is not just comfortably the other but is rhetorically made to occupy both positions.

I take seriously the critical commonplace that sees Medea (like Phaedra and Hekabe) as a sympathetic character for the first half of the play.[6] As the other elements are mixed, so too is there mixture on the axis of

2. Hirsch, *Mother/Daughter Plot*, p. 170.

3. See McDermott, *Euripides' "Medea"*; duBois, *Centaurs*, pp. 110–24. Williamson, "Woman's Place," puts it in the context of public and private, as does Walsh, "Public and Private."

4. My analysis shares a great deal with that of McDermott, *Euripides' "Medea,"* who calls it "a purposely paradoxical blend." She goes on, however, to link not the divine so much as the passionate individual with other women: "Right from the start of the play, Euripides is at some pains to portray Medea not solely as a woman whose immoderate passion will drive her beyond the accepted limits of human behavior, but . . . as spokeswoman for the fears and pressures faced by ordinary fifth-century Athenian wives in a male-dominated world" (pp. 43–44, 129 nn. 4–5). Yet in the end she treats the play as gender-neutral because Euripides has challenged the category male/female.

5. DuBois, *Centaurs*, pp. 118–19.

6. McDermott, *Euripides' "Medea,"* p. 70, recognizes that Jason is "more sympathetic, but he is not good, nor even grand." Michelini, *Euripides*, p. 93, notes that the play of sympathy is part of a "dangerous game," through which Euripides toys with the audience, "luring them in with pathos and charm, but chilling their sympathy always, just at the crucial moment when the watchers would have become incapable of detaching themselves from the dramatic illusion." On the similarity to the other plays, see, e.g., Page, *Medea*, p. xvii; Michelini, *Euripides*, pp. 288, 292–93 on *Medea* and *Hippolytos*.

sympathy: Jason gains in sympathy, although not in stature; Medea is frightening even when she is sympathetic; and an important part of the play's effect is that even when she is terrifying, we cannot forget that we found her sympathetic. That sympathy itself can then work to reinforce the threat. Psychoanalytically speaking, it is the threat that the mother will kill her young instead of nurturing them; culturally, it is the threat that women will escape the nets of male domination.

Levels of Reading

We will be aided in dealing with this play by remembering that there are different levels on which we approach any work of representational art. Two levels emerge because every work of mimesis functions by presenting itself as something it is not: a piece of canvas as a landscape, an invented narrative as a true diary. Appreciation of the work as art involves an awareness of both levels at once. As readers, we are what Peter J. Rabinowitz has called the "authorial audience," aware that the work being performed is only an "imitation."[7] On this level, we know that the words we hear were written by a playwright and are spoken by actors. At the same time, we act as a "narrative audience," pretending to believe that the story before us is literally true. The distance and balance between the two sorts of audience are controlled by the poet, thus constituting a major rhetorical tool.

On the so-called narrative level, Euripides clearly establishes sympathy for Medea in the first half of the play. He opens with her partisans and has them stress her ill fortune and her suffering. For example, the Nurse asserts that "Jason has betrayed her and the children to bed down in royal marriages" (*eunazetai*, 17–18). She describes Medea as "lying without eating, giving up her body to suffering, continually melting away in tears" (24–25); she is a poor wretch (*hē talaina*, 34, see 59; cf. *tlēmōn*, 115).[8] Our sense of Medea's suffering is refracted first through her servant's eyes, who says she feels doubly the sufferings of her mistress (54–58); then we hear her grieving voice directly. Both Nurse and Chorus shape the audience's response by the way they respond to Medea, with compassion but also fear. For instance, the Nurse sees that Medea is fearsome in the way that rulers typically are (*deina turannōn lēmata*, 119–21). Similarly, the

7. For the full working out of this theory, see Rabinowitz, *Before Reading*.

8. At the same time, each of these references to her sufferings is paired with a terrifying possibility that is made good on in the second half of the play. She is *deinē* as well as *talaina*, a doer as well as a sufferer.

Corinthian women of the Chorus have heard her crying and hope they
can get her to listen to them and "to let go of her temper that oppresses
her heart and her mind's rage" (*baruthumon organ kai lēma phrenōn metheiē*,
176–77). They are her loyal friends (*prothumon philoisin*, 178–79), but
they are also aware of her terrible temper.

Though the Nurse and Chorus are clearly afraid of what she might do,
Euripides plays down the fearfulness as he establishes Medea's right to
sorrow and anger. The Nurse, the Chorus, Tutor, and Aigeus are all her
supporters. Each sees that Jason is wrong, and each accepts the premise
that she is entitled to justice. As the Chorus says, "Justly you will exact
payment from your husband, Medea" (267–68). The Tutor is more dis-
creet, but even he sees her as a victim (*talaina, mōros*, 59, 61) and wishes
that she and the children were not going to be exiled (73). Aigeus finds
Jason shameless (695) and is shocked that he would allow his children to
be exiled (707). Their sympathy clearly directs the audience to find at least
some vengeance acceptable.

Medea commands affection and loyalty from the narrative audience; she
effectively manages to persuade the Chorus, Kreon, Aigeus, and Jason
himself to help her by portraying herself as a victim, like "everyone else."
She first gains the support of the Corinthian women by identifying herself
as a woman among women. In one of the most famous speeches of the
play (214–66), she speaks to the Chorus, detailing the hardships of
women, showing what they have in common. Medea admits her rhetorical
purposes in such a way as to disarm suspicion: she is addressing them lest
they suspect her of standoffishness simply because she lives quietly (215–
18). She frames the speech in terms of the outsider/insider dichotomy,
not denying but rather asserting that as a stranger she is in a more delicate
position than they are (*chrē de xenon men karta proschōrein polei*, 222).

She not only gains their pity but likens her situation to theirs: "Women
are the most wretched creatures of all" (231). Though not everything she
says applies directly to her, her argument is an incisive analysis of the
typical Athenian woman's position. A woman leaves behind everything
she could have called her own, purchases a husband she doesn't really
know, and must seek to learn his ways. If she is reasonably successful, she
is lucky. But even if things go well for a time, she can still lose her husband,
for if he is not satisfied at home (literally, within, *endon*, 244), he can go
outside its bounds (*exō*, 245) "to ease his heart's desire." He can turn to
a *philos*, a dear friend or perhaps a family member, or someone his own
age (*philon tin' ē pros hēlika trapeis*, 246). The wife, however, cannot take
a new companion herself, but must "look only to one soul" (*mian psuchēn
blepein*, 247). The rationale behind this double standard is the old excuse

that men protect women and that women must therefore submissively accept their behavior. Euripides has Medea deny that women need that protection; after all, was she not Jason's savior? In fact, men have the easier task, and she would rather stand behind a shield in battle three times than bear one child (250–51).

This speech is indeed an exercise in rhetoric calculated to persuade the Chorus, but it need not be specious. Indeed, it must be substantially correct, since it achieves its end: the Chorus does not demur. The details fit Medea in important ways.[9] She bought Jason with the Golden Fleece (233); she left her natal family and had to adopt new customs and laws (238–39); she is certainly vulnerable to his departure. Later, to ensure the silence of the Nurse and the Chorus, she again appeals to them as women: "You will say nothing of my plans if you think well of your mistress, and if you are born a woman" (822–23).

Having established her commonality with other women, Medea faces her first adversary. The scene with Kreon is staged as a suppliant action in which the villainous ruler with all the power exiles a "defenseless" woman and her children. Medea tries to make herself seem helpless, discounting as much as possible her reputation for wisdom, but Kreon is still afraid of her (*dedoika s'*, 282). Nonetheless, he is approachable on the grounds of their common parenthood (344–45). Euripides makes her a shrewd psychologist; she brings up what will appeal to others, unerringly reaching her target. Again, the Chorus shows us where we should situate ourselves as listeners when they cry: "Unfortunate woman [*dustane gunai*, 357], woe, woe for your grievous suffering; where will you turn? What friend or house or land will be your salvation in these evils? Medea, thus has some god brought you into this uncrossable wave of evils" (357–63).

In Medea's remarks following this scene, Euripides begins to let her victim's mask slip ever so slightly. She points out that she would not have fawned and flattered thus (*thōpeusai*, 368) if she did not expect some profit from it. She lays out the possible objects of her revenge, including "the father, the maiden, and her husband," but the Chorus is not yet put off. Rather, they then sing of a time to come when song will stop recounting women's faithlessness (*mousai de palaigeneōn lēxous' aoidōn / tan eman hum-neusai apistosunan*, 421–22). After Medea's open dispute with Jason, they and we are still on her side, the Chorus singing: "Jason, even though you have made pretty speeches, all the same, it seems to me, even if I speak beyond good judgment [*para gnōmēn*, 577], that you are betraying your wife and not acting with justice" (576–78). The contrast here of words

9. See Page, *Medea*, p. 80 on line 231; cf. Michelini, *Euripides*, p. 87.

and deeds, and the implication that the members of the Chorus stand to lose if they speak against him, predispose the audience not to trust Jason. Therefore, we remain firmly with Medea.

At the play's midpoint, Medea is still sympathetic as the woman wronged.[10] In the scene with Aigeus, Euripides creates a further opportunity for her to narrate her wrongs, starting with Jason's gratuitous betrayal of her (692) and ending with his complicity in her exile (708). She again plays the suppliant, begging Aigeus to pity her (*oiktiron oiktiron*, 711) because she is unfortunate and deserted (*erēmon*, 712). So long as Medea is the *victimized woman*, then, she has support for her revenge. As members of the narrative audience, we feel that she has suffered grievously, and the structure of the play calls on us to side with her.

But what is happening on the authorial level? Medea attempts to persuade the characters, but what is Euripides doing by shaping her in this way? There is reason to make this interpretive move to the authorial level of response. Aristotle criticized two points in the play: the arrival of Aigeus, and the escape in the dragon-drawn chariot. Significantly, the very scenes he found objectionable most strongly call forth the authorial level of response, removing us from the reality of the play and encouraging us to consider the events of its plot symbolically. Aristotle calls Aigeus's entrance improbable (*Poetics* 25.31[1461b]); as T. V. Buttrey says, he comes from nowhere, is unannounced, and has no reason to be in Corinth.[11] In the terminology I have introduced, Aigeus disrupts the narrative level of the audience's experience. Buttrey convincingly dismisses the plot and thematic connections of the scene and finds structural significance instead. But these are precisely significant only when we are distant from the action and responding primarily on the authorial level: that is, when our response is based on our awareness that we are watching a play.[12] Such structural relevance only heightens our awareness that the scene is "unnatural" and works not against the scene's alleged "irrationality" but with it. I would

10. Critics speak of her as a universal: the "woman scorned." See, e.g., Musurillo, "Euripides' *Medea*," pp. 52, 61; and Page, *Medea*, p. xviii: "And there is another aspect of Medea's character to consider. She is a woman scorned. . . . Though her emotions are natural to all women of all times in her position, their expression and the dreadful end to which they lead are everywhere affected by her foreign origin."

11. Buttrey, "Accident and Design," pp. 4–5. Actually, Aigeus is tied in with the thematics of children; she promises him young as she kills her own.

12. Buttrey, ibid., points out that the audience expects a speedy resolution to the plot, since Aigeus enacts the conventions of the messenger or some sort of savior; my point is that messenger speeches after the third episode reflect not real life but the conventional life of the theater.

argue that the very arbitrariness of the scene is a reminder of the artificiality of our experience, a reminder to us of our role as audience at a play.[13]

The authorial level becomes even more prominent when we turn our attention to Aristotle's second objection: Medea's escape. Euripides arranges it through a device that underlines the story's folktale origins. On the narrative level, the sun god's dragon chariot signifies that Medea is returning to the realm of the fantastic and supernatural. But there is another implication for the authorial audience: to arrange for escape by a mythic conveyance drawn by mythic beasts is to remind us of the play's connection to representation, and thus to stress its existence as a cultural artifact.[14] Moreover, the plot does not require both scenes: if Aigeus can give her asylum, presumably he could provide a vehicle; if Helios can give her a vehicle, presumably he could provide asylum.[15] Given its redundancy and the significance of the reference to myth, we should take this interruption in the narrative fabric as a sign to stress our role as authorial audience.

In doing so, however, we are deterred from taking the character of Medea as real. By emphasizing the authorial level of response, Euripides interrupts the audience's initial sympathy and in many ways distances us from her, so that what might have inspired a critique of the institution of marriage from her point of view tends to inspire instead a fear of the strong female he has represented. From this perspective, the compassion previously built up in the audience seems misplaced; it is evidence of Medea's persuasive power—a terrifying power, as we shall see.

Triple Binaries

Euripides further undermines our compassion by manipulating his representation of Medea. The character initially gains sympathy by representing herself as "like everyone else": like the Chorus, a woman; like Kreon, a parent. Euripides then undercuts that sympathy by revealing her difference. The audience has three levels of questions about her ontological status: is she mortal or immortal? is she foreign or Greek? in the end, is

13. Thematic claims for its integration—e.g., that Aigeus's childlessness underlines the issue of infanticide—are also authorial.

14. Cf. Pucci, *Violence of Pity*, p. 159: "Euripides shows here that Medea is not merely a woman but also a character of myth." His conclusion about the significance of that fact differs from my own, however: "Myth, being itself a discourse, cannot escape questioning the relationship between self and other" (p. 160).

15. Buttrey, "Accident and Design," p. 2; Walsh, "Public and Private," p. 298.

she like or unlike other Greek women? The very device Euripides employed to gain our sympathy for her, her similarity to other women, makes her most terrifying, for she is not a victim and not vulnerable—that is, not feminine—yet she has been identified as and with other women.[16] To the extent that she is nonetheless a woman like other women, she destabilizes the category "woman."[17]

On the axis mortal/immortal, Euripides deploys her divinity so as to make her as threatening as possible. There is a strong tradition that Medea had been a divinity in the past.[18] As Louis Séchan says, her divine nature is involved in her magical powers and mastery over charms.[19] He points to alternate traditions in Corinth and Thessaly, but in both places her roots are divine.[20] What kind of divinity was she? First, she was the granddaughter of Helios the sun god, the daughter of Aietes, and the niece of Circe. Although solar imagery and light predominate here, Aietes is simultaneously a chthonic figure. Second, we hear that Medea, attempting to render her children immortal, hid them in the sanctuary of Hera at Corinth; in one version of their death at Corinth, they died by her error during this process (alternatively, Hera fails her). Her attempt to render a child immortal shares the goals of rites of initiation; she seems then to be a *kourotrophos*, nurturer of youth, one of those figures that Henri Jeanmaire links to initiation.[21] Third, one variant shows her as the wife of Zeus in the period before Hera's worship took over at Corinth; as such, she had power over life and death. As a pre-Hellenic deity, then, the mythic Medea had a terrifying strength.

Medea shares important traits with Metis, another pre-Olympian female divinity, who is significantly a figure of devices (*mēchanē*), and one who

16. McDermott, *Euripides' "Medea*," p. 51, makes similar observations about this interplay.

17. On Medea as a hero, see Knox, *"Medea* of Euripides"; Burnett, *"Medea"*; Foley, "Medea's Divided Self."

18. Visser, "Medea," pp. 158, 164 nn. 55–56, notes the connection to Ino and cauldrons as a remnant of the Mother Goddess cult. She cites E. Will, *Korinthiaka* (Paris, 1955) pp. 118–29, to the effect that there were two separate Medeas and that Euripides "lets the first part of the story provide the circumstances and the background for the second." See also Roussel, "Médée"; Kerényi, *Goddesses*, pp. 20–40; Burkert, *Structure and History*, pp. 9–10, 148 nn. 27–29; McDermott, *Euripides' "Medea*," pp. 44, 129 n. 5, and 51 on deemphasis.

19. Séchan, "Légende de Médée," p. 234. See Roscher, *Aus führlicher Lexicon der griechischen und römischen Mythologie*, 2.2.c.2486, citing Alcman fragment 106 (Bergk); Hesiod *Theogony* 961–62, Pindar *Pythian* 3.9ff.; Lewis Farnell, *Cults of the Greek States* (Oxford: Clarendon Press, 1896, 1986), I:201–4.

20. Séchan, "Légende de Médée," p. 237, citing Robert, *Griechische Heldensage*, pp. 185–86 and Wilamowitz-Moellendorf, *Griechische Tragödie*, on Medea, p. 20. Page, *Medea*, p. xxix, cites Nicolaus Wecklein's edition of the play to the effect that Medea was a Phoenician moon goddess, but he himself emphasizes her foreignness (e.g., p. xix).

21. Jeanmaire, *Couroi et courètes*, pp. 296–99; Visser, "Medea," pp. 158–59.

finds paths (*poros*) across the sea.[22] As Metis was married to Zeus (and gave him her powers, after he swallowed her), so Medea was married to Zeus in some stories. Like Metis she is liminal, crossing boundaries, and therefore she seems to pose a threat. A relationship to Metis is consistent with her position in the play as a figure full of contrivances, who first enables Jason to win the Golden Fleece but then discovers devices to gain her own revenge.[23] Medea retains the liminality of Metis even in her capacity as an ogre's daughter, like other figures at the border: Alcestis and Ariadne, for instance, daughters who help the hero.

We will never know how Medea would have been constructed in the cultures in which she was a divinity, because the culture that produced her is lost in the past. Since the Olympian order won and their world view predominated, we can see this earlier time only through the eyes of that later victorious order. Euripides might have made Medea a divinity from the first, like Aphrodite in *Hippolytos* or Dionysos in *The Bacchae*; their power is brutal, but the terror is of a different sort because it has not been brought into the human circle. Since he does not do so, it is commonly agreed that Euripides deemphasizes Medea's role as a goddess.[24] The result is that even feminist critics Sandra Gilbert and Susan Gubar persist in calling her "merely witch."[25] And when critics emphasize the escape in the chariot at the end of the play, they tend to regard Medea's divinity there as the objective correlative of the inhumanity of the infanticide. Anne Burnett and Eilhard Schlesinger specifically see the device as signifying her loss of womanhood.[26] The point is surely that when the demoted goddess of a former age walks the earth with the creators of the new moral order, she looks like Medea. Such powerful and independent women are called witches, or as Jean-Pierre Vernant and Marcel Detienne put it, "a long line of women who are experts in the use of poisons, love-philtres,

22. Detienne and Vernant, *Cunning Intelligence*, pp. 57–58 (on Metis), 189, 193 (on Medea). They do not see Medea as a divinity but do point out the importance of her connections to Corinth and Sisyphus, both of which Euripides also uses.

23. See Gernet, *Anthropology*, pp. 93–96, on the Golden Fleece.

24. E.g., Lesky, *Greek Literature*, p. 369; Conacher, *Euripidean Drama*, p. 186; Kitto, *Greek Tragedy*, p. 208; Knox, "*Medea* of Euripides," esp. pp. 214–15; Reckford, "Medea's First Exit," pp. 329ff.; Schlesinger, "On Euripides' *Medea*," pp. 33–35.

25. Gilbert and Gubar, *Madwoman*, p. 68. Page says: "Because she was a foreigner, she could kill her children, because she was a witch she could escape in a magic chariot (*Medea*, p. xxi). For similar views of her as witch, see Grube, *Drama*, pp. 152–54; Elliot, *Medea*, on lines 395, 1317; Cunningham, "Medea *apo Mēchanēs*," p. 153; Reckford, "Medea's First Exit," pp. 333, 347. Conacher, *Euripidean Drama*, p. 186, finds her more woman than witch; cf. Shaw, "Female Intruder," p. 259, who points out that she is a woman in her use of drugs.

26. Schlesinger, "On Euripides' *Medea*," p. 89: "Medea the woman is dead." Cf. Burnett, "*Medea*," p. 22: "no longer a woman." See also Cunningham, "Medea *apo Mēchanēs*," p. 152; Knox, "*Medea* of Euripides," p. 209.

spell-binding magic, *pharmaka mētioenta*" and who hark back to an earlier period, (mis?)recognized as terrifying.[27]

To have delineated Medea from the start as a goddess would have prematurely eliminated the basis for sympathy. Euripides chooses to develop her first as a woman, to whom we respond on the narrative level, then to reveal her as a divinity, to whom we respond more appropriately on the authorial level. Emily McDermott makes a similar observation, using different terminology: "Such a [supernatural] Medea would appeal to our intellects, to that part of our literary sensibility which seeks out and thrives on metaphors and allegories. Since she need not in that case be judged ultimately as a human being, her 'existence' in the play would not create such a sense of moral turmoil." McDermott also claims that "beings who live outside the realm of human life, whether gods, demigods, or mortals with supernatural powers, naturally live beyond the bounds of human ethics as well."[28] I would argue that Euripides appeals to two levels at once; he asks us to respond with our intellects, by appealing strongly to the authorial audience, only after he has gotten us involved emotionally; he does not use her divinity as he might but, rather, downplays her ancestry.

There are, however, two significant allusions. First, Medea claims Helios as the source of the robe she will present to Kreon's daughter as well as of the dragon-drawn chariot in which she escapes. This claim minimizes her potential as a *female-centered divinity* by pointedly inscribing her in patrilineal, not matrilineal, relationships. The robe is from her father's house: "this robe [*kosmon*] which Helios, father of my father, gave to his [masculine] descendants [*ekgonoisin hois*]" (954–55). Second, her heritage is intertwined with her status as a representative of women. Early in the play, talking to herself, Medea calls her actions appropriate to "one from a noble father and Helios" (406); in the same breath, however, she is made first to assert her human womanliness and women's danger to men. She swears not by Zeus or Themis, as she had done earlier, but by Hekate; having thereby associated herself with magic, she makes the link between herself and all other women and their capacity for evil: "No, by the mistress whom I honor, Hekate, who inhabits the inner regions of my hearth [*hestias emēs*, 397], no one will rejoice at my heart's suffering. I will make those marriages painful.... You see what I suffer? You shall not provide an object of mockery for these Sisyphean weddings of Jason, being of a

27. Detienne and Vernant, *Cunning Intelligence*, p. 189.
28. McDermott, *Euripides' "Medea*," p. 51.

noble father and Helios. You know this well, and we are moreover women, with least resources for good, and the most sophisticated contrivers of all evil" (395–409). Thus, we can see that her noble/divine patriliny is linked to her worship of Hekate on the one hand and to her vengeance on the other. It all comes together in an evil that is gendered female.

Because the immortal aspects of Medea are repressed, her methods seem to be those of a woman (as she herself argues); the traces of the goddess then percolate through the representation of the mortal woman and make her awful. She possesses particular powers, *poros* and *mēchanē*, that are traits of Metis, but in the play, these appear troublesome aspects of her femininity. Our sympathy for her is in large part based on what she has done for Jason, and his disloyalty in the face of that generosity, but those same powers also make her an uncanny enemy. Metis was swallowed by Zeus when he founded his rule, but Jason is not the man to control Medea's powers. Unless Euripides does the job for him, Medea's devices will run wild.

Euripides stresses the legend of the Argonauts, making Medea Jason's savior, as in the Nurse's opening lines: "Would that the ship Argos had never winged its way into the land of Kolchis, of the dark Symplegades [crashing rocks, 2] nor had the cut pine trees fallen in the glades of Pelias, nor had the hands of the best men ever plied the oars, those who came for the Golden Fleece for Pelias. For then my mistress Medea would never have sailed to the towers of Iolkos stricken by eros for Jason" (1–8). As savior, Medea is again like the cosmogonic Metis, a figure for finding the way; she is the one who can find a way *between* the wandering rocks. The Chorus emphasizes the issue of boundaries: "Having suffered unjustly, she calls on the gods, on the the Justice of Zeus that belongs to the oath, which moved her across the track [*antiporos*] into Hellas, through the inky night of the sea to the infinite [*aperantos*] salty gate of Pontos" (207–13). They envision her as someone who makes paths, for her departure from her father's house led her through the double rocks (432, the second reference to the Symplegades) where she makes a boundary (*horisasa*, 432). The gate of the sea is infinite, without tracks—that is impassable, without signs—and requires a Medea to navigate it; on the human level, these signs are provided by the law, Themis, and the oaths that Jason has broken.[29]

The trackless sea and the one who makes tracks, with a cluster of other sea

29. See Burnett, *"Medea,"* on Jason as destroyer of order; cf. McDermott, *Euripides' "Medea."*

images, make up a backdrop on which the characters then place themselves with respect to one another.[30] In her bid for sympathy, Medea misrepresents herself as a poor woman instead of a wily divinity. In her opening appeal to the Chorus, Medea depicts herself as someone who has lost any anchorage (*methormisasthai*, 258; cf. 442) since sailing away from her father's home (255–58). Nurse and Chorus emphasize her sailing (*epleus'*, 7; *epleusas*, 431). The absence of a harbor serves as an impulse for her, and she intends to find a way, some *poros* or *mēchanē* (260); she asks Kreon for one day so that she can locate a harbor for her children (342). (Here Jason is the one without care or forethought for his children: *mēchanēsasthai teknois*, 343.) Her troubles are like a sail let loose (278) and an uncrossable (*aporos*) sea of troubles (362). When Aigeus supplies a harbor for her (*limēn*, 769), she says she can now attach her sails to him (770). But we see the deception in this self-presentation when she lashes out against Jason as the storm itself; her ability to find her own way is clear.

Euripides, in this play as in so many others, contrives to have it both ways. Although the female divinity has been repressed by Hellenic civilization, the text of the play, precisely by subordinating Medea's divinity to her status as mortal woman, makes the audience fear the return of that repressed. She becomes a woman with fearful powers rather than a deity.

On the axis of outsider/insider, Euripides could have made Medea unequivocally a stranger, and at first it would appear that he has done so. He seems to have displaced what would have pertained to her as a goddess onto her foreignness, which is emphasized as the divinity is deemphasized. From the first we are told that she came from Kolchis (2, 132); she is *xenos* not *astos* (222–23, 297, 388, 434), and *barbara* (536; cf. 540, 591). As Denys Page says: "Euripides' Medea is just such a woman as his audience would expect a foreign princess to be. She has nearly all the features of the type—unrestrained excess in lamentation, a readiness to fawn upon authority, the powers of magic, childish surprise at falsehoods and broken promises." He thinks that Medea's feeling about broken promises is part of her depiction as barbarian and takes the "contrast of truthful barbarian and lying Greek" as a commonplace.[31] Although it is no longer possible to say with Page that Medea is "simply" a barbarian princess, there is no doubt that she is strongly characterized as such.[32]

30. Obviously, I disagree with Barlow, who finds repeated reference to the sea a cliché, lacking "some special dramatic exigency" (*Imagery*, p. 98). See also Musurillo, "Euripides' *Medea*," pp. 67–71. Blaiklock, "Nautical Imagery," observes that Medea's use of the image pattern makes her a victim and is "tragic, Jason's response is comic" (p. 236).
31. Page, *Medea*, p. xix.
32. As Visser, "Medea," p. 151, says, "Hardly anyone today would insist that we should

Instead of treating her as the representative of a full-blown culture of her own, however, Euripides presents Medea within a Greek setting and point of view.[33] While the play loudly proclaims Medea to be a foreigner, it assumes that she is Greek; she is perfectly easily understood by the Greek characters, and she swears by the same gods. Thus there is a constant interplay between outsider and insider (as there is between divine and mortal), conforming to what Helen Bacon has seen as general to Euripides: "With Euripides the actual concrete foreigner—Ethiopian, Persian, Egyptian—disappears, and we have instead the symbolic foreigner. . . . the fact of foreignness, the problems it creates, and the mood of romance and unreality it can be used to evoke, are never to be forgotten. Where Aeschylus and Sophocles are realistic, Euripides is thematic and symbolic."[34]

What would it mean to see the events from the Kolchian perspective? Herodotus mentions that Kolchis was first an Egyptian settlement; according to this evidence, then Medea was not only a foreigner but also a woman of color and, more important, a member of a well-established civilization, not at all "barbaric."[35] In Kolchis, Medea would not be an exotic; her wisdom would be a strength, to be sure, but not a weird knowledge.

It is the suppressed Kolchian perspective that shapes her dependence on oaths, which, as others have noted, are thematic in the play. Not only are there references to Jason's broken oaths, but Medea ostentatiously extracts a new one from Aigeus.[36] Anne Burnett refers to their "primordial" significance: "Oaths stood like the primeval pillar that supports the sky, a link that could at the same time hold off a possibly angry weight. The oldest doctrine was that oath-breaking was twin to kin-murder, these two being initially the only human crimes of interest to the pre-Olympian divinities."[37] Medea's belief in the importance of oaths marks her not merely as a barbarian, as Page would have it, but as a being from an earlier time. As Gernet argues, the oath comes from a period of pre-law; it is based on concrete objects and is tantamount to the statement "I will do something for you that creates an obligation."[38]

Jason, however, is part of the Olympian order that has taken over. Thus,

explain the actions of Euripides' Medea as entirely those of a barbarian witch. Medea now has many supporters, and few people pretend that they do not understand her."

33. See Bacon, *Barbarians*, p. 144: "As a rule Euripides in characterizing barbarians disregards differences in manners and social institutions."

34. Ibid., pp. 168–69.

35. Herodotus *Histories* 2.104; Snowden, *Blacks in Antiquity*, pp. 155, 161.

36. Flory, "Medea's Right Hand."

37. Burnett, "*Medea*," p. 13.

38. Gernet, *Anthropology*, pp. 172, 148.

he and Medea have different assumptions about the meaning of the oath. An oath *does* as well as *says* something; in speech-act terminology, it is a performative and thus must be judged differently from constatives. Speech acts are appropriate or inappropriate, not true or false. From this perspective, we can see that Jason and Medea fail to meet one of the requirements that J. L. Austin sets out: "The particular persons and circumstances in a given case must be appropriate for the invocation of the particular procedure invoked." Medea and Jason are not members of the same speech community; coming from different communities and even different strata of history as they do, it seems likely that they never shared the same assumptions about oaths—hence the impossibility of their successfully swearing an oath together. Even though the words were uttered, we have an example of a "misfire."[39]

Because social institutions (especially marriage and promising) depend on efficacious speech acts, the flouting of the speech conventions in these cases is tantamount to a destruction of social reality. Jason believes that he granted Medea a great good by bringing her to Greece, but that benefit all has to do with language, law, and fame.[40] Civilization equals language, which is why the Greeks defined as babbling (the root of "barbarian") the speech of anyone who lacked their language. But from Medea's standpoint, Jason has eroded civilization, for he has broken the oaths that sustain it; in her view there was another moral order sustained by another concept of language. What we have is not the difference between civilization and its absence but between two different civilizations, for Kolchis had an ancient culture of its own.

As Medea's position as a former goddess renders her a preternaturally powerful "woman," so her position as an outsider makes her a distorted representative of Greek beliefs about femininity. Despite her speech to the Chorus, she is clearly an anomaly: she was never given in marriage in the way that an Athenian woman would have been; there was no ritual of betrothal, no exchange of gifts between men. Rather, she chose Jason. This action is doubly significant, for it not only raises her to Jason's status as an equal—no one gives her in marriage; she has no male guardian (*kurios*)—but also shows her to have sexual desire and to act on it.[41]

39. Austin, *How to Do Things with Words*, pp. 14–19; there is another class of "infelicities" that applies here, that of "abuses where the act is professed but hollow." I am arguing that Jason and Medea were not in a position to swear and that therefore it was a misfire. His later behavior, however, is an abuse of marriage. For a discussion of speech communities, see Fish, *Is There a Text*, p. 215.

40. Burnett, *"Medea,"* p. 13, takes Medea's point of view, accepting Jason as the "man of injustice"; McDermott, *Euripides' "Medea,"* emphasizes Medea's role as the destroyer of order.

41. Flory, "Medea's Right Hand," p. 71: "She is a larger-than-life female whose contract

Admittedly, since Medea is a foreigner and one who has literally killed her brother to help her husband, she is not typical. But her action is an exaggeration of, not different in kind from, that required of other women. As the text makes explicit, Medea is both like and unlike other mortal women.[42] The fact that she was not exchanged but is yet recognizably feminine underlines the risks in marriage by exchange: she is the extreme case of the outsider woman who marries into the family, the woman located at the hearth who threatens the very *oikos* she comes to stand for.[43] Her loyalty to Hekate, goddess of the underworld, not Hestia, goddess of the hearth, makes the point. Medea's situation may be anomalous, but it nonetheless points out a crux in the problematic relationship of women's desire to the institution of marriage.

Much of what is true of her as an individual confirms Greek negative stereotypes about women as sexual and dangerous, especially given the text's tendency to generalize about women and to identify her with them. Medea's passion for Jason is repeatedly asserted as a cause of the action. The Nurse, who takes her mistress's part throughout, says, "In Kolchis she acted out of a soul [*thumon*] burning with desire for Jason" (8); the Chorus attributes her sailing forth from her father's house to her "maddened heart" (432). Jason goes further: since Aphrodite alone was responsible for all that Medea did for him, he therefore owes Medea nothing; only her passion led her to help him (527–31). Although Medea is in many ways exceptional, we have nonetheless seen her successfully claim commonality with other women (214–66). Her passion, therefore, seems to apply to them; in fact, the Chorus is afraid that such desire will afflict

---

with Jason takes on the character not just of a marriage settlement but of a treaty between sovereign states." In a typical betrothal, as discussed in the Introduction and Chapter 2, the men shake hands; as Flory, "Medea's Right Hand," says "no Athenian woman could enter into such a contract on her own behalf" (p. 70). See also Burnett, "*Medea*," p. 13; Williamson, "Woman's Place," pp. 18–19.

42. Michelini, *Euripides*, p. 87, makes similar connections: "[Medea] does follow her sexual desires, choosing her husband at dreadful cost to her family of birth; and in punishing Iason's sexual infidelity with an atrocious crime, she inverts the moral rule by which women must subordinate sexual impulse to family needs. When this figure defends the female sex, she is persuasive and offensive at once and in almost equal measure; but her arguments are largely false to her own circumstances, a fact which qualifies both offense and persuasion." For the most part, critics seem to focus on the contrast of witch and woman, conflating this with the contrast of foreigner and Greek. The threat to the Athenian male comes, however, from the possible overlap of the two categories. For recent consideration, see McDermott, *Euripides' "Medea*," chap. 3; Musurillo, "Euripides' *Medea*," who calls her a mere woman; Knox, "*Medea* of Euripides," pp. 214–15, who observes that her speech locates the play in a social situation. For the play of gender roles, see Burnett, "*Medea*"; and Foley, "Medea's Divided Self," p. 73, who notes the dialectic between heroic masculine and helpless feminine.

43. On this point, see duBois, *Centaurs*, p. 115. Visser, "Medea," cites Vernant's work as well.

them (627–41). Medea not only generalizes about desire but relates it to her vindictiveness, saying that "once a woman suffers injustice in bed, no other heart [*phrēn*] is more bloodthirsty" (265–66). In this she agrees with Jason who believes that "women think only about their bed" (569–73), and, in fact, that they are "bitten" (*knizēi* 555, 568), a word implying a visceral reaction to matters of the bed.[44]

What does it mean that Medea and Jason both say women are focused on the marriage bed? It does not mean that they are in fundamental agreement, for the couch, *lechos* or *eunē*, can stand for desire, as Jason thinks, but it can also stand for status, position.[45] Medea's explanation of this "obsession" centers not on sexuality but on the exchange of women in matrimony. For the reality is that men, not women, pursue pleasure: according to Medea's self-justifying speech to the Chorus, not only does a woman "have to buy a husband, a master for her body," but then, whereas he can stray when dissatisfied, she cannot (232–33, 244–47). Medea denies the desire that Jason imputes to women, although she agrees with him about the effects. Women are obsessed with "the bed" because it is the source and site of their position in the house.

Jason seems to believe that his relationships to the princess and to Medea could have coexisted but for Medea's passion. In his scenario, she desires him, while he merely desires heirs and is trying to do what is best for them. In other words, heterosexual desire is ascribed to women; men are motivated by a homosocial drive for sons. Through this logic, Jason distinguishes himself as a rational being from Medea as a passionate one; he argues that his purpose in his new marriage is not the gratification of sexual longing but the procreation of royal progeny (563–65, 593–97; cf. 876–78, where Medea deceitfully agrees) whose noble position will support his children by Medea. He believes that he can reassure her and eliminate her sexual jealousy, but it is too late, for her passion has caused an avowedly rational problem: where can she and her children go if she is no longer his wife (511–13)?

Jason is now consummating a perfectly conventional marriage, one based neither on oaths nor on desire for the partner but on desire for the connection the marriage offers. Kreon says he has heard Medea cursing "the one giving, and the one marrying, and the one being married" (288); this formulation stresses the kind of marriage taking place, as does Medea's telling Kreon to give his daughter to whomever his heart desires (309–10). The word marriage, as it appears over and over again in the play,

44. On reason and Medea, see Foley, "Medea's Divided Self," esp. pp. 64–66. She argues against seeing the play in terms of reason and passion, and for a maternal versus an avenging Medea who combines rationality and irrationality (p. 73).

45. On the confusion of meanings, see Loraux, *Enfants*, pp. 215–16.

usually refers to Jason's new relationship, not to his union with Medea (but see 1341). In this typical union the bride is not even named but is simply the daughter of the king, for it is the king that Jason is interested in. He stresses the fact that he is marrying the king's daughter (554; see *lektra basileōn*, 594) because he is concerned for his lineage (*genos*, 564). Medea agrees, telling Aigeus that Jason is unfaithful to his oaths because he wants to ally himself with the king (698–700; cf. 778, 876–77).

Medea's theory is that Jason has decided his "foreign marriage bed" (*lechos*) does not suit him at his age (591–92). In fact, Jason was looking for a throne all along, and her original appeal was her power to invest him with one through the Golden Fleece. Since he failed to get what he wanted by consorting with this creature from the border,[46] he tries the more conventional route of an alliance with a king's daughter. If Mc-Dermott is right that as a typical fifth-century Athenian male he is a cad but not a criminal,[47] then it is particularly tempting to make connections to the problematic legislation surrounding marriage in the period. The 451 law stipulating that Athenian citizens had to be born of two native parents was still on the books; an Athenian audience might have drawn the analogy between Jason's situation and their own. Even if that law had fallen into disuse, surely an Athenian audience would recognize Jason's desire for legitimacy as familiar. Moreover, there is evidence that Athenian men could keep if not two wives then a wife and a concubine; again, Jason's plan would have been familiar. The Chorus believes that Medea suffers what many women suffer ("it is common," 157), but Medea comes with a different set of assumptions and is not willing to put up with it.

Jason is now making an ordinary Athenian marriage, but the transaction is interrupted by the eruption of Medea's desire; given the represented similarity between her and other women, on the authorial level it would seem that women's sexuality is dangerous to the very institution that requires it. The text both ascribes sexual desire to women and renders that desire problematic.

Monstrous Revenge

The most obvious strategy for rendering the formerly sympathetic Medea frightening is through the construction and representation of her

---

46. See Burnett, "*Medea*," p. 16.

47. McDermott, *Euripides' "Medea*," p. 30: "No matter how much we may indict Jason for his ingratitude, his weasely manner, and his self-interested rationalizations, he is no worse, really, than the middling man. A cad, yes; a criminal, no."

revenge. Medea's revenge, like Hekabe's and Phaedra's, is inscribed as excessive: betrayed by one, she kills four, not one of them her primary antagonist. The narration of the murders of the princess and Kreon, taken together with the murder of the children, creates a Medea monstrous in her powers. The two parts of her vengeance are intertwined; working as they do on both the authorial and narrative levels, they also depend on the mixtures I have been analyzing of mortal and immortal, Greek and foreign. Euripides depicts the murder of the princess and Kreon in ways calculated to distance us from the Medea with whom we have identified and consequently make her morally problematic. The means he has her select highlight both her divinity and her foreign status, but they are also established as belonging to her as a woman; thus the representation once again confirms negative stereotypes of women. I have already discussed Medea's relationship to Metis, goddess of *poros* and *mēchanē*, and her persuasive abilities. Rhetoric is her device of choice, and it is closely tied to her form of revenge; not only does Euripides make her vengeance terrifying, but to the extent that she has been identified with other women, their language and wisdom are also implicated in that vengeance and therefore rendered terrifying.

Early on in the play, Medea's words seem to have caused her trouble; Kreon was afraid and exiled her because he heard that she was cursing his family (287–89); Jason taunts her with the fact that her own words are responsible for her exile (450, 457). The imagery of speech fits in with that of the sea; from having been a savior to Jason, Medea has become the wave of words that he must navigate: "It is necessary for me to be no bad speaker, it would seem, but like the trusty pilot of the ship with the topmost edges of the sail to outrun your noisy talking, woman, that makes the tongue ache" (522–25).

For much of the play, Medea is simply persuading the mortals who populate her world: she persuades Kreon to give her a one-day reprieve; she persuades Aigeus to give her asylum; she persuades Jason to take her children to Kreon's daughter with the poisoned gifts, and the gifts are designed to persuade the princess to let them stay in Corinth. In each case, we are shown the extent to which she can disguise her intentions, in large part because, like Hekabe, she is able to play on common beliefs about women.[48] Had Medea been only divine, the Greek male audience could have avoided taking her threat to heart, but instead, everything that might mark her as divine is ascribed to femaleness; the possibility is there-

---

48. Foley, "Medea's Divided Self," p. 74: "She successfully feigns being the helpless woman." Musurillo, "Euripides' *Medea*," p. 61, talks about her feminine charm.

fore raised that all women merely feign powerlessness in order to corroborate men's beliefs and thereby achieve female ends.

Since the discourse of rhetoric is connected to sexuality; each is contaminated by the other.[49] For instance, Euripides' Medea sees that it is
Jason who has wandered from her bed, thus betraying the oaths, making
lies of his promises. She links male sexuality with linguistic duplicity and
comes down most firmly against the person who is unjust but a talented
speaker (580–81); she accuses Jason of being an empty rhetorician (582–
85), and thinks her initial mistake was being "persuaded by the words of
this Greek man" (800–802). But like Hekabe in her confrontations, Medea
is the more talented speaker; thus she stands accused by her own words.[50]
Since she has also said that women will do anything if they are upset about
matters having to do with the bed, and since her sexuality is believed to
be at the root of her revenge, to the extent that her revenge is accomplished
through persuasion, female speech is tied to female excesses in the bed.

Medea's rhetoric, definitely dangerous and malevolent, also goes beyond
mere words, for it is tied up with the murders and the way in which she
proceeds: that is, through drugs. As we saw earlier, though we might view
her methods as suitable to a Metis figure, Euripides has her assert that
they are merely those favored by her sex. She sees many murderous paths
(*hodous*, 376)—some direct, others indirect—but feels a special affinity for
the use of drugs, in which women are *by nature* wise or experienced
(*pephukamen sophai malista*, 384–85).

The gifts that Medea uses also evoke her troublesome duality, her immortal origins as well as her existence as an ordinary woman. Like her
vengeance itself they are doubled, and that doubling suggests overdetermination. First, the gifts are intended as another form of persuasion, for
"gold is stronger than countless words with mortals" (965). As persuasion
is both divine and mortal, so are the gifts. Second, women are associated
with weaving, and thus the robe she gives the princess is appropriate to
her as a woman; at the same time, since the robe comes from Helios, it
is divine. Moreover, it may connote her wiliness, since the weaving of
cloth and the weaving of a plot are metaphorically the same. The trick
(*doloisi*, 783) does not refer simply to the poison but also to the robe and
crown themselves. The word *leptos*, meaning "fine," can apply as easily to

49. Two parts of Hippolytos's great diatribe (see Chapter 5) are divided between the
two protagonists: Medea wishes for the sure sign between gold and counterfeit to distinguish
liars and truthtellers (516–19, cf. *Hippolytos* 616–17 on women as counterfeit, 925–31 on
the desire for two voices); Jason wishes for a way to reproduce without women (573–75;
cf. *Hippolytos* 618–24).

50. Cf. Williamson, "Woman's Place," p. 28.

a fabric as to an intelligence or speech: the robe is *leptos* (786, 1188) and, according to Jason, so is Medea's mind (529). The messenger reports that the "robes were *poikilos*" (1159), an almost untranslatable word meaning "dappled" in color but also used to describe a shifting intelligence like that of Odysseus. Even the crown is *plokos*, "plaited" (786, 1186), as is the plot of a play (Aristotle *Poetics* 18.9[1456a9]); it is an *anadesmē*, which literally means a snood but also evokes the magic powers of binding and loosing (978; cf. *sundesma*, 1193).

Weaving as divine and as symbolic of an artful femininity do not exhaust the significance of the gifts, for their giving is also deployed in a system of circulation and exchange. Here the duplicitous gifts become a sign of value in the debate between Jason and Medea. Medea has to persuade Jason to send the gifts to his princess and therefore argues that the robe is not ordinary but well worth having, a gift from Helios, handed down in the father's line (954). Jason takes this as an insult to his new household and replies that they do not need her gifts but have a sufficiency of goods; he challenges her own wealth, saying that she is a fool to "empty her hands" (959–61). Not only has Medea given an oath that she supposed meant something, not only has she acted independently on her desire, but she further claims her independence here; she asserts her right and ability to give gifts, to participate in the community.

At the same time, her success in persuading Jason to accept the gifts is a public enactment of the internal effects the gifts will have on the princess, Kreon, and Jason and Medea's children. This circulation of precious gifts, like the circulation of women's sexuality, is dangerous: the *pharmaka* that anoint them are contagious, afflicting not only the father but the children.

Still we must ask, why two gifts where one would have been sufficient?[51] A robe is a typical female gift, as well as a typical offering to a female deity; it also forms part of the wedding dowry (*phernas*, 956), which of course is a display of familial wealth and status, part of the contest between Jason and Medea here. But why the crown as well? Euripides foreshadows the wedding by that gesture, so that Medea seems to intervene in the relationship between the king's daughter and Jason, dressing her for the wedding in order to kill her.[52] By this device, giving her the "adornment of Hades" (980–81), she makes the bride a bride to Hades (985). Medea pretends to work together with Jason in his courting of the princess in

---

51. On the doubleness of the gifts, see Musurillo, "Euripides' *Medea*," p. 63 n. 10; Page, *Medea*, p. xxvi.

52. We cannot be sure of the relative chronology between this play and Sophocles' *Women of Trachis*, in which Deianeira "inadvertently" kills Herakles with a poisoned robe. On the ritual of wedding and sacrifice in that play, see Segal, "Mariage et sacrifice."

order to rescue the children (946), and the nature of the gifts suggests
that she is also forwarding the marriage as she says she should have done
sooner ("I should have stood by the bed and rejoiced in attending your
bride," 887–88).[53] By alluding to marriage in the double gifts, Euripides
alludes as well to the power of women to turn marriage into death. At
the same time, we can see here an unsettling trace of Medea's quasi-divine
powers. As a *kourotrophos* and pre-Hellenic Hera, she would have been
responsible for initiation; in garbing the princess, she parodies marriage
as an initiation for the bride.[54]

Euripides has so far adumbrated Medea's power and supported the
vengeance she exacts; the full horror is now revealed. Medea emerges as
the playwright orchestrating the deaths from a distance, and her desire is
emblematized by the excesses of the Messenger's speech in reporting eroticized violence. Euripides slowly builds up to the gruesome murder, but
not before he has inscribed the princess as cold and narcissistic; he still
lets us think that she perhaps deserves what she gets. Her behavior at any
rate supports Medea's fears for her children, for while the servants dandled
the children and patted their hair, the new mistress was not kind to them—
until she saw the dress (1141–42, 1147–56). The impression of her greed
and vanity is reinforced when she puts on crown and dress: she looks at
herself in the mirror and admires her legs (1161–66). The combination
of these ordinary, commonplace events with a grotesque death heightens
the paradoxical pleasure in pain.[55]

Posing thus, the princess becomes a spectacle first for her own gaze,
then for the imagination and ears of Medea, and finally for the audience.
The Messenger's horror at the "sight terrible to behold" (1167) com-
municates itself to us. He draws out the description to great length, showing how the dress affects first its wearer and then Kreon. To the extent
that the audience has taken Medea's side, it must now retreat from her,
for Medea not only planned the death but is also inscribed as the audience
of the Messenger's narration. She gets pleasure from his telling: "You will
please us twice as much if they died very wretchedly" (1134–35). Moreover, listening to the account of these deaths does not lead her to suicide
(as is the case for other wives such as Eurydice, Jocasta, or Deianeira) but

53. The multiple meanings of the word *kēdeuousan* (take charge of: lay out a corpse or
contract a marriage) at 888 are all in play simultaneously, for she is referring to the wife
who will be a corpse, thus to the laying out of the corpse, but also to the fact that a marriage
is being contracted.

54. On initiation and Medea, see Visser, "Medea," pp. 158–59, but she does not make
the connection to the murder.

55. For a more thorough working-out of the pornographic implications of this passage,
see Rabinowitz, "Tragedy."

rather confirms Medea in her plan to kill the children before someone else does.

Which brings me to one last question: why does Euripides have Medea kill her children? That is, what motives does he give her, and what are his motives? The position of the child murder in the legend has been and continues to be debated.[56] Euripides probably invented this part of the story; for one thing, his version has been so successful that it seems likely we would have heard of it if it had been current before his *Medea*. It is clearly an important part of his design, whether or not he invented it. At the least, then, we must concur with P. E. Easterling that "the most uncompromising feature of all is Euripides' handling of the story, his design which makes the murder of the children the centrepiece of the play. This horrific act is something from which we naturally recoil."[57]

What does Euripides gain by having Medea murder her children? The infanticide is the final way in which he makes Medea excessive, and he uses it, I would argue, to ensure that the audience does not continue to applaud her and validate her words and wisdom. Once again we can take our cue from the Chorus, for the women were firmly behind her when she planned to attack Jason, his bride, and her father, but they recoil when she announces that the plot includes the murder of the children. They ask Medea not to do what she contemplates, not to break the human norms (812–13); she goes too far in her vengeance when she takes her (male) children as her victims. By addressing her as "woman" (816), they foreground the conflict of roles and expectations.

Euripides does not present Medea simply and straightforwardly as the killer of her young, however; he rather plays with the audience, heightening our involvement, lessening our distance. To this end, he has the Chorus base its horror in part on the presumed pain to *her*: "How can you bear to kill your own seed, woman?" Medea replies, "For thus will my husband be most eaten up." But the Chorus reminds her that she "will be the most wretched of women" (816–18). This exchange raises the question first for the narrative audience, who will want to understand why Medea the character kills her children. Let us try to follow her reasoning. Having persuaded Kreon to give her one day, Medea discusses her options with the Chorus; she realizes that there are many ways of reaching her goal, to get back at "those making new marriages" (366–67). Infanticide is not inevitable, however, for when she first sketches out the possibilities,

56. See discussion in McDermott, *Euripides' "Medea,"* chaps. 1–2. I agree with McDermott but also think that the importance of the device does not depend on our proving that Euripides invented it.

57. Easterling, "Infanticide," p. 177.

the children don't enter into the equation at all. She tallies up the direct and the indirect ways of taking revenge and decides to use the indirect means, at which she is more skilled, only if she has found a place of refuge (376–94). Her concern is that she not be a laughingstock (*gelōn*, 383; *gelōta*, 404). Once Aigeus has come and gone, promising her and the children a harbor, she decides on duplicity.

But duplicity turns out to entail infanticide: she moves from having found a harbor (769), to sending for Jason (774–75), to asking that the children remain—"not so that leaving them in a hostile land my enemies can insult them, but so that with my devices I can kill the child of the king" (*paidas, paida*, 780–83). After describing that plan, she announces her intention to kill her babies (*tekna*, 792). Thus, the promise of safety for her is ironically the death sentence for the children. But why can't she take the children if she has a safe place to hide, and more particularly, why can't she take the children in the chariot with her? Medea later asserts that they must die and therefore better at the hands of the one who bore them than at someone else's (1240–41), but the narrative audience must remember that the only reason they must die is that she used them as intermediaries with the princess. And even then it is possible that Jason could have saved them, as he tries to do, not knowing what has happened (1301–5).

On one level the remaining motive, that she kills the children to get back at Jason, does not make any more sense; he has been willing to abandon them and thus cannot be supposed to care much about them. For the narrative audience, there is no explanation if we simply assume that Medea loves her children. The Nurse, however, foreshadows what will happen with her early emphasis on Medea's possible aggression against the children (36–37); her fear suggests that Medea kills them because they are the visible signs of her relationship to Jason.[58] We must return then to the different grounds of marriage; Jason does not have a physical tie to the children in the present, but they do represent the future to him. Medea kills his bride and his sons not because he cares about them but to make sure that his house will be destroyed (794, 803–5).[59]

A rationalizing tone characterizes the speeches preceding the vengeance action; the tone shifts sharply when Medea faces the children and when she faces the implications of what she has put in motion. Euripides wrests the last bit of pathos from the plot, for he still gives us hope and extends

58. See Burnett, "*Medea*," p. 22, who refers to Clytemnestra's similar language, speaking of Orestes, in the *Oresteia*.
59. Musurillo, "Euripides' *Medea*," p. 65.

our sympathy for Medea by showing her deliberating and thus revealing to us what it costs her to do this deed. In her great monologue in which she again talks to herself, she is divided between a masculine, heroic warrior self that adopts those values and will not be a laughingstock, and a maternal self that feels for the children and would take pity on them and let them live (1019–80).[60] The Messenger's speech leads Medea immediately to arm herself like a hoplite (*hoplizou*, 1242) and to forget her children; warrior spirit is set off against childbearing (*exephusamen* and *etiktes*, 1241, 1247). If she forgets them only for a minute, she can then spend the rest of her life mourning them (*thrēnei*, 1249).

The victimized woman with whom we had felt sympathy is in combat with the victimizer, whom we abhor. By making her both for and against the murder, Euripides extends our sympathy for her, but at the same time, he casts the debate in such terms that she is threatening to the categories of male and female. Like the plays of sacrifice (and the *Hippolytos* as well), the *Medea* raises a fundamental question as to whether and how a woman can have access to those virtues esteemed by Greek culture; Medea's role as a woman is in direct conflict with her desire for a warrior's glory. As Helene Foley says, there is only a "male model if she wishes to act authoritatively and within *timē*."[61] Euripides puts Medea in this predicament by making her accept heroic values. There seem to be only two positions, both undesirable: to kill her own children, or to be a laughingstock. Euripides then makes her horrifying: is it better or worse that they die at her hands, that she who gave life will also take it? Her choice makes sense only in the logic that they are an extension of her and that their capture would tarnish her honor.

On the narrative level, the infanticide is terrifying because it is so incomprehensible: this "woman" is willing to hurt herself in order to injure her husband. She seems consciously to choose that which is against at least part of her self-interest. Medea is even more threatening to the established order than Agave in Euripides' *The Bacchae*, for she kills her son while in a Bacchic trance, and the "true" villain is Dionysos. Medea is not mad but calculating, and she uses her children in a plot against her husband.[62]

60. Foley, "Medea's Divided Self," p. 74, relates the two, noting that for the Chorus, protection of the children from harm is an ultimate part of the self-interest of mothers. On the development of the heroic side, see p. 76. On the speech and the heroic Medea, see Knox, "*Medea* of Euripides"; Burnett, "*Medea*"; McDermott, *Euripides' "Medea."*

61. Foley, "Medea's Divided Self," p. 79; she also refers to the heroic masculine and helpless feminine (p. 73). See also Knox, "*Medea* of Euripides"; and Burnett, "*Medea.*"

62. Although in epic men are avengers, in tragedy, women predominate. In *The Bacchae*, Euripides subjects the effeminate god to the treatment he gives Phaedra, Hekabe, and Medea,

But let us remember that Euripides has created this character, and consequently he makes her make herself suffer and makes her a threat. Reading
on the authorial level, the audience takes her as general, symbolic; the
threat to her own children becomes a threat to all men's children. It is
instructive again to mark the contrast with Agamemnon, the similarity to
Clytemnestra; Iphigenia sacrifices herself voluntarily, but not so Medea's
sons. Moreover, although Medea once refers to her murder as a sacrifice
(*thumasin*, 1055), there are none of the other trappings of ritual death,
no divine order, no altar or libation; the boys are merely "sacrificed" to
her sense of honor. When the woman is violent, then, the sense of sacrality
is undermined; there is no cause worth dying for.[63] As Clytemnestra's
justifiable motive is forgotten by the end of the *Oresteia*, so Medea's vengeance is made to seem to go too far.

Euripides' Medea not only kills her children; she escapes. As I have
argued, the authorial level is heightened by the escape; moreover, it further
marks the infanticide as unnecessary and seemingly willful violence. The
final tableau discloses a mortal female standing in the position usually held
by some divinity at the end of Euripidean drama.[64] The scene might well
provoke male anxiety at the specter of the dominating female, for the
anticipated remorse does not materialize; instead, Medea pours forth
hatred. As Jacqueline de Romilly has pointed out, the violence at the end
of this play seems gratuitous.[65] Although Medea occupies the position of
a goddess, and the chariot comes from Helios, the audience cannot erase
the strong delineation throughout the play of Medea as a woman. Thus,
for the authorial audience what she does will seem general: if women (or
slaves?) are willing to hurt themselves to gain revenge, there is no way to
stop them.

What is the effect of this structuring of the action? First, Medea seems
to have established a dangerous subjectivity for herself through her powerful acts. But second, like Phaedra and Hekabe, this Medea loosens her
claims on audience sympathy by the vengeance she exacts. As Page and
others have noted, Jason, by contrast, becomes more sympathetic toward

---

making him at first a sympathetic victim but then an unsympathetic victimizer. Medea
combines in herself both the roles of Dionysos (avenger) and Agave (child murderer).
Musurillo, "Euripides' *Medea*," p. 62, makes the *Bacchae* comparison as well and calls Euripides "the master of pure horror."

63. McDermott, *Euripides' "Medea,"* esp. p. 76, discusses the sacrificial motif at length,
comparing the treatment of the boys' death with that of Iphigenia's. I agree with her on the
facts but focus on why Euripides chooses to depict Medea in this way.

64. Medea here diverges from Clytemnestra, who in Aeschylus's treatment is in the end
at least superficially subordinate to Aegisthus.

65. Romilly, *Modernité*, p. 78.

the end of the play.[66] Having exchanged positions with Medea, victimizer becoming victim, he also has a less mediated relationship to the children, expressing for the first time the sensual feelings for them that have heretofore been characteristic of Medea. Although he had been willing to allow them to go into exile, he now wants to touch their bodies. He becomes more human as she becomes less so. Medea's divine status must make the audience identify with Jason; after all, we are humans like him, not deities like her. This gain in sympathy may lead the audience to accept his point of view, to see her as a dragon or Skylla (1342–43).[67] As in the *Hekabe*, the problem is displaced from the faithless male to the terrifying female.

What are the consequences of this move from a sympathetic Medea to a terrifying Medea and a sympathetic Jason? To the extent that she gets away with murder, the play does represent a form of successful female subjectivity; it nonetheless supports the continued control of actual women because it makes Medea's very freedom terrifying.[68] One lesson to be learned is that the woman who is not exchanged, who is not controlled by a man, who acts on her own sexual desire, will kill her own children to get back at him. For men, as Emily McDermott says, "any even slight recognition by a male audience member of silently smoldering resentment in his own or others' housebound women might be precipitated by this catalyst into queasy *phobos* for himself, his sex, and the social order of fifth-century Athens."[69] The play, then, might well encourage men to control actual women by portraying the disaster that occurs when a woman is out of control.

Yet to the extent that Medea was made sympathetic and seemed to suffer, women in the audience must be ambivalent; she buys her freedom at the price of the murder of her own children, which is represented in the text as a form of self-mutilation. As the virgins sacrifice themselves because they have accepted the ideology of glory and tried to win it in the only way possible for them, so Medea's vengeance is a kind of self-sacrifice. Euripides gives her a warrior sensibility that values honor above

---

66. Page, *Medea*, p. xvii. McDermott, *Euripides' "Medea*," pp. 67–70, takes the amelioration of Jason as a sign to the audience that it was wrong to see the fight as male against female; I take it as an integral part of that fight. For other statements of Jason's sympathetic presentation, see also Foley, "Medea's Divided Self," p. 81; Palmer, "Apology," p. 49.

67. As Burnett says, for instance, he allied himself with forces he was meant to oppose ("*Medea*," p. 16).

68. The implied critique of masculine values is, I believe, substantially undercut by making her so terrifying. But cf. Foley, "Medea's Divided Self," pp. 80–83.

69. McDermott, *Euripides' Medea*, p. 31; Musurillo, "Euripides' *Medea*," posits that the demonic Medea is only the Fury "beneath the skin of every woman" (p. 69).

all; she can achieve it only by killing her young and part of her self, as is made clear in her monologue.

The Power of Song

At the same time that the text renders Medea's wisdom and language dangerous, it insistently raises the question of the power and status of poetry. For instance, the members of the Chorus initially ask the Nurse if Medea "will come into our view and receive our words"; the Nurse doubts that she will be able to persuade her and she then launches into her discourse on the efficacy of poetry.

> You would not be wrong to consider those mortals of earlier times stupid and not at all wise, those who in song for festivities, banquets, and dinners dicovered the delightful music of life; but no one ever found in music and song a way to stop the hateful sufferings of mortals, with which death and fortune trip up their houses.
> And yet, it would be a profit for men to be cured by song; but where there are well-spread feasts, why raise the voice? For the amplitude of a feast has its own present delight for mortals. (190–203)

The Nurse here challenges the usefulness of songs of such poets as the Homeridai and Pindar, who sang at feasts and claimed to be able to make people forget their troubles. She concedes that song would be beneficial if it were a cure but sees no reason to add it as merely one more pleasure to the pleasures of the banquet. That she is willing to address Medea but is not optimistic about influencing her, seems to emphasize the Nurse's lack of faith in language, not its power.[70]

The second prominent reference to poetry is in a choral ode and gives evidence *for* the relationship between power and song. The Chorus takes as its topic the falsity of men's songs.

> The sources of the holy rivers flow upward and the law in all things twists back on itself [*palin strephetai*]. For the counsels of men are deceitful [*doliai*], the oaths on the gods do not hold. The legends will twist so

---

70. Pucci, *Violence of Pity*, pp. 25–32, 45–46, analyzes the remedial purpose of song at length; he translates the Nurse's line this way: "And yet it is a gain that men heal these by means of songs." For him, however, the mechanism involves self-inflicted pain and an advantage gained by controlling it. He relates this speech to Euripides' claims for his own poetry. See also Walsh, *Enchantment*, pp. 111–15.

that my way of life will have good fame; honor will come to the female race; no longer will an evil-sounding fame hold women.

The Muses of the singers of old will leave off singing my faithlessness. Never to our power of thought did Phoibos, leader of song, give the inspired ode of the lyre; for I would have sung an opposing song to the race of men. Long time has much to say of our lot and of men. (410–30)

The Nurse has already introduced Medea by wishing away the entire quest of the Argonauts; her view of that adventure coheres well with her view of poetry. The Chorus and Nurse agree that the old epic songs celebrating the heroic adventures of men have to go; hymns will then stop exalting the exploits of faithless men like Jason.

The question is whether or not Euripides means his play to constitute this "opposing" new song.[71] Perhaps yes. Since tragedy is the characteristic art form of Athens, we may glean a third allusion to art in the Chorus's praise of Athens after Medea has revealed her plan. They glorify it for its integration of wisdom, Harmony, and the Muses with Aphrodite and the Desires (824–32). When they fully believed in Medea, they called on the holy rivers to reverse their course; here they once again mention holy rivers (846), but now in the context of wondering how such a land can welcome Medea, a child murderer, and still (we extrapolate) maintain its purity.[72]

What is a feminist critic to do with this play? It is imperative that we find a place to stand, escaping the agonistic view of Jason versus Medea. It may seem attractive to look at the ambivalent Medea as having been constructed so as to avoid binarisms, as a precursor of post-structuralist versions of the "feminine." Is Medea a figure of the poet? Page suggests: "Foreshadowed, too, already in *Medea* is the great burden of unpopularity which was to oppress the poet throughout his life."[73] If Euripides is indeed using Medea in this way, however, it is still an example of what Gayatri Spivak has called "double displacement," a strategy by which the male poet occupies all the positions.[74]

For Medea and the "feminine" have not much to do with real women. In the time of the play's production, women could not write plays, and

71. Knox, "*Medea* of Euripides," pp. 223–24, e.g., believes he does.

72. On the optimistic reading that Athens is great because it *can* integrate her, see Burnett, "*Medea*," p. 23: "Evidently the city that had swallowed up the Aeschylean Furies would be able to digest one more demon of punishment; it is even suggested that, like the Furies, Medea might undergo a transformation and join the company of benevolent forces, since her promise to Aegeus, like theirs at the end of the *Eumenides*, is one of fruitfulness (714–15)."

73. Page, *Medea*, p. xii.

74. Spivak, "Displacement."

the character of Medea was enacted by a man pretending to be a woman who pretends to be feminine but who is motivated by the masculine ideal of honor. As I have argued in earlier chapters, the honor code for men did not apply to women, who in general merely passed honor to their children through their chastity. The character Medea may be of the female sex but is of the male gender.

I would submit, then, that Euripides is not doing what his Chorus claims needs to be done for women. This is not a case where women have taken the lyre into their own hands, to tell their own stories, but rather one in which a man has written the parts for men and women. The version of myth we have before us was presented in Athens at an Athenian dramatic contest in which only men were primary players. If Aigeus welcomes Medea to Athens, Euripides makes it difficult for Athenians to do so (after all, in the sequel to the play she did manipulate Aigeus, getting him to marry her and getting him killed). To the extent that the authorial audience sees Medea as standing for all women, the vengeance will be generalizable, and she will seem to pose a threat to marriage as well: her act may raise the specter of all women killing the sons of their faithless husbands. Medea, refusing to allow Jason to come close, contests the Greek fathers' control over their sons. The threat is not merely that mothers will kill sons, depriving the father of legitimate progeny, but that they will do so on the grounds of betrayed sexual desire and through a formidable rhetorical power.

Coming to terms with Medea means coming to terms with masculine control of representation, the ability of the dominant order to construct the female and femininity in ways consistent with its needs. It is important to understand what Euripides is trying to do: the murder of the children is his choice, not Medea's. What better way to make her justifiable rage terrifying to Athenian men and women than to make her kill her children? However hard the Nurse wishes away the story of the Argonauts, we always see Medea through the eye of the Greek hero; after all, it is only through the legend of the Argo that she sails into view.

But the Euripidean text is not the only factor determining how we read, for each reader brings to it certain predispositions. For instance, to the extent that this play presents a choice between freedom and connectedness, "writing" and motherhood, it plays into the dilemma of the academic woman in our own time. It may be difficult to resist Euripides' plot, difficult to avoid seeing Medea as witch, but we can be on our guard first by remaining aware of what Euripides has done to create that character. Having analyzed his deployment of the audiences and our engagement, we have choices to make, for finally the text cannot totally control the reader. We can read primarily as authorial audience, avoiding the play of sympathy and emphasizing the symbolic level of meaning. We can, alternatively, accept Euripides' dare and embrace Medea as a revolutionary figure instead of resisting her.

Given the realities of child abuse in our own time, however, I find it problematic simply to applaud Medea's infanticide and escape. The difficulty here is both personal (I am a mother and find the vision of Medea troubling) and moral (do we want to endorse infanticide as a solution?). As a further alternative, having recognized Euripides' design, we can stress Medea's repressed divinity and the other culture to which she belongs. In this way we can use the play to expose the constraints of patriarchy that shape Medea.

All these readings are more or less removed from the play's strong appeal to the audience's emotions, an appeal it was surely meant to have. If we ignore the narrative level and reinstate the positive "feminine" elements suppressed by fifth-century Athens, we seriously underestimate its power. Rather, we must do the hard work of uncovering the ideological implications of the text and the ways in which it attempts to construct its audience, even as we try to erode that construct; we can look for the traces of female subjectivity, but let us not fool ourselves that Euripides applauds it.

5 Sacrificial Son and Vengeful Destroyer: Hippolytos and Phaedra

While sexuality is thematic in the representation of the dangers of Hekabe and Medea, it is even more structurally relevant to the *Hippolytos*; here too we see the woman's threat to the sons, since Phaedra causes the death of her husband's son. Like many of his other heroines, Euripides' Phaedra also seeks a form of glory and subjectivity, one that is denied her; as a result of her quest, though, women's speech is again problematized. Hidden assumptions in the text enable the dominant codes of behavior to seem adequate; unveiling them shows that the *Hippolytos* empowers men and reaffirms their authority by celebrating relations between them and by displacing the female.

Even a bald summary of Euripides' text reveals some of its peculiarities. The goddess Aphrodite opens the play, announcing that in revenge for Hippolytos's rejection of her and the marriage bed, she has filled Theseus's wife, Phaedra, with an illicit desire for her stepson.[1] Phaedra is silently starving herself in her chambers. When she is persuaded by her Nurse to speak and to act, Phaedra sanctions the use of a drug to cure her. The Nurse instead intercedes for her with Hippolytos; he replies with a misogynist diatribe (616–68) that leads Phaedra to take revenge; she leaves a suicide note accusing him of rape and then hangs herself. When her husband, Theseus, returns and reads the note, he calls on his putative father, Poseidon, to kill his son with one of the three wishes the god has granted to him; he himself condemns Hippolytos to exile. The play ends with a telling conjunction of gestures: Artemis appears *ex machina* to promise a marriage ritual in Hippolytos's honor, and father and dying son embrace in loving forgive-

---

1. Line numbers refer to the edition of W. S. Barrett.

ness. Chapter 6 further examines the question of why a misogynist youth is rewarded, and rewarded in these particular ways.

The antithesis chastity/sexuality, played out against a grid of male/female, is not symmetrical but hierarchical; the female emerges as carnal, her language and activity curtailed.[2] I shall argue that when Artemis promises Hippolytos a marriage ritual in his honor, we have the representation of an institution that will reproduce these asymmetries, mystified but not eliminated. Significantly, the resolution realized on stage takes place between men, father and son, and it is made possible through the control of Phaedra's sexuality and speech.[3]

The text seems to propose two possible models for women: either passive and virtuous but denied the rewards of the culture (in this case, fame), or active and malicious but denied the rewards just the same. These are the parameters Phaedra accepts for her behavior: starvation (a slow death) or hanging (a sudden one), silence (which acts out the misogynist's denial of activity for the female protagonist) or speech (which deprives her of the honor she covets). In this way, the text reaffirms Hippolytos's fantasy (618–24) and makes of the woman a counter to be exchanged by men. The play (and functionalist/ritualist criticism that applauds the marriage cult as a constructive cultural given) makes both Phaedra and the virgins of the cult accept as inevitable a male vision of themselves, their sexuality, and reality.

Hippolytos's Diatribe

The play presents at least one perplexing feature: why should the misogynist Hippolytos be rewarded with the worship of virgins on their wedding night and with the forgiving embrace of his father? The structure (prologue by Aphrodite, epilogue by Artemis) and the plot (Hippolytos is punished by Aphrodite for his devotion to Artemis) might suggest that the play hinges on an antagonism between the divinities, seen as a polarity representing an eternal conflict between sexuality and chastity.[4] In such a

2. For an extensive consideration of speech and silence as themes of the play, although without a discussion of the gender roles involved, see Knox, "*Hippolytus* of Euripides." See also Goff, *Noose*, chaps. 1–2; Zeitlin, "Power of Aphrodite," pp. 52–58, esp. pp. 52–54. On women's speech and sexuality in antiquity, see Bergren, "Language and the Female."
3. Others take a more optimistic view of the ending: e.g., Segal, "The Tragedy of the *Hippolytus*," p. 156; Knox, "*Hippolytus* of Euripides," p. 31; Reckford, "Phaethon," p. 419; Conacher, *Euripidean Drama*, p. 46; Winnington-Ingram, "Hippolytus," p. 191. See also Chapter 6.
4. See, e.g., Segal, "Tragedy of the *Hippolytus*," p. 160, and "Solar Imagery," pp. 151–61; and for a slightly different model, Burnett, "Hearth and Hunt."

structuralist reading, the chaste Hippolytos can stand for female resistance to marriage and can even help to overcome that resistance.[5] But Hippolytos can adequately represent female virgins only if we forget the sexual antagonism at the play's heart. This blindness behind the strategies of interpretation so often applied to the play may hint that contemporary criticism shares the ideological functions of the texts it studies.

To grasp the peculiarity of the conjunction of Hippolytos with marriage cult, we must analyze his diatribe against women.[6] In his view, women are counterfeit coin, they are oversexed, and they talk too much. These three themes are interrelated: all suggest that women's activity or mobility is problematic, and all reflect a male desire to control culture by controlling their circulation. Hippolytos's speech is not merely a sign of his madness and cannot be discounted as idiosyncratic; rather, it heightens and starkly expresses the cultural beliefs that define the ways in which the female threatens social structures, and therefore define as well the place she is supposed to occupy according to male desire.

The polemic begins with a cry to Zeus asking why he "set this counterfeit coin, woman, in the light of the sun as an evil to men" (616–17).[7] Hippolytos would choose to buy offspring by leaving gifts of precious metals in the temples. His preference for using the metals themselves bespeaks his desire to eliminate currency, thereby establishing some absolute value system instead of coin, which is arbitrary and therefore corruptible.[8] But more important, his fantasy soon brings him to his second topic: buying children would bypass women's sexuality, which from his point of view is an unfortunate concomitant of the predominant mode of reproduction, and which he like other misogynists finds excessive. Of course, any female desire is ex-cessive because it goes outside women's necessary role in the reproduction of heirs. According to Hippolytos, the wife easiest to bear

5. See Foley, *Ritual Irony*, p. 22; Reckford, "Phaethon," p. 415; Corelis, "Hippolytos with the Garland," pp. 84–85, 133: "Since Hippolytos is virginity made incarnate and destroyed, it is appropriate for girls to cut their hair in mourning for him at their marriage."

6. On the irony of the pairing, see Zeitlin, "Power of Aphrodite," p. 65. Segal, "Pentheus and Hippolytus," sees the ending as creating an "ironic inversion" correcting Hippolytus's life, but neither he nor Reckford, "Phaethon," who also emphasizes the ritual, takes into account the hatred for women that Hippolytos expresses. Vellacott, *Ironic Drama*, pp. 115–17, 234, does remark on the problematic discontinuity.

7. Irigaray, *Speculum*, p. 125, seems almost to give a gloss of the image of woman as counterfeit: "A woman's special form of neurosis would be to mimic a work of art, to be *a bad (copy of a) work of art* . . . which has to be condemned because it is a forgery. A society has the duty to ban forgeries." Thus, Phaedra's hysteria leads to the production of her deceitful text.

8. Corelis, "Hippolytos with the Garland," refers to a possible Freudian interpretation of the image, which links money and feces.

is literally a nothing (*to mēden*), who is at least harmless although of no benefit in her silliness; he reserves his hatred for the *sophē* (the one who thinks thoughts surpassing a woman's station) because "Kypris gives birth to more evildoing in the clever. The witless [*amēchanos*, literally "without devices"] woman is freed from lust by her half-wittedness" (642–44). Finally, because women use intelligence solely in the service of lust, their speech—the distinguishing sign of human intelligence—is closely tied to sexuality. Having asserted that women's sexuality is rampant, Hippolytos concludes that they must be isolated indoors and must not even have servants to go in and out but only "the silent bite of beasts," so that no one will be able to speak to them, nor will anyone have to hear their voices (645–50). Because of Phaedra's filthy desires, her words have sullied his ears, with the result that he "must purify himself with running water" (653–54), as if even hearing words so incompatible with his purity could make him low or bad (*kakos*). Thus, women and their words pollute by virtue of their sexuality.

We can see that Hippolytos is in agreement with many of the values of his day if we analyze his speech as enumerating three systems of exchange—financial, sexual, linguistic—from which women must be excluded or in which they must be controlled.[9] A verbal echo reveals the disturbing irony: because women are the objects of exchange (*apallachthēi*, 629), they cannot be trusted, and men run the risk that they will traffic (*sunallagas*, 652) in beds not to be touched. The larger culture and the rest of the text confirm this connection of exchange and traffic. In the *Hippolytos* the Lévi-Straussian formulation discussed in my Introduction seems explanatory: women are seen as gifts exchanged by men to cement relations between men. "Woman" has an ambiguous status as an object in this exchange, constitutive of male culture, yet as a human participant in culture. Also invoked is the contradictory position, noted by Lévi-Strauss, of women as both signifiers and the manipulators of signs.[10] One way to resolve the contradiction would be to follow Hippolytos's suggestion to deprive women of speech altogether; then they would simply be signifiers of male honor, like the other gifts that men exchange. However ironically he means the word, by calling the wife a

9. Zeitlin, "Power of Aphrodite," pp. 87–89, discusses the passage in similar terms but sees marriage as "reciprocity" as well as exchange, whereas I see it as a relation of unequals. While I agree that Phaedra is defined as other for Hippolytos, I give priority to her femaleness in accounting for that categorization.

10. See the Introduction, pp. 15–17; Lévi-Strauss, *Elementary Structures*, esp. pp. 115, 496; Zeitlin, "Power of Aphrodite," p. 87.

treasure (*agalmati*, 631), Hippolytos participates in this redefinition of women.

Structuralist analysis and Greek myth are in agreement: the wife does have special status, but since a man's honor can be tarnished through her, she must be carefully watched.[11] Women can both make and unmake culture. The Hippolytos myth is a variant of the Potiphar's Wife story group, in which the woman is as a rule older and seductive. But this mythic assertion of women's sexuality conflicts with the male practice analyzed more fully in the Introduction: marriage for the purpose of engendering legitimate heirs. Because of the conflict between male needs for sons and this ascription of overweening desire to women, women have to be restrained. At the same time that (and perhaps because) the mythology and misogynistic poetry devalue woman as "sexual," the ideology prescribes that she be chaste, stay at home, be silent. Thus, the *Hippolytos* supports the Periclean motto that the best fame a woman can hope for is not to be spoken of among men (Thucydides 2.45.2): if she is chaste and stays at home, she will not be spoken of and will not threaten the stability of a culture based on her exchange.

Phaedra's Virtuous Silence

So far I have been documenting the connections between Hippolytos's misogyny and the organized exchange of women by men. But what are the results of this pattern for Phaedra? She accepts what her culture and its misogynistic representative Hippolytos say is appropriate for a woman and seeks to repress her desire, to die without speaking; sharing Hippolytos's estimation of women, she is condemned to self-hatred. Yet she is further placed in contradiction because if she achieves the goal of total self-effacement, she will not fulfill her desire for good fame (*eukleia*).

Before we see Phaedra, we hear that she is suffering silently (40), has taken to her bed, keeps herself inside the house (*entos echein oikōn*, 131–32), covers up her head, and has not eaten for three days (131–40). She confirms this version of her behavior in her apologia to the Chorus: she tried first to be silent (394), then to conquer her desire (399), then to commit suicide (401). Death by starvation is particularly appropriate for one who feels the shame of the body; the choral language is revealing, for

11. Pitt-Rivers, *Fate of Shechem*, p. 118; on this problem in Sophocles' *Trachiniae*, see duBois, "Horse/Men," pp. 35–49; for an economic understanding of the transaction, see Irigaray, *Speculum*, p. 122.

it indicates that she purifies herself by fasting (136–38). At the same time, starvation as a means of death shows her poverty (she has only herself as material) and indicates passive resistance (she will not forward life but does not yet take an active step against her life).

We can easily recognize that Phaedra has accepted the values of the patriarchy and her place in it,[12] and she sounds like Hippolytos—his exchange systems of currency, sex, and speech are analogous to her triad of food, sexuality, and language. Consequently, the only safe course for her is total withdrawal; she must close all her openings, and then be enclosed within the house. Language is forbidden to her, tied as it is to acting on desire. As silence means that no sound goes out, so fasting means that no food comes in; by these devices Phaedra maintains the integrity of her boundaries.[13] By abstaining from the physicality of sexual desire and food at the same time that she determines not to speak, she makes sure that if her mind sins, her mouth will not.

Like Hippolytos's diatribe against her, Phaedra's position is embedded in a generalized disdain for women. First of all, her acceptance of what is socially acceptable leads her to self-destruction. Beyond the suicide, though, we hear female self-hatred expressed by Nurse, Chorus, and Phaedra. Not only do they stress Phaedra's destructive passion as a female inheritance from her mother and sister (337, 339, 341), but she is also aware that she inherits the sufferings of her sex (669–70; cf. the Chorus's sentiments, 161–64). Moreover, Phaedra recognizes that others judge her as a woman, hateful to all (*misēma pasin*), and that as a result even her laudable struggle against her love will be viewed negatively (405–7). There is no strength for Phaedra in this community of women; her shared suffering leads her instead to condemn others as she condemns herself. Thus finally she attacks other women. First, when she analyzes what leads people not to do the right even though they know it, she refers specifically to those temptations facing women in her situation: talk and leisure (381–83).[14] In this she is again like Hippolytos, who would deprive women even of servants with voice. Second, she takes the male point of view when she blames the first adulteress (407–9), not an adulterer (like her husband

12. Winnington-Ingram, "Hippolytus," p. 183, discusses the social definition of Phaedra; other critics in considering the two forms of shame (*aidōs*) have come close to an analysis of the effect of convention on the formation of Phaedra's character. See Segal, "Shame and Purity"; Pigeaud, "Euripide."

13. Cf. Zeitlin, "Power of Aphrodite," p. 74: "Rather, the secret, confined and repressed, confines her to her bed, and blocks all the normal forms of domestic exchanges and those of the body itself in that food can neither enter in nor can the secret issue forth."

14. On the femaleness of the pleasures described, see Winnington-Ingram, "Hippolytus," pp. 176–77; Barrett, *Hippolytos*, p. 229 on lines 381–85.

in the mythic tradition and in other plays on the theme). As she does in her own case, she locates the problem in women's use of language: women's gossip will lead to disaster. As if to underline her subservience, Euripides has her make a connection between speech and going out of the house by repeating *thuraia*: the tongue that is "out of doors" (395), the woman who seeks a bed "outside her home" (409). Third, she reviles aristocratic women (411) who give lip service to chastity but are capable of anything in the shadows (413, 417).

As a model wife and mother, Phaedra has thus launched herself on a respectable and deathly line of action, embracing the dark inner chambers, silence, and deprivation. By doing so she hopes to secure her good reputation. Her concern with her good fame (*eukleia*) is well established in the text and in the commentary. To give merely a few examples: Aphrodite introduces her by saying that she must die even though she is *eukleēs* (47); she seeks to leave *eukleia* for her children (423); she wants her good deeds known and no witnesses for her shameful ones (403–4). The question is, where does this desire for reputation come from, and where does it lead? To a certain extent, Phaedra seems to model herself on the Homeric hero, who wants glory and fame and who defines those externally.[15] The conflict is caused by gender: as a woman, only if she is totally passive will she die nobly, but then she would surely have no fame at all. As R. P. Winnington-Ingram puts it, "If honour is everything, what is the point of virtuous action, if it is known to none...?"[16] The private sphere does not lend itself readily to the concept of glory.

Euripides ensures that Phaedra will not enjoy the good fame she desires, because she fails her own (self-loathing) standard of behavior.[17] Although she has vowed silence, the play depicts her move into language—first with unwilling speech, then with mediated spech, then with writing. Moreover, although she remains chaste, her failure to be silent seems a sexual impropriety because the dramatic necessity for her public appearance joins women's sexual role to their role in language.[18]

15. Claus, "Phaedra," pp. 235–36; Knox, "*Hippolytus* of Euripides," p. 20.

16. Winnington-Ingram, "Hippolytus," p. 79; Knox, "*Hippolytus* of Euripides," p. 13.

17. Most critics see that Phaedra's honor is tarnished in some way: e.g., Winnington-Ingram, "Hippolytus," pp. 181, 185; Knox, "*Hippolytus* of Euripides," pp. 13–14, 17–18; Matthaei, *Studies*, p. 89; Conacher, *Euripidean Drama*, p. 41; Dodds, "*Aidos* of Phaedra," p. 103. Gill, "Articulation," p. 87, notes that "Phaedra thus sees herself as an aspiring and, in the end, a failed version of Hippolytus, as regards their shared objective of being—and being seen to be—*sōphrōn* [chaste]."

18. Zeitlin, "Power of Aphrodite," pp. 74–76, comments on Phaedra's entrance, placing it within the the duality inside/outside, although she does not see Phaedra's action as failure.

When Phaedra recounts her thoughts and analyzes her reasoning, she asserts that she will not be diverted from the path she has taken—from her opinion—by any drug (388–90). But she is in fact vulnerable because she has already departed from her original path of total privacy and silence. Knowing as we do that Phaedra has been suffering silently within, we find even her entrance a break in that absolute integrity, but her first entry tells us further that she is changeable, even fickle, and weakened, for the Nurse says that she cannot make up her mind about what she wants (e.g. 181–82). Vacillating between her initial desire and subsequent shame, her behavior forges links between sexuality and speech, chastity and silence.

She speaks outside, and her whole first address emblematizes her repressed desire to throw off restraint. She does so in speech, if not in deed. So, for instance, having begged the Nurse to bring her into the light, she asks for the release of her hair (202), and her wording indicates her craving for freedom. She wants relief from the burden of her headdress, wants her hair free, and asks the women to support her ("lift up my head," 198). Yet propriety demands the headdress and requires that the hair be bound up. Further, her feeling that the yoke of her limbs is loosened (199) suggests more than prostration, for in Greek, yoking connotes the marriage bed, and loosened limbs imply sexual passion.

In the lucid introduction and conclusion to these hallucinatory ravings, we see a milder version of what she says in her trance. As she hallucinates, the sexual implications of her speech expand.[19] She gets further and further out of herself, so that her speaking almost accomplishes her goal in leaving the confines of the house. She imagines herself in places associated with Hippolytos, because she longs to share his freedom as much as to possess him.[20] The language is strongly marked as erotic, but even if it were not, the desires expressed do not suit a woman of Phaedra's rank and therefore brand her mad. The Nurse's response underlines the inappropriate desire for freedom characterizing these ravings: she knows that royal female thirst must be satisfied by the domestic waters of the palace, not waters from a spring (225–27). Thus when Phaedra "comes to herself," completing the frame around her rhapsodizing, she wants to hide her head (243) and with it the hair she has let down, to go inside and resume her silence. She sees her speech, connected as it is with desire, as shameful (*aidoumetha,*

19. For extensive documentation of the eroticism of this speech, see Corelis, "Hippolytos with the Garland," pp. 44–48, 57 n. 15; Glenn, "Fantasies," pp. 435–42; Knox, "*Hippolytus* of Euripides," p. 6; Segal, "Tragedy of the *Hippolytus*," pp. 124–25, 130, 144–47.
20. See Irigaray's rereading of Freud: "And if she is no male, because she sees—he says, they say—that she doesn't have one, she will strive to become him, to mimic him, to seduce him in order to get one" (*Speculum,* p. 84).

ep' aischunēn, 244, 246) because with it she is breaking the codes of silence, privacy, and inaction.[21]

Phaedra's Destructive Speech

Although Phaedra struggles against activity in the form of speech and sexuality, the text negates her wish to be faithful. In the next two scenes the Nurse seeks to persuade her to action. Since speech explicitly leads to Hippolytos, Phaedra, in keeping with her resolution, fights it for as long as she can. Even though her unconscious has already given voice to her longings, she will not willingly state her problem. She has distinguished between her pure hands and impure thoughts (317), and here she keeps her lips clean by making the Nurse speak Hippolytos's name (352), while she merely refers to him as the son of the Amazon (351; cf. 310). Thus, in this first persuasion or interrogation scene, we can see that Phaedra does attempt to regain her stance of silence, initially broken by the desire to come into the light, but cannot do so. Instead, Euripides and the Nurse make her an accomplice in pronouncing the name of her beloved. The name, standing for the person, has an almost magical power; Phaedra resists it to no avail.

After Phaedra's address to the Chorus, in which she presents a discourse on the possible reasons for nonperformance of a known good, the Nurse returns, and Phaedra becomes an example of her own theory: she knows what is right, but lacks the strength to do it. In this persuasion scene, sexuality contaminates language, for the Nurse wants to cure her by procuring for her. She appears to seduce Phaedra away from her noble purpose; the Nurse seems to be like those sophists who made the worse appear the better, speaking words that are pleasant but not good and that will not preserve her mistress's reputation. The Nurse is blunt: "Why are you so prissy [literally, why do you talk so piously]? What you need is not well-turned phrases, but the man" (490–91). Phaedra, afraid that she will be "taken" as the adulteress she has already spoken against (note the verbal echo between *alō* and *analōthēsomai*, 420, 506), asks the Nurse to lock up her mouth, calls her speech shameful, and fears lest she be con-

---

21. As I pointed out in Chapters 1 and 3, the separation of spheres is emphasized in tragedy. When Aeschylus's Clytemnestra comes outside and speaks to Agamemnon, she makes much of the extraordinariness of what she does (*Agamemnon* 855–60); similarly, it is irregular for Euripides' Clytemnestra to talk to Achilles and clearly embarrasses him (*Iphigenia in Aulis* 819–24).

vincing. The lock is off Phaedra's door and mouth, but she still hopes to prevent further damage by controlling the Nurse.

The traditional connection of language and sexual enchantment is underscored by the Nurse's words for her potions: she calls them incantations and "softening words" (478), "softening charms of love" (509). Thus, she uses speech to convince Phaedra to give in to her desire, as she plots to use words on Hippolytos. We must construe speech here as an action, whether moving toward Hippolytos or saving Phaedra's life, as the Nurse claims (497, 501). Phaedra, because she has adopted a masculine aristocratic definition of herself according to which such actions as coming out of the house and speaking are breaches of honor,[22] finds that language is killing the only thing she had sought to salvage, itself a word: her good name.

Up to this point, Phaedra has resisted, but after hearing Hippolytos's vituperative attack on all women, she asserts herself; her privacy taken away from her, she wields the tools of the culture. The extent of her implication in the Nurse's address to Hippolytos is unclear,[23] but there is no doubt of her responsibility for his death, for there is a final link in the chain of female sexuality and destructive words: the tablet. Fearing the name of whore that Hippolytos will give to her, Phaedra names him instead as her attacker (Theseus says "he has dared to touch my marriage bed with force," 885–86). She thus reassigns the desire that the playwright through the goddess assigned to her.[24] Moreover, whereas earlier she maintained a noble idealism and opposed the Nurse's pragmatism, Phaedra now becomes increasingly like the Nurse. She too deals in the *logos*, boasting that she will discover new plans (*kainōn logōn*, 688) to make Hippolytos catch her illness (730). Her speech is as duplicitous as was the Nurse's to her; and as the Nurse got Hippolytos unwittingly to swear an oath of silence (603, 611), Phaedra now demands the same from the Chorus (710–15). But Phaedra goes further and decides to defend herself and her children in the only way she can, by a preemptive strike against her enemy. Ironically perhaps, she acts in good epic style, where the only thing that counts is to do good to your friends and harm to your enemies.

Phaedra's assumption of "sexual subjectivity" leads to language that is

22. Winnington-Ingram, "Hippolytus," p. 40, refers to the "first breach in her honorable silence."

23. Barrett, *Hippolytus*, p. 256 on lines 516–21; and Conacher, *Euripidean Drama*, pp. 33, 40, assert that she preserved her resistance to the end. Winnington-Ingram, "Hippolytus," p. 180, implies that she gives in because she "longs for this in the very depths of her soul."

24. Zeitlin, "Power of Aphrodite," p. 65, notes that she redefines herself as subject, him as object.

not only deceptive but destructive, thus confirming Hippolytos's view. Earlier she had spoken only under pressure and with difficulty even to women; now she writes to men. Not only does her text enter the public realm of the men, but because of the double meaning of *deltos* as female sexual parts and tablet[25] and because of her message, it appears that her sex as well as her text is circulating freely. It is the combination that is lethal: neither Aphrodite nor Phaedra's desire kills Hippolytos; it is rather the written document, the *tablet* with its presumably clear message, that does the deed. In this way the play seems to corroborate Phaedra's and Hippolytos's view that female language is evil. The Nurse's *pharmakon* does not cure, and Phaedra's *deltos* merely provides the logical conclusion to the Nurse's destructive act of taking Phaedra's name into the public arena where, according to the aristocratic system of values, neither she nor it belongs.

Evaluation of characters is always problematic, but it is particularly important to attempt it in this case, because concern for her reputation was Phaedra's prime motivation for her actions. The play is set up so that the audience cannot offer the praise Phaedra so badly desires. We may understand her passion for revenge, but we are not intended to admire it. As woman and character, Phaedra is destroyed by speech and writing; she loses her honor and her moral superiority to Hippolytos.[26] Artemis reserves the crucial word *eukleia* for Hippolytos (1299), whereas Phaedra is merely excused as the goddess's victim and granted a kind of nobility (*tropon tina gennaiotēta*, 1300-1301)—only a qualified nobility because, out of her fear of being questioned, she has written lies (1310–11). The most noble course for Phaedra would have been to die without having spoken, but then where would the *kleos* (fame) of *eukleia* come from?

Rhetorical Consequences

I have been engaged in understanding how the character Phaedra's sexuality is identified with language, defined as destructive, and controlled within the text: she is in an irresoluble dilemma caused by cultural demands for passivity and her own desire for fame. Now I want to step back and examine the assumptions and implications of this analysis and the problems it poses for the meaning of the text—where meaning in-

25. Aristophanes *Lysistrata* 151; Artemidorus *Oneirocritica* 2.45. For modern criticism, see Zeitlin, "Travesties," p. 326, and "Power of Aphrodite," pp. 76–77; duBois, "Horse/Men," pp. 41–42. Cf. Iphigenia, who is like the tablet (Chapter 1) to be written on.

26. For the critical discussion, see notes 17 and 23 above.

cludes but is not limited to the uses culture makes of it. One strand of
contemporary criticism seeks to locate the "feminine" in textuality, identifying the feminine with the imaginary, that which precedes and is dis-
ruptive of the phallocentric rule of *logos*. Indeed, it would be tempting to
see Euripides as identifying with female voices; surely Phaedra and Medea
(see Chapter 4), for example, are among his most philosophical creations.
If that is the case, however, then the connection must be to himself as
impotent, for the play shows the disturbing possibilities of female writing
and then makes the world safe again by doing away with the active woman
and her text. If the play takes sides, it is the side of the father and his
word (see Chapter 6).

Let us look at the limits on Phaedra at her most active, when she replaces
and imitates the Nurse. First, she is limited in what she writes.[27] That is,
she may inscribe her own tablet, but the only way she can be effective at
all is to speak of the misuse of her body. She capitalizes on her privileged
place in the system of exchange; by narrating the violation of the system
and herself, she can invoke the wrath of the father. And she must do so,
because it is only by recourse to his power that she can achieve her ends.
Her tablet is inscribed by her but with male language, so that to win even
her self-defeating victory, she must inscribe there the story of another
unlawful inscription—on her body. She makes the lying fable of a true
shame to cover the true story of an imagined shame, using the only power
given to her by the patriarchy. Similarly, although she has taken authority
for herself, she can claim it only by signing herself with her death, for
only her corpse makes Theseus absolutely sure that this is her true letter.
The text draws our attention to the authenticity of the letter, and Theseus
describes her seal at length, its curves and the *typoi* on it. The marks on
seals like those on coins, must come from a proper authority to have value;
the seal on her *deltos qua* genitals is her husband's,[28] and though the seal
on Phaedra's *deltos qua* tablet may be distinctively her own, her "lips" speak
the language given to her by her culture.

Furthermore, the text controls Phaedra's attempt at authorship; not
only does Artemis correct her lie, but Euripides inscribes her story within

27. For a radical statement of the position that "there has not yet been any writing that
inscribes femininity" and of the forces that have made of women the "precocious, we the
repressed of culture, our lovely mouths gagged with pollen, our wind knocked out of us,
we the labyrinths, the ladders, the trampled spaces," see Cixous, "Laugh of the Medusa,"
p. 282.

28. Clytemnestra's fulsome talk about having kept the seals unbroken on the vessels in
Agamemnon's storehouse, while she at the same time boasts about her nonexistent chastity,
seems to give further license to this speculation (*Agamemnon* 609–10). Cf. Zeitlin, "Power
of Aphrodite," pp. 76, 198 n. 66.

Hippolytos's apotheosis. First, Phaedra's fate is merely a part of Hippolytos's; as Aphrodite makes explicit, Phaedra is a tool she uses to get back at the acolyte of Artemis (47–50). Second, the structure of the play, by giving Hippolytos both first and last scenes, minimizes Phaedra's importance. Finally, Phaedra's writing will be forgotten, and only her love will be remembered in the cult song honoring Hippolytos (1429–30). If Euripides was speaking through his female characters in the beginning, by the end he has eliminated them or subordinated them to the males.[29]

Written speech makes apparent what is a concealed truth about speech and language in general: it is of no use unless it is in some sense public or shared. Except when construed as harmful (and poison pen letters justify recriminations), this public use of the word was denied to Greek women.[30] Their problematic relationship to language was linked to an assigned status as objects to be exchanged by men and to confer honor on men. In this play, where our attention is drawn to the *typoi* on the seal of a *deltos*, we are led to consider the connections between writing, coinage, and female genitals. As we have seen, Phaedra is very limited in what she can say, and as a woman she can be sure of being believed only when she speaks from the dead. Thus, the possibilities for meaningful speech are nil: given the ideology of their sexuality, women can be either silent (as Phaedra was at the beginning of the play), or seductive (as only the Nurse is here, while in Euripides' earlier play on the theme Phaedra approached Hippolytos herself),[31] or deceitful (as Phaedra is in the tablet).[32] Women's texts lie; they are counterfeit coins whose circulation will drive down value. Women must be exchanged only once between father and husband; then they take their stamp from one man, stay his. But if the woman/coin stays at home, what use is she/it?

The play then participates in keeping women silent even while it allows Phaedra to speak, because it confirms the misogynist view that the lips of women unleash or are themselves a harmful drug (*pharmakon*). As I show more fully in Chapter 6, the ending of the play completes the process by founding its resolution on the basis of father-son reunion, indicating that Phaedra is important only in relation to the men. The combination of father-son bond and marriage ritual restores a status quo, comforting to

29. For a consideration of the suppression of Artemis, see Rabinowitz, "Aphrodite and the Audience."

30. For a development of this common notion in feminist theory, see Kaplan, "Language and Gender," p. 21; and Irigaray, *Speculum*, p. 125.

31. Zeitlin, "Power of Aphrodite," pp. 52–55, gives extensive consideration to this *Hippolytos* as palinode of the earlier text.

32. For a contemporary version of this list of possibilities, see Gallop, "Snatches," pp. 274–75.

men, in which the desires ascribed to Phaedra are effectively kept down. Men may be hailed as a subject by ideology; women are rather failed as subject and hailed as object, in a text such as this one.

The epilogue fixes Phaedra in an attitude of praise for Hippolytos and assures that she will be heard or seen only from that perspective.[33] The virgins imitate Phaedra and not Hippolytos in that they marry and cut their hair, as she wore the matronly headdress; but by making them worship the woman-hating Hippolytos, Euripides' text reaffirms the cultural practice of rendering invisible women's connections to other women. Although Phaedra is more human and more philosophical than Hippolytos, and a female world is strongly articulated from the beginning, the mundane life of women is not valorized by the women or the text, so that its path is not a real possibility for her.[34] Unlike Medea or Hekabe, who are threatening because they succeed, Phaedra can have no triumph, no victory.

We must ask ourselves who has made the figure Phaedra a girl who can't say no, what caused her to become enamored of Hippolytos in the first place—and the answer of course is the playwright and the myth behind him. Aphrodite is not some general sexuality but the sexuality that means heterosexuality for women and the exchange of women between men. Hippolytos continues to privilege male embrace even in death; this asymmetry is then at the heart of the institution of marriage as established here. Phaedra's emblematic status renders her a screen for the enacting of male desires; we have no way of knowing her point of view.

This play assumes and makes "natural" at least three ideological assertions: that all ties between women are willingly subordinated to their ties to men; that women's voices are contaminated by their carnality; and that in their text the word is made flesh—destructive because deceitful. Similarly ideological is the wedding ritual established at the end; it promises a resolution to the disharmony of the play, if only because of our expectations as critics of literature. But in actuality it incarcerates the brides in an institution whose goal is the production of male heirs, as is shown by the father-son embrace that accompanies it. Euripides' Phaedra is a victim of the ideology she accepts: although she fails to uphold her own values,

33. On the play as a monument to Hippolytos, see Pucci, "Euripides' *Hippolytus*," esp. pp. 184–85.

34. On the Chorus's characteristically female activities, see Burnett, "Hearth and Hunt"; and Segal, "Tragedy of the *Hippolytus*," p. 160. Irigaray, although not speaking of this play, points out that as part of the suppression of the feminine, "the need, the charm felt for one's like will be repressed, denied, turned into their opposites in what is labeled 'normal femininity' " (*Speculum*, p. 104).

she does not question them, so she is doomed to hate herself as well. By making the audience admire that same system of values, this text can participate in silencing women and rendering them invisible in a dark chamber identified with them and apparently chosen by them. The trick for the feminist reader, then, is to problematize the assumptions, revealing potential female strength, even if it is not left standing at the play's conclusion.

PART III *Men United*

6 Renegotiating the Oedipus: Theseus and Hippolytos

In the preceding chapter, I approached the *Hippolytos* by considering the representation of Phaedra and female sexuality. Another trajectory to that text, however, inscribes the power of the father in the patriarchal order, with significant consequences for son and wife. This text, like others, pretends to represent females and their desire while in fact enacting male desire. The question I would put forward is, as Gayatri Spivak has worded it, "What is man that the itinerary of his desire creates such a text?"[1] It is my claim that the desire of men for other men, especially of the father for a son, is primary in Greek tragedy, and that a textual economy is worked out to form that relationship while excluding the sexual female.

Since Freud, the Oedipal narrative has exercised a strong power over our imagination, but as Luce Irigaray notes, there are other stories: "When Freud describes and theorises, notably in *Totem and Taboo*, the murder of the Father as the foundation of the primitive tribe, he forgets a more archaic murder, that of the woman-mother necessitated by the establishment of a certain order in the city."[2] As in the Oedipus story the hostility of father and son is linked with a postulated desire for the mother, so in the *Hippolytos* the desire of father and son is linked with a hostility for the mother. Euripides' *Hippolytos* contains a false Oedipus story and, under that surface, an eroticized charge between father and son; the wife/mother is displaced so that these two can be alone together.

But surely the *Hippolytos* is a classic representation of, not a repression

1. Spivak, "Displacement," p. 186.
2. Irigaray, *Corps-à-corps*, pp. 15–16.

of, female desire. After all, does Phaedra not die for love? In the plot that
Aphrodite outlines, Phaedra loves and suffers so that Hippolytos can be
punished; his refusal and her passion are coupled as necessary for the play's
action. Heterosexual desire is ascribed to the woman by goddess, myth,
and playwright, with the result that in the end she suffers and punishes
herself. The structure of desire organizing the play, however, is actually
the male desire for the one like himself, for legitimate heirs coined in the
father's image, and for a concomitant security of meaning. Significantly,
the play does not end with Aphrodite's victory, the suffering of Theseus
and Hippolytos. The playwright adds a reassuring epilogue. Although I
agree with critics who argue that the text is about marriage,[3] I would add
that it is about marriage as an arrangement between men, in which the
goal is the relationship not between husband and wife but between father
and son. This relationship dominates the play's conclusion; the wife, having served the function of bringing the men together, is displaced and
done in.

The play has much to tell us about Greek culture and our own, for both
are founded on the exclusion of women from the important sites of culture,
those places where men speak together and make decisions: the Academy,
the agora, the theater. The masculine orientation of Greek society, where
the mature woman functioned only as the mother of future soldiers or the
manager of the household, was matched by an erotic organization as well.
In this respect, there are important differences between ancient Greek
society and our own. In particular, Greek society did not use the word
"homosexual" and did not fear and discriminate against men who loved
other men, but rather accommodated both a well-worked-out system of
male sexual relations with other men *and* marriages producing heirs.[4]
Current scholarly acceptance of the normative position of pederasty in the
culture leads me to a fresh scrutiny of father-son relations, since the lover
as educator in some sense stands in place of the father. The possibility or
probability of an erotic charge between father and son was denied in
antiquity because that relationship founded the social order. Horizontal
desire for one like oneself is the repressed, unconscious desire of this text;
it is gratified by being transformed into a vertical (asexual) desire of father
for son.

3. A recent treatment with a good bibliography of the scholarship on this play is Zeitlin,
"Power of Aphrodite." On marriage as thematic, see, e.g., Reckford, "Phaethon"; Segal,
"Pentheus and Hippolytus," 138–39, and "Solar Imagery"; Burnett, "Hearth and Hunt."

4. See the Introduction and works cited there, esp. Sedgwick, *Between Men*, for an analysis
of homosocial desire. On this point, see Dover, *Greek Homosexuality*, esp. pp. 1, 171; Sergent,
Homosexuality; Licht, *Sexual Life*, p. 445.

The Father's Story

While the primary antagonists in the drama are Aphrodite and Hippolytos or Aphrodite/Phaedra and Artemis/Hippolytos, Theseus is necessary to Aphrodite, and the relationship of father and son is crucial to the play's resolution. As in so many other Greek tragedies, the father is not just a father but *the father*, as function: his psychological and biological relationship to his son are paralleled by a social role. To recognize this clustering in the play, we have only to remember the position of Theseus, national hero of Athens and, like Herakles and Perseus, a killer of monsters. As a king, Theseus is supported by Zeus, the Olympian king, the patron of his representatives on earth; therefore, Theseus in his discovery of Phaedra's note asserts that Hippolytos has shamed not only his father but also the august eye of Zeus (886). Celebrated in Athenian ritual, himself a figure for initiation, Theseus brings together the psychological and sociopolitical elements in fatherhood.

By using Theseus in her plan to take revenge on Hippolytos, Aphrodite makes of him a great sufferer. This much is clear when Artemis, hearing him groan, says, "It bites you, this story?" (1313), and names him as one of the three primarily affected by the events of the play (1403–5). Although Theseus suffers the loss of wife and son, in psychological, sociopolitical, and discursive terms, his wishes are granted. Thus, he simultaneously loses and wins.

Despite his later grief at what he has done, Theseus wants the death of Hippolytos. There is ample evidence that this father is hostile to his son and that Theseus stands in relation to Hippolytos as does Laius to Oedipus. As Artemis points out, Theseus causes his own suffering through his rashness and stubbornness: "Too soon you hurled curses and killed your own son" (1323–1324); he should have waited to see what divine signs would attend Hippolytos's oath (1321–23). Why doesn't he wait? His haste is well motivated if we consider it the result of a prior hostility to his illicit offspring. Certainly there is evidence of an inheritance of paternal antagonism, since Theseus kills his son through the agency of his own father: "O Father Poseidon, those three curses that you once promised me, with one of them make an end of my son; may he not escape this day" (887–90). Given that Theseus has already cursed him thus, why does he doubly punish his son, adding exile (a lesser sentence) to death? The excess or supplement marks psychological and dramatic overdetermination and acts also as a signifier of paternal violence.

The tone of the interaction between Hippolytos and Theseus further suggests that a history of distance lies behind the immediate episode; we surmise that the two men are not suddenly at odds, following a history of trust, but rather have never been "close."[5] Theseus saves his emotion for the Chorus and the audience, giving Hippolytos only silence and then cold generalizations from which Hippolytos must infer what is wrong. Moreover, though Hippolytos calls on Theseus again and again as his father (905, 923, 983, 1041, 1348, 1362–63, 1378), Theseus never names the relationship. The two are at odds in part because of the difference between them. Theseus is fleshly and scornfully ascribes to Hippolytos the asceticism of Orpheus (953). Because the father is so entrenched in his own world view, he cannot trust his son; he does not believe in his holiness any more. Rather, he accuses Hippolytos of hypocrisy, of claiming great purity when he is really, so Theseus thinks, a great sinner: "You the extraordinary man who keeps company with the gods? You the virtuous one, untouched by evil?" (948–49). Theseus counters in advance an argument that men are not sexual, while women are (966–67), by asserting that "young men are no more secure than women when Kypris stirs up their young heart" (968–69). Hippolytos's great defense, of course, is the implausibility of his having touched Phaedra. First, he is not like other men—he has a "virgin soul" (1006) and no knowledge of sex except through books and pictures (1004–5). Further, he claims no interest in affairs of state which could have led him to desire Phaedra for the position she might confer; rather, he prefers "Hellenic contests" (1016–17) to political power.

Theseus rejects these answers; everything he knows about Hippolytos is irrelevant as he reconstructs his son according to his own nature and "masculinity" in general. Hippolytos cannot be tolerated as different from or other than his father. The play in this way exposes the often forgotten truth that patriarchy does not give power to all men equally. If we see Theseus as a castrating father who is actually hostile to his son, we can see that he has succeeded even when he seems to have failed.

This violence satisfies Theseus's other, more conscious, desires—most important, those for himself and his position. His lack of concern for Phaedra herself is striking. When he returns from his visit to the oracle and hears the women's cries, he thinks first about his father, a natural enough mistake, and then about his children: "Woe, has something stolen the life of my children?" (799). But at no point does he think of Phaedra,

---

5. E.g., Norwood, *Essays*, p. 89, suspects that there was never any feeling between them. On the splitting of the father into Pittheus (grandfather) and Theseus, see Segal, "Pentheus and Hippolytus," p. 135.

or grieve for what has happened to her. His subsequent mourning is mostly for himself: "Woe for my sufferings; I have suffered the greatest of evils" (817–18); "I wish I were below earth" (836); "You have destroyed [me], and worn me away" (839). Finally, when he reads Phaedra's message, he is most anxious not about her fate but about his honor: "Hippolytos has dared to touch my bed, dishonoring the august eye of Zeus" (885–86). We can say then that Phaedra matters not for herself but for what she signifies about Theseus. In sum, the shame is not the woman's but the husband's and father's.[6]

Theseus's social position makes his reputation especially important. His role as culture hero is alluded to in the text (34–37, 977–80) and would have been well known to an Athenian audience. It was Theseus who conquered the Minotaur with the help of Ariadne, and fought the Amazons. Not only did he triumph over monsters and in this way imitate the cosmogonic acts of Zeus, but he was a civilizer. He brought order to the road between Troezen and Athens and founded Athens as we know it; he settled all the inhabitants of Attica in the city, making them a people, and instituted the coining of money.[7] As city founder and representative of Zeus, then, Theseus must uphold his name; as he says, he must punish Hippolytos because if he does not, the monsters he has tamed will deny his accomplishments (977–80).

But since the city founder must also establish a lineage, an underlying issue remains as to who will rule in Athens—the legitimate sons of Phaedra or the illegitimate son of the Amazon. The other sons are mentioned repeatedly (305–9, 421–25, 717, 799, 847, 858) and cause the plot to take shape. Concern for them leads Phaedra first to speak and then to write her telling lie. Theseus takes as axiomatic "the enmity between bastard and legitimate" (962–63); Hippolytos mourns for his mother's birth pangs that brought forth a bastard (1082–83).[8] Theseus's defense of his honor and position in the city would require protection, even if it meant killing his son, but in this instance the son sacrificed is the illegitimate one, one who is not capable of carrying on that name in any case.

Theseus's hasty curse settles another paternity case as well, inasmuch as he not only gets rid of the illegitimate son constituted as threat to his

6. Ann Michelini has pointed out that his response is largely a matter of convention, but that convention is then open to the same interpretation.

7. Plutarch *Theseus* 24, 27.

8. For the point of view that the bastardy is irrelevant, see Barrett, *Hippolytos*, p. 363. See also Rankin, "Euripides' Hippolytos," pp. 75, 78; Grube, *Drama*, p. 184; Fitzgerald, "Misconception," pp. 27, 29.

honor but is also reassured about his own father. According to widely
known legend, he had two fathers, Aigeus and Poseidon.[9] In this text the
death of Hippolytos functions to resolve Theseus's doubt in this matter.
When Poseidon heeds his call and punishes Hippolytos, Theseus treats it
as evidence that Poseidon "was truly my father, since he has heard my
prayers" (1169–70).

Theseus's use of his father's curse links paternity to language—is it a
sure curse? is Poseidon his father?—in a way typical of patriarchy. Assurance that one's son is one's own means that he bears the father's name,
and as Spivak remarks, "The desire to make one's progeny represent his
presence is akin to the desire to make one's words represent the full
meaning of one's intention."[10] The text explicitly focuses on these issues:
Theseus's longings for honor and reputation, for legitimate heirs to rule
Athens, to know his own father, are analogous to his desire for clear
meaning. Ordinarily, words tend to have a shifting relationship to deeds,
feelings, thoughts.[11] Theseus is troubled by his recognition of this problem
and has the fantasy that "men should have a sure token established of their
friends . . . to tell who is true and who is not, and all humans should have
two voices, one just and one however it falls out, so that the one thinking
unjust thoughts would be refuted by the just, and we would not be deceived" (925–26, 928–31).

The text fulfills his fantasy in two ways. First, his own word has power,
granted to him by his father. Having disdained Hippolytos's demand for
oaths, calling him a "magician," he himself becomes a magician: through
the power of his father, his curse is a performative and, like magic, works
instantaneously.[12] We see the devastating force of paternal language. Second, he ultimately gets the voice he longs for. Although Theseus believes
that Phaedra's body and the tablet with her story are sure proof ("clearest
witness of the corpse here," 972) and the voice giving Hippolytos the lie,
he is wrong. Nonetheless, he *does* get the voice he asked for, for Artemis,
a detached voice, tells him the whole story. Even if he does not like what
he hears, hearing it resolves his epistemological concern, and he is no
longer in doubt as to how he knows what he knows.

Thus far we have seen that Theseus's implicit and explicit desires are

9. See Plutarch *Theseus* 3, and Bacchylides 13 (Edmonds), for legends.
10. Spivak, "Displacement," p. 169.
11. The play is full of references to the search for signs or clarity: 269, 371 (*asēma*,
Phaedra's illness is without sign), 346 (*saphōs*), 386 (*saphēs*), 585 (*saphes*), 857–58 (*deltos . . .
sēmēnai*), 925–26 (*tekmērion saphes*), 972 (the corpse); by contrast, because of Phaedra's and
Hippolytos's vows of silence, much necessarily remains hidden. For an analysis of speech
and silence in the play, see Chapter 5 as well as Knox, "*Hippolytus* of Euripides."
12. Knox, "*Hippolytus* of Euripides," comments that Theseus's speech becomes fact.

gratified, despite his apparent suffering at the hands of Aphrodite. To the extent that he was hostile to his son because of the latter's difference from him, he desires his death; to the extent that the son was a threat to him and his legitimate line, he is also satisfied. In the process of killing his illegitimate son, he is reassured about his own dubious paternity. Finally, as paternity is established, so is meaning made stable, for he has won sure signs from the goddess Artemis.

In the ending contrived by Euripides, he makes further gains from his losses. Let me note first that the playwright has gone to considerable lengths to create the concluding tableau of the father cradling his broken son in his arms.[13] Plays on the Phaedra-and-Hippolytos theme do not always end thus, and it is awkward to accomplish: the messenger says first that Hippolytos "is no longer" and then has to modify that statement to allow for his entrance (1162–63). The very awkwardness is a signal of how important it must be, and indeed is. First, the father-son Pietà accomplishes the displacement of the mother (specifically, Phaedra), for the traditionally feminine gesture of cradling one's child is here performed by Theseus. Second, the appearance of Hippolytos—on the point of death, but not yet dead—makes possible the representation of both the rupture and the reunion of father and son. Hippolytos frees his father from blame and denies any claim of vengeance (1449); moreover, he wishes that Theseus might have such noble legitimate sons (1455). This double gesture simultaneously covers up evidence of the earlier hostility and reminds us of the question of rule implied by his illegitimacy.

In these last words Hippolytos participates in a cultural and textual tendency to bolster the institution of marriage by identifying its problems with the female. As a bastard Hippolytos would ordinarily be a primary sign of the instability of marriage, and as I have mentioned, the text shows a persistent concern with bastardy. In fact, however, Theseus is responsible for the vulnerability of this marriage, since it was his excessive desire that led to the rape of the Amazon and the birth of Hippolytos, which has threatened his own legitimate line. Theseus's consistently sexual adventures include the seduction of Phaedra's sister Ariadne, as well as the rape of twelve-year-old Helen and the attempted rape of Persephone (Plutarch *Theseus* 29, 30, 31).

But all of this must be muted in a play about the Athenian hero for an Athenian audience. In order to allay concern about the purity of the line,

---

13. Others have noted the importance of the ending, finding a humanistic comfort in it: e.g., Knox, "*Hippolytus* of Euripides," esp. p. 31; Winnington-Ingram, "Hippolytus," esp. p. 191; Segal, "Tragedy of the *Hippolytus*," p. 156; Rivier, *Essai*, pp. 57–58.

Theseus's lechery is projected onto Phaedra in the form of maternal desire for the son. Instead of presenting men raping women who are interested only in other women (Theseus and the Amazon), the play represents female desire as dangerous and overspilling its bounds: Phaedra's desire attacks marriage as it attacks her. The exchange of women lies at the center of marriage rules designed to mediate between extreme exogamy (bestiality) and extreme endogamy (incest), both of which are represented in the extended Hippolytos story: out of desire for a sacred bull Phaedra's mother, Pasiphae, gave birth to the Minotaur (a clear case of excessive exogamy), and Phaedra's desire for her adoptive son verges on the incestuous (excessive endogamy). Theseus as culture hero serves as a focal point for these institutional stresses of excess in either direction. In Greek culture, and in this play, problems of illegitimacy and incest (which break the rules for appropriate partners) seem to male eyes to come from women: the woman once exchanged may not stay so.[14] Anxiety lest female desire throw paternity into question requires monogamy as a way for men to control female sexuality.

The play *Hippolytos* confirms the father in his desire for a son just like himself, rather than for the female other. It affirms that Theseus made a mistake in believing his wife's words when he should have trusted his son's. In the end the tie to the son becomes supreme. Although Theseus risked losing what he really wanted (a son) for honor (through the perishability of woman's fidelity), he is forgiven by his son, and he achieves reunion with Hippolytos. His loss turns out to be a gain. The Father's desires—to get rid of the illegitimate, to retain his honor, to consummate a relationship with a noble heir, to establish the truth through a divine voice—are satisfied.

The Son's Story

Hippolytos, the son, goes through a similar double path: he is punished by the goddess but rewarded by the playwright. The play presents a double vision: he both understands and totally misunderstands what is demanded of him. In Aphrodite's scheme Hippolytos looks for a moment like one with incestuous desires who must be punished for them, but in Euripides' plot he successfully renegotiates this Oedipal configuration and gains the symbolic as his kingdom; although his flesh is torn from him, he is embraced by the father. The son's filial fantasy is fulfilled by convincing his father

14. Cf. Bergren, "Language and the Female," p. 78.

that he is not a rival but rather a loyal subject. And for having shown obedience to the law (after all, he did not touch his father's bed), he gains a marriage cult and songs in his honor. The ambiguity and rivalry that shadowed the father-son relationship are done away with by Artemis at the play's end. Although the price is great, Hippolytos wins reconciliation with his father and continuing recognition for nobility of spirit and repression of the body.

According to Aphrodite, Hippolytos must suffer because he alone of mortals calls her "the worst of divinities" and "refuses the bed and will not touch marriage, preferring instead the company of Artemis, Phoibos's sister, Zeus's daughter" (13–15). We see him act out Aphrodite's claim by refusing to pay his respects to her altar, saying, in effect, to each his own taste in goddesses (104).

But what does he value in worshipping Artemis?

> To you, o Mistress, I bring this woven crown, having put it together [ordered, *kosmēsas*] from your untouched meadow, where no shepherd would think to graze the flock, nor does any iron [implement] come there; untouched, only the honeybee passes through the meadow in spring, and Reverence [*Aidōs*] tends it with river waters. It is lawful only for those to whom nothing is taught but who naturally exercise moderation [*sophrosune*] always in all things; it is lawful for them, not for the low. But o beloved mistress, receive this band [*anadēma*] for your golden head from my pious hand. This gift is mine alone among men; I am with you and I exchange words with you, hearing your voice, though not looking on your eye. May I turn the end of my life as I began it. (73–87)

Hippolytos desires the eternal and spiritual, eschews the ephemeral and physical. On the simplest level, he worships chastity by his reverence for Artemis; therefore, he invokes her as the "most beautiful of maidens" (66). As the play unfolds, we find that he divides women into two classes, the sexual and the chaste, epitomized by Aphrodite and Artemis.[15] He despises the desiring female principle, the goddess of the night, and respects his Amazon mother and patron goddess. This maidenhood, however, seems to be an existential as well as a sexual category, for Hippolytos is an absolutist: while Aphrodite implies the possibility of lip service to her, Hippolytos stresses his purity and the possibility of corruption from any

---

15. Rankin and Smoot, in "Hippolytus as Narcissus," consider Hippolytos with Narcissus; Sergent, *Homosexuality*, pp. 87–101, places Narcissus with Hyacinthus as a model of the beloved.

contact with her. He can only greet such a goddess from afar (102) lest her "nighttime" activities rub off on him.

Moreover, in several ways his worship seems evidence that he wants to stay the same. First, he covets a form of stasis in the meadow, which is twice referred to as "untouched," therefore unchanging. It does not give fruit or grain, because it is not cultivated; it is not useful for animal grazing. Second, those who are with him there are perfect by nature—that is, they do not have to learn virtue—and thus they do not change (compare Chapter 3, on *Hekabe* and custom, *nomos*). Third, his relationship with Artemis is also immune to change in that it is divorced from the body: he can only hear her voice. In sum, the garden of his reverence is unchanging, the object of his worship is incorporeal, and he desires to end life as he began it; Hippolytos seems to avoid the physical as a sign of change and flux.[16]

The sexual is apparently absent in his attention to the chaste goddess, but there are signs that it is only repressed, not nonexistent. The meadow brings with it the resonance of lovemaking; it is, says J. M. Bremer, "par excellence a place where lovers meet."[17] The meadow as a site for eros here figures a different desire, most strongly that for Artemis but also possibly for those of his fellows who accompany Hippolytos. The prologue depicts him as rejecting Aphrodite and what she stands for, and, because he "ever wishes to be with the maiden" (17), as "falling in with company more than mortal" (19). The language used of Hippolytos's desires for Artemis has sexual connotations, which are acceptable to him because she is an absent figure. As a voice (86), Artemis does not separate him from the company of his age mates but rather provides them with a pretext for being together in their worship of her. Although Hippolytos is not sexually active, his companions in the hunt and the age mates to whom alone he speaks (987) constitute his appropriate charmed circle. He does not discount all humankind, only those who are unworthy. Those who naturally moderate themselves (*sophronein*) can inhabit the garden (80).

Hippolytos's perspective is intimately associated with his age. His servant tries to excuse his arrogance by reminding the goddess that Hippolytos is young (114–19). In his idealization of changelessness and his desire to die as he began, we also see signs of an adherence to youth and a resistance to maturity. This same inclination is echoed later in the play

16. Segal, "Tragedy of the *Hippolytus*," pp. 139, 160.
17. Bremer, "Meadow of Love," p. 279. See also Pigeaud, "Euripide"; Corelis, "Hippolytos with the Garland," p. 15, who adds violence to the pattern of imagery.

when he defends himself to his father by saying that he does not wish to rule the city but far prefers contests (1016), for athletics are the province of youth, rule that of maturity.

At a central point in the play when, having heard the Nurse's proposition, he launches into his vitriolic castigation of women, we get an explicit statement of his desires. This outburst leads to his downfall by making Phaedra his enemy, but the same desires are ironically fulfilled by the play's structure. Although I discussed the speech in Chapter 5, I will here emphasize the main points. Hippolytos's fantasy bespeaks his desire for a male world, though not one with a totally static population. His wish "to buy children from the temples of the gods by giving a weight of bronze or iron or gold" (620–622), if granted, would enable male parents to possess male heirs without having relationships with women. He would avoid even the intermediary of money, for the metals are not struck into coin; coinage has been contaminated by the counterfeit female (616–17). His desire for a single *Aidōs* in a garden that is never cut is appropriate to a man who reviles woman as a false coin.

Hippolytos, then, implicitly desires youth and explicitly hates women because of the sexuality he has (dis)placed onto them. We may hypothesize that it is his anxiety about his own position that has led him to imagine woman as a counterfeit coin. Is he not the counterfeit, since the bastard son does not have the stamp of the legitimate? What happens to him in the course of the play? Aphrodite never wins Hippolytos's respect or even acknowledgment; rather, he says, "The words of my father must be obeyed" (1182). As a result of his filial piety, he is accepted by his father, and that concern can be laid to rest. A new intimacy based on claims of nobility is finally established, according to which Hippolytos can be acknowledged and legitimized.

The play does not demand that Hippolytos give up his misogyny or accept women; he gives up his circle of boys in order to enter into a socially acceptable relationship with an older man. In this he seems to identify with the other, chaste, exceptional woman.[18] His characterization of Artemis as a most holy maiden (61, 66) matches his sense of himself (his maiden soul, 1006; his holiness, 1364). He reveres Artemis for those traits that he shares. Named after his mother, the Amazon Hippolyta, he calls on her, recalling her bitter labor that brought him forth (*pikrai gonai*, 1082); he then seems to suffer like her, for he applies a term for birth

18. On identification with the mother or woman, see Barnes, *Hippolytus*, p. 111; Loraux, "Le lit, la guerre"; Segal, "Tragedy of the *Hippolytus*," pp. 141, 160; Zeitlin, "Power of Aphrodite," pp. 77–78, and "Playing the Other."

pangs to himself (*oduna*, 1371). In his first scene with Theseus, he lacks
the speech that would persuade his father, even as he would have deprived
the woman of speech by keeping her and her servants within.[19]

Thus, it is as a woman-identified boy that he suffers. And like his mother,
herself raped by Theseus, he is hurt by the power of the father, the masculine man. In his death the purely destructive power of the phallus stands
revealed: "And with its very deluge and mountainous surge, the wave put
forth a bull, a wild and fierce wonder; the whole earth was full of its voice
shiveringly echoed, a sight revealed more than our eyes could look on.
Straightaway fear seized the horses" (1210–17). The sexual symbolism of
the bull cannot be missed. But what is the nature of the sexuality so
inscribed? When Poseidon appears in the form of the bull, it is adult male
sexuality that rises before us. The potential violence of masculine sexuality,
defined as dominance, is here unleashed against a youth; this scene seems
to inscribe paternal sadism against the son, leading us to interrogate again
the repressed desire propelling the text.

But it is not the bull itself that kills Hippolytos. Rather, it causes Hippolytos's horses to pull him apart by entangling him in the reins. Here is
what the Messenger has to say:

> The master, experienced with horses, pulled on the reins. . . . The horses
> took the fire-fashioned bit in their jaws by force. . . . They would not be
> turned, neither by the hand of the captain, nor by the horsebands, nor
> by the well-built chariot. . . . until in the end he [the bull] tripped up
> and overturned it, throwing the wheel of the chariot against the rock.
> All was confused . . . and the driver, wretched man, was dragged bound
> in a bond hard to unravel, smashing his own head against the rocks and
> tearing his flesh, and crying out things terrible to hear. (1218–39)

This passage calls to mind a similar passage in Plato's *Phaedrus*, a somewhat later text but one similarly preoccupied with relationships between
men. Hippolytos is like the Platonic hero who has gone through the
initiation and triumphed. In the *Phaedrus* the soul is described as tripartite,
imagined as a charioteer and two horses, one chaste and one wanton. The
latter, "heeding no more the driver's goad or whip leaps and dashes on
. . . with head down and tail stretched out he takes the bit between his
teeth and shamelessly plunges on." But the charioteer conquers the wanton
horse, bringing him to his knees: "The driver with resentment stronger
than before, like a racer recoiling from the starting rope, jerks back the
bit in the mouth of the wanton horse with an even stronger pull, bespatters

---

19. On the effeminate man and the way in which pederasty was meant to keep the stigma
of femininity or softness from the boy beloved, see Winkler, *Constraints*, chap. 2.

his railing tongue and his jaws with blood, and forcing him down on legs and haunches, delivers him over to anguish."[20]

In controlling the lecherous horse distracted by the beauties of a youth, the Platonic figure gains the lofty reaches of the dialectic and philosophy. Julia Kristeva's reading of Plato underlines the sexuality inherent in that scene: "Love means always and indistinguishably *love of young people, love of the Good, and love of true discourse.*"[21] In Plato the erotic is dominated but nonetheless represented in the process of domination; in Euripides the two moments are separated in that an erotic force is represented as domination (a kind of rape) and then sublimated.

If we look at the *Hippolytos* through the lens provided by Plato and Kristeva, we can see that Hippolytos, like his father, is confirmed in his desire for that which is like himself, for the masculine. Having briefly survived the father's murderous wish, he is crowned by his touch. The homoerotic content of the Platonic scene is sublimated into philosophy; Hippolytos's homoeroticism is sublimated into religion; philosophy and religion themselves mirror the actual all-male spaces of the gymnasium or the city. Even as the Platonic figure gains an immortal soul through his efforts, Hippolytos is given immortality through fame. Artemis promises that he "will not be anonymous" (1429): girls will dedicate their hair to him on the eve of their wedding. The meadow of his Artemis worship is allowed to remain uncut, suggesting that he does not pass puberty, but the girls must cut their hair, symbolizing their move to womanhood. Without his participating in the hetero-sexual relationship here established, cult and songs will assure his eternal reputation. In this way he gains a name, which ordinary mortal men generally gain through having sons to carry on the line. And in the present, he is reassured by his father, who recognizes him and accepts him: "Woe is me, what a pious and virtuous mind" (1454). "O, you regions of Athens, you are deprived of a priceless man" (1459–60). Finally, Hippolytos's cries of "father" are met this time with Theseus's long-awaited response of "child" (1456). The trial that Hippolytus goes through leads, like his father's, to gratification. Having undergone dismemberment, he is eligible for apotheosis.

The Murder of the Woman-Mother

In conclusion, let me return once again to the murder of the woman-mother, the murder that Irigaray (as noted above) asserts is necessary for

20. Plato, *The Collected Dialogues*, p. 500.
21. Kristeva, *Tales of Love*, p. 62; see pp. 59–69 for discussion.

the "establishment of a certain order in the city." Euripides' play brings it to pass in a number of subtle ways. First, the myth attributes heterosexual desire to women. Second, that desire is then seen as excessive and uncontrollable (even monstrous in the case of Pasiphae's passion for the bull): it is a spur, a goad (39, 1300), driving Phaedra. And like Io who wanders out of her course,[22] Phaedra turns hysteric, thanks to this visitation of the goddess of love. But her madness does not disrupt the order for long; it soon closes in over her head. Third, in this series of strategic moves, Phaedra sentences herself to death before she even acts on her desire. The men do not kill her; the story rather requires that she kill herself, thus making the dominant male morality appear to be accepted even by its victims. Her suicide relieves Hippolytos of the blame for matricide, but it is a form of matricide nonetheless, one that serves to eliminate the figure of the passionate woman. Hippolytos's dream of a world where men can procreate without women is realized when father and son hold one another without a woman present. Both forms of eros associated with Aphrodite—destructive (525–64, 1268–81) and constructive (442–50)—converge on the two men, enacted in their embrace at the behest of Artemis. This device displaces the mortal woman and appropriates the goddess in a script for men only.

Linguistic and social order arise on the basis of this violent treatment of the feminine. As the quest for stability of heirs correlates with Theseus's longing for a truthful voice, so Phaedra's desire has its linguistic correlative. Not only does her desire work through speech and writing, but she and Hippolytos differ significantly around issues of speech and silence: he keeps his vow of silence even at his peril, while she relinquishes hers. Moreover, while he is defined by the garden that does not grow or change, with one Reverence or *Aidōs* in charge of it, she regretfully acknowledges that there is confusion in the word *Aidōs* and that the same signifier can have two referents. Since she accepts the lack of clarity that men resist, since she inscribes the death sentence on her tablet, she makes women seem the source of what men cannot, but nonetheless wish to, control about language as well as sexuality.[23]

Legitimacy was an important concern in fifth-century Athens; the Periclean law of 451 relates citizenship and legitimacy since both mother and father had to be Athenian for offspring even to be legitimate (Demosthenes 59.17). Although that law was not enforced during the period of the

22. Clément and Cixous, *The Newly Born Woman*, p. 20.
23. For a full development of this relationship between sexuality and language, see Chapter 5; on Euripides' frustration of the audience's desire, see Goff, *Noose*.

Peloponnesian War, the issues it addressed did not simply disappear. This play gains some of its force from the discourse around legitimacy. Euripides unsettles Theseus, Athenian hero par excellence, in order to resettle him more securely, having satisfactorily dealt with Hippolytos. Theseus mourns that the "glorious boundaries of Pallas and Athens" have lost Hippolytos (1459–60), but what would Athens have done with him had he lived? Living, he would have been a challenge to the lawful offspring of Theseus; dead, he can simply be the hero. Theseus's heroic deeds included the conquest of the Amazons; his city-founding gesture is secure now because his line is secure.

Artemis leaves, unable to be near Hippolytos while he suffers. While the female characters (woman and goddesses) thus disappear, and while the male bond is enacted on stage, (simultaneously establishing the legitimacy of Theseus's heirs), this play then inserts the institution of a new marriage cult in honor of Hippolytos.[24] Artemis's fiat normalizes what is really quite strange: a male icon worshiped by maidens, an imagined heterosexual union balanced by a staged rapprochement between men. Ceremonial cutting of hair also took place at funerals and at the Apatouria festival of Athens, when boys and girls were registered in the deme but only boys in the clan (phratry). Construing marriage as initiation, we are face to face with the asymmetry of male and female: initiation for girls leads to heterosexual union; initiation for boys leads to the world of men. If Hippolytos is a figure for initiation, we can see new significance in the violence of the bull and horse, since at least Spartan and Cretan rituals included homosexual rape by an older lover.

The civic gains are matched for the son, who gains access to the father's power symbolically and thus gains the discourse denied to him in their agon. Because of the power of the father, the son is constructed within a very narrow range; he must give up the youthful group of his age mates. But if he does that, the rewards are great: a cult of his own and eternal remembrance. He is re-membered for his forgiveness of his father. We see that the *Hippolytos* enacts the story of the destruction of (not the desire for) the mother, and the desire for (not the destruction of) the father. The heterosexual rape of Phaedra is after all a fiction; the truth of the tale is the (dominant-submissive) violence of incest repressed between father and son. Oedipus's is not the only story; the

---

24. Foley, *Ritual Irony*, p. 22, views the ritual as assisting brides in their "potentially painful transition to marriage;" cf. Pucci, "Euripides' *Hippolytos*"; and Corelis, "Hippolytos with the Garland," pp. 4, 84–85.

narrative of Orestes is an alternative to it, in which the attachment and affinity of father and son transcend their hostility. This is the thread leading into the labyrinth of culture as defined by the exchange of women; how can we find our way out without simply reinventing Ariadne?

7 Raped or Seduced?
and Abandoned:
Kreousa, Ion, Xouthos

The *Ion* is a tragedy that is almost a romance. As a result, it shares many structural features with the somber *Hekabe*, *Medea*, and *Hippolytos* as well as the tragicomic *Alcestis*; in it the mother's murder of the son is almost enacted, but then averted.[1] Here once more the vindictive mother who would murder her young is coupled with the father-son plot.

The play opens with the god Hermes informing the audience about past and future events. Years ago, he explains, Apollo raped and impregnated the Athenian princess Kreousa, who abandoned her child in a basket. At Apollo's request, Hermes brought the infant to Delphi, where he was reared by his Priestess, the Pythia (29–49). Kreousa was subsequently married to Xouthos, a powerful military ally of Athens, but they are childless; at the play's opening, they have come to Delphi to consult the oracle about this problem. Hermes tells the audience that Apollo plans to give Ion to Xouthos and so secure the boy's inheritance (69–71). Kreousa will be introduced to Ion only after they have returned to Athens, "so that coming into the house of his mother he will be known to Kreousa, and the union with Apollo will be secret, and the child will have his inheritance" (71–73). It is not clear, however, whether Ion is to be known as Xouthos's son or Kreousa's.[2]

---

1. On form, see Burnett, *Catastrophe*; Knox, "Euripidean Comedy," pp. 250–67; Troiano, "*Ion*," pp. 49–51, with references.

2. Owen, *Ion*, p. xxi, says, "If Hermes is to be trusted, Apollo meant her never to know." On line 71, he says: "The best-laid schemes, even of gods, gang aft agley. Apollo's programme is upset, for the recognition takes place in Delphi" (p. 74). After the intervention of Kreousa, Athena says that Ion was meant to know in Athens (1568); Kreousa's knowledge is not specified. As Sinos, "Characterization," says, "The phrase is purposefully left vague" (p. 129).

Apollo's plan is in any case derailed. Kreousa prematurely discovers that
Xouthos has been "given" Ion as his son; fearing for her own position,
she tries to kill the young man. He is on the point of killing her in
retaliation, when Apollo's priestess interrupts the tragic action, bringing
out the basket and tokens of his birth so that mother and son can recognize
each other. The play ends with Athena, Apollo's emissary, predicting the
generations to come from Ion's stock, and with Kreousa agreeing to keep
her relationship to him secret.

Because the false recognition is allowed almost to run its course before
the "true" recognition is enacted, the *Ion* appears both tragic and comic;
like the *Alcestis*, it also affects female and male differently. In the potentially
tragic plot, Euripides constructs Kreousa on the model of the other excessively vindictive women: like Hekabe, Medea, and Phaedra, Kreousa
is shifted from the position of sympathetic victim to the position of unsympathetic monster when she is represented as attempting the murder
of her son.[3] In the tragedies of *Hekabe* and *Medea*, which make it abun-
dantly clear that heirs are of primary importance to the Greek male, the
aggression of the women denies the fulfillment of that desire; in this
interrupted tragedy, the desire of father for son is granted.[4]

The *Ion* is most like the *Hippolytos*, for both represent the reunion of
father and son. Moreover, both plays begin and end with speeches by the
gods; in each an incomplete prologue prophecy is followed by a promise
for the future; in each the lineage at Athens is in question, and the relationship of purity to bastardy is explored. Like Hippolytos, Ion is obsessed
with purity; he is devoted to the god of light, and Hippolytos to that
god's sister, Artemis. Like Hippolytos, Ion makes a long speech in which
he articulates the reasons not to accept secular power (585–606), thus
seeming to share Hippolytos's desire to remain a youth forever. Each of
them has a mother who was raped, and each was separated from that
mother at birth. Ion is a son who almost kills his mother and whose
mother almost kills him; in the *Hippolytos* the stepmother does in effect

3. Owen, *Ion*, p. xxvii, comparing her with Medea and Hermione in Euripides' *Andromache*, says: "Creusa is one of those women that Euripides is especially fond of drawing,
who become completely unbalanced when they feel that they have been grievously wronged."
Doolittle, p. 31 in her translation of *Ion*, calls Kreousa "mother of sorrows," but like Hekabe
she moves to the position of one who would inflict sorrows on others.

4. Forehand, "Truth and Reality," points out the interconnection of dynastic and psychological motives: "Xuthus has dynastic reasons for wanting a son, but the needs of his
self-concept are even more powerful. The existence of a son confirms his virility and dra-
matically relieves him." He notes that the Aegeus scene in the *Medea* reveals "the dominant
place of this need in the male ego" (p. 180). Grube, *Drama*, pp. 19, 21, connects the
importance of father-son ties to male same-sex desire, as does Poole in "Male Homosexuality,"
pp. 115–16.

murder the son. In the *Hippolytos* active female sexuality is closely related to female speech, which is in consequence deemed dangerous; Phaedra is ultimately displaced in favor of the father-son bond. The *Ion* too requires female silence and works through a strategy of displacement to satisfy the (misogynistic) Greek male desire to reproduce male from male.[5]

The *Ion* develops a double story line, the story of Kreousa and that of Ion, and both of them seem to end happily: Kreousa finds her son (giving Athens a properly autochthonous heir); Ion finds a biological as well as a surrogate father.[6] Like the *Alcestis*, however, the *Ion* achieves its comic effect only by covering over the woman's loss; in fact, her gain depends on her not saying what has happened to her. In *Alcestis* the joke Herakles plays on Admetos clearly depends on Alcestis's silently acceding to her own exchange (see Chapter 2); erasing the violence done to Kreousa makes possible the happy resolution to the *Ion*. Critics have typically discussed Apollo's morality and his vision (or lack thereof); such issues not only intersect with questions of the play's genre, but should also be seen as mapped on the ground of the woman's body. That grounding, however, is often ignored. For instance, George Gellie mingles the questions of rape and genre in a revealing way: "Our pleasure in the repeated story [of rape] derives largely from our condemnation of Apollo. . . . But the one thing nobody could do was to condemn Zeus (or Apollo) for immorality in a story about the supplying of divine forebears to a human society. That is the thing one cannot do; so, in a comedy, Euripides does it. This exposes the game that is being played and advertises the degree of contrivance to which poet and audience are party. It makes the joke all the better."[7] He

5. Like Oedipus, Ion was exposed at birth; his mother seems to convey the rule to her consort; he knows only one thing (311); as Oedipus claims to be a child of Luck (*Tuchē*), Ion calls on *Tuchē*, who saved him from acting unworthily (1514); and not only is he a creature of Apollo, but he too is anxious lest his mother turn out to have been a slave (1382). Still, they differ: Ion's desire for his mother is explicit and appropriate, and his attempted murder is based on ignorance, whereas Oedipus runs off to attack Jocasta precisely because of who she is. Further, unlike Oedipus, Ion cannot read Kreousa's cryptic speeches (429–30), nor has he tried to track down his mother. He lacks the heroic qualities that make for the suffering of Oedipus. Wolff notes in "Design," p. 170, that "this plot turns on revelations of the truth about the past, on knowledge and recognitions (recalling, in this respect, the story of another foundling, Oedipus)." Cf. Knox, "Euripidean Comedy," p. 258.

6. For consideration of the happy ending, see especially Burnett, "Human Resistance"; Rosivach, "Earthborn"; Wolff, "Design."

7. Gellie, "Apollo," pp. 94–95; Saxonhouse, "Myths," p. 260, argues that Euripides "has also asserted a new vision, one that introduces the female into the origins of the cities and reveals the city's contradictory needs for mutuality and openness as well as for exclusiveness"; in a note she observes, "Although the ending may be satisfying on the political level, this does not mean that all questions are resolved, particularly in terms of Apollo's role in the events and the relationship between humans and the gods."

ignores the fact that the joke, as in the *Alcestis*, requires the complicity of the female character and consequently places the woman in the audience in a predicament. What happens to the spectator as she participates in Gellie's "audience contrivance"? Is she complicit in her own metaphoric rape?

Who Are the True Parents?

Like the other plays I have studied, the *Ion* also performs important cultural work; it asks the question "Who is the true parent?" and resolves it in favor of the father, the public community, and the Athenian empire while *simultaneously* enacting a mother-son reconciliation.[8] We see reenacted Ion's birth and early attachment to the maternal figure, then his shift to the father. On the one hand, it is crucial that Ion be born of Kreousa in order to reaffirm Athenian claims of autochthony, that is, their claims that they were the indigenous people of Attica, for she is one of the line of rulers literally born from the earth (Gegenes meaning earth-born). On the other hand, this essential physical bond to the mother is recuperated by the realm of the symbolic for that relationship is rendered private and silent in deference to the tie to the father, who is a stranger.

As Loraux points out, the "exclusion of the female," the male desire to reproduce without women, is always at issue in the Athenian myth of autochthony.[9] DuBois argues that Euripides challenges the claim of autochthony; it seems to me, however, that he attempts to satisfy the requirements of both autochthony and legitimacy. In order to make Ion genuinely autochthonous, and thus appropriately the heir to the Athenian throne, he must be born from Kreousa, who is the native; but legitimacy, name, and inheritance must still come through the father.[10] As Zeitlin says: " . . . Teleologically speaking, the law of the father is maintained on both sides and even advanced through adoption. On the other hand, the play dramatises the role of maternity and the bond between mother and

8. Ferguson, "Tetralogies," gives a less abstract version of this question, noting that Euripides does not provide an unequivocal answer to the question "Who are Ion's parents?"
9. I am indebted throughout this book to the thinking of Loraux on the problems of "birth from one, birth from two" and here particularly to *Enfants*, pp. 129–31, on "le nom Athénien," as well as the chapter "Créuse autochtone." I disagree, however, with the conclusions she draws and her assertion that Kreousa dominates the piece (pp. 204–7, but cf. p. 232).
10. DuBois, *Sowing*, p. 80. Conacher, "Paradox," sees the chief paradox of the play in the contrasting effects of its national-dynastic theme and its treatment of Apollo; Saxonhouse, "Myths," privileges the mother.

child and insists on the necessary reunion of the pair just at the moment when Ion's age should dictate their separation."[11]

Nonetheless—and, I would argue just as necessarily—that separation of mother and son does take place. The pre-oedipal phase of Ion's life is marked by his closeness to Delphi, the navel (*omphalos*, 223) of the world; in Athens, he will be known only as the son of his father. As we shall see, this resolution privileges the symbolic—the Name of the Father—at the *expense* of the body and the mother, while seeming to privilege the mother-son reunion. The myth of autochthony excludes the human female from the ideal of reproduction yet retains the earth, a privileged metaphor for a female body. The play, however, reduplicates the exclusion of the female. The political agenda of the play, its support of Athenian claims of auto-chthony and divine origins, rests on violence to the mother in the past and displacement of her in the present.

Who are the parents of Ion? Kreousa, Apollo, the Pythia, and Xouthos are all named.[12] The text first cites Kreousa and Apollo; but Apollo is absent, and Kreousa soon abandons the infant in the cave of his birth (10–21). That momentary mother-son dyad then dissolves into another, for in the second stage Hermes rescues the baby and brings him to Delphi, where he is discovered by the Priestess. These acts of discovery create two surrogates who give life, if not birth, to the babe, for the Priestess nurtures Ion (*trephō*, 49; *ethrepse*, 319), who then calls her his mother (321, 1324). She acts like the woman of Apollo's house (the temple is repeatedly called a house: *domos*, 34, 129, 249); like a wife, she guards the treasury (*thē-saurōn*, 1141; *thēsaurismasin*, 1394).[13] Third, Ion says he has always con-sidered Apollo his father (*genetōr patēr, pateros . . . Phoibou*) because he feeds him and is his benefactor (136–40). Apollo thus replaces Hermes as the "surrogate" father.

Euripides deliberately increases the number of candidates as, fourth, Ion and Kreousa generate two shadows, his "mother" and her "friend"; in the process of telling each other their sad stories, they conjure up a mother-son reunion which, as Zeitlin observes, "serves retrospectively as the con-vincing rehearsal for the joyful reunion at the end."[14] Then comes the fifth pairing, the one that precipitates the crisis and "the recognition," for

11. Zeitlin, "Mysteries of Identity," p. 181; she critiques the partial truths held both in Bachofen, *Myth*, who points out the evolution of fictive fatherhood here, and in a similar view of autochthony expressed in Saxonhouse, "Myths."

12. Zeitlin, "Mysteries of Identity," pp. 169–74, convincingly adds others, notably the Old Man and Hephaistos.

13. See duBois, *Sowing*, pp. 107–9, on treasury.

14. Zeitlin, "Mysteries of Identity," p. 150.

when Xouthos hears the prophecy, he believes that he is the father of Ion (536, 537). Since Xouthos cannot at first remember any specific liaison with a woman, Ion claims Earth as his mother (542). Xouthos discounts that possibility summarily, but it is of course the central tenet of Athenian autochthony. This father-son pair then dissolves, after the threatened violence, into the original one of mother and son—but not for long: their relationship is to be secret so that Ion can inherit through his father.

Such slippage and repetition are possible because parenthood is seen to derive from both nature and nurture.[15] The answer to the question "Who are the parents of Ion?" is "All of the above," for they have all acted as parents in one sense or the other. Apollo alone is represented as establishing a relationship to the child in both senses: he acknowledges Ion as his own (*emos gar estin*, . . . *ho pais*, 35), but he is named by Ion as parent not because of the biological tie but because Apollo feeds him (*boskonta*, 137). Ion considers the Priestess his mother because she has brought him up (*hē d'ethrepse me . . . mēter'hōs nomizomen*, 319, 321). Kreousa, on the other hand, has an exclusively physical relationship to the child; she carried him in her womb (*gastros diēnegk' ogkon*, 15) and gave birth to him (*tekous'*, 16) but did not nurture him; to emphasize the disjunction, the Greek says she bore the infant but also bore it off to die (*diēnegk'*, 15; *apēnegken*, 16). When Ion and Kreousa discuss her "friend," the same duality predominates: the woman gave birth (*eteke*, 340; *tekousa*, 355), but perhaps the god brought the child up (*ektrephei*, 357). Significantly, Ion is separated from any biological tie: he does not know the mother who bore him (*tekousa*, 308, 324) and has not nursed at any breast (318–19).[16]

The replication of parents is due, then, to the splitting of the social and biological aspects of parenting. The division is promoted by replacing the woman's body at each stage with representations of it. For instance, after his birth from Kreousa's belly (*gastron*, 15), Ion is placed in two other hollows, a cradle within a cave (*antron, koilēs . . . antipēgos*, 17, 19).[17] Euripides clearly gives prominence to the hollow vessel, for Hermes describes it twice and mentions it several times (*ek koilēs petras, aggei*, 31–32; *kutos*,

15. See ibid., p. 171, on modes of reproduction, and p. 180 on nature/nurture. On bearing and nursing, see Daladier, "Mères aveugles," pp. 241–43; this essay asks the larger question of why mothers don't recognize their sons in tragedy and finds the answer in the cultural silence about the sexuality of mothers, who are effectively neutralized as women (p. 244).

16. Hillman, "Abandoning," pp. 393–95, analyzes the need for both mother and nurse from a Jungian perspective.

17. Saxonhouse, "Myths," discusses the parallels between Erichthonius and Ion, emphasizing the shift between womb, cradle, cave. She focuses on the elevation of maternity, calling the *Ion* a "play that primarily extols the unity of the mother and the child" (p. 267). Obviously, I disagree.

37, 39–40). The words *koilē* and *kutos* can refer to any hollow space and sometimes denoted the uterus itself; thus Ion is symbolically born again when the Priestess removes him from the hollow container and again when he meets Xouthos as he leaves the inner sanctuary, the *adutōn* (662), which is, like a woman's body, a *muchos* or innermost recess (228) closed to outsiders. The sanctuary also resembles the vessel it has guarded, for both are decorated with wreaths (*stemmasi enduton*, 224; *antipēg' en stemmasin*, 1338).[18]

Not only can a man have many metaphorical mothers, then, but a male can play the mother by co-opting one of these substitutes. All these hollows that hold the child and therefore replace the woman's body are in fact usurped by the male god: the cave is turned into the site of the rape and exposure; the basket is taken over by Hermes for Apollo; in the temple at Delphi itself, which once belonged to Earth (see the *Eumenides* account of Delphi's history), the female presence has been reduced to a voice speaking Apollo's words and acting as his surrogate. The many answers to the question "Who are Ion's parents?" rest on a textual manipulation of signs for the female body that forwards a cultural effort to displace the female. For the male, the possibility of having many parents means a certain troublesome indeterminacy of identity (see below), but at the same time it holds out two positive possibilities: rebirth, and centrality of the father.

The Mother's Story: Victim, Victimizer, and Silent Partner

The simultaneously divine and autochthonous origins of Athens rest on an incident involving violence to a woman, but the problem of the play, at least as it is discussed in the literature, is in large part the reputation of the god. As we shall see, the two are connected. The play does indeed attempt to redeem Apollo, first by legitimizing that initial moment, making rape seem like seduction, then by representing Kreousa as a would-be murderer and Apollo as the one who rescues her from her own intentions.[19] The "tragic" story thus vilifies her and makes her a suitably monstrous descendant of the Gegenes. She gives up her revenge, however, and becomes "a good woman," a willing accomplice in Apollo's plan; in doing so, she reconfigures her own history in order to hand down her noble autochthonous heritage to her son. A representation of a physical woman

---

18. On *aduton* and *muchoi*, and Ion's rebirth, see Loraux, *Enfants*, pp. 248–50, 252.

19. On the negative construction of Kreousa's resistance to Apollo's plan, see Rosivach, "Earthborn"; Burnett, "Human Resistance."

is necessary for this masculine project, but then even the child is taken away from her. Mother and son will have a closeted relationship, so to speak.[20]

The system of exchange and objectification of women which is at work in Euripides both facilitates and depends on (1) male appropriation of the female body, (2) the appropriation of the product of a woman's labor (the baby), and (3) the construction of knowledge. Catharine MacKinnon argues that "sexuality is to feminism what work is to marxism: that which is most one's own, yet most taken away."[21] In this view, the alienation of the woman from her body makes her like a member of the proletariat. If the woman in heterosexual relations is like the worker, the product of her labor—that is, the child—is also taken away, so that reproduction becomes a form of alienated labor. As MacKinnon points out, much feminist thinking and organizing has focused on issues of the body: abortion, battering, and rape, for instance. Her analysis of cultural domination of women works out best on the subject of rape, for there a woman's sexuality is most obviously not her own.[22]

Rape and the attendant problem of defining consent bring MacKinnon (and us) face to face with the way claims of knowledge are made, with legal standards of evidence, and with the relationship of epistemology to ideology. In general, the nature of rape makes a witness to the event unlikely; without such confirming testimony, judge and jury are left with only competing versions of the truth. Whom should they believe? That will depend on how we define rape. If, with the law, we take it to be nonconsensual sexual intercourse, we must ask who defines consent. Is it not rape if he says he did not mean it as rape, if he thought she consented? Patricia Cholakian remarks: "From a practical point of view, this distinction hinges on whether the woman experienced desire for intercourse before the rape or pleasure during it. In other words, in order to prove that she was raped, the victim is obliged to prove that she did not want to be raped."[23] As MacKinnon argues in her essays, men in authority have been in a position to legislate their "meaning" as truth: hence the epistemological dimension to male power. Male epistemology is female ontology—they know it, we live it.[24] Such modern theoretical questions condition and frame my analysis of Kreousa.

20. For another view, see Loraux, *Enfants*, esp. p. 202, but cf. p. 232, where she notes that the women in the end retreat to silence.
21. MacKinnon, "Feminism...Theory," p. 227.
22. For this analysis, see MacKinnon, "Feminism...Jurisprudence."
23. Cholakian, *Rape and Writing*, p. 117.
24. See MacKinnon, "Feminism...Theory," p. 249: "The parallel between representa-

As I noted when discussing the connection between sacrifice and marriage (Chapter 1), consent distinguishes sacrifice from murder; similarly, consent distinguishes seduction from rape. In animal sacrifice, as we saw, there was considerable latitude in how the community obtained and interpreted that consent: an animal victim was considered to have consented if it nodded its head; but in order to procure the nod the officiating priest might legitimately splash its head with water. As I argued in Chapters 1 and 2, the culture (and in particular the drama) had its ways of constructing female consent to sacrifice in order to take the blame off the men who demanded that sacrifice; the same sleight of hand is at work in the *Ion*. If a woman has been raped, *male* sexual morality is put in question; if a woman has been seduced, *female* sexual morality is put in question. It is important to the line descended from Kreousa that she be above reproach and thus that she was raped; it is important to the reputation of the god that he be above reproach and thus that she desired him. The *Ion* occupies an ambiguous middle ground in this paradox.

Was Kreousa raped or seduced? The text begins by giving a clear answer to this question—she was raped—but then undermines it, subtly blaming the victim the better to praise Apollo. As the prologue speaker in this play, Hermes appears to give "the facts." He says: "Phoibos forcefully yoked in union Kreousa, child of Erechtheus" (10–11). There is no question of consent; Apollo used force. The story of Kreousa's rape is told and retold throughout the play, however, causing the theater audience to revise its conclusions.[25]

Kreousa herself repeats the story, getting different responses. She first talks to Ion, pretending that she is describing a friend's experience. Distancing the events from herself (334–58), she notes merely that the god "mixed" with her friend (*migēnai*, 338); all the suffering (*athlia*, 342, 355) centers on what happened to the child. And, as I will show in the next section, when they finally recognize one another, this same emphasis is maintained. A third account of the rape occurs after Kreousa has heard of Apollo's prophecy to Xouthos; she is speaking to her own people and expounds at length on how she suffered. On this occasion, Kreousa makes the crucial claim: this bed was without desire (literally, grace or charm, *lektrōn prodotas acharistous*, 880). Apollo's song is always associated with

tion and construction should be sustained: men *create* the world from their own point of view, which then *becomes* the truth to be described. . . . *Power to create the world from one's point of view is power in its male form.*"

25. See also Troiano, "*Ion*," p. 47; Wolff, "Design," p. 170. Gellie, "Apollo," p. 94, says, "Euripides seems to believe that the more often we are told about the rape the happier we will be."

the Graces (Charis) and the Muses, but not her bedding with him. In her later exchange with the old man, she goes over the details less poetically, again asserting her unwillingness (*xunēps' akousa dustēnon gamon*, 941).

Not only does the poet make Kreousa vacillate about Apollo's use of force; he even inscribes ambiguity into her accusation.[26] In the long lament she intones on hearing that Xouthos alone has received a son from Apollo (774–75), Euripides has Kreousa cite the attributes of Apollo (881–86), ostensibly to assert a contradiction between his reputation for song and what he did to her. But the appeal of the god is simultaneously inscribed and therefore impresses and remains with the audience: "You came to me with shimmering golden hair, as I gathered yellow petals blossoming with golden light in the lap of my robe; you planted your hands on my white wrists [punningly, implanted with white fruit]; my divine bedpartner besting me led me into the bed of the cave, me shouting a cry of mother, doing a service to the shameless Aphrodite. A wretch, I bore a son to you, which in fear of my mother I threw into your bed, where you yoked unfortunate, sorrowful me in that couch of sorrow" (887–901). She glorifies the god and simultaneously eroticizes him with the attribute of shimmering golden hair, which matches the golden flowers she gathers and thus seems to lodge in her lap. In this version, constraint is oblique, "hands on wrists" compared to Hermes' "force" (*bia*).

Kreousa's ambivalent and ambiguous description is consistent with the cultural attitudes represented in the text: it is not clear that she was a victim. Because of the illicit nature of the union, darkness hides the entire transaction. Secrecy dominates almost from the first (*lathraion*, 45). Kreousa subsequently asks for a hidden prophecy (*krupton*, 334), and she describes the birth as secret (340). This secrecy is the corollary of the force used, following as it does from the fact that it was not a lawful union. Kreousa feels shame and is ashamed to speak (*aidoumetha*, 336; *aidous*, 861; *aischunē*, 395; *aischunomai*, 934). Her silence, then, corresponds to modesty; thus she asks whether she should now maintain that silence or, abandoning her modesty (*aidous*), make public her "shadowy bedding" (860–61). That modest silence in turn makes it difficult to know her point of view. We are never told, for instance, the precise nature of the force used.

The term *aidōs* is almost untranslatable; Liddell and Scott, the standard

Greek lexicon, give this definition: "moral feeling, *reverence, awe, respect* for the feeling of others or for one's own conscience, and so *shame, self-respect*" (emphasis added). But the word is differentially applied to male and female virtues: what a Greek man was ashamed to do differed from what a Greek woman was ashamed to do. In general, a man has "respect" (*aidōs*) for those entitled to his protection—women, slaves, children—whereas a woman's *aidōs* has to do with sexual shame or chastity, the way in which it is crucial that she show self-respect and self-control.[27] In Greek, "shame" does not have a strictly sexual significance, but it does often have that significance for a woman, since as a noun "the shameful thing" (*to aidoion*) means the (mostly female) genitals.[28] Kreousa is represented as feeling ashamed even though she was not at fault, for female honor requires chastity and silence.[29] The silence surrounding rape leads to ambiguity and to precisely the sort of epistemological problem that MacKinnon points out. As in modern times, so here, the rape victim must be questioned: what is she hiding, her desire or her victimization?

The doubts expressed in the text tell us that a woman talking of rape by a god is not to be trusted. Though a mortal coupling with a god may seem patently absurd from a modern point of view, these things "did happen" in antiquity; the questions put to Kreousa may thus be revealing about Athenian attitudes toward female sexuality. For instance, Ion asks whether Kreousa's "friend" might not have suffered injury from some man instead of the god (341; cf. 325). In their later discussion of the incident, Ion suggests further that she may be concealing her own youthful folly: "Did you not slip up in the failings common to maidens, into some hidden unions [*gamous*], then put the blame on the god?" (1524–25). In such a case, her secrecy would hide her own error (and eros). The Priestess, who has kept the basket and its contents safe, not knowing the father, draws the same inference (*noson kruphaian . . . lathra*, 944).

Certain cultural advantages accrue by characterizing this event as not a rape. To accept Apollo as a rapist could result in increased distrust of the

27. There is a striking similarity between the Greek system and what Lila Abu-Lughod found in her study of Bedouin culture: "To have moral worth, these people must show modesty (*hasham*), which must be understood as voluntary deference to those in the system who more closely embody its ideals" (*Veiled Sentiments*, p. 33). She argues that sexual purity is the form most closely associated with women's modesty (pp. 108–45).

28. See Chapter 5 on Phaedra. For a brief consideration of *aidōs*, see Carson, "Putting," pp. 142, 161 n. 20. Phaedra's speech on the two forms of *aidōs* has generated some scholarly interest: see Winnington-Ingram, "Hippolytus"; Segal, "Purity and Shame"; Pigeaud, "Euripide"; and Lombard, "Aspects."

29. For an expert working-out of this problem in the *Heptaméron*, see Cholakian, *Rape and Writing*.

oracle, a distrust already inscribed in the text.[30] After all, should a god
take part in a cover-up? But Ion suggests that Apollo would, when he
says, "This business is shameful; do not ask him . . . . It is not possible that
any one will prophesy about these things to you . . . Give it up, woman.
The god cannot be made to give prophecies against himself [*tananti' ou
manteuteon*]" (367, 369, 372–73). Similarly, Athena comes in the god's
place because "some blame might attach to him" (*mempsis*, 1558).

The stigma spreads, moreover, from the god's worship to the entire
human realm of sexual conduct, as Ion makes clear after Kreousa leaves
the stage: if Apollo has really been guilty of rape (*parthenous biai gamōn
prodidōsi*, 437–38), then "it is not right to call men wrong for imitating
behaviors the gods deem good, but those who teach these things" (449–
51). Moreover, the way Apollo treated (and treats) Kreousa is conflated
with the treatment she anticipates from Xouthos; she suffers the same
"charmless [*acharistous*] betrayals of the bed from men and gods" (878–
80).[31] The Chorus makes the connection between the wrongs of Apollo
and the projected wrongs of Xouthos, when it speaks of "hat[ing] men
who contrive evil, making their sins look good with decorative devices"
(832–34).

In point of fact, Apollo's behavior is consistent with assumptions about
male behavior, as articulated at several points in the play. So, for instance,
Kreousa's experience is analogous to that of Ion's imaginary mother; it is,
moreover, assumed that Xouthos has had illicit sexual encounters (545,
813–16) and that his unknown partner abandoned the child at Delphi.
Then too, Kreousa, like Medea, believes that her experience is like that of
other women: "Oh long-suffering women, oh the daring of gods. What
then? Where shall we get justice if we suffer injustice from those in power?"
(252–54). Other textual generalizations about women are based on her
experience: women are used badly by men, who hate the good with the
evil; "thus we are all by nature unfortunate [*dustucheis pephukamen*]" (398–
400).

30. Ferguson, "Tetralogies," p. 114, points out that Apollo is discredited "not so much
because of his treatment of Creusa as because he, the god of prophecy, fails to foresee the
course of events." I do not want to get embroiled in the historical question of Euripides'
position on the oracle at Delphi; nonetheless, the alleged rape does make up part of the
evidence against the god: see Verrall, *Euripides the Rationalist*, pp. 133–36; Norwood, *Greek
Tragedy*, p. 238; Murray, *Euripides*, p. 121. Others find this a misguided approach: Wasserman, "Divine Violence," pp. 590, 602; Burnett, "Human Resistance," p. 97. Hanson,
"Euripides' *Ion*," p. 42, takes the play as unflattering to Apollo but feels that the attack is not
Euripides' main point; Conacher, p. 33, finds that the attacks are answered but that the god
nonetheless looks shabby. For a thorough consideration, see Lloyd, "Divine and Human."

31. LaRue, "Creusa's Monody," p. 130, points out that "betrayal" here (*prodotas*) echoes
the same word at 864 and links Apollo to Xouthos.

Especially given these generalizations, the play suggests not only that rape was not exceptional but that it was not so different from marriage. In some cases, in fact, the vocabulary of rape was indistinguishable from that of marriage: *gamos* (union) and *zeuxein* (to yoke) described both,[32] though in the case of rape the legitimizing rituals were absent, replaced by force (*bia*) and secrecy.[33] But how much power did the bride wield in marriage by exchange? Kreousa was given in legal marriage to Xouthos as a prize for his aid in war. Ion asks, "Did he come as an ally? For which he married you?"; Kreousa replies, "Receiving thus a dowry of war and a prize for his spear" (*phernas polemou, doros labōn geras*, 297–98). She is won by the spear as much as Andromache and the Trojan women were. Heterosexual relations were not ordinarily an arena for the exercise of female power.

We must be careful of anachronism here: rape did not carry the same meaning in fifth-century Athens as it does now in the European and North American context after long and arduous feminist organizing and education. In Athenian law, rape was a less severe crime than adultery or seduction: the man involved in adultery could be put to death; he only paid a fine in the case of rape.[34] But for the woman, the potential punishment was the same in either case: expulsion (literally dishonor, *atimia*). If the body of the citizen man represented the boundary at which, as David M. Halperin says, "the operation of almost all social and economic power halted,"[35] the body of the woman was constructed as legitimately permeable depending not on the woman's experience but on the degree of injury to her male guardian. To a present-day feminist, the text might seem to suggest that all heterosexual intercourse is a form of rape; the ancient view seems rather to legitimize rape through this same slippage.

Blame the Victim-izer

When Kreousa asserts, as she does just before her final exit, that Apollo has done well, she renounces not only her anger at the god's betrayal but her perception of his violent assault. This resolution, whereby the revised narrative can erase earlier violence ex post facto, underwrites a later ro-

---

32. Loraux, *Enfants*, p. 216, discusses the confusion of marriage and sexuality, meant to be separate, but women's sexuality is constructed as submission in both rape and marriage.

33. Against which the citizen woman was supposed to be protected by the law. See Halperin, *One Hundred Years*, p. 92.

34. Lysias 1.32–33. Cf. Xenophon *Hiero* 3.3–4; Harrison, *Law*, pp. 34–35; Dover, "Classical Greek Attitudes," p. 62; Cohen, "Seclusion."

35. Halperin, *One Hundred Years*, p. 96.

mance tradition in which the rapist/hero renders his behavior acceptable by marrying his victim. Euripides further redeems Apollo by displacing masculine guilt onto Kreousa both in the past and in the present. Since her attempted murders are recounted, the audience experiences them even though the catastrophe is in each case avoided—and Apollo gets even more credit by preventing them.[36]

First, in the quasi-Marxist terms of MacKinnon, after the rapist god dispossessed Kreousa of her body, a second alienation took place, for Kreousa gave away the valuable "product" of her labor. Divine intercourse always leads to birth; the text thus conflates rape with birth and infanticide, through the shared attributes of secrecy, silence, shame. As I mentioned earlier, Athena explains Apollo's absence by remarking that if he had come, he might have been blamed (1558–59), but she does not say for what. The audience must read between the lines; if temporality implies causality, she does suggest that it would be for sexual misconduct when she says in the very next line: "Thus this one bore you from father Apollo" (1560).[37] The potentially problematic sexual wrong is canceled out by Ion's rescue, which is emphasized.

Insofar as illegitimate birth is made tantamount to the exposure of the infant, emphasizing the birth over the rape tends to foreground Kreousa's culpability rather than her victimization. The parallel usage of the word for "wrong" indicates that there are two wrongs: Apollo's to her (e.g., *adikei*, 355; *adikēsanta*, 972), which leads to the wrong done to the infant (*adik' epaschen ex emou*, 963); the secret sexual encounter leads to the secret birth, and then to murder. When Kreousa tells Ion her story after they have identified each other, she emphasizes the secrecy of the bedding and does not mention force (1484, 1487, 1489). She spends twelve lines describing what happened to the infant, only two recounting what happened to her. Moreover, no matter how the sexual encounter is defined, whether as rape or seduction, the attempted infanticide is always linked to it. Finally, the references to the exposure are further increased because Ion, the victim of real and imaginary abandonment, also alludes to his deprivation. Thus, the exposure is referred to more often than the rape.

Psychoanalytic theory speculates that the infant, denied the milk of the mother (either because he is biting and hurting her or because another child has come along to take his place), responds with aggressive fantasies

36. As Burnett notes, "Human Resistance," p. 94, Apollo acts to prevent the characters from destroying one another, but, I would add, only when his sanctuary is at risk.

37. The blame is tricky to pin down, for it is bound up with the god's behavior to Kreousa, the inefficacy of his plan, and his false prophecy. As discussed below, Ion's parentage is bound up with the validity of the oracle.

of destroying her but justifies his own hostility by simultaneously imagining that she is harming him. Euripides, taking the part of the son, creates a scenario in which the mother does harm the infant first.[38] Euripides justifies Ion's attack on Kreousa by depicting her as the aggressor.

The text inscribes Kreousa's defense, to be sure, for "will" was taken from her in both these early moments of her womanhood (*akousa*, 941, 1499). Not only was she an unwilling victim, but she was isolated; without any support, she *had* to abandon the baby. The necessity of hiding the birth from her parents was decisive; from the first we are told that the birth was unknown to her father (14) and later that she was in fear of her mother (898). She gave birth alone (948–49; cf. 957, 1486–87), apart from her mother (1489). Like Persephone, she was gathering flowers, but the difference between these victims of rape is telling. Demeter responded to her daughter, whereas Kreousa's cries to her mother go unanswered (893).[39] Her isolation is thus stressed at both moments in this story of womanhood: rape and birth.

Because her labor and the birth (like the rape) were secret, hidden first in the cave and then in the temple where Hermes took the basket, hermeneutic difficulties surround their interpretation as well. Euripides introduces two somewhat troubling discrepancies. First, Hermes says that Kreousa gave birth at home (*en oikois*, 16), but Kreousa tells the Old Man that she delivered the child in the cave where she was raped (899, 949). Second, she speaks of the painful birth (869, 900–901), but Athena says that the god made it painless (1596). By an act of condensation, the secrecy of the rape slips into the secrecy attendant on illegitimate birth; the pain of the rape is made visible only in the birth pangs, and then those are erased as well in the greater (imagined) pain that the son suffered.

On one level, the very existence of these divergent narratives exposes the difficulty of knowing what another has experienced. But on a second level, each version reflects also the rhetorical agenda of the speaker. For instance, the question of the place of Ion's birth gives A. S. Owen the occasion to say that Kreousa's goal "may have been to make her tale to the old man more pathetic. She does not always adhere strictly to the truth."[40] So, Athena's goal is to exculpate Apollo, whereas Kreousa must justify herself. Kreousa in her anger alludes to Apollo's own birth from Leto, which is traditionally associated with general fruitfulness (919–22), and the Chorus mentions the easy birth of Athena (452–56). If Kreousa's

38. Roheim, "Dragon." I use the masculine following Euripides and the theorists.
39. On Kreousa's affinities to the other goddesses, see Loraux, *Enfants*, pp. 245–46; also Zeitlin, "Mysteries of Identity," p. 159.
40. Owen, *Ion*, p. 69 on line 16.

birth experience was difficult, then she is distinguished from the divine models. If not, she is like them and does not need or deserve our pity.

Even if Owen is correct and Kreousa has misnamed the place of birth, she need not be lying; she collapses the sites of rape, birth, and exposure, for from her point of view they are analogues or even identical. Her pain comes from her isolation, pointed up by the difference from other births. It is not simply that she is duplicitous, as Owen suggests, but that she has had a different experience. And yet the audience is left with Athena's colonizing "master narrative," a version of the events that elides both the rape and the pain. And Kreousa accepts that account.

In the text's deployment of the motif of exposure, then, Kreousa is alternately excused and blamed. Euripides goes further, however, in darkening her reputation. He has her reenact that assumed "murder" ("I killed you unwillingly," 1499). Euripides could have brought about the recognition at any point, as could Apollo. He/they choose to wait until Kreousa has once again launched a plot against her son; he/they choose to torment her further by seeming to give Xouthos a son who is his alone, whereupon Kreousa resists the god's plan and disrupts what Hermes has announced as a sure future because she feels betrayed by her husband and by the god (*posis hēmōn prodotēs*, 864; *prodotas*, 880).

How is the audience to judge Kreousa? On the one hand, it must feel sympathy; it is led to support her because the internal audience, the Old Man and the women of the Chorus, do so. The latter, for instance, are loyal to her as a woman; in a move unprecedented in tragedy, they break the silence enjoined on them by Xouthos and support her decision to take preventive measures (758–62).[41]

The text fully represents the position that Kreousa is legitimately defending herself because of the harsh material and ideological reality of women's situation. Since the wife's function was to reproduce and provide heirs, Kreousa's "childlessness" might well have been held against her. Had she continued to be infertile, Xouthos could have divorced her and taken a new wife. Speculating on how Xouthos begot Ion, for instance, the Old Man asserts that Xouthos should have asked for a new wife rather than sneaking off (839–41); similarly, Medea believes that Jason would have been justified in marrying the princess if she, Medea, had given him no heirs.

Kreousa's concern for her "childlessness" is at least in part a concern for her position in the household; she talks about her isolation, "inhabiting

41. For considerations of gender in the play, see also Zeitlin, "Mysteries of Identity," pp. 164–65; Saxonhouse, "Myths."

a wasteland of orphaned halls" (789–91), and fears that she will be deprived of house as well as children (*steromai d'oikōn, steromai paidōn*, 865). Both she and the Old Man fear that Ion, as the outsider, will be an enemy to the house (813–16, 836–38, 1291, 1293). The Old Man predicts that she will be insulted and thrown out (808–11; cf. 1295); she thinks she will be killed (1301). Hearing his own good fortune, Ion pities Xouthos's wife, who has the bitter misfortune to be childless, and he anticipates that he will be hated by her (610–11). Because he appreciates her plight, he fears that she will attack him. Although Ion does not intend to dislodge her—as he says, "I did not come with weapons into your land" (1292)—everything in her experience combines to make her believe this of him. Finally, Kreousa expects to be accused of murder if Ion dies in Athens, whether she is guilty or not, because stepmothers are thought to be murderous to children (1025).[42] The Priestess simply acknowledges this hostility as a fact and as a reason for Ion to overlook Kreousa's plot against him (1329–31). In short, if one wife is childless, she is seen as a failure; if two women both have children, then there will be a conflict over inheritance.

In these ways, Euripides establishes sympathy and understanding for Kreousa. At the same time, however, that sympathy is undercut in large measure by the overarching structure of dramatic irony. That is, the audience knows, first, that Ion is really her son, not an impostor, and second, that he does not intend to threaten her. All the violence she fears is imagined, not to say projected. Clearly there is no immediate physical danger to her.

The Old Man is most obviously excessive, for he goes so far as to suggest that they burn down Apollo's sanctuary. Although she resists the attack on Apollo, Kreousa is nonetheless infected by such violence; she directs her hostility to the child instead. Here too we can see a choice made by Euripides, for the plot is discovered in time, but the audience nonetheless sees its effects. The doves associated with the sanctuary are mentioned in the prologue as constantly befouling the temple that Ion as constantly must clean (106–8); they are in this way his opposite number. In the scene of attempted murder, one dies in his place. As the Servant reports, just when the Old Man had poisoned Ion's drink (1184–86), someone uttered a blasphemy (1189); the pious Ion bade all those present to throw out their wine. When a dove drank Ion's spilled wine, "straightaway his

---

42. As a consequence of this set of beliefs and practices, the enmity of stepmother to stepchild was taken for granted in antiquity. We can see this in *Hippolytos* and *Medea*, as well as in this play.

body shook and took on a Bacchic frenzy; his voice screamed out moaning incomprehensibly; the whole crowd of feasters wondered at the labors of the bird" (1204–6). In this way the audience experiences even the murder that does not kill and is made viscerally aware of the intended consequences of Kreousa's actions.

Though it is Apollo's actions—silence and withdrawal—that have twice made this woman a would-be killer, Euripides constructs her as violent. Moreover, the audience is encouraged to see Kreousa (like Medea) as representative of women in general, because the text underlines gender. For instance, Kreousa calls on the women of the Chorus for assistance as "women of my loom and shuttle" (747). Even her murder plot is tied to her femininity, since as in the other plays the use of poison is represented as typically a woman's deed (*gunaikeion*, 843; cf. 616–17). By affiliating her revenge with women's devices, Euripides gives her behavior more general significance when she acts on what must seem like paranoid fantasies.

Kreousa is not, however, entirely like other women; she is an Erechtheid and partakes of a further ambivalence that is built into the imagery of the Earthborn.[43] On the one hand, the Gegenes were the noble progenitors of Athens, as the play reminds us by recounting the story of Erichthonios. Hephaistos attempted to rape Athena; failing, his seed fell to the ground, where it took the form of Erichthonios; Athena brought up this ancestor of the Athenians, who are thus connected to her (269). Kreousa, as a daughter of his son (or grandson) Erechtheus, has nobility written on her face (238–39). Euripides goes out of his way to give us this information; Ion has already heard the stories and only wants confirmation of the truth of these incredible tales. ·

Not only is her lineage thus exalted, but as a child Kreousa was even more extraordinary, for in the familial story of virgin sacrifice, she is inscribed as saved (279): the daughters of Cecrops died because they looked at the babe Erichthonios (272), and the other daughters of Ere-chtheus were sacrificed for the land (*pro gaias*, 278); Kreousa escaped because she was an infant herself (280).[44]

But this status, too, fluctuates. As a baby, outside the cycle of exchange, Kreousa was exempt from the fate of her sisters, but at later moments in life she was, as I have shown, vulnerable; nobility does not, therefore,

---

43. On the ambivalence of the Gegenes, see Loraux, *Enfants*, p. 239 with n. 178; duBois, *Sowing*, p. 80. Zeitlin, "Configurations," p. 135, makes the connection between centaurs, Amazons, and Giants in the context of rape.

44. On Erichthonius and women as alternative sources of the name of Athens, see Loraux, *Enfants*, pp. 121–22.

counter the effects of gender. Thus, as Kreousa tells Ion, her lineage was of no help to her in the past (268). It did not save her from the effects of divine male power; her experience of sexuality has been one of submission to violence. Nonetheless, it is important not to lose sight of the ways in which Kreousa was and is exceptionally powerful. For instance, although she was given as a prize to Xouthos, he came to her city; she did not share the fate of the typical woman who left her natal family for her husband. Her power is limited, however, for even though Xouthos gains access to the city only by marrying Kreousa, he then assumes possession of the house, and it is only through him that Ion can inherit.

When Xouthos alone is awarded a child by the oracle, Kreousa does not acquiesce; rather, she attempts to activate her powerful Earthborn heritage. In the form of revenge she chooses, she is shown acting out of a monstrous aspect of that ancestry—like the monstrous children of Earth alone, who are enemies of the Olympians (987–88), and who had to be fought in order to establish culture. The battle against the earthborn Giants, for instance, is commemorated in the metopes described in the play.[45] Euripides also refers to the Gorgon as an offspring of earth (989) and relates it to Kreousa's actions. The radical ambivalence of the Gorgon is apparent: alive she was Athena's enemy; dead, her skin becomes the goddess's aegis. From the Gorgon come two drops of blood, one healthful, one poisonous (1003, 1015).

The beneficent aspect of the Gorgon leads to its association with life. Two of Ion's three "birthplaces" are thus identified, for the omphalos is flanked by Gorgons (224), and Kreousa embroidered a Gorgon on the robe she gave to Ion as an infant (1421). She attempted to use the positive power of the Gorgon, meaning the cloth to act like the aegis (1423) and protect as Athena protected Erichthonios.[46] Even more, Kreousa tried to identify with Athena, not her monstrous opponents, by giving the baby a necklace of golden snakes, like the one the goddess gave Erichthonios.

But Kreousa both gives birth to *and* tries to kill her young; like other threatening female figures of myth, she is imagined as monstrous when she lashes out. "O the bull-shaped eye of her forefather Kephis. What an echidna [see 1233] you have engendered, a bloody scourge, or a dragon

45. Owen, *Ion*, p. 84 on line 190: "The conquest of earthborn monsters by gods and Heroes would be appropriate in the place where Apollo conquered Python." Bromios too is represented killing monstrous offspring of Earth (216–17). The battle with the Giants was also depicted on the ceremonial robe given to Athena in the Panathenaia, a celebration of the civic order established by conquering the monsters. See duBois, *Centaurs*, esp. pp. 53, 55.

46. Wolff, "Design," p. 182. On repetitions of the Erichthonios story, see Zeitlin, "Mysteries of Identity"; and Loraux, *Enfants*.

with flashing glance of fire, she who has dared all, nothing less than the drops of the Gorgon, with which she intended to kill me. Grab her, so that the rocks of Parnassus can card well through the uncut locks of her hair when she is thrown like the discus from the rock" (1261–68). Ion invokes the image of the snaky-haired Gorgon, thus feminizing her plan while making it monstrous. The poison Kreousa employs clearly corresponds to the monstrous side of the Earthborn; using her inheritance from the Gorgon to kill, she becomes Athena's potential enemy and the image of Gorgon to her son. Euripides represents Ion here as the hero and athlete, Kreousa as the monster and object hurled.

DuBois argues that "the myth of Medusa is a myth of fear of women, fear of their archaism, their self-sufficiency, their buried power. . . . Creusa, implicated in the autochthony myth of the Athenian people, is a variant of the Medusa figure and contaminates the Athenian legends with some of the misogyny and ambivalence associated with that figure."[47] The ambiguity attaching to Kreousa as an Erechtheid is symptomatic of the way a male-dominated myth system represents female power. Maternal energy itself appears to be threatening, for allowed to recreate endlessly by herself, Earth would engender monsters.[48] Since Earth is both origin of life and repository of the dead (in a culture that buries), to be born of Earth is to be double and close to death. When Euripides represents Kreousa as attempting to kill her own child, he represents her as moving from the positive to the negative aspect of her noble heritage.

The instability in the definition of the Earthborn allows Euripides to construct Kreousa as double, as uncanny and gorgonish. In the course of the play she resists the silence her fate has necessitated, first by speaking and then by acting. The oscillation between positive and negative does not continue interminably, however; rather, Euripides satisfies convention and provides closure, this time by bringing the action back to the positive pole. That is, Kreousa is "rescued" from her inscribed violent desires. For this "happy" ending to work, however, she must consent to her own repression.

The denouement is brought about in two stages, by the Pythia and by

---

47. DuBois, *Sowing*, pp. 92–93; see her chap. 4 for an analysis of the rewriting of "the most traditional metaphor for woman's body, the earth" (p. 65).

48. On productive earth as demonstration of "the primacy of the maternal body," see ibid., p. 3. DuBois further observes: "The body is like the earth, autonomously productive; like stone, part of the earth's landscape, guardian, virginal" (p. 109). In her autonomy the earth is potentially dangerous; thus, Hesiod represents Earth going on to produce the monster Typhoeus, who is the last challenger to Zeus (*Theogony* 821).

Athena: both females who, while *parthenoi* (unmarried females, or "virgins") and thus seemingly independent of male power, are simultaneously identified with male power. The Pythia gets her prophetic abilities from Apollo and speaks only what he wishes; Athena, born directly from the head of Zeus, takes her power from him as she says in Aeschylus's *Eumenides*. As is typical of the goddess, she devalues her representative.[49]

The Priestess emphasizes the god's forethought and affirms his planning: he required not only that she bring the baby up but also that she save his wrappings (1357–63). Even though Ion still knows neither mother nor father, the god is inscribed as "savior" (*sōsai*, 1349). Athena then addresses Kreousa, predictably asserting that "Apollo has done all things well; first he made your childbirth painless, so that your family would not know; when you had borne this child and put it from you in its swaddling clothes, he bade Hermes snatch the infant up in his arms and bring him here, and he nursed him up and would not let him breathe out his life" (1595–1600).

The clear consequence is that Kreousa should now "be silent" (*siōpa*, 1601; see her earlier "*pōs sigasō?*" ["how can I be silent?"] 859). The shameful secret that she has guarded has been brought to light, but it will be buried again so that her son can inherit Athens. Kreousa acknowledges that Apollo was right: "Listen to my words now: I praise Phoibos, never having praised him before, because he gives back to me the son he had neglected. These gates and this oracle of the god seem friendly, although hostile before" (1609–12).[50]

The mother's story is written as one first of violence and subsequently of repression and complicity. Euripides renders her dangerous and murderous (she has the snakes of Medusa); then the audience witnesses her taming and her accession to the wisdom of the god who raped her. The text suggests that Kreousa was twice hostile to her son and that the god was twice benign in redeeming her errors (once through Hermes, once through Athena) and in granting her the son she would have killed. By emphasizing Euripides' choices, one can see the ways in which the poet constructs Kreousa; she is a plaything of the playwright as well as of the god. In Athens—the scene for the audience, after all—shame and honor will continue to require the woman's silence about what has happened to her "own" body.

49. Loraux, *Enfants*, p. 153: "The victory of Athena always devalues the maternity of Athenian women."

50. Of course, Apollo does not agree that he was ever careless; see his words as quoted in Hermes' speech, "take care" (*melēsei*, 36) vs. "he took care" (*ēmelēse*, 1610).

From the Body of the Mother to the Name of
the Father

As should be clear, I believe that the *Ion* does not tell a gynocentric
story of female desire, but rather figures aspects of female experience so
as to satisfy certain needs of the male. The plot movement revolves around
Ion's discovery of his parentage, a version of the "family romance," in
which the foundling finds his true parents and, despite irregularities, inherits the throne. Fears of maternal power have been given their due by
the construction of a hostile Kreousa; they are then allayed by her mol-
lification, her cooperation, and her praise for Apollo.

The significance of the comic plot becomes clearer if we think of the
play as a mini-*Oresteia*, in which Ion plays the role of the heroic Orestes;
he is identified with the same divinities (Apollo, Hermes, and Athena)
and against a monstrous mother, similarly viewed as a Gorgon and
dragon.[51] He too moves toward his father and separates from his mother.
But this play is a wish-fulfillment fantasy. Ion, unlike Orestes, does not
have to kill in order to found his line and come into relationship with the
masculine. Rather, Euripides enacts a coming-of-age ritual for Ion; the
tragic possibility of misrecognition allows him to play the cosmogonic
hero; he imitates Orestes' city founding by building a tent (*skēnē*, probably
with punning reference to the theater) in which the Amazon tapestries
furnish a ceiling that imitates the sky, and by founding an empire through
his offspring (74–75, 1575–94). Crucially, the text of *Ion* puts into practice
Apollo's abstract reasoning in the *Oresteia*—that the mother is merely the
nurse to the father's seed. In the play's past the biological father, Apollo,
has in fact been nurse as well as inseminator; in its future the nonbiological
father's claim will be publicly realized. The silent Kreousa, successor to
her own aggression, will be a beneficent resident of Athens, as the Erinyes,
successors to Clytemnestra's and their own aggression, will be beneficent
residents of Athens.

The son's relationship to the mother goes through several stages in the
drama: separation, reunion, separation. In consequence, both male protagonist and male audience member get what they want: their worst fears
are played out, but the conclusion is reassuring. Whatever one might think
about the more general applicability of Lacanian theory, it well describes
Ion's entry into the symbolic. Tragedy is like psychoanalytic theory in that
the woman is always seen from the male point of view; both are instructive
about what men have fantasized about women. While for Jacques Lacan

---

51. On Clytemnestra as dragon, see Rabinowitz, "From Force to Persuasion."

the mother is only a lack, Euripides bodies forth her fearful power; imagining her first as powerful and then as subsumed under the law of the father (which the son stands to inherit) is even more flattering to the narcissism of the male child.

It is clear that Kreousa's narrative is inscribed within the coming-of-age story, or ritual rebirth, of the son. As a result of this masculine focus we hear more about the exposure of the child than about the rape of the woman. Similarly, since the female body coincides with the maternal body, descriptions focus on what would be of interest to the infant: breasts and arms. Not only does the text stress the physical bond to the mother (as opposed to rearing; see the discussion of Ion's parents, above), but it inscribes her body as missing.[52] For instance, Kreousa asks Ion, "And which one of the Delphic maidens nourished you with milk?" He replies: "I never knew the breast" (318–19). Then the Chorus uses the same terminology to tell Kreousa of her own prophesied childlessness: "You are never to clasp a child to your breast, or hold one in your arms" (761–62). The Old Man echoes those terms when he envisions the infant reaching out for breast and the cradling nook of her arms (*maston, agkalais*, 962). Ion regrets his own mother, who did not offer him the breast because of secret bridals (1372), and Kreousa echoes him, summing up breast and milk as "motherly nurture" (*tropheia matros*, 1493). Elsewhere, there are references to the arms alone (1375, 1454, 1598), always signifying loss. Kreousa's body is defined as absent even when she is on stage, because it is only the body of the m/other, not that of a subject.

Physical mothering itself is thus established as an absence; as a result, longing for it and nostalgia form the predominant tropes of these scenes.[53] Much of Ion's initial meeting with Kreousa is given over to discussion of his missing mother, and Kreousa's supposed friend. But it is even more striking that on meeting Xouthos and hearing that Apollo has declared him to be his father, Ion is overcome with longing (*pothos*) for his mother: "O dear mother, when will I look on your face? Now I long to see you more than before, whoever you are, but perhaps you have died, so that we will never be able to [meet]" (563–65; cf. 572–75). Once he has accepted Xouthos, their conversation also turns on speculations as to the identity of his mother, and Ion leaves expressing his concern for her (668–75).

Because the mother is absent, the symbolic order of the father is un-

52. For the Lacanian analysis of the relationship between this absence, desire, and language, see Lacan, "Signification of the Phallus."

53. Wolff, "Design," pp. 172–74, finds that doubling and nostalgia dominate the play as a whole, including its treatment of myth and Athens.

contested.[54] The mother-son reunion literally takes place in the symbolic, for the Greek word for Ion's telltale wrappings and basket is *sumbola* (1386); the time for nursing is long past. Ordinarily, a woman would be the one to know with certainty the identity or origin of a child,[55] but in this world even the woman does not know her son and lives entirely in the symbolic realm.[56] Thus, in this scenario, the mother as well as the son submits to the law of the father; her traditionally privileged biological tie is subordinated to the social tie, one of seeming (*dokēsis*, 1602); the physical mother is given back her child by means of signs (*mētros sumbola*, 1386), which she must read. The Gorgon now takes on a signifying function, referring not to the fearsome mother, the return of the repressed, or the *unheimlich* but simply to Kreousa's own childhood. The pieces of evidence, each relevant to her Athenian story, enable her to communicate with Ion but also enable him to fulfill the criteria of rule at Athens. Thus her body is not sufficient; she requires these signs to give Ion rights as a native to the Athenian throne, an inheritance denied him as a result of his illegitimacy.[57] Their failed biological relationship becomes a successful cultural relationship, as she interprets the gifts that she gave to him.

The mother-son recognition scene cannot be the basis for a future relationship, however, for the culture in fact requires their separation.[58] The initial alienation of son from mother is repeated, this time by the intervention of Apollo, who first gives Ion to Xouthos and then reasserts that gift through the action of Athena. Euripides depicts a privileging of the paternal over the maternal on the basis of very real material benefits.[59] So, for instance, Ion's emotional attachment to the absent mother attenuates

---

54. On the entry into the symbolic and the intervention of the Name of the Father, see Lacan, "Mirror-Stage."

55. Acceptance of the maternal as decisive is attested by the Athenian law prohibiting marriage of maternally, but not paternally, consanguine siblings (Harrison, *Law*, pp. 22–23). On Plato's usurpation of maternity, see Halperin, *One Hundred Years*, chap. 6, esp. p. 139 with n. 164.

56. On misrecognition of the mother, see Daladier, "Mères aveugles."

57. Loraux, *Enfants*, in the chapter "Créuse autochton," stresses Kreousa's usurpation of the Athenian father's rights.

58. There is a Jungian corollary as well. Hillman, "Abandoning," p. 379, notes a "similarity of metaphor . . . between Aristotle's entelechy, Leibniz' monad, and Jung's self of which the child is a primary image. Entelechy, monad and self coincide in this fantasy of independence."

59. I claim not that Euripides has understood some universal truth about the human condition, but rather that he has laid bare certain structures at work in his own gendered reality. Flax, *Thinking Fragments* (esp. p. 79), among others, has noted the limitations of Freud and Lacan: "By privileging the oedipal phase and denying the power of the first object relation, Freud participates in and rationalizes an act of repression both typical of and necessary to the replication of patriarchal culture" (p. 81).

when he is about to find her; having found a noble father—Xouthos is a son of Zeus—he is unenthusiastic about discovering that he may be the son of a slave woman, and he almost hides the basket containing evidence he might use to track her down.[60] This class dynamic coexists with the sex/gender structure and reinforces it, since class and nationality are both at issue for the one who wishes to inherit a place in Athens.

Euripides depicts Ion as reborn from his father. Others have noted the extent to which Ion's story follows the pattern of rebirth, a psychological or social birth, not a physical one; the play enacts a coming-of-age ritual with a twist, since Ion gains a new name and a father.[61] Xouthos is going to celebrate the rituals omitted at the boy's birth (*genethli'*, 653). He has reached maturity and is a "full-grown youth" (*ektelē neanian*, 780), the age at which he can fulfill a man's obligations, or inherit, as in the case of Orestes. Moreover, the action of the play follows a legal model of historical adoption, whereby an Athenian man without heirs could adopt a boy or man to inherit his estate.[62] Ion moves from the house of the god—his "functional" father, as he thought—to that of the man he at first sees as his real father but who turns out to be a surrogate.

To the extent that Xouthos gains a son, this text grants the misogynist wish expressed by Jason and Hippolytos, the wish to escape the need for women in procreation. As a result of the splitting of parenting into biological and social functions, the son need not be born to the man but can be a gift between men: is Ion Xouthos's child by birth or by gift (*pephukenai men ouchi, dōreitai de se hautou gegōta*, 1534–35; cf. 536–37, 781, 1561)?

Ion's relationship to Xouthos is quite explicitly "in name only": that is, symbolic, existing only in language. It is the result of a prophecy (*muthos*, 529; *ainigma*, 533). But in fact, "in name only" comes to mean virtually everything, since the name of the father is what is necessary for inheritance (*onoma patros*, 1543; cf. *mētros sumbola*, 1386). Without an Athenian mother, he might not have speaking rights in the assembly (*parrēsia*, 672), as he fears. But such rights are less important than having a known father, as Kreousa explains to him: "Listen to what has come to me, my son; Loxias has done you a good turn, establishing you in a well-born house;

60. Although Ion is, like Oedipus, a foundling, he is not a tracker; Euripides spares him the tragic version of the story, making his desire acceptable and eliminating parricide. For more on the similarities, see above, n. 5, as well as Hanson, "Euripides' *Ion*," pp. 28–29.

61. On Ion's development, see Hanson, "Euripides' *Ion*." On death and rebirth, see Loraux, *Enfants*, pp. 200–201; Burnett, "Human Resistance," p. 97; Wolff, "Design," p. 171. Flax, *Thinking Fragments*, p. 111 discusses psychic as opposed to physical birth in psychoanalytic terms, citing Winnicott, *Through Pediatrics to Psychoanalysis* (New York: Basic Books, 1975).

62. On adoption, see Owen, *Ion*, p. 176 on line 1535; Harrison, *Law*, pp. 84–96.

if the god had not spoken [*tou theou de legomenos*, 1541], you would not
have your allotted house nor the name of a father. How would you, when
I myself had hidden my union and killed you secretly? He does you a
good turn by giving you to another father [*prostithēs'*]" (1539–45).

The question of name is prominent in the text, for Ion gets his name
in the course of the action, and only by virtue of his relationship not to
his mother but to his new "father." Hermes predicts what it will be (74),
but it is Xouthos who names him Ion (661) because he sees him going
out from (*exionti*) the temple.[63] Having acquired his name by his own
motion, as it were, he is destined to hand it on (74–75). Significantly,
there is little mythology surrounding Ion except that which names him as
the eponymous hero of the Ionians. In justifying Apollo to Ion, Kreousa
stresses inheritance and name, or legitimacy (1543). To endow him with
both is the motivating force behind the play.

Establishing the primacy of Ion's patriliny also helps to define and
construct a masculine community, a vexed concept in the play. What
constitutes the group, who will eat with whom, who will share pleasure
and pain with whom? Looking at the usage of the term *koinia*, we can see
how it shifts. First, Ion suggests to Kreousa that Apollo might, unknown
to her, have raised her son; she feels that given the "intimacy" she had
shared with him, they should have made a community and asks why Apollo
would keep that pleasure to himself instead of sharing it (*ta koina . . . monos*,
358; cf. 1284). Then, the father-son pair constitutes an eating community
when Xouthos plans his shared dinner with his new son (652, 807); the
Old Man asks whether the son is theirs in common (*koinōnos*) or whether
only Xouthos is fortunate, leaving Kreousa alone in her childlessness (771–
72). In reaction to this prophecy, Kreousa mobilizes the community of
women; the Chorus takes her side and together they plan the murder
(*koinoumenē*, 858) to take place at that feast. As a result of the acknowledgment that Kreousa has something in common with Apollo (*koinon*,
1284), she and Ion share common feelings (*koinōs*, 1462). Although he
does not use the same term, Ion wishes to establish a trinity and would
like to share the pleasure of his recognition of Kreousa with his putative
father (1468).[64]

The questions about community correlate with the similar theme of
xenia or guest friendship (so important in the *Alcestis*): Xouthos is a

63. For references to name see 75, 81, 139, 259, 661, 800, 830, 855, 996–97, 1278,
1372, 1543, 1555, 1577, 1587. Loraux, *Enfants*, pp. 200–201 stresses that Xouthos isn't
even the first one to give him that name.

64. On *koinia* and *xenia*, see Zeitlin, "Mysteries of Identity," pp. 177–79. On the Athenian politics, see Saxonhouse, "Myths"; Walsh, "Rhetoric of Birthright."

stranger/guest-friend (*xenos*) at Athens (293, 813), or outsider (*thuraios*, 702); he intends to make offerings not only for the birth but for the *xenia* of his new-found son. In contrast, Kreousa is marked as the *xenē* at Delphi (1221). But the Athens of this text is not hospitable to outsiders; in fact the Chorus of Athenian women and the Old Man find the idea of an outsider son of Xouthos very threatening. While it was bad enough that an Erechtheid like Kreousa would marry an outsider, it is worse that a non-Athenian would inherit. Because Ion is without place, (*atopos*, 690), and from elsewhere, he is other (*allos*, 1058, 1069–73); as a consequence, he is not welcomed by these insiders (676–724).[65]

The play resolves this conflict by giving Ion both a hidden biological Earthborn parent and a public symbolic outsider parent. While in the time of the play the biological level seems dominant, in the time to come the symbolic will come to the fore, thereby facilitating ties of male *xenia* and *koinia*. Thus Athena's propitiating speech has mostly to do with the establishment of rule and empire. She orders Kreousa to return, to "inhabit the tyrant's thrones," because Ion will rule rightly, being born from an Erechtheid (1571–75). Ion goes from having been anonymous to having a name to becoming eponymous; he gains the power of the phallus, establishing "four lines from one root" (1576).[66]

Epistemological Consequences

In the play's conclusion, linguistic and conventional ties finally take precedence over "dubious" biological ones. Ion's relationship to Xouthos suggests the possibility of the exchange of children between men. This transaction is not grounded in the body; in consequence, the characters find themselves in a shifting realm attractive to a postmodern sensibility: there is no originary parent. In the Greek tradition radical cultural doubt about paternity is symptomatic. It goes back at least to Telemachos's questions about Odysseus: doubt about the identity of his father leads Telemachos out of the house, on to the sea, and into the world of masculine *xenia*.[67] We might say that uncertainty about the father precipitates him into the realm of the exchange of gifts and of the symbolic. Similarly, through Kreousa's rape and the subsequent exposure of Ion, knowledge

65. On this topic, see Saxonhouse, "Myths"; Walsh, "Rhetoric of Birthright."
66. While *rizē* (root) does not literally mean penis, the allusion is made more likely in the context "root of family" and close to the word *sperma*. Cf. Pindar *Olympians* 2.46, Isthmian 8.61; Aeschylus *Agamemnon* 966; Sophocles *Ajax* 1178.
67. Zeitlin, "Mysteries of Identity," p. 147, makes the same connection.

of the mother is lost, leaving the characters in the realm of circulation, representation, and illusion.

It is significant that the play begins under the sign of Hermes, a divinity associated not only with luck and travel but also with exchange.[68] Apollo and Hermes are close, as is clear from the Homeric "Hymn to Hermes"; they are simultaneously opposite and alike. It is not surprising that Euripides has Apollo use this brother to rescue his son. But why does Euripides choose him to open the play? On the narrative level, there is no reason for his presence at Delphi, aside from curiosity. To the authorial audience, his presence powerfully supports the image of rebirth by repeating the moment when he first saved Ion. At the same time, however, this strategy must imply that Apollo has dropped into Hermes' world from his own realm of clarity, prophecy, and revelation. In terms of plot, Hermes is present because Apollo is absent. But why is Apollo absent? As I have mentioned before, the narrative audience believes that Apollo stays away because he is ashamed (*mempsis es meson molei*, 1558).[69] Metaphorically, however, the transcendental signifier can never be seen; he is the source of the seed and visions but works through women's bodies—his prophetess and Kreousa. In the end, Apollo speaks through Athena in order to ordain a world of seeming in which what was revealed as true by nature is once again concealed. The hidden and deceptive dominate this story of secret conception, birth, and nurturance.

The alternation of the two gods helps characterize Ion as well, for while he serves Apollo, he lacks fixity and is appropriately under Hermes' care.[70] In many ways, he resembles his uncle more than his father. Hermes was the god of lucky finds; Ion *is* a lucky find, and words for finding are repeated frequently in the text (575, 588, 651, 669, 1302, 1349, 1441, 1518). Hermes watched over roads; Ion is defined as a wanderer (*ēlat'*, *ēlateian*, 53, 576) and like the god Hermes is a servant to Apollo (*latris*, 4, 124, 152, 1343). But, as would also make sense in a world dominated by Hermes, Ion's role is not stable. He is called "no account" (*ana-rithmēton*, 837) by the Old Man; he is indeed a cipher, suitable occupant of many different positions. First he is the recipient of gifts from his mother, then the gift itself; first, as an exposed infant, he would have made a likely meal for birds, next he guards the sanctuary against birds, then he is the beneficiary of the bird who drinks the poison intended for

---

68. On Hermes, see Kahn, *Hermès*; Loraux, *Enfants*, pp. 212–13.
69. See Wolff, "Design," p. 188. Sinos, "Characterization," p. 133, sees him as "amoral."
70. On Hermes as god of ambiguous identity, see Loraux, *Enfants*, p. 200 nn. 11–12.

him.[71] Moreover, he almost defiles the altar he is supposed to protect when he is about to kill Kreousa when she claims suppliant rights. This shiftiness is characteristic of exchange; the god who claims to reveal the truth is absent, represented by the god of exchange himself.

Xouthos and Kreousa's desire for a prophecy sets the plot in motion; as a result, issues of knowledge and truth and falsity seem to inform the play. J. O. de Graft Hanson makes the connection to Ion: "at the bottom of Ion's new awareness is a need for certainty of knowledge; the doubt and questionings engendered by his recent experiences have revealed to him the inadequacy of his previous simple faith, and the narrowness of his simple view of life."[72] These issues are immediately related to parenthood, for that is the form of the literal questioning. In fact, the play constructs truth claims as claims of identity, for the oracle is *true* if Xouthos is *really* Ion's father.[73] If the oracle is not true, then Ion's belief in the god will be shaken: "Is the god true or does he prophesy falsely? This shakes me" (1537–38). Kreousa's double answer—that he was a gift to Xouthos, because only in that way could he inherit (1534, 1539–45)—does not satisfy him. He intends to ask the oracle directly who his father is (1546–58); he is stopped only by the appearance of Athena. She, asserting again what Kreousa has said, convinces him (*ouk apistiai . . . peithomai*, 1606–7).

In an attempt to control circulation and get this family back on track, Euripides and Apollo consign the play's conclusion to Athena, a virgin goddess who was born from the single masculine principle. Athena rescues Ion from his status as nonentity or cipher, rendering him *anarithmeton* in another sense of the word as well, for his importance is "immeasurable." In the end, Ion's position in Athens is assured. Athena's presence fixes both knowledge and parentage—but only by consigning the mother to silence (*siōpa*, 1601). As in MacKinnon's theory, sexuality and epistemology intersect.

Euripides is self-conscious about the importance of gender, and about the relationship between poetry, power, and gender. As the Chorus of the *Medea* recognizes, men have the power of the lyre, and the one who gets to tell the story determines in large part what its meaning will be. Euripides represents the Chorus of women here as similarly wishing for a new song, accusing poets of singing "of our unholy and unlawful unions and loves"

---

71. On Ion and the birds, see Zeitlin, "Mysteries of Identity," pp. 144–45; Hanson, "Euripides' *Ion*," pp. 31–32.

72. Hanson, "Euripides' *Ion*," p. 39; see also p. 41. On epistemology and the play, see Forehand, "Truth and Reality," esp. pp. 175–78 on Ion's quest for identity.

73. On the play's deployment of themes of identity, see Zeitlin, "Mysteries of Identity."

(1092–93). They claim to exceed the unjust race of men in righteousness. "Let there be a song that speaks ill of the unions of men" (1097–98).

Is this play that new song?[74] We must be cautious in answering this question, first looking at the other explicit references to art or song. In doing so, we see that masculine creativity is writ large. The Chorus begins with elaborate praise of Delphi and a description of its metopes.[75] The scenes mentioned depict heroes battling monsters: Zeus and the Hydra, Herakles and Iolaos in action, Bellerophon and the Chimera, the Olympian battle with the Giants, Athena and Enkelados. Euripides conjures up the bringing of order by the taming of the monstrous other;[76] as a warrior, Athena participated in the Giant battle, that struggle of Olympians against the Earthborn which confirmed Zeus's rule. Thus, even in the metopes we see an adumbration of the duality involved in being born from the Earth, and Kreousa is, as I showed earlier, identified with the monstrous enemy until she is pacified.

Similarly, Euripides includes an elaborate description of the tent erected for his hero's ritual of initiation (1141–65).[77] In constructing the tent like a world, with sky above and earth scenes on the sides, Ion imitates the actions of the gods in constructing a world. The hangings depicting earth emphasize the struggles of nature and culture, Greek and "others," for there are images of ships opposing Greeks, of creatures half animal and half human, and of contests between animal and human. The tent also represents empire in the sources of the tapestries that Ion uses: the conquered Amazons furnished the material for the ceiling; barbarians supplied that of the walls, and Athens donated the central showpiece at the entrance, which shows Cecrops and his daughters wreathed with snakes.

Set against this public form of art, which is a mimesis of cosmogony, is women's weaving. As the members of the Chorus admire the metopes, they remember that they have woven some of these stories into their own handiwork (*emaisi mutheuetai para pēnais*, 196–97); from stories and woven fabrics, they know that no good comes of mortals mingling with immortals (506–8). Not only do women learn by weaving, but women's crafts unite them; as I noted above, Kreousa's Chorus is a group of women of the shuttle, and it is only with the courage she gains from that com-

---

74. Loraux, *Enfants*, pp. 205–6, is convinced that it does fulfill their wish.

75. On myth and Euripides' representation, see Wolff, "Design," pp. 181–82.

76. DuBois, *Centaurs*, p. 53 on Giants, as juxtaposed with Amazons and Centaurs, pp. 49–77. Rosivach, "Earthborn," pp. 284–88, notes that the battle with Kreousa is analogous to these battles.

77. For other explanations of this long description, see Burnett, "Human Resistance"; Wolff, "Design," p. 180; Zeitlin, "Mysteries of Identity," pp. 165–69 (on p. 147 she calls it a "correlation of self-fashioning and world-making").

munity that she can act. Kreousa too wove as a girl; like the glorious tapestries of Ion's tent (*huphasmath', huphantai grammasin toiaid' huphai*, 1141, 1146), her weaving (*huphasm' huphēn'egō, huphasmata, huphasma* 1417, 1418, 1424) is withdrawn from the treasury (1394; cf. 1141), though as a product of girlish craft (1425), her work has only private significance. Euripides recognizes the support women may get from other women in the private sphere, but the plot moves Kreousa away from these friends and toward her son and husband.

In/conclusion

In order for her son to inherit, Kreousa must be co-opted by or co-operative with the male divinity and his male-identified surrogates, the Pythia and Athena. Kreousa accepts her son gratefully and renounces her rebellion; after all, something is better than nothing. The son, on the other hand, truly gets it all, for Euripides ends his play as a wish-fulfillment fantasy. What has been solved? Ion will still be the son of an outsider to all of Athens except the Chorus, and he will still be a bastard.[78] On that level we see Euripides' sleight of hand; the anxiety about the murderous mother, however, is assuaged, for she has been persuaded to comply with the system that puts the patriliny first.

In the end, Euripides has it both ways: he acknowledges that Ion inhabits a world of apparent parents—seeming (*dokēsis*), not being—yet neither hero nor audience has to remain in doubt. For although Kreousa's resistance sets up a detour before Apollo's plot can work itself out, Athena removes the signs that such a deviation ever took place. She is posited as speaking a single truth, answering with certainty the question of who Ion's parents *really* are.

In this tragedy that is part comedy, Euripides teases out the "negative" possibilities before effecting a "positive" conclusion; he thus increases the emotional impact of his drama on the audience. As another consequence, however, he gives a great deal of space to Kreousa's strength, for her violence is an effect of the tragic plot. Modern readers committed to social change may choose to read in opposition, taking as negative what the text proposes as positive. They would then value Kreousa's self-assertion by understanding what it is that necessitates its taking the form of near murder.

The *Ion* subsumes many of the topics raised in my consideration of the

78. See Loraux, *Enfants*, p. 218. On the debate about the status of bastards in Athens, see Harrison, *Law*, pp. 63–65; MacDowell, *Law*, pp. 89–91; Rhodes, "Bastards," pp. 89–92.

other plays. For instance, as in *Alcestis* and *Hippolytos* as well as *Iphigenia in Aulis*, the traffic in women creates a bond between men; the primary legitimate desire is the father's for the son, or the host's for the guest, to which end the female drops out. Like the sacrificial virgins, Kreousa is represented as willingly ceding her place to Xouthos. Like the other active women, she represents a deathly threat to the male lineage. Finally, as in *Alcestis*, the "happy ending" is dependent on the woman's silence.

Let me return to the twice-expressed wish for an art that takes the side of women. As masculine creations, produced by and contributing to a masculine culture, these plays do not seem likely candidates to be those much desired women's texts. Indeed, I would say that in appearing to make this claim, Euripides makes a preemptive strike and occupies all the positions, feminine as well as masculine, by seeming to speak for women at the same time that the plays structurally support the dominant sex/gender system.

Where are feminists then to position ourselves? In David Hwang's *M Butterfly* (Penguin, 1989), a play about the scandalous affair between a French diplomat and a Chinese cross-dressing opera singer, there is this interchange:

> *Song*: Miss Chin? Why, in the opera, are women's roles played by men?
> *Chin*: I don't know. Maybe, a reactionary remnant of male—
> *Song*: No. Because only a man knows how a woman is supposed to act. (2.7)

Thus, in the *Ion*, for Kreousa to have been raped by Apollo, to have had to abandon her child, to have lived childless, and then to praise the god and give up public acknowledgment of her child: this is what men want. For feminists to think that Euripides might have been writing her story is naive; it is wishful thinking on the part of male critics.

But isn't this reading just the old woman-as-victim scenario that I supposedly eschewed in my Introduction? Where is my third position now? When I presented my work at a conference several years ago, someone in the audience asked why we should continue to teach and read this material. I admit that that is a problem for me, given the competition for scarce resources in the curriculum, for example. My position, however, is that feminists must keep our claim on this powerful canonical material, not give it over to the tender mercies of the educational conservatives.

It is possible for feminist readers to use these texts, as I have been trying to do, not by denying Euripides' agenda but by inscribing our own. As

I have stressed throughout, the reader/spectator has a power: we can refuse to "get the joke." The text we create will depend then on our own point of view. For me it consists of recognizing the female strength (or male perceptions of it) which has necessitated such strategies of control, realizing at the same time that classical Athens did not celebrate that strength. Though the texts did grow out of a patriarchal milieu and were used to build a cultural elite in the intervening centuries, the anxiety about female power is itself significant.

What is the source of that power? When Freud finally recognized the potential separateness of female sexuality, he made the analogy to antiquity: "Our insight into this early, pre-Oedipus, phase in girls comes to us as a surprise, like the discovery, in another field, of the Minoan-Mycenaean civilization behind the civilization of Greece."[79] As Athenian marriage depended on its construction of that sexuality, so the Olympian gods and Athenian civilization depended on dominating that past. It is no accident that in researching Iphigenia, Alcestis, Medea, Phaedra, I have come back to pre-Hellenic goddesses, or that Hekabe is represented as close to Hekate and the crone.[80]

In the sacrificial model, Euripides the ironist comes together with Euripides the fetishist. He questions the dominant morality by showing the corruption of the leadership (in *Iphigenia in Aulis* and *Hekabe*, in particular): the heroes do not live up to their own standards. Because irony is primarily not positive but negative, however, there is no new system of values offered; instead, fetishism works to complete the irony. The praise for the sacrificial maidens then co-opts their strength. As a result, in those chapters on the sacrificial model, I have stressed resisting the fetishism that would seem to glorify these women while requiring their death. Our task instead is to read for the strength Euripides encodes but to insist on seeing that it could have ended otherwise than with their sacrifice. We must problematize the traffic in women (the imposition of the heterosexual imperative), asking what would have happened if these girls had been inscribed in woman-centered circles; we must resist the rupture of the bond between women. Perhaps in those bonds we can find a new set of values.

In looking at the vindictive heroines, it is not difficult to see the strength; the trick is to retain sympathy by remembering the author (and culture) who makes them the way they are. Self-consciousness about the strategies

79. Freud, "Female Sexuality," p. 226.
80. On the goddess and classical antiquity, see Zweig, " 'Primal Mind,' " and Passman, "Out of the Closet."

of the text then will have longer-lasting results, for again it may help us to see the world otherwise—which is what we need, of course, in order to effect change. Again, the strategy at this point will depend on the reader. Some may view Euripides as a feminist who has understood the problems with marriage as an institution and who is writing Medea's story. Others may resist Euripides simply by cheering for Medea. Or we can read against the text at least by giving Medea our understanding and refusing it to Jason.

The third position then is the middle, reading for the strength that lies at the heart of the anxiety Euripides so carefully veils. At the same time there is another risk in looking to the past in the way I have just laid out: are we embracing a strength that seems to reduce women once again to gendered biology? As must be clear, I prefer to interpret that strength not as the power to give birth but as women's (pre-Oedipal?) identification with other women, a nascent form of resistance to patriarchy.

Jack Winkler wrote about the double consciousness of Sappho, her consciousness in the face of "masculine norms of behavior, her attitude to the public ethic and her allusions to private reality."[81] This hermeneutic cannot really apply to Euripides, who after all was a man writing for men; Athenian women may nevertheless have had such a double consciousness. Though we have no women's texts from classical Athens, there was a women's world of ritual which may have prepared women in the fifth century to receive the resistant message I have put beside Euripides' masculine agenda. Women in antiquity did live what Adrienne Rich called the double life.[82] We can read these texts differently by reading them double ourselves.

81. Winkler, *Constraints*, p. 164.
82. Rich, "Compulsory Heterosexuality," p. 162.

Works Cited

Abrahamson, Ernst L. "Euripides' Tragedy of *Hecuba*." *Transactions and Proceedings of the American Philological Association* 83 (1952): 120–29.

Abu-Lughod, Lila. *Veiled Sentiments: Honor and Poetry in a Bedouin Society*. Berkeley: University of California Press, 1986.

Adkins, Arthur. "Basic Greek Values in Euripides' *Hecuba* and *Hercules Furens*." *Classical Quarterly* 16 (1966): 193–219.

Althusser, Louis. "Ideology and Ideological State Apparatuses." In *Lenin and Philosophy and Other Essays*, 127–88. New York: New Left Books, 1971.

Appleton, R. B. *Euripides the Idealist*. New York: J. M. Dent, 1927.

Ardener, Edwin. "Belief and the Problem of Women." In *Perceiving Women*, ed. Shirley Ardener, 1–18. New York: Wiley, 1975.

——. "The 'Problem' Revisited." In *Perceiving Women*, ed. Shirley Ardener, 19–27. New York: Wiley, 1975.

Arripe, Marie-Laure. "Contribution à une critique de l'échange des femmes." In *La dot, la valeur des femmes*, 67–81. Toulouse: Service des publications de l'Université de Toulouse-Le Mirail, 1982.

Arrowsmith, William, ed. and trans. *Alcestis*. New York: Oxford University Press, 1974.

——. "Euripides' Theater of Ideas." In *Euripides: A Collection of Critical Essays*, ed. Erich Segal, 13–33. Englewood Cliffs, N.J.: Prentice-Hall, 1968.

Arthur, Marylin B. "'Liberated Women': The Classical Era." In *Becoming Visible: Women in European History*, ed. Renate Bridenthal and Claudia Koonz, 62–89. Boston: Houghton Mifflin, 1977.

——. "Review Essay: Classics." *Signs* 2 (1976): 382–403.

Assaël, Jacqueline. "Misogynie et féminisme chez Aristophane et chez Euripide." *Pallas* 32 (1985): 91–103.

Austin, J. L. *How to Do Things with Words*. 2d ed. Cambridge, Mass.: Harvard University Press, 1962.

Bachofen, J. J. *Myth, Religion, and Motherright*. Trans. Ralph Manheim. Princeton: Princeton University Press, 1967.

Bacon, Helen. *Barbarians in Greek Tragedy*. New Haven: Yale University Press, 1961.

Bain, David. "The Prologues of Euripides' *Iphigeneia in Aulis*." *Classical Quarterly* 27 (1977): 10–26.

Bal, Mieke. *Death and Dissymmetry: The Politics of Coherence in the Book of Judges*. Chicago: University of Chicago Press, 1988.

Barlow, Shirley. *The Imagery of Euripides*. London: Methuen, 1971.

Barnes, Hazel. *Hippolytus of Drama and Myth*. Lincoln: University of Nebraska Press, 1960.

Barrett, W. S., ed. *Euripides: Hippolytos*. Oxford: Oxford University Press, 1964.

Bartky, Sandra Lee. "Foucault, Femininity, and the Modernization of Patriarchal Power." In *Foucault and Feminism*, ed. Irene Diamond and Lee Quinby, 61–86. Boston: Northeastern University Press, 1988.

Bassi, Karen. "Gender and the Ideology of Greek Histrionics." In progress.

———. "Helen and the Discourse of Denial in Stesichorus' *Palinode*." *Arethusa* 26 (1993): 51–75.

Bates, W. N. *Euripides: A Student of Human Nature*. Philadelphia: University of Pennsylvania Press, 1930.

Belsey, Catherine. *The Subject of Tragedy: Identity and Difference in Renaissance Drama*. London: Methuen, 1985.

Benjamin, Jessica. *Bonds of Love: Psychoanalysis, Feminism, and the Problem of Domination*. New York: Pantheon, 1988.

Benveniste, Emile. *Le vocabulaire des institutions indo-européennes*. Vol. 1. Paris: Minuit, 1969.

Bergren, Ann. "Language and the Female in Early Greek Thought." *Arethusa* 16 (1983): 69–95.

Bernal, Martin. *Black Athena: The Afroasiatic Roots of Classical Civilization*. Vol. 1. New Brunswick, N.J.: Rutgers University Press, 1987.

Beye, Charles. "Alcestis and Her Critics." *Greek, Roman, and Byzantine Studies* 2 (1959): 109–27.

———. *"Alcestis" of Euripides*. Englewood Cliffs, N.J.: Prentice-Hall, 1974.

Bickerman, E. J. "La conception du mariage à Athènes." *Bullettino dell 'Instituo di Diritto romano* 78 (1975): 1–28.

Blaiklock, E. M. *The Male Characters of Euripides: A Study in Realism*. Wellington: New Zealand University Press, 1952.

———. "The Nautical Imagery of Euripides' *Medea*." *Classical Philology* 50 (1955): 233–37.

Blanchot, Maurice. "Two Versions of the Imaginary." In *The Gaze of Orpheus and Other Essays*, trans. Lydia Davis, ed. P. Adams Sitney, 79–90. Barrytown, N.Y.: Station Hill Press, 1981. Trans. of "Les deux versions de l'imaginaire," in *L'espace littéraire*, 1955.

Blok, Josine. "Sexual Asymmetry: A Historiographical Essay." In *Sexual Asymmetry: Studies in Ancient Society*, ed. Josine Blok with Peter Mason, 1–57. Amsterdam: J. C. Gieben, 1987.

Boardman, John, and Donna Kurtz. *Greek Burial Customs*. Ithaca: Cornell University Press, 1971.

Bonnard, André. "Iphigénie à Aulis, tragique et poésie." *Museum Heleveticum* 2 (1945): 87–107.

Booth, Wayne C. *A Rhetoric of Irony*. Chicago: University of Chicago Press, 1974.

Boswell, John. "Concepts, Experience, and Sexuality." *Differences* 2.1 (1990): 67–87.

Bourdieu, Pierre. *Algeria 1960*. Trans. Richard Nice. Cambridge: Cambridge University Press, 1979. Trans. of *Algérie 60 (i.e. Soixante)*, 1977.

——. *Outline of a Theory of Practice*. Trans. Richard Nice. Cambridge: Cambridge University Press, 1977. Trans. of *Esquisse d'une théorie de la pratique*, 1972.

Bradley, Edward. "Admetus and the Triumph of Failure in Euripides' 'Alcestis.' " *Ramus* 9 (1980): 112–27.

Bremer, J. M. "The Meadow of Love and Two Passages in Euripides' *Hippolytus*." *Mnemosyne* 28 (1975): 268–80.

Bremmer, Jan. "Scapegoat Rituals in Ancient Greece." *Harvard Studies in Classical Philology* 87 (1983): 299–320.

Buffière, Félix. *Eros adolescent: La pédérastie dans la Grèce antique*. Paris: Les Belles Lettres, 1980.

Burkert, Walter. "Greek Tragedy and Sacrificial Ritual." *Greek, Roman, and Byzantine Studies* 7 (1966): 87–121.

——. *Homo Necans: The Anthropology of Ancient Sacrificial Ritual and Myth*. Trans. Peter Bing. Berkeley: University of California Press, 1983. Trans. of *Homo Necans: Interpretationem altgriechischer Opferiten und Mythen*, 1972.

——. *Structure and History in Greek Mythology and Ritual*. Berkeley: University of California Press, 1979.

Burnett, Anne. *Catastrophe Survived: Euripides' Plays of Mixed Reversal*. Oxford: Oxford University Press, 1971.

——. "Hearth and Hunt in Euripides' *Hippolytos*." In *Greek Tragedy and Its Legacy: Essays Presented to D. J. Conacher*, ed. Martin Cropp, Elaine Fantham, and S. E. Scully, 167–86. Calgary: University of Calgary Press, 1986.

——. "Human Resistance and Divine Persuasion in Euripides' *Ion*." *Classical Philology* 57 (1962): 89–103.

——. "*Medea* and the Tragedy of Revenge." *Classical Philology* 68 (1973): 1–24.

——. "The Virtues of Admetus." *Classical Philology* 60 (1965): 240–55.

Buttrey, T. V. "Accident and Design in Euripides' 'Medea.' " *American Journal of Philology* 79 (1958): 1–17.

Buxton, R. G. A. *Persuasion in Greek Tragedy: A Study of Peitho*. Cambridge: Cambridge University Press, 1982.

Buxton, Richard. "Le voile et le silence dans *Alceste*." *Cahiers du GITA* 3 (1987): 167–78.

Calame, Claude. *Les choeurs de jeunes filles en Grèce archaïque*. Rome: Ateneo and Bizzarri, 1977.

Cantarella, Eva. *Bisexuality in the Ancient World*. New Haven: Yale University Press, 1992.

Carson, Anne. "Putting Her in Her Place." In *Before Sexuality: The Construction of Erotic Experience in the Ancient Greek World*, ed. David Halperin, with John J. Winkler, and Froma I. Zeitlin, 135–69. Princeton: Princeton University Press, 1990.

Cartledge, Paul. "The Politics of Spartan Pederasty." *Proceedings of the Cambridge Philological Society* 27 (1981): 17–36.

Case, Sue-Ellen. *Feminism and Theatre*. New York: Methuen, 1988.

Castellani, Victor. "Notes on the Structure of Euripides' *Alcestis*." *American Journal of Philology* 100 (1979): 487–96.

——. "Warlords and Women in Euripides' *Iphigenia at Aulis*." In *Drama, Sex and Politics*, ed. James Redmund, 1–10. Cambridge: Cambridge University Press, 1985.

Chant, Dale. "Role Inversion and Its Function in the *Iphigeneia at Aulis*." *Ramus* 15 (1986): 83–92.

Chantraine, P. "Les Noms du mari et de la femme du père et de la mère en grec." *Revue des Etudes Grecques* 59 (1946): 219–50.

Chodorow, Nancy. *The Reproduction of Mothering: Psychoanalysis and the Sociology of Gender*. Berkeley: University of California Press, 1978.

Cholakian, Patricia. *Rape and Writing in the "Heptaméron" of Marguerite de Navarre*. Carbondale: Southern Illinois University Press, 1991.

Cixous, Hélène. "Laugh of the Medusa." Trans. Keith Cohen and Paula Cohen. In *Signs Reader: Women, Gender, and Scholarship*, ed. Elizabeth Abel and Emily Abel, 279–97. Chicago: University of Chicago Press, 1983.

Claus, David. "Phaedra and the Socratic Paradox." *Yale Classical Studies* 22 (1972): 223–38.

Clément, Catherine, and Hélène Cixous. *The Newly Born Woman*. Trans. Betsy Wing. Minneapolis: University of Minnesota Press, 1986. Trans. of *La jeune née*, 1975.

Cohen, David. "Seclusion, Separation, and the Status of Women in Classical Athens." *Greece and Rome* 36 (1989): 3–15.

Collard, C. "Formal Debates in Euripides' Drama." *Greece and Rome* 22 (1975): 58–71.

Comaroff, John L. "Sui Genderis: Feminism, Kinship Theory, and Structural Domains." In *Gender and Kinship*, ed. James Collier and Sylvia Yanagisako, 53–85. Stanford, Calif.: Stanford University Press, 1987.

Conacher, D. J. *Euripidean Drama: Myth, Theme, and Structure*. Toronto: University of Toronto Press, 1967.

——. "Euripides' *Hecuba*." *American Journal of Philology* 82 (1961): 1–26.

——. "The Paradox of Euripides' 'Ion.'" *Transactions and Proceedings of the American Philological Association* 90 (1959): 20–39.

Corelis, Jon. "Hippolytos with the Garland: Myth, Ritual and Symbolism in Euripides' *Hippolytos*." Diss., Stanford University, 1978.

Cowie, Elizabeth. "Woman as Sign." *M/f* 1 (1978): 49–63.

Cunningham, Maurice. "Medea *apo Mēchanēs*." *Classical Philology* 49 (1954): 151–60.

Daitz, Stephen. "Concepts of Freedom and Slavery in Euripides' *Hecuba*." *Hermes* 99 (1971): 217–26.

Daladier, Nathalie. "Les mères aveugles." *Nouvelle Revue de Psychanalyse* 19 (1979): 229–44.

Dale, A. M., ed. *Euripides: Alcestis*. Oxford: Clarendon Press, 1954.

de Lauretis, Teresa. *Alice Doesn't: Feminism, Semiotics, Cinema*. Bloomington: Indiana University Press, 1984.

——. *Technologies of Gender*. Bloomington: Indiana University Press, 1987.

Delebecque, Edouard. *Euripide et la guerre du Péloponnèse*. Paris: Klincksieck, 1951.

Derrida, Jacques. *Dissemination*. Trans. Barbara Harlow. Chicago: University of Chicago Press, 1981. Trans. of *La dissémination*, 1972.

——. *Spurs: Nietzsche's Styles*. Trans. Barbara Harlow. Chicago: University of Chicago Press, 1979. Trans. of *Eperons: Les styles de Nietzsche*, 1978.

Detienne, Marcel. *Gardens of Adonis*. Trans. Janet Lloyd. Atlantic Highlands, N.J.: Humanities Press, 1977. Trans. of *Les jardins d'Adonis*, 1972.

Detienne, Marcel and Jean-Pierre Vernant. *Cunning Intelligence in Greek Culture and Society*. Trans. Janet Lloyd. Atlantic Highlands, N.J.: Harvester Press, 1978. Trans. of *Les ruses d'intelligence: La mètis des Grecs*, 1974.

Devereux, George. *Dreams in Greek Tragedy*. Berkeley: University of California Press, 1976.

Doane, Mary Ann. *The Desire to Desire: The Woman's Film of the 1940's*. Bloomington: Indiana University Press, 1987.

———. "Film and the Masquerade: Theorising the Female Spectator." *Screen* 23 (1982): 74–87.

Dodds, E. R. "*Aidos* of Phaedra and the Meaning of the *Hippolytus*." *Classical Review* 34 (1925): 102–4.

Donaldson, Laura. "The Miranda Complex: Colonialism and the Question of Feminist Reading." *Diacritics* 18.3 (1988): 65–77.

Doolittle, Hilda, ed. and trans. *Ion*. Boston: Houghton Mifflin, 1937.

Douglas, Mary. *Purity and Danger: An Analysis of Concepts of Pollution and Taboo*. 1966; London: Routledge & Kegan Paul, 1978.

Dover, K. J. "Classical Greek Attitudes to Sexual Behavior." *Arethusa* 6 (1973): 59–73.

———. *Greek Homosexuality*. Cambridge, Mass: Harvard University Press, 1978; Vintage Books, 1980.

Dowden, Ken. *Death and the Maiden: Girls' Initiation Rites in Greek Mythology*. New York: Routledge, 1989.

Dubisch, Jill. *Gender and Power in Rural Greece*. Princeton: Princeton University Press, 1986.

duBois, Page. *Centaurs and Amazons*. Ann Arbor: University of Michigan Press, 1982.

———. "On Horse/Men, Amazons, and Endogamy." *Arethusa* 12 (1979): 35–49.

———. *Sowing the Body: Psychoanalysis and Ancient Representations of Women*. Chicago: University of Chicago Press, 1988.

du Boulay, Juliet. *Portrait of a Greek Mountain Village*. Oxford: Clarendon Press, 1974.

Easterling, P. E. "The Infanticide in Euripides' 'Medea.' " *Yale Classical Studies* 25 (1977): 177–91.

Ehrenberg, Victor. *The People of Aristophanes*. Oxford: Blackwell, 1951.

Ellen, Roy. "Fetishism." *Man* n.s. 23 (1988): 213–35.

Elliot, Alan, ed. *Euripides: Medea*. London: Oxford University Press, 1969.

Euripides. *Fabulae*. Vols. 1–3. Ed. Gilbert Murray. 2d ed. Oxford: Oxford University Press, 1913.

Falkner, Thomas. "The Wrath of Alcmene: Gender, Authority, and Old Age in Euripides' *Children of Heracles*." In *Old Age in Greek and Latin Literature*, ed. Judith de Luce and Thomas Falkner, 114–31. Albany: State University of New York Press, 1989.

Ferguson, John. *A Companion to Greek Tragedy*. Austin: University of Texas Press, 1972.

———. "Tetralogies, Divine Paternities, and the Plays of 414." *Transactions and Proceedings of the American Philological Association* 100 (1969): 109–17.

Fetterley, Judith. *The Resisting Reader: A Feminist Approach to American Fiction*. Bloomington: Indiana University Press, 1978.

Fish, Stanley. *Is There a Text in This Class?* Cambridge, Mass.: Harvard University Press, 1980.

Fitzgerald, G. J. "Misconception and Hypocrisy in the *Hippolytus*." *Ramus* 2 (1973): 20–40.

Flax, Jane. *Thinking Fragments: Psychoanalysis, Feminism, and Postmodernism in the Contemporary West*. Berkeley: University of California Press, 1990.

Flory, Stewart. "Medea's Right Hand: Promises and Revenge." *Transactions and Proceedings of the American Philological Association* 108 (1978): 69–74.

Foley, Helene. "The Conception of Women in Athenian Drama." In *Reflections of Women in Antiquity*, ed. Helene Foley, 127–67. New York: Gordon & Breach Science Publishers, 1981.

———. "Marriage and Sacrifice in Euripides' *Iphigenia at Aulis*." *Arethusa* 15 (1982): 159–80.

———. "Medea's Divided Self." *Classical Antiquity* 8 (1989): 61–85.

———. *Ritual Irony: Poetry and Sacrifice in Euripides*. Ithaca: Cornell University Press, 1985.

———. "Women in Greece." In *Civilization of the Ancient Mediterranean: Greece and Rome*, ed. Michael Grant and Rachel Kitzinger, 3: 1301–17. New York: Scribner, 1988.

Forehand, W. E. "Truth and Reality in Euripides' *Ion*." *Ramus* 8 (1979): 174–87.

Foucault, Michel. *Power/Knowledge: Selected Interviews and Other Writings 1972–1977*. Ed. Colin Gordon; trans. Colin Gordon, Leo Marshall, John Mepham, and Kate Soper. New York: Pantheon Books, 1980.

———. *The Use of Pleasure*. Vol. 2. of *The History of Sexuality*. Trans. Robert Hurley. New York: Random House, 1985. Trans. of *L'usage des plaisirs*, 1984.

Freud, Sigmund. "Family Romances" (1909 [1908]). In *The Standard Edition of the Complete Psychological Works of Sigmund Freud*, ed. James Strachey et al., 9: 235–41. London: Hogarth Press, 1953–74.

———. "Female Sexuality" (1931). In *Standard Edition*, 21:225–43.

———. "Femininity" (1933 [1932]). In *Standard Edition*, 22:112–35.

———. "Fetishism" (1927). In *Standard Edition*, 21:152–57.

———. "Infantile Genital Organization" (1923). In *Standard Edition*, 19:141–48.

———. *Jokes and Their Relation to the Unconscious* (1905). In *Standard Edition*, Vol. 8.

———. "Medusa's Head" (1940 [1922]). In *Standard Edition*, 18:273–74

———. "The Taboo of Virginity" (1918a [1917]). In *Standard Edition*, 11:193–208.

———. "Three Contributions to the Psychology of Love: A Special Type of Choice of Object Made by Men" (1925). In *On Creativity and the Unconscious*, 162–205. New York: Harper and Row, 1958.

———. "Three Essays on the Theory of Sexuality" (1905). In *Standard Edition*, 7:135–243.

———. "The Uncanny" (1919). In *Standard Edition*, 17:217–52.

Galinsky, G. Karl. *The Herakles Theme*. Totowa, N.J.: Rowman & Littlefield, 1972.

Gallop, Jane. "Snatches of Conversation." In *Women and Language in Literature and Society*, ed. Sally McConnell-Ginet, Ruth Borker, and Nelly Furman, 278–83. New York: Praeger, 1980.

Gardner, Jane. "Aristophanes and Male Anxiety: The Defense of the *Oikos*." *Greece and Rome* 36.1 (1989): 51–62.

Gellie, George. "Apollo in the *Ion*." *Ramus* 13 (1984): 93–101.

———. "Hecuba and Tragedy." *Antichthon* 39 (1980): 30–44.

Gernet, Louis. *The Anthropology of Ancient Greece*. Trans. John Hamilton, S.J., and Blaise Nagy. Baltimore: Johns Hopkins University Press, 1981. Trans. of *Anthropologie de la Grèce antique*, 1968.

Gilbert, Sandra, and Susan Gubar. *The Madwoman in the Attic*. New Haven: Yale University Press, 1984.

Gill, Christopher. "The Articulation of the Self in Euripides' *Hippolytos*." In *Euripides, Women and Sexuality*, ed. Anton Powell, 76–107. New York: Routledge, Chapman & Hall, 1990.

Girard, René. *La violence et le sacré*. Paris: Grasset, 1972.

Gladstone, Ralph, trans. *The Heracleidae*. In *The Complete Greek Tragedies*, vol. 3, ed. David Grene and Richmond Lattimore, 110–55. Chicago: University of Chicago Press, 1959.

Glenn, Justin. "The Fantasies of Phaedra: A Psychoanalytic Reading." *Classical World* 69 (1976): 435–42.

Goff, Barbara E. *The Noose of Words: Readings of Desire, Violence, and Language in Euripides' "Hippolytos."* Cambridge: Cambridge University Press, 1990.

Gold, Barbara. " 'But Ariadne Was Never There in the First Place ': Finding the Female in Roman Poetry." In *Feminist Theory and the Classics*, ed. Nancy Sorkin Rabinowitz and Amy Richlin. New York: Routledge, 1993.

Golden, Leon. "Euripides' *Alcestis*: Structure and Theme." *Classical Journal* 66 (1970–71): 116–25.

Goldhill, Simon. "The Great Dionysia and Civic Ideology." In *Nothing to Do with Dionysos*, ed. John J. Winkler and Froma I. Zeitlin, 97–129. Princeton: Princeton University Press, 1990.

Gomme, A. W. "The Position of Women in Athens in the Fifth and Fourth Centuries." *Classical Philology* 20 (1925): 1–25.

Gould, John. "Law, Custom, and Myth: Aspects of the Social Position of Women in Classical Athens." *Journal of Hellenic Studies* 100 (1980): 38–59.

Gregory, Justina. "Euripides' *Alcestis*." *Hermes* 107 (1979): 259–70.

——. *Euripides and the Instruction of the Athenians*. Ann Arbor: University of Michigan Press, 1991.

Grube, G. M. A. *The Drama of Euripides*. London: Methuen, 1941.

Guépin, J. P. *Tragic Paradox: Myth and Ritual in Greek Tragedy*. Amsterdam: Hakkert, 1968.

Haigh, Arthur. *The Attic Theatre*. Oxford: Clarendon Press, 1898.

Halperin, David M. *One Hundred Years of Homosexuality and Other Essays on Greek Love*. New York: Routledge, 1990.

Halperin, David M., ed., with John J. Winkler and Froma I. Zeitlin. *Before Sexuality: The Construction of Erotic Experience in the Ancient Greek World*. Princeton: Princeton University Press, 1990.

Hanson, J. O. de Graft. "Euripides' *Ion*: Tragic Awakening and Disillusionment." *Museum Africum* 4 (1975): 27–42.

Harrison, A. R. W. *The Law of Athens*, vol. 1, *The Family and Property*. Oxford: Oxford University Press, 1968.

Harrison, Jane. *Themis: A Study of the Social Origins of Greek Religion*. Cambridge: Cambridge University Press, 1912.

Hartsock, Nancy. "Foucault on Power: A Theory for Women?" In *Feminism/Postmodernism*, ed. Linda Nicholson, 157–75. New York: Routledge, 1990.

——. *Money, Sex, and Power: Toward a Feminist Historical Materialism*. Boston: Northeastern University Press, 1985.

Havelock, Eric A. *The Literate Revolution in Greece and Its Cultural Consequences*. Princeton: Princeton University Press, 1982.

Hekman, Susan J. *Gender and Knowledge: Elements of a Postmodern Feminism*. Boston: Northeastern University Press, 1990.

Henrichs, Albert. "Human Sacrifice in Greek Religion: Three Case Studies." In *Le sacrifice dans l'antiquité*, ed. Jean Rudhardt and Olivier Reverdin, 195–242. Geneva: Fondation Hardt, 1980.

Herzfeld, Michael. "Semantic Slippage and Moral Fall: The Rhetoric of Chastity in

Rural Greek Society." In *Symbolic Aspects of Male/Female Relations in Greece*, ed. Loring M. Danforth, 161–71. *Journal of Modern Greek Studies* (special issue) 1 (1983): 161–71.

Hillman, James. "Abandoning the Child." *Eranos* 40 (1971): 357–407.

Hirsch, Marianne. *The Mother/Daughter Plot*. Bloomington: Indiana University Press, 1989.

Hoffmann, Genevieve. "Pandora: La jarre et l'espoir." *Etudes Rurales* 97–98 (1985): 119–32.

Hogan, James C. "Thucydides 3.52–68 and Euripides' 'Hecuba.' " *Phoenix* 26 (1972): 241–57.

Horney, Karen. "The Dread of Woman." In *Feminine Psychology*, 133–46. 1967; New York: Norton, 1973.

Hughes, Dennis D. *Human Sacrifice in Ancient Greece*. New York: Routledge, 1991.

Humphreys, Sally. *The Family, Women, and Death*. London: Routledge & Kegan Paul, 1983.

Irigaray, Luce. *Le corps-à-corps avec la mère*. Montreal: La Pleine Lune, 1981.

——. *Ethique de la difference sexuelle*. Paris: Minuit, 1984.

——. *Speculum of the Other Woman*. Trans. Gillian Gill. Ithaca: Cornell University Press, 1985. Trans. of *Speculum de l'autre femme*, 1974.

——. *This Sex Which Is Not One*. Trans. Catherine Porter. Ithaca: Cornell University Press, 1985. Trans. of *Ce sexe qui n'en est pas un*, 1977.

Jameson, Fredric. *Marxism and Form: Twentieth-Century Dialectical Theories of Literature*. Princeton: Princeton University Press, 1971.

Jardine, Alice. *Gynesis: Configurations of Women and Modernity*. Ithaca: Cornell University Press, 1985.

Jeanmaire, Henri. *Couroi et courètes*. Lille: Bibliothèque Universitaire, 1939.

——. *Dionysos: Histoire du culte du Bacchus*. Paris: Payot, 1970.

Jones, D. M. "Euripides' *Alcestis*." *Classical Review* 62 (1948): 50–55.

Joplin, Patricia Klindienst. "The Voice of the Shuttle Is Ours." *Stanford Literature Review* 1 (1984): 25–53.

Jouanna, Jacques. "Réalité et théâtricalité du rêve: Le rêve dans l'*Hécube* d'Euripide." *Ktèma* 7 (1982): 43–52.

Just, Roger. "Conceptions of Women in Classical Athens." *Journal of the Anthropological Society of Oxford* 6.1 (1975): 153–70.

Kahn, Laurence. *Hermès passe ou les ambiguïtés de la communication*. Paris: Maspero, 1978.

Kaplan, Cora. "Language and Gender." In *Papers on Patriarchy*, ed. Ros Coward, Sue Lipshitz, and Elizabeth Cowie. London: Women's Publishing Collective, 1976.

Kappeler, Susanne. *The Pornography of Representation*. Minneapolis: University of Minnesota Press, 1986.

Kerényi, Karl. *Goddesses of Sun and Moon*. Trans. M. Stein. Irving, Tex.: University of Dallas, 1979. Trans. of *Töchter der Sonne Betrachtungten über griechiesche gottheiten*, 1944.

Keuls, Eva C. *The Reign of the Phallus: Sexual Politics in Ancient Athens*. New York: Harper & Row, 1985.

King, Katherine C. "The Politics of Imitation: Euripides' *Hekabe* and the Homeric Achilles." *Arethusa* 18 (1985): 47–64.

Kirk, G. S. "Pitfalls in the Study of Ancient Greek Sacrifice." In *Le sacrifice dans l'antiquité*, ed. Jean Rudhardt and Olivier Reverdin, 41–89. Geneva: Fondation Hardt, 1980.

Kirkwood, Gordon M. "Hecuba and Nomos." *Transactions and Proceedings of the American Philological Association* 78 (1947): 61–68.

Kitto, H. D. F. *The Greeks.* Harmondsworth: Penguin, 1951.

——. *Greek Tragedy: A Literary Study.* Garden City, N.Y.: Doubleday, 1954.

Knox, Bernard. "Euripidean Comedy." In *Word and Action: Essays on the Ancient Theater*, 250–74. Baltimore: Johns Hopkins University Press, 1979.

——. "Euripides' *Iphigenia in Aulide* 1–163 (in that order)." *Yale Classical Studies* 22 (1972): 239–61.

——. "The *Hippolytus* of Euripides." *Yale Classical Studies* 13 (1952): 3–31.

——. "The *Medea* of Euripides." *Yale Classical Studies* 25 (1977): 193–225.

——. "Second Thoughts in Greek Tragedy." In *Word and Action: Essays on the Ancient Theater*, 231–50. Baltimore: Johns Hopkins University Press, 1979.

Kofman, Sarah. "Ça Cloche." In *Lectures de Derrida*, 117–51. Paris: Galilée, 1984.

——. *The Enigma of Woman: Woman in the Writings of Freud.* Trans. Catherine Porter. Ithaca: Cornell University Press, 1985. Trans. of *L'énigme de la femme: La femme dans les textes de Freud*, 1980.

Kovacs, David. *The Heroic Muse: Studies in the "Hippolytus" and "Hecuba" of Euripides.* Baltimore: Johns Hopkins University Press, 1987.

Kramer, Samuel, ed. and trans., with Diane Wolkstein. *Inanna.* New York: Harper & Row, 1983.

Kristeva, Julia. "Stabat Mater." In *The Female Body in Western Culture*, ed. Susan Suleiman, 99–118. Cambridge, Mass.: Harvard University Press, 1986.

——. *Tales of Love.* Trans. Leon S. Roudiez. New York: Columbia University Press, 1987. Trans. of *Histoires d'amour*, 1983.

Lacan, Jacques. "The Mirror-Stage as Formative of the Function of the I." In *Ecrits*, trans. Alan Sheridan, 1–7. New York: Norton, 1977.

——. "The Signification of the Phallus." In *Ecrits*, trans. Alan Sheridan, 281–91. New York: Norton, 1977.

Lacey, W. K. C. *The Family in Classical Greece.* Ithaca: Cornell University Press, 1968.

La Fontaine, Jean. *Initiation.* Manchester: Manchester University Press, 1986.

LaRue, Jene. "Creusa's Monody: *Ion* 859–922." *Transactions and Proceedings of the American Philological Association* 94 (1963): 126–36.

Lattimore, Richmond, trans. *Agamemnon.* In *The Complete Greek Tragedies*, vol. 1, ed. David Grene and Richmond Lattimore, 35–90. Chicago: University of Chicago Press, 1953.

Lebeck, Anne. *The Oresteia: A Study in Language and Structure.* Washington, D.C.: Center for Hellenic Studies, 1971.

Le Maître, J. "De la prétendue misogynie d'Euripide." *Ho Luchnos: Revue de l'Association Connaissance Hellenique*, July 1981, 20–21.

Lesky, Albin. "*Alkestis:* Der Mythos und das Drama." *SAWW* 203.2 (1925): 1–86.

——. *A History of Greek Literature.* Trans. James Willis and Cornelis de Heer. 2d ed. New York: Thomas Y. Crowell, 1963. Trans. of *Geschichte der Griechischen Literatur*, 1957–58.

Lévi-Strauss, Claude. *Elementary Structures of Kinship.* 2d ed. Trans. James Bell, John Sturmer, and Rodney Needham; ed. Rodney Needham. Boston: Beacon Press, 1966. Trans. of *Les structures élémentaires de parenté*, 1949.

Licht, Hans [Paul Brandt]. *Sexual Life in Ancient Greece*. Trans. J. H. Freese. London: Abbey Library, 1932. Trans. of *Sittengeschichte Griechenlands*, 1925.

Lloyd, G. E. R. "Hot and Cold, Dry and Wet in Early Greek Thought." In *Studies in Presocratic Philosophy*, ed. David Furley and R. E. Allen, 255–80. 1970; London: Routledge & Kegan Paul, 1975.

——. *Polarity and Analogy*. Cambridge: Cambridge University Press, 1966.

——. *Science, Folklore, and Ideology: Studies in the Life Sciences in Ancient Greece*. Cambridge: Cambridge University Press, 1983.

Lloyd, Michael. "Divine and Human Action in Euripides' *Ion*." *Antike und Abendland* 32 (1986): 33–45.

Lloyd-Jones, Hugh. "Artemis and Iphigeneia." *Journal of Hellenic Studies* 103 (1983): 87–102.

Lombard, D. B. "Aspects of *Aidos* in Euripides." *Acta Classica* 28 (1985): 5–12.

Longo, Oddone. "The Theater of the Polis." In *Nothing to Do with Dionysos*, ed. John J. Winkler and Froma I. Zeitlin. 12–19. Princeton: Princeton University Press, 1990.

Loraux, Nicole. *Les Enfants d'Athéna*. Paris: Maspero, 1981.

——. "Herakles: The Super-male and the Feminine." In *Before Sexuality: The Construction of Erotic Experience in the Ancient Greek World*, ed. David M. Halperin, with John J. Winkler and Froma I. Zeitlin, 21–52. Princeton: Princeton University Press, 1990.

——. *The Invention of Athens: the Funeral Oration in the Classical City*. Trans. Alan Sheridan. Cambridge, Mass.: Harvard University Press, 1986. Trans. of *L'invention d'Athènes: Histoire de l'oration funèbre dans la cité classique*, 1981.

——. "Le lit, la guerre." *L'Homme* 21 (1981): 37–67.

——. "Sur la race des femmes." *Arethusa* 11 (1978): 43–69.

——. *Tragic Ways of Killing a Woman*. Trans. Anthony Forster. Cambridge, Mass.: Harvard University Press, 1987. Trans. of *Façons tragiques de tuer une femme*, 1985.

Luschnig, C. A. E. "Euripides' *Hecabe*: The Time Is Out of Joint." *Classical Journal* 71 (1976): 227–36.

MacDowell, Douglas M. *The Law in Classical Athens*. Ithaca: Cornell University Press, 1978.

MacKinnon, Catharine. "Feminism, Marxism, Method, and the State: An Agenda for Theory." In *Signs Reader: Women, Gender and Scholarship*, ed. Emily Abel and Elizabeth Abel, 227–56. Chicago: University of Chicago Press, 1983.

——. "Feminism, Marxism, Method, and the State: Toward a Feminist Jurisprudence." *Signs* 8.4 (1983): 635–58.

Mandel, Ruth. "Sacrifice at the Bridge of Arta: Sex Roles and the Manipulation of Power." *Journal of Modern Greek Studies* 1.1 (1983): 173–84.

Marsh, Terri. "The (Other) Maiden's Tale." In *Pornography and Representation in Greece and Rome*, ed. Amy Richlin, 269–84. New York: Oxford University Press, 1992.

Marx, Karl. "Fetishism of Commodities." In *Selected Writings*, ed. David McLellan. Oxford: Oxford University Press, 1977.

Mason, Peter. "Third Person/Second Sex: Patterns of Sexual Asymmetry in the *Theogony* of Hesiodos." In *Sexual Asymmetry: Studies in Ancient Society*, ed. Josine Blok with Peter Mason, 147–89. Amsterdam: J. C. Gieben, 1987.

Masqueray, Paul. *Euripide et ses idées*. Paris: Hachette, 1908.

Mastronarde, D. J. "Iconography and Imagery in Euripides' *Ion*." *California Studies in Classical Antiquity* 8 (1975): 163–76.

Matthaei, Louise E. *Studies in Greek Tragedy*. Cambridge: Cambridge University Press, 1918.

Mauron, Charles. *Psychocritique du genre comique*. Paris: J. Corti, 1964.

Mauss, Marcel. *The Gift*. Trans. Ian Cunnison. New York: Norton, 1967. Trans. of *Essai sur le don*, 1925.

Mauss, Marcel, and Henri Hubert. *Sacrifice: Its Nature and Function*. Trans. W. D. Halls. London: Cohen & West, 1964. Trans. of *Essai sur la nature et fonction du sacrifice*, 1899.

McDermott, Emily. *Euripides' "Medea": The Incarnation of Disorder*. University Park: Pennsylvania State University Press, 1989.

Mehlman, Jeffrey. "How to Read Freud on Jokes: The Critic as *Schadchen*." *New Literary History* 6 (1975): 439–61.

Méridier, Louis. *Euripide*. 2 vols. 8th ed. Paris: Les Belles Lettres, 1989.

Meridor, Ra'anana. "Euripides' *Hec.* 1035–38." *American Journal of Philology* 96 (1975): 5–6.

———. "The Function of Polymestor's Crime in the 'Hecuba' of Euripides." *Eranos* 81 (1983): 13–20.

———. "Hecuba's Revenge: Some Observations on Euripides' *Hecuba*." *American Journal of Philology* 99 (1978): 28–35.

Meuli, Karl. *Gesammelte Schriften*. Vol. 2. Basel: Schwabe, 1975.

Michelini, Ann. *Euripides and the Tragic Tradition*. Madison: University of Wisconsin Press, 1987.

Moore, Henrietta. *Feminism and Anthropology*. Minneapolis: University of Minnesota Press, 1988.

Morris, Ian. *Burial and Ancient Society*. Cambridge: Cambridge University Press, 1987.

Mulvey, Laura. *Visual and Other Pleasures*. Bloomington: Indiana University Press, 1989.

Murray, Gilbert. *Euripides and His Age*. London: Williams & Norgate, 1918.

Musurillo, Herbert, S.J. "*Alcestis*: The Pageant of Life and Death." *Studi Classici in Onore di Quintino Cataudella* 1 (1972): 275–88.

———. "Euripides' *Medea*: A Reconsideration." *American Journal of Philology* 87 (1966): 52–74.

Myres, J. L. "The Plot of the *Alcestis*." *Journal of Hellenic Studies* 37 (1917): 195–218.

Nancy, Claire. "Pharmakon sōtērias: Le mécanisme du sacrifice humain chez Euripide." *Théâtre et Spectacles dans l' Antiquité*, November 1981, 17–30.

Nielsen, Rosemary. "Alcestis: A Paradox in Dying." *Ramus* 5 (1976): 92–102.

Nietzsche, Friedrich. *The Birth of Tragedy and the Genealogy of Morals*. Trans. Francis Golffing. New York: Doubleday, 1956. Trans. of *Die Geburt der tragödie*, 1872.

Norwood, Gilbert. *Essays on Euripidean Drama*. Berkeley: University of California Press, 1954.

———. *Greek Tragedy*. London: Methuen, 1920.

Nussbaum, Martha. "Therapeutic Arguments and Structures of Desire." *Differences* 2.1 (1990): 46–65.

O'Higgins, Dolores. "Above Rubies: Admetus' Perfect Wife." *Arethusa* 26 (1993: 77–97.

Olender, Maurice. "Aspects of Baubo." In *Before Sexuality, The Construction of Erotic Experience in the Ancient Greek World*, ed. David Halperin with John J. Winkler and Froma I. Zeitlin, 83–114. Princeton: Princetoon University Press, 1990.

Orban, Marcel. "*Hécube*: Drame humain." *Les Etudes Classiques* 38 (1970): 316–30.

Owen, A. S., ed. *Euripides: Ion*. 1939; Oxford: Oxford University Press, 1963.

Page, Denys, ed. *Euripides: Medea*. 1938. 2d ed. Oxford: Clarendon Press, 1961.

Pajaczkowska, Claire. "Heterosexual Presumption: A Contribution to the Debate on Pornography." *Screen* 22.1 (1981): 79–94.

Palmer, Robert. "An Apology for Jason: A Study of Euripides' *Medea*." *Classical Journal* 53 (1957–58): 49–55.

Pandiri, Thalia. "*Alcestis* 1052." *Classical Journal* 7.2 (1974): 50–52.

Parke, H. W. *Festivals of the Athenians*. Ithaca: Cornell University Press, 1977.

Passman, Tina. "Out of the Closet and Into the Field: Matriculture, the Lesbian Perspective, and Feminist Classics." In *Feminist Theory and the Classics*, ed. Nancy Sorkin Rabinowitz and Amy Richlin. New York: Routledge, 1993.

Pateman, Carole. "Women and Consent." *Political Theory* 8.2 (1980): 149–68.

Patterson, Cynthia. "*Hai Attikai*: The Other Athenians." *Helios* 13 (1986): 49–68.

——. "Marriage and the Married Woman in Athenian Law." In *Women's History and Ancient History*, ed. Sarah Pomeroy, 48–72. Chapel Hill: University of North Carolina Press, 1991.

——. *Pericles' Citizenship Law of 452–450 B.C.* New York: Arno Press, 1981.

Pearson, A. C., ed. *Fragments of Sophocles*. Vol. 2. Cambridge: Cambridge University Press, 1917.

Pearson, Lionel. *Popular Ethics in Ancient Greece*. Stanford, Calif.: Stanford University Press, 1962.

Perlman, Paula. "Acting the She-Bear for Artemis." *Arethusa* 22.2 (1989): 111–34.

Pickard-Cambridge, Arthur. *The Dramatic Festivals of Athens*. 2d ed. Oxford: Clarendon Press, 1968.

Pigeaud, J. "Euripide et la connaissance de soi." *Les Etudes Classiques* 44 (1976): 3–24.

Pitt-Rivers, Julian. *The Fate of Shechem, or the Politics of Sex*. Cambridge: Cambridge University Press, 1977.

——. "Honour and Social Status." In *Honour and Shame: The Values of Mediterranean Society*, ed. J. G. Péristiany, 21–77. Chicago: University of Chicago Press, 1966.

Plato. *The Collected Dialogues*. Ed. Edith Hamilton and Huntington Cairns. Bollingen Series 71. New York: Pantheon Books, 1961.

Pohlenz, Max. *Die griechische Tragödie*. Leipzig: Teubner, 1930.

Pomeroy, Sarah. *Goddesses, Whores, Wives, and Slaves: Women in Classical Antiquity*. New York: Schocken Books, 1975.

——. "The Study of Women in Antiquity: Past, Present, and Future." *American Journal of Philology* 112 (1991): 263–68.

Poole, Howard Michael. *The Unity of Euripides' 'Hecuba' by Way of the Image of Hecuba as an Earth Mother*. Diss., Florida State University, Tallahassee, 1979.

Poole, William. "Male Homosexuality in Euripides." In *Euripides, Women, and Sexuality*, ed. Anton Powell, 108–50. New York: Routledge, Chapman & Hall, 1990.

Pucci, Pietro. "Euripides' *Hippolytos*: The Monument and the Sacrifice." *Arethusa* 10 (1977): 165–95.

——. *Hesiod and the Language of Poetry*. Baltimore: Johns Hopkins University Press, 1976.

——. *The Violence of Pity in Euripides' "Medea."* Ithaca: Cornell University Press, 1980.

Rabinowitz, Nancy Sorkin. "Aphrodite and the Audience: Engendering the Reader." *Arethusa* 19.2 (1986): 171–85.

——. "From Force to Persuasion: Aeschylus' *Oresteia* as Cosmogonic Myth." *Ramus* 10 (1981): 159–91.

——. "Paths of Song in Aeschylus' *Oresteia*." *Classical Bulletin* 60 (1984): 20–28.

——. "Tragedy and the Politics of Containment." In *Pornography and Representation in Greece and Rome*, ed. Amy Richlin, 36–52. New York: Oxford University Press, 1992.

Rabinowitz, Peter J. *Before Reading*. Ithaca: Cornell University Press, 1987.

Rankin, Anne. "Euripides' Hippolytos: A Psychopathological Hero." *Arethusa* 7 (1974): 71–94.

Rankin, Anne, and Jean J. Smoot. "Hippolytus as Narcissus: An Amplification." *Arethusa* 9 (1976): 35–51.

Raymond, Janice G. *A Passion for Friends*. Boston: Beacon Press, 1986.

Reckford, Kenneth. "Concepts of Demoralization in the *Hecuba*." In *Directions in Euripidean Criticism*, ed. Peter Burian, 112–28. Durham, N.C.: Duke University Press, 1985.

———. "Medea's First Exit." *Transactions and Proceedings of the American Philological Association* 99 (1968): 329–59.

———. "Phaethon, Hippolytus, and Aphrodite." *Transactions and Proceedings of the American Philological Association* 103 (1972): 405–32.

Redfield, James. "Notes on the Greek Wedding." *Arethusa* 15 (1982): 181–201.

Rhodes, P. J. "Bastards as Athenian Citizens." *Classical Quarterly* 28 (1978): 87–92.

Rich, Adrienne. "Compulsory Heterosexuality and Lesbian Existence." In *Signs Reader: Women, Gender, and Scholarship*, ed. Elizabeth Abel and Emily Abel, 139–68. Chicago: University of Chicago Press, 1983.

———. *Of Woman Born: Motherhood as Experience and Institution*. New York: Norton, 1976.

Richlin, Amy. "Zeus and Metis: Foucault, Feminism, Classics." *Helios* 18 (1991): 160–80.

Richter, Donald. "The Position of Women in Classical Athens." *Classical Journal* 67 (1971): 1–8.

Ritoók, Zsigmond. "Euripides: Alcestis, a Comedy or a Tragedy?" *Acta Litteraria Academiae Scientarum Hungaricae* 19 (1977): 168–78.

Rivier, André. *Essai sur le tragique d'Euripide*. Paris: Boccard, 1975.

Robinson, Sally. "Misappropriations of the 'Feminine.' " *SubStance* 59 (1989): 48–70.

Roheim, Geza. "The Dragon and the Hero." Pts. 1–2. *American Imago* 1.2–3 (1940): 40–69, 61–94.

Romilly, Jacqueline de. *La modernité d'Euripide*. Paris: Presses Universitaires de France, 1986.

Rosaldo, Michelle. "The Uses and Abuses of Anthropology: Reflections on Feminism and Cross-cultural Understanding." *Signs* 5 (1980): 389–417.

———. "Woman, Culture, and Society: A Theoretical Overview." In *Woman, Culture, and Society*, ed. Michelle Rosaldo and Louise Lamphere, 17–42. Stanford, Calif.: Stanford University Press, 1974.

Rose, H. J. "The Bride of Hades." *Classical Philology* 19 (1925): 238–43.

———. *Handbook of Greek Literature*. London: Methuen, 1934.

Rose, Peter W. *Sons of the Gods, Children of Earth: Ideology and Literary Form in Ancient Greece*. Ithaca: Cornell University Press, 1992.

Rosenmeyer, Thomas. *The Masks of Tragedy*. Austin: University of Texas Press, 1963.

Rosivach, Vincent. "Earthborn and Olympians: The Parodos of the *Ion*." *Classical Quarterly* 27 (1977): 284–94.

———. "The First Stasimon of the 'Hecuba,' 444ff." *American Journal of Philology* 96 (1975): 349–62.

Roussel, P. "Médée et le meurtre de ses enfants." *Revue des Etudes Anciennes* 22 (1920): 157–71.

——. "Le rôle d'Achille dans l'*Iphigénie à Aulis*." *Revue des Etudes Grecques* 28 (1915): 234–50.

——. "Le thème du sacrifice volontaire dans la tragédie d'Euripide." *Revue Belge de Philologie et d'Histoire* 1 (1922): 225–40.

Rousselle, Aline. "Observation féminine et idéologie masculine: Le corps de la femme d'après les médecines grecs." *Annales: Economies, Sociétés, Civilisations* 35 (1980): 1089–1115.

Rubin, Gayle. "The Traffic in Women: Notes on a 'Political Economy' of Sex." In *Toward an Anthropology of Women*, ed. Rayna Reiter, 175–210. New York: Monthly Review Press, 1975.

Rukeyser, Muriel. *The Collected Poems*. New York: McGraw-Hill, 1978.

Saïd, Suzanne. "Féminin, femme, et femelle dans les grands traités biologiques d'Aristote." In *La femme dans les sociétés antiques: Actes des Colloques de Strasbourg*, 93–123. Strasbourg: Université des Sciences Humaines de Strasbourg, 1983.

Sanday, Peggy. *Female Power and Male Dominance: On the Origins of Sexual Inequality*. Cambridge: Cambridge University Press, 1981.

Saxonhouse, Arlene W. "Myths and the Origins of Cities: Reflections on the Autochthony Theme in Euripides' *Ion*." In *Greek Tragedy and Political Theory*, ed. J. Peter Euben, 252–73. Berkeley: University of California Press, 1986.

Schaps, David. *Economic Rights of Women in Ancient Greece*. Edinburgh: Edinburgh University Press, 1979.

——. "The Women Least Mentioned: Etiquette and Women's Names." *Classical Quarterly* 27 (1977): 323–30.

Schlesinger, Eilhard. "On Euripides' *Medea*." In *Euripides: A Collection of Critical Essays*, ed. Erich Segal, 70–89. Englewood Cliffs, N.J.: Prentice Hall, 1968.

Schmitt, Johanna. *Freiwilliger Opfertod bei Euripides*. Giessen: A. Töpelmann, 1921.

Schmitt, Pauline. "Athéna Apatouria et la ceinture: Les aspects féminins des Apatouries à Athènes." *Annales: Economies, Sociétés, Civilisations* 32 (1977): 1059–73.

Schmitt-Pantel, Pauline. "Histoire du Tyran." In *Les marginaux et les exclus dans l'histoire*, ed. Bernard Vincent, 17–31. Paris: Union Générale d'Éditions, 1979.

Schor, Naomi. "Female Fetishism: The Case of George Sand." In *The Female Body in Western Culture*, ed. Susan Suleiman, 363–72. Cambridge, Mass.: Harvard University Press, 1985.

——. "Fetishism and Its Ironies." *Nineteenth-Century French Studies* 17.1–2 (1989): 89–97.

Scodel, Ruth. "*Admetou Logos* and the *Alcestis*." *Harvard Studies in Classical Philology* 83 (1979): 50–62.

——. "Old Women and the Greek Sexual Economy." Paper presented at the 1991 meeting of American Philological Association.

Séchan, Louis. "La dévouement d'Alceste." Pts. 1–2. *Revue des Cours et Conférences* 17–18 (1927): 490–514, 329–53.

——. "La légende de Médée." *Revue des Etudes Grecques* 40 (1927): 234–310.

Sedgwick, Eve Kosofsky. *Between Men: English Literature and Male Homosocial Desire*. New York: Columbia University Press, 1985.

——. *Epistemology of the Closet*. Berkeley: University of California Press, 1990.

Segal, Charles. "Cold Delight: Art, Death, and the Transgression of Genre in Euripides' *Alcestis*." In *The Scope of Words: In Honor of Albert S. Cook*, ed. Peter Baker, Sarah Webster Goodwin, and Gary Handwerk, 211–28. New York: Peter Lang, 1991.

——. "Euripides' *Alcestis*: Female Death and Male Tears." *Classical Antiquity* 11.1 (1992): 142–58.

——. "Greek Tragedy and Society: A Structuralist Perspective." In *Greek Tragedy and Political Theory*, ed. J. Peter Euben, 43–75. Berkeley: University of California Press, 1986.

——. "Mariage et sacrifice dans les *Trachiniennes* de Sophocle." *L'Antiquité Classique* 44 (1975): 30–53.

——. "Pentheus and Hippolytus on the Couch and the Grid." *Classical World* 72 (1978): 129–48.

——. "Shame and Purity in the *Hippolytus*." *Hermes* 98 (1970): 278–99.

——. "Solar Imagery and Tragic Heroism in Euripides' *Hippolytus*." In *Arktouros*, ed. Glen Bowersock, Walter Burkert, and Michael Putnam, 151–61. Berlin: De Gruyter, 1979.

——. "The Tragedy of the *Hippolytus*: The Waters of Ocean and the Untouched Meadow." *Harvard Studies in Classical Philology* 70 (1965): 117–69.

——. "Violence and the Other: Greek, Female, and Barbarian in Euripides' *Hecuba*." *Transactions and Proceedings of the American Philological Association* 120 (1990): 109–32.

Sergent, Bernard. *Homosexuality and Greek Myth*. Trans. Arthur Goldhammer. Boston: Beacon Press, 1986.Trans. of *Homosexualité dans la mythologie grecque*, 1984.

Shaw, Michael. "The Female Intruder: Women in Fifth-Century Drama." *Classical Philology* 70 (1975): 255–66.

Sicking, C. M. J. "Alceste: Tragédie d'amour ou du devoir?" *Dioniso* 41 (1976): 155–74.

Siegel, Herbert. "Agamemnon in Euripides' *Iphigenia at Aulis*." *Hermes* 109 (1981): 257–65.

——. "Self-Delusion and the Volte-Face of Iphigenia in Euripides' *Iphigenia at Aulis*." *Hermes* 108 (1980): 300–21.

Simon, Stephen. "Euripides' Defense of Women." *Classical Bulletin* 50 (1973–74): 39–42.

Sinos, Dale. "Characterization in the *Ion*: Apollo and the Dynamism of the Plot." *Eranos* 80 (1982): 129–34.

Sissa, Giulia. *Greek Virginity*. Trans. Arthur Goldhammer. Cambridge, Mass.: Harvard University Press, 1990. Trans. of *Le corps virginal*, 1987.

Skinner, Marilyn. "Classical Studies, Patriarchy, and Feminism: The View from 1986." *Women's Studies International Forum* 10 (1987): 181–86.

——. "Classical Studies vs. Women's Studies: *Duo Moi ta Noēmmata*." *Helios* 12 (1985): 3–21.

——. "Sapphic Nossis." *Arethusa* 22 (1989): 5–18.

——. "Woman and Language in Archaic Greece; or, Why Is Sappho a Woman?" In *Feminist Theory and the Classics*, ed. Nancy Sorkin Rabinowitz and Amy Richlin. New York: Routledge, 1993.

Slater, Philip E. *The Glory of Hera: Greek Mythology and the Greek Family*. Boston: Beacon Press, 1968.

Smith, Wesley. "Iphigeneia in Love." In *Arktouros*, ed. Glen Bowersock, 173–80. Berlin: De Gruyter, 1979.

——. "The Ironic Structure in *Alcestis*." *Phoenix* 14 (1960): 127–45.

Snowden, Frank. *Blacks in Antiquity: Ethiopians in the Greco-Roman Experience*. Cambridge, Mass.: Harvard University Press, 1970.

Snyder, Jane. *The Woman and the Lyre: Women Writers in Classical Greece and Rome.* Carbondale: Southern Illinois University Press, 1989.

Solmsen, Friedrich. *Intellectual Experiments of the Greek Enlightenment.* Princeton: Princeton University Press, 1975.

Spelman, Elizabeth V. *Inessential Woman: Problems of Exclusion in Feminist Thought.* Boston: Beacon Press, 1988.

Spivak, Gayatri. "Displacement and the Discourse of Woman." In *Displacement: Derrida and After,* ed. Mark Krupnick, 169–95. Bloomington: Indiana University Press, 1983.

Stinton, T. C. W. "Euripides and the Judgment of Paris." Society for the Promotion of Hellenic Studies, supplementary paper #1. 1965.

Thury, Eva. "Euripides' *Alcestis* and the Athenian Generation Gap." *Arethusa* 21.2 (1988): 197–214.

Troiano, Edna. "The *Ion*: The Relationship of Character and Genre." *Classical Bulletin* 61 (1985): 45–52.

Turner, Victor. *The Ritual Process: Structure and Anti-Structure.* 1969; Ithaca: Cornell University Press, 1977.

Tyrrell, William Blake. *Amazons: A Study in Athenian Mythmaking.* Baltimore: Johns Hopkins University Press, 1984.

van Gennep, Arnold. *Rites of Passage.* Trans. Monika B. Vizedom and Gabrielle L. Caffel. Chicago: University of Chicago Press, 1960. Trans. of *Les rites de passage,* 1909.

Vellacott, Philip. *Ironic Drama: A Study of Euripides' Method and Meaning.* Cambridge: Cambridge University Press, 1975.

———. "Woman and Man in Ancient Greece: The Evidence from Tragic Drama." *Carleton Miscellany* 18.2 (1980): 7–20.

Vernant, Jean-Pierre. "City-State Warfare." In *Myth and Society in Ancient Greece,* trans. Janet Lloyd, 19–44. Atlantic Highlands, N.J.: Humanities Press, 1980. Trans. of *Mythe et société en Grèce ancienne,* 1974.

———. "Hestia-Hermes: The Religious Expression of Space and Movement in Ancient Greece." In *Myth and Thought among the Greeks,* trans. Janet Lloyd, 127–75. London: Routledge & Kegan Paul, 1983. Trans. of *Mythe et pensée chez les grecs,* 1965.

———. "The Historical Moment." In *Tragedy and Myth in Ancient Greece,* trans. Janet Lloyd, 1–5. Sussex, N.J.: Harvester Press, 1981. Trans. of *Mythe et tragédie en Grèce ancienne,* 1972.

———. "Introduction." In Marcel Detienne, *Gardens of Adonis,* trans. Janet Lloyd, i–xxxv. Atlantic Highlands, N.J.: Humanities Press, 1977. Trans. of *Les jardins d'Adonis,* 1972.

———. "Marriage." In *Myth and Society in Ancient Greece,* 45–70. Atlantic Highlands, N. J.: Humanities Press, 1980.

———. "The Myth of Prometheus." In *Myth and Society in Ancient Greece,* 168–85. Atlantic Highlands, N.J.: Humanities Press, 1980.

———. "The Representation of the Invisible and the Psychological Category of the Double: The Colossos." In *Myth and Thought among the Greeks,* 305–20. London: Routledge & Kegan Paul, 1983.

———. "Théorie generale du sacrifice et mise à mort dans la *thysia* grecque." In *Le sacrifice dans l'antiquité,* ed. Jean Rudhardt and Olivier Reverdin, 1–30. Geneva: Fondation Hardt, 1980.

2

39

Vernant, Jean-Pierre, and Pierre Vidal-Naquet. "Tensions and Ambiguities in Greek Tragedy." In *Tragedy and Myth in Ancient Greece*, trans. Janet Lloyd, 6–27. Sussex, N.J.: Harvester Press, 1981. Trans. of *Mythe et tragédie en Grèce ancienne*, 1972.

Verrall, A. W. *Euripides the Rationalist: A Study in the History of Art and Religion.* Cambridge: Cambridge University Press, 1895.

Versnel, H. S. "Self-sacrifice, Compensation, and the Anonymous Gods." In *Le sacrifice dans l'antiquité*, ed. Jean Rudhardt and Olivier Reverdin, 135–94. Geneva: Fondation Hardt, 1980.

——. "Wife and Helpmate: Women of Ancient Athens in Anthropological Perspective." In *Sexual Assymmetry: Studies in Ancient Society*, ed. Josine Blok with Peter Mason, 59–85. Amsterdam: J. C. Gieben, 1987.

Vidal-Naquet, Pierre. *Black Hunter.* Trans. Andrew Szegedy-Maszak. Baltimore: Johns Hopkins University Press, 1986; Trans. of *Le chausseur noir: Formes de pensée et formes de société dans le monde grec*, 1981.

——. "La tradition d'hoplite athénien." In *Problèmes de la guerre*, ed. Jean-Pierre Vernant, 161–81. Paris: Mouton, 1968.

Visser, Margaret. "Medea: Daughter, Sister, Wife, and Mother: Natal Family *versus* Conjugal Family in Greek and Roman Myths about Women." In *Greek Tragedy and Its Legacy: Essays Presented to D. J. Conacher*, ed. Martin Cropp, Elaine Fantham, and S. E. Scully, 149–65. Calgary: University of Calgary Press, 1986.

von Fritz, Kurt. "Euripides *Alkestis* und ihre modernen Nachahmer und Kritiker." In *Antike und moderne Tragödie, neun Abhandlungen.* Berlin: De Gruyter, 1962.

Walker, Barbara. *The Crone: Woman of Age, Wisdom, and Power.* San Francisco: Harper & Row, 1985.

Walker, Susan. "Women and Housing in Classical Greece: The Archaeological Evidence." In *Images of Women in Antiquity*, ed. Averil Cameron and Amélie Kuhrt, 81–91. Detroit: Wayne State University Press, 1983.

Walsh, George B. "Public and Private in Three Plays of Euripides." *Classical Philology* 74 (1979): 294–309.

——. "The Rhetoric of Birthright and Race in Euripides' *Ion.*" *Hermes* 106.2 (1978): 301–15.

——. *The Varieties of Enchantment.* Chapel Hill: University of North Carolina Press, 1984.

Wasserman, Felix. "Agamemnon in the *Iphigenia at Aulis*: A Man in the Age of Crisis." *Transactions and Proceedings of the American Philological Association* 80 (1949): 174–86.

——. "Divine Violence and Providence in Euripides' *Ion.*" *Transactions and Proceedings of the American Philological Association* 71 (1940): 587–606.

Webster, T. B. L. "Euripides' Trojan Trilogy." In *Essays in Honor of Francis Letters: For Service to Classical Studies*, ed. Maurice Kelly, 207–13. Melbourne: F. W. Cheshire, 1966.

——. *The Tragedies of Euripides.* London: Methuen, 1967.

Weil, Henri. *Alceste.* Paris: Hachette, 1891.

West, D. J. *Homosexuality.* London: Duckworth, 1968.

Wilamowitz-Moellendorf, Ulrich von. *Griechische Tragödien.* Vol. 3. Berlin: Weidmann, 1919–23.

Williams, Linda. "Fetishism and the Visual Pleasure of Hard Core: Marx, Freud, and the 'Money Shot.'" *Quarterly Review of Film and Video* 11.2 (1989): 23–42.

Williamson, Margaret. "A Woman's Place in Euripides' *Medea*." In *Euripides, Women, and Sexuality*, ed. Anton Powell, 16–31. New York: Routledge, Chapman & Hall, 1990.

Willink, C. W. "The Prologue of the *Iphigenia at Aulis*." *Classical Quarterly*, n.s. 21 (1971): 343–64.

Wilson, John, ed. *Euripides' "Alcestis": A Collection of Critical Essays*. Twentieth Century Interpretations. Englewood Cliffs, N.J.: Prentice-Hall, 1968.

Winkler, John J. *The Constraints of Desire: The Anthropology of Sex and Gender in Ancient Greece*. New York: Routledge, 1990.

———. "The Ephebes' Song: *Tragoidia* and *Polis*." In *Nothing to Do with Dionysos*, ed. John J. Winkler and Froma I. Zeitlin, 20–62. Princeton: Princeton University Press, 1990.

Winnington-Ingram, R. P. "Hippolytus: A Study in Causation." In *Entretiens sur l'antiquité classique 6: Euripide*, 169–97. Geneva: Fondation Hardt, 1960.

Wolff, Christian. "The Design and Myth in Euripides' *Ion*." *Harvard Studies in Classical Philology* 69 (1965): 169–94.

Wolff, Hans. "Marriage Law and Family Organization." *Traditio* 2 (1944): 43–95.

Zeitlin, Froma I. "Configurations of Rape in Greek Myth." In *Rape*, ed. Sylvana Tomaselli and Roy Porter, 152–73. Oxford: Blackwell, 1986.

———. "Cultic Models of the Female: Rites of Dionysus and Demeter." *Arethusa* 15.1–2 (1982): 129–57.

———. "Euripides' *Hekabe* and the Somatics of Dionysiac Theater." *Ramus* 20.1 (1991): 53–94.

———. "The Motif of Corrupted Sacrifice in Aeschylus' *Oresteia*." *Transactions and Proceedings of the American Philological Association* 96 (1965): 463–508.

———. "Mysteries of Identity and Designs of the Self in Euripides' *Ion*." *Proceedings of the Cambridge Philological Society* 35 (1989): 144–97.

———. "Playing the Other: Theater, Theatricality, and the Feminine in Greek Drama." *Representations* 11 (1985): 63–94.

———. "Postscript to the Sacrificial Imagery in the *Oresteia*." *Transactions and Proceedings of the American Philological Association* 97 (1966): 645–53.

———. "The Power of Aphrodite: Eros and the Boundaries of the Self in the *Hippolytus*." In *Directions in Euripidean Criticism*, ed. Peter Burian, 52–111. Durham, N.C.: Duke University Press, 1985.

———. "Travesties of Gender and Genre in Aristophanes' *Thesmophoriazeusae*." *Critical Inquiry* 8.2 (1981): 301–27.

Zweig, Bella. " 'The Primal Mind': Using Native American Models for the Study of Women in Ancient Greece." In *Feminist Theory and the Classics*, ed. Nancy Sorkin Rabinowitz and Amy Richlin. New York: Routledge, 1993.

Index

Library of Congress Cataloging-in-Publication Data

Rabinowitz, Nancy Sorkin.
    Anxiety veiled : Euripides and the traffic in women / Nancy Sorkin
Rabinowitz.
      p. cm.
    Includes bibliographical references and index.
    ISBN 0–8014–2845–9.—ISBN 0–8014–8091–4
    1. Euripides—Characters—Women. 2. Greek drama (Tragedy)—
History and criticism. 3. Mythology, Greek, in literature.
4. Feminism and literature—Greece. 5. Women and literature—
Greece. 6. Women—Mythology. I. Title.
    PA3978.R33 1993
882′.01—dc20
93–17257